SMALL FIRMS

NATIONAL SMALL FIRMS'
POLICY AND RESEARCH CONFERENCES

Available from:
Paul Chapman Publishing
144 Liverpool Road
London
N1 1LA

Telephone 071 609 5315/6
Fax 071 700 1057

Towards the Twenty-First Century: *The Challenge
for Small Business*
edited by
Martyn Robertson, Elizabeth Chell and Colin Mason
(ISBN 0 9519230 0 5).
Selected papers from the 13th National Small Firms' Policy
and Research Conference 1990.

Small Enterprise Development: *Policy and Practice in Action*
edited by
Kevin Caley, Elizabeth Chell, Francis Chittenden and Colin
Mason   (ISBN 1 85396 215 5).
Selected papers from the 14th National Small Firms' Policy
and Research Conference 1991.

SMALL FIRMS

Recession and Recovery

edited by
Francis Chittenden, Martyn Robertson
and David Watkins

Published on behalf of
The Institute for Small Business Affairs
by
Paul Chapman Publishing

P·C·P
Paul Chapman
Publishing Ltd

Paul Chapman Publishing Ltd
144 Liverpool Road
London
N1 1LA

British Library Cataloguing in Publication Data
Small Firms: Recession and Recovery
  I. Chittenden, Francis
  658.02

ISBN 1 85396 249 ×

Typeset by Setrite Typesetters, Hong Kong
Printed and bound by The Cromwell Press, Wiltshire.

A B C D E F G H 9 8 7 6 5 4 3

Contents

FOREWORD

The Small Business sector is of major importance to the UK, contributing 17 per cent of national output and accounting for 35 per cent of private sector employment.

As a sector it is extremely dynamic. In the current recession, there have been, on average, 400,000 small businesses starting up each year but this has to be viewed against a high rate of business closures. Overall, the market is showing signs of decline but these figures have to be set against an almost 51 per cent increase in the stock of UK businesses over the past decade from 1.79 million in 1979 to 2.70 million in 1991.

With large businesses streamlining their core activities, it is small businesses which have the capability to reduce UK unemployment as the locally based supplier competes to provide these services.

For small businesses to survive and grow in this rapidly changing marketplace there is a need for continued research, to help policy makers in Government and Business better understand the reasons for success and failure, to add to our knowledge of how this diverse and complex sector functions, and to assess what training and developmental needs they have now and for the future.

NatWest welcomes the opportunity to sponsor publication of this selection of papers presented at the 15th National Small Firms Policy and Research Conference in Southampton last year under the auspices of The Institute for Small Business Affairs.

Jane Bradford
Head of Small Business Services
National Westminster Bank

CONTRIBUTORS

M.R. Binks, Department of Economics, Nottingham University, Nottingham.

R.A. Blackburn, Small Business Research Centre, Kingston University, Kingston Hill, Kingston upon Thames, Surrey KT2 7LB.

F. Chittenden, Business Development Centre, Manchester Business School, University of Manchester, Booth Street West, Manchester M15 6PB.

R. Cressy, Centre for Small and Medium Sized Enterprises, Warwick University Business School, The University of Warwick, Coventry CV4 7AL.

J. Curran, Small Business Research Centre, Kingston University, Kingston Hill, Kingston upon Thames, Surrey KT2 7LB.

D. Deakins, Department of Financial Services, University of Central England Business School, Perry Barr, Birmingham B42 2SU.

K. Dickson, Management Studies, University of West London (Brunel), Kingston Lane, Uxbridge, Middlesex UK8 3PH.

C. Gallagher, Trends Business Research, St Thomas Street, Newcastle NE1 4LE.

C. Gray, School of Management, Open University, Walton Hall, Milton Keynes MK7 6AA.

R. Holliday, Department of Management, University of Central England Business School, Perry Barr, Birmingham B42 2SU.

G. Hussain, Department of Financial Services, University of Central England Business School, Perry Barr, Birmingham B42 2SU.

D. Jones-Evans, Centre for Entrepreneurship in the Service Sector, Durham University Business School, Mill Hill Lane, Durham City DH1 3LB.

A. Kennon, Business Development Centre, Manchester Business School, University of Manchester, Booth Street West, Manchester M15 6PB.

J. Kerr, St Mary's House, Sheffield S1 4PQ.

D.A. Kirby, Centre for Entrepreneurship in the Service Sector, Durham University Business School, Mill Hill Lane, Durham City DH1 3LB.

R. Leigh, Centre for Enterprise and Economic Development Research, Middlesex University, Queensway, Enfield, Middlesex EN3 4SF.

S. Lloyd-Smith, School of Social Science, Kingston University, Penrhyn Road, Kingston upon Thames, Surrey KT1 2EE.

S. Mahindru, Business Development Centre, Manchester Business School, University of Manchester, Booth Street West, Manchester M15 6PB.

N. Meager, Institute of Manpower Studies, University of Sussex, Mantell Building, Falmer, Brighton BN1 9RF.

D. North, Centre for Enterprise and Economic Development Research, Middlesex University, Queensway, Enfield, Middlesex EN3 4SF.

D. Purdy, Future of Work Research Group, Faculty of Business, Management and Social Studies, 35 Marylebone Road, London NW1 5LS.

M. Ram, Department of Management, University of Central England Business School, Perry Barr, Birmingham B42 2SU.

G. Robson, Management Division, School of Business Management, Armstrong Building, University of Newcastle upon Tyne NE1 7RU.

M. Robertson, Leeds Business School, Leeds Metropolitan University, 80 Woodhouse Lane, Leeds.

D. Smallbone, Centre for Enterprise and Economic Development Research, Middlesex University, Queensway, Enfield, Middlesex EN3 4SF.

J. Sparrow, Department of Business Policy and Marketing, University of Central England Business School, Perry Barr, Birmingham B42 2SU.

J. Stanworth, Future of Work Research Group, Faculty of Business, Management and Social Studies, 35 Marylebone Road, London NW1 5LS.

D. Storey, Centre for Small and Medium Sized Enterprises, Warwick University Business School, The University of Warwick, Coventry CV4 7AL.

P.A. Vale, Centre for Management Development, Durham University Business School, Mill Hill Lane, Durham City DH1 3LB.

P. Wilson, New Enterprise Partnership, 15 Park House, 140 Battersea Park Road, London SW11 4NB.

A. Woods, Management Studies, University of West London (Brunel), Kingston Lane, Uxbridge, Middlesex UK8 3PH.

N. Zafiris, Future of Work Research Group, Faculty of Business, Management and Social Studies, 35 Marylebone Road, London NW1 5LS.

1.

SMALL FIRMS: PUBLIC POLICY ISSUES IN RECESSION AND RECOVERY

Francis Chittenden and Martyn Robertson

INTRODUCTION

Small Business in Britain (DoE 1992) identifies six areas of research which are of particular interest to public policy makers. These are:

- The internal and external barriers to growth facing small businesses.
- Small and medium-sized enterprises (SMEs) demand for and access to finance, including equity.
- Inter-relationships and interdependence between small and large firms, and between small businesses.
- Training within small firms.
- The impact of BS 5750 and other standards.
- The impact of growth in the SME sector on overall economic performance.

All of these topics were the subject of presentations and discussion at the 15th National Small Firms' Policy and Research Conference hosted by the Southampton Institute in November 1992 and organised on their behalf by David Watkins, with the support of Hampshire Training and Enterprise Council.

This chapter draws upon a selection of papers from that conference and a broad range of the topics identified above are considered. As might be anticipated, a recurrent theme is the impact of recession on the SME sector and the policy issues which require to be addressed in order to assist small businesses in leading the economy into sustained recovery.[1]

This chapter is divided into seven sections; recent research on six specific facets of small firms policy is first presented and then summarised in an agenda for action. The contribution of small firms to economic performance is considered initially, focusing particularly on their capacity for job creation. The external factors influencing formation, growth and churning within the sector are next examined, in the context of regional policy and performance. Thirdly, the propensity of small firms to interact with one another, with larger businesses and within their locality is discussed. Fourthly, there is a review of recent evidence on the behavioural factors influencing performance, particularly the growth orientation of owner managers. No evaluation would be complete without consideration of the most widely reported barrier to growth, the need for appropriate types and quantities of finance. Penultimately, two recent studies have identified the existence of gaps in the support services available to certain types of SMEs. Finally, the conclusions from these studies are summarised together with recommendations for policy action.

ECONOMIC PERFORMANCE

In Chapter 2 Storey demonstrates that the high levels of self-employment observed in the UK, following a decade of virtually continuous growth, are unlikely to result in strong performance either in terms of increases in employment, or reductions in unemployment. A continued switch of resources from support for start-ups to a more focused strategy to nurture established small firms with growth potential is called for. It does seem that DTI policies have moved some way along this route and the analysis concludes by outlining a strategy which Training and Enterprise Councils (TECs) could adopt to implement these proposals. The tactics require TECs to identify fast growing firms in their area and approach these to identify whether they:

1. Intend to continue to expand.
2. Face constraints or risks associated with growth.
3. Wish to work with the TEC in identifying managerial solutions to these difficulties.

This policy is radical as it requires TECs to provide demand- rather than supply-led services and to work consistently with the owners of a relatively small number of firms[2] over several months. It is also radical as there has been long debate on the practicality of identifying the minority of small businesses which will be responsible for the majority of new growth.

During the conference there were a number of other papers on this theme, some providing further insight into the selection of businesses and entrepreneurs with the greatest propensity to generate growth, others explaining the strategies that are presently being adopted to achieve these objectives (see for example Bartlett 1992).

Continuing the theme of the impact of SME policy on economic performance, Meager (Chapter 3) received the Stan Mendham Prize for the best conference paper, awarded annually by the Forum of Private Business, for an outstanding analysis of the growth in self-employment across Europe and an appraisal of the effectiveness of the Enterprise Allowance Scheme. This research documents the increases in self-employment observed during the 1980s and concludes that government programmes such as the Enterprise Allowance Scheme (now the Business Start-up Scheme) do have a positive impact on the propensity to establish new businesses.

The paper reaches two interesting conclusions. Firstly, that unemployment push is almost certainly not the primary reason for increases in self-employment (as evidenced by current experience in the UK). Secondly, that there may be more effective methods for encouraging lasting self-employment than subsidising new business owners' incomes. In particular there is a contrast with the French experience, where firms qualifying for support receive a grant towards capital equipment, thus encouraging business formation in sectors where the barriers to entry might otherwise be beyond the reach of the unemployed. This is an interesting approach which accords more closely with current Training and Enterprise Councils (TECs) policies towards the Business Start-up Scheme.

This extensive study of self-employment is complemented by the work of Stanworth et al (Chapter 4) which reviews the performance of established SMEs and compares job generation and financial performance in periods of growth (1984–1988) and recession (1989–1992). Those sectors which exhibited the most rapid growth in employment are also the sectors exhibiting the largest decline during the recession. Nonetheless there is, at this stage of observation, still evidence of a net increase in employment from these firms across the whole period under review.

The study also examines the barriers to growth identified during the boom years based upon the Nat West/Small Business Research Trust (SBRT) quarterly surveys and contrasts these results with experiences in recession. Predictably, lack of skilled staff was the major barrier in 1988 as noted by about 1/6 of respondents. However, in 1992 almost 44% of the sample reported low turnover or lack of business as the major constraint, with the smallest businesses being affected most.

The sensitivity of small business owners to possible changes in the economic environment was observed by comparing the employment increases anticipated in 1989 with the levels actually achieved by 1992. Survey participants were generally over-optimistic, and appeared to fall into two categories, with the results being bimodal. About 20% overestimated future employment potential by 0−25%, whilst 35−40% were in error to the extent of 100% or more! However, it must be said that SMEs were not alone in expecting 'more of the same' when the recession had only just started.

EXTERNAL FACTORS INFLUENCING PERFORMANCE

Thus far, at the macro-level, a fairly dismal picture has been painted of the plight of SMEs in the current recession. In addition Chapter 4 presents regional analyses of performance, and this work is complemented by Gallagher et al (Chapter 5), who provide a detailed review of spatial variations in the populations of small firms by size, and Paul Westhead and Sue Birley (1992) who examine the regional patterns of VAT deregistrations.

Chapter 5 studies the constitution of the SME population by regions, based upon data provided by Dun & Bradstreet for the period 1987−1989, and concludes that, as well as many similarities, there are important variations in the distribution (and performance) of businesses in this heterogeneous sector. For example, in such a period of economic growth, low concentration of employment in small firms in a region appears to lead to strong job creation by existing firms. However, overall more than 50% of jobs were created by small firms in the 1−4 employment band. In other words, micro-firms have (despite the high level of churning in this sector) been significant contributors to employment growth.

Finally the paper clusters regions of the UK by firm density and GDP per capita, identifying three groups:

1. The South East, in a rank of its own.
2. An intermediate group made up of East Anglia, the East Midlands, the North West, the South West, the West Midlands and Yorkshire.
3. The North, Scotland and Wales.

Regional groupings are also presented in the methodologically interesting Westhead and Birley (1992) paper. This analysis uses VAT deregistration data to monitor and evaluate the propensity of firms to decrease in size, recognise reduced prospects or cease to be economically active; for which VAT deregistrations are taken to be an adequate surrogate. The analysis concludes by identifying 14 factors which contribute to and explain 83% of the level of deregistrations across regions.

The key factor influencing the number of deregistrations was, predictably, the number of registrations, and there were other factors which might be associated with rapid economic growth followed by steep decline. Higher levels of deregistrations were associated with regions which had exhibited high levels of employment and earnings. At the same time, there was a range of causal relationships associated with deregistration which were typical of declining urban areas. These include high levels of long-term unemployment, dense population, high domestic rates and rapid change in the industrial base, presumably associated with a shift away from traditional but contracting sectors.

Factors associated with lower rates of deregistrations include regional specialisation of the industrial base, population growth, growing total and manufacturing employment and good levels of education as evidenced, for example, by the proportion of children staying on at school beyond the age of 16. These could perhaps be categorised as volume factors (e.g. population growth) and quality factors (e.g. high educational achievement); however they are likely to be interdependent.

The analysis concludes by providing a classification of seven regions with distinctive patterns of deregistrations. The areas faring best are the more remote parts such as Lincolnshire, Cornwall, Cumbria and counties in North Wales, whereas the worst performers are the large urban conurbations including Greater Manchester, the West Midlands, Merseyside and Tyne and Wear; with London coming a close second.

The conclusions of these two papers appear to be that the heterogeneity observed in the small business population is mirrored in the constitution and performance of local economies. As a result TECs and Local Enterprise Companies (LECs) should adopt policies with distinctive focus and resources in order to meet the particular needs of their regions' economic environment. It will be interesting to observe the extent to which policies can be contrasted between one locality and another.

INTER-RELATIONSHIPS AND INTERDEPENDENCE

Following this commentary relating to the external factors influencing the performance of the SME sector, it is appropriate to consider issues relating to the inter-regional and intra-regional relationships of small businesses with consumers and organisations of all sizes.

Small businesses and local economies are often perceived as inextricably linked (Pyke et al 1990). It is frequently assumed that small businesses serve almost exclusively local markets and, more recently, a good deal of theorising and research has studied the role of the small enterprise in sustaining and regenerating local economies. Larger enterprises and organisations have also received attention, for instance, in terms of their ability to influence the whole character of a local economy, or to alter it fundamentally following changes in corporate policy.

Curran & Blackburn (Chapter 6) have examined the role of 410 small service and manufacturing firms in seven local economies, with an emphasis on small/large firm relations. In addition, data from interviews with representatives of 16 large enterprises in the public and private sectors is presented.

The research concludes that in the seven economies studied, rather than them behaving as interdependent industrial districts, there exists a range of fragmented economic patterns which are dependent upon the type of activities conducted and the management strategies of the small and large businesses towards their wider economic environment. For most firms the economic imperatives of price, quality and delivery were of paramount importance in choosing trading partners.

Often small firms did not serve only local markets and when they did relationships were frequently purely functional. It is well known that small business owners are highly independent and this trait could be observed in the self-imposed distancing of their enterprises from the wider economy. Involvement in the business and social community through organisations such as Chambers of Commerce were limited. Inter-trading between large and small businesses was also restricted with both parties expressing reservations about their ability to forge successful commercial relationships. It appears that the models of harmonious regional economies comprising firms of various sizes supporting one another in supplying the needs of the market place are of limited practical relevance.

Complementing this analysis Smith et al (Chapter 7) report the results of a study which examines the manner in which small firms from four unrelated service sectors interact with other firms within their sector. This is a sociological study which examines the behaviour patterns of small business owners and discusses the extent to which they influence or are influenced by the established behaviour patterns within their sector. The paper concludes that business owners are strongly influenced by the operating dynamics of their trades which fall into two types. Type A firms, including employment and training agencies and advertising and design companies, do not interact in a supportive manner with their competitors, whereas Type B firms, garages and plant hire businesses, do co-operate with one another.

An interesting extension to the conclusions from Chapter 6 resulting from this study is that the propensity to serve local markets is highly specific to the industry sector. The garage and plant hire firms (Type B) definitely served local industrial districts while advertising and design, and Employment and Training Agencies (Type A firms) had neither strong local or national links. Research conducted by Morrison (1992) demonstrates that this lack of industry networks can represent a source of competitive disadvantage for small firms. In the hotel industry, small business owners may have to discard a measure of their independence and participate in co-operative marketing schemes in order to survive.

Finally in this section, Jones-Evans & Kirby (Chapter 8) present the result of a study examining the growth of small technical consultancies in the UK. This analysis starts with the hypothesis that small firms of this type will have multiplied in number partly because larger organisations are externalising certain corporate functions. There has been extensive research in the UK of businesses involved in technologically innovative activity (see for example, Oakey 1984). However less attention has been paid to technology-based services even though the growth in business services stands out as the single most important component of expansion of the SME sector in the 1980s (Keeble et al 1992).

This study focuses on businesses in high technology manufacturing, computer services, professional/technical services and research and development; sectors in which technical consultancies are believed to thrive. Very rapid rates of growth in the number of small firms in each of these sectors are identified; together with an overall shift in employment towards technical and computing services between 1981–1989, and rapid employment growth in the period 1987–1989. However, the results of this study were equivocal. The observed growth could be due to 'externalisation' by large companies creating opportunities for employees to establish specialist organisations serving their former employers. Alternatively, the advance of technology may be creating niches in which small businesses can operate successfully.

BEHAVIOURAL FACTORS INFLUENCING PERFORMANCE

Gray (Chapter 9) challenges some traditional concepts when he explores the propensity of small business owners to expand their organisations. The study examines the established stages of growth models (see for example Churchill and Lewis 1983) and finds that they have limited relevance to the small businesses observed in the SBRT quarterly surveys.

This paper draws on the well-known phenomenon that small business owners, particularly the self-employed, are primarily concerned to retain their independence (Stanworth and Curran 1973), although this term may have different meanings for the various types of business owners (Gray 1990, 1992). The latest labour force survey revealed that self-employment declined by 4% in 1991, and that of the UK's 3,282,000 self-employed, 70% have no staff whatsoever.

Applying the constructs of motivational theory to the development of small business owners it is concluded that although firms are seldom founded with the objective of establishing a large enterprise these aspirations may develop as a consequence of strong business performance. However, Gray argues that few small business owners wish to expand their firms beyond the 25 employee range, the point around which management style must become 'professional' with considerable delegation of responsibility and authority.[3] Reluctance to raise external equity to fund the rapid expansion of the business is also seen as a significant barrier.

In support of this theory, analysis of the motivations of survey respondents shows that growth-orientated firms have owners whose business objectives are more profit-centred than those of less dynamic firms where security or an improving lifestyle were of greater importance. Interestingly, the stated importance of profit orientation for the business was sometimes in conflict with owners' personal objectives of security or improved lifestyle. However, the relationship between commercial objectives and business performance appears to be the more important.

The paper concludes that workforce size/maturity models alone may not be adequate to describe small firm growth. It is apparent that some owners have higher commercial awareness than others. This is reflected in the fact that the growth-orientated firms tended to be more business minded and this proactive approach is manifested in greater appreciation of the need to address the key issues of growth, including delegation and acquiring external finance.

Some evidence is presented which suggests that the confidence which results from running a small business successfully may help provide the impetus for future growth. This is a fundamental point which is underlined in work by Macnabb and McCoy (1992) who explore the core values and conflicts facing business owners at different stages of the business lifecycle. The need to stimulate and sustain growth orientation is also one of the objectives of expert systems currently being developed (Fuller and Heslop 1992). Whilst it will be some time before the impact of this technique can be fully evaluated, the general point that maximising the potential of the SME sector is bound up with owner-managers' experiences in running their businesses must not be lost from view. A volatile economic environment, burdensome compliance regime and intractable barriers to growth (such as failure of the factor market for finance) simply ensure that economic performance will be constrained by the modest aspirations of a large number of small business managers.

Continuing discussion of the attitudinal factors affecting growth potential, Ram and Holliday (Chapter 10) present an interesting operational review of managerial behaviour in family firms, which account for 80% of partnerships and almost 2/3 of limited companies in the SME sector (Chittenden 1991). For some, the notion of the family firm presents an image of harmony in the workplace; moreover family ties are seen as an important source of commitment and flexibility. Others, however, view family involvement as little more than a cover-up for exploitative practices which are believed to be dominant in small firms.

Using an ethnographic approach (Holliday 1992, Stockport and Kakabadse 1992) this paper explores how the notion of the family is actually operationalised at the level of the workplace. Interestingly 'extended' family relationships were found to influence managerial behaviour even in firms which would not normally be regarded as family businesses. Based upon this research it appears that 'the family' is crucial to the under-standing of the pattern of social relations within small firms, but is much more complex and contested than commonly portrayed. 'The family' was found to act as both a resource and a constraint; management benefited from the flexibility afforded by familial ties, but the 'family' also imposed obligations which occasionally conflicted with wealth maximisation objectives. The diffuse nature of such arrangements meant that 'negotiated paternalism', rather than an 'autocracy of harmony', more accurately depicted the pattern of work. The familial culture also bounded the development of the management teams and their values and resulted in replication of the gender roles often found in natural family units.

FINANCE AND THE SMALL FIRM

Having reviewed some of the papers relating to the contribution of small firms to the UK economy, particularly their contribution to employment, and the external and internal factors which influence this role, the discussion now turns to what is often referred to as the greatest external barrier to growth, the need for sufficient quantities and appropriate forms of finance to be made available to the sector.

Whilst the provision of debt capital has received significant media attention over the past few years, for most small firms with growth prospects this is probably not the ideal form of finance. Limited proprietorial capital, modest personal resources, few marketable assets and relatively high risk all signify a primary need for greater equity resources (Mason and Harrison 1992).

This issue is addressed by Binks and Vale in Chapter 11 which draws heavily on the authors' theoretical treatise on entrepreneurship (Binks and Vale 1990) in which new ventures are classified in accordance with a typology of entrepreneurial acts. The point is made that not all new firms have the same potential to contribute to economic development. In an extreme case, it is argued, certain entrepreneurial events may accelerate the process of decline within a particular industrial sector.[4]

This is inductive rather than empirical work which concludes that the entrepreneurial events likely to have the most positive economic impact[5] in the medium term require sources of equity which reflect the risk profile of those investments. This is a significant conceptual leap, akin perhaps to the principle of matching of funds for debt finance. There is substantial evidence of the need for such an approach, as the provision of modest sums of equity for small firms is seriously constrained as a result of market failure (Binks and Vale 1990, Camp and Sexton 1992). However, the mechanisms proposed in this paper, including the use of a national 'risk capital lottery', are highly controversial in their current form and unlikely to attract wide support.

The proposed scheme also involves the provision of tax relief for investment in certain classes of business through a recognised fund. A variety of mechanisms have provided tax relief for investment in small businesses over the past few years, including the Business Start up and Expansion Schemes. Sadly none of these have permitted investment or re-investment in businesses by their owners, or their lineal antecedents or descendants.

There are a number of constraints on small firms attracting external equity funds, including, but certainly not exclusively, owners' desire for independence (Binks and Vale 1990), information asymmetries[6] and agency costs[7] (Peterson and Shulman 1987). Any scheme which ignores these and restricts incentives to third parties will be constrained to having limited application.

Pursuing the theme of ensuring adequate finance for small businesses as the recession eases, Deakins and Hussain (Chapter 12) investigate the criteria adopted by banks appraising new business propositions. The authors found a wide variety of responses to a real business plan, with limited consistency in either the analytic criteria employed or bankers' decisions to offer financial support or reject the proposal.

Of eight factors frequently considered by the bankers 75% related to the financial characteristics of the proposition or the owner. 'Industry contacts' ranked only fourth and small business experience was mentioned by just one banker in 10. This latter point is surprising as evidence provided by ACOST (1990) indicates that large firm managers may not operate effectively in the small firm sector, supporting the view that small firms are not little big firms (Welsh and White 1981).

The research concludes that the bank staff interviewed were more concerned about avoiding the provision of financial support for businesses which fail (Type 1 errors) than declining to support potentially successful ventures (Type 2 errors). This is no doubt rational behaviour in the face of considerable uncertainty with the prospects for success further constrained by a weak economy. For banks there is a limited return on successful propositions, portfolio management of small business loans was found to be rudimentary and the administrative hassle associated with non-performing accounts bears little relationship to the level of funds advanced. The paper concludes by making a number of policy recommendations to overcome the adverse selection problem, in particular the application of more sophisticated portfolio management techniques for small business loans.

A recent review of the small firms loan guarantee scheme (SFLGS) concluded that its initial purpose had been superseded, primarily because of the striking increase in bank lending during the 1980s, and recommended that the scheme should be scaled down or abolished altogether (NERA 1990). However, the scale of provisions made by the banks against their small business loan portfolios during this recession means that the recently announced extensions to the SFLGS could provide a useful tool for avoiding Type 2 errors, if only the banks will embrace this opportunity with enthusiasm. The appeal of the SFLGS might be further enhanced by the introduction of a secondary market in Government guaranteed loans, similar to the one which operates successfully in the USA. The risks associated with high opportunity businesses could also be reduced through partnerships with TECs providing additional managerial resource as proposed by Storey (see Chapter 2).

In the absence of such initiatives, banks face a limited number of options:

1. To minimise risk, for example by maximising security.
2. To maximise margins by charging as large a risk premium as permitted by market forces.
3. To maximise margins by minimising administration costs and passing these on to the customer wherever possible.
4. To reduce the risk by better informed selection criteria.

All banks are simultaneously attempting to improve management of each of these processes. Failure to do so would be tantamount to surrendering market presence in this sector to more determined and better informed competition. Cressy (Chapter 13) reports the early results of a study commissioned by market leader National Westminster Bank aimed at improving lending decisions to new businesses.

This study is based upon a sample of 2000 randomly selected start-up propositions supported by Nat West in 1988. Of these, approximately half were still trading by the end of the first quarter of 1992. The result is an econometric study employing five simultaneous equations which produce some interesting results. For example, probability of survival is improved for older, more appropriately qualified proprietors (human capital), providing higher value security (commitment), taking advice from professionals. Certain industry sectors had lower exit rates than others and multi-banked borrowers were more likely to cease trading.

This is a fascinating exercise involving a unique data set providing longitudinal as well as cross-sectional data. No doubt the full results will not be published for some considerable time, as they represent competitive advantage for Nat West. However, it must be recognised that competitive forces alone will not be adequate to redress market failure in the factor market for finance. Public policy initiatives are essential, to quote the Bolton Committee (1971):

> Moreover what is required for the health of the (small firms) sector is an economic and taxation system which will enable individuals to acquire or establish new businesses out of personal resources and to develop these on the base of retained profits. Without this no institutional financing arrangement can preserve the small firms sector

Finally, attention shifts to the management of cashflow by SMEs. There has been considerable public debate on the impact of and need to control late payment of commercial invoices. One of the earlier contributions in the field came from the Forum of Private Business (1987) which has been lobbying hard for legislation to control these practices through a statutory right to interest. A more recent study, conducted for National Westminster Bank (Chapter 14), seeks to determine the extent of the slow payment problem and to evaluate its impact on small firms and the economy as a whole. This analysis concludes that the long-established practice of offering trade credit to support customers' stock holdings and thereby ease the flow of goods through the supply chain whilst simultaneously reducing the administrative burden of immediate payment is generally beneficial to the economy.

However, the research shows that these objectives have been lost from view. Trade credit is now more strongly associated with funding trade debtors, which results in a multiplier effect leading to rising financing costs and less predictable income for the majority of firms. The analysis demonstrates that prompt payment would improve the aggregate operating cashflow of UK firms although some sectors and businesses would benefit at the expense of others. Evidence is provided that small businesses in France and Germany would also gain from improved payment practices, which could be an important element in sustaining economic recovery.

A fundamental problem relating to payment periods is that, in the UK, time of payment is not automatically a condition of commercial contracts, even though time of delivery often is! Thus suppliers who are paid late can only recover interest by taking legal action against customers and persuading the court to award an appropriate sum in damages. This is slow, administratively cumbersome and only a viable option when suing for recovery of the principal as well as the interest. Most EC states already have legislation which provides an automatic right to interest in respect of late payments. Whilst simply introducing legislation does not necessarily provide a solution, carefully drafted laws would provide substantial impetus towards improving UK payment practices which are reportedly the worst in the EC (Chittenden et al 1993). An increasing number of representative bodies (e.g. The Forum of Private Business, Association of British Chambers of Commerce) and leading lawyers (e.g. Lord Alexander of Weedon) now publicly support the introduction of legislation on this matter.

SME POLICY – BRIDGING THE SUPPORT GAP

Smallbone, North and Leigh (Chapter 15) provide a policy agenda for mature SMEs based upon analysis of a sample of 306 firms (at least 10 years old at the time of interview), located in Greater London, outer metropolitan locations and remote rural areas. Of the 306 firms in the panel, 54% showed real turnover growth over the decade and 37% more than doubled sales. Employment generation was closely related to output growth, being particularly concentrated in those firms which more than doubled output.

In accordance with the analysis by Storey (Chapter 2), this sample consists of firms which are of particular interest in the current policy environment. Only just over half (55%) of the firms interviewed had used external support over the decade, and very few regularly used assistance from any source, reflecting once more the independence of small business owners. It might be argued that this behaviour could have resulted from the fact that the economic environment had generally been favourable over this period (1979–1990). Perhaps the firms felt that they did not require assistance.[8]

In fact 25% of the mature SMEs were able to identify particular problems over the decade where external assistance could have been useful, but was not available. On the basis of this evidence the authors conclude that a support gap appears to exist. One obvious target group for such assistance is those firms seeking to grow but experiencing difficulty in realising this goal. Such firms accounted for just over 1/4 of the sample! A second priority group would be firms growing very rapidly (Storey and Johnson 1987) as this may in itself be a high risk strategy (North et al 1991).

The mature SMEs interviewed required distinctive patterns of support usually beyond the scope of Enterprise Agencies. In particular it is necessary for advisers to gain the respect of client companies quickly (Carswell 1990) and, in the view of business owners, specialist sectoral expertise is especially valued (Leigh et al 1991). Sector-based support and advice has not merely a higher chance of being acceptable to clients, thus encouraging take-up, but also of making more of a real impact on the business.

Experience of both public sector support and subsidised consultancy was patchy. The TECs had not been established long enough to have had a measurable impact. It is recommended that in order to maximise the beneficial influence of consultants there should be a move away from quick in-and-out studies so that longer term relationships can contribute to the learning of the managers. The most obvious role model identified is the Rural Development Commission, which offers a mixture of financial support and ongoing advice widely appreciated by its clients.

A support gap has also been identified in a survey of 50 Asian-owned SMEs conducted by Ram and Sparrow (Chapter 16). The analysis concludes that Asian SMEs do have particular needs not necessarily typical of other sectors. In particular racial discrimination is found to influence the ways in which ethnic business owners approach potential markets and specialist marketing support is required to mitigate some of these difficulties. TECs must also examine their own personnel management policies and ensure that ethnic minorities are appropriately represented, especially in positions with responsibility for interfacing with local employers.

CONCLUSIONS AND RECOMMENDATIONS

Based on international comparisons there is little evidence that the high levels of self-employment observed in the UK, following a decade of virtually continuous growth, are likely to result in strong performance either in terms of increases in employment, or reductions in unemployment. Employment growth is provided by a minority of businesses, with 4% of firms generating 50% of new jobs and 18% of firms creating 92% of net new employment (Chapter 2, Gallagher and Miller 1991). The switch of resources from support for start-ups to a more focused strategy to nurture established small firms with growth potential should be continued.

A detailed analysis of the Enterprise Allowance Scheme and its equivalent in other European countries identifies that there may be more effective methods for encouraging lasting self-employment than subsidising new business owners' income. In particular there is a contrast with the French experience, where firms qualifying for support receive a grant towards capital equipment, thus encouraging business formation in sectors where the barriers to entry might otherwise be beyond the reach of the unemployed. Government should continue to encourage TECs to use the Business Start-up Scheme flexibly.

Analysis of the motivations of respondents to the SBRT quarterly surveys shows that growth-orientated firms have owners whose business objectives are more profit-centred than those of less dynamic firms where security or an improving lifestyle were of greater importance. Interestingly, the stated importance of profit/growth orientation for the business was sometimes in conflict with owners' personal objectives of security or improved lifestyle. However, the relationship between commercial objectives and business performance appears to be the more important. Public policy should focus attention on those businesses seeking to maximise profits through business growth.

In 1992, almost 44% of the small businesses responding to the National Westminster Bank/Small Business Research Trust surveys reported low turnover or lack of business as the major constraint, with the smallest businesses being affected most. The economic and social policy cocktail which guarantees sustained growth has yet to be discovered in the UK, if indeed such policies exist. However, over the past 30 years (excluding the oil shock of the early 1970s) the two periods of decline in real GDP have occurred since 1980.[9] It thus appears that the downside swings in the economy are becoming more pronounced. The recent reductions in interest rates are helpful in encouraging recovery; however Government must also seek to develop policies which smooth rather than accentuate fluctuations in the levels of economic activity.

Based upon two extensive studies of the regional variations in performance of SMEs, it is concluded that the heterogeneity observed in the small business population is mirrored in the constitution and performance of local economies. TECs must be given the freedom to adopt policies with distinctive focus and resources in order to meet the particular needs of their local economic environment. It will be interesting to observe the extent to which their policies can be contrasted between regions and over time.

Areas exhibiting the highest rates of business (VAT) deregistrations were the major conurbations, including Greater Manchester, Merseyside, the West Midlands and Tyne and Wear, with London not far behind. A number of these areas are now benefiting from City Challenge funds. It is essential that these resources are carefully deployed to ensure that the adverse impact of disruption during redevelopment does not further damage the already fragile stock of small businesses.

Eighty per cent of partnerships and almost 2/3 of small limited companies are family-owned and managed (Chittenden 1991). As a result the family is crucial to the understanding of the pattern of social relations within small firms. In addition small businesses which are not family-owned may, nonetheless, espouse family values in their management style and these relationships are much more complex and contested than commonly portrayed. 'The family' acts as both a resource and a constraint; management benefits from the flexibility afforded by familial ties, but the family also imposes obligations which occasionally conflict with wealth-maximisation goals. The diffuse nature of such arrangements means that 'negotiated paternalism', rather than an 'autocracy of harmony', more accurately depicts the family at work. Policy makers, TEC advisers and small business consultants must be aware of the impact of familial relationships and values on small firms' decisions.

A variety of mechanisms have provided tax relief for investment in small businesses over the past few years, including the Business Start-up and Expansion Schemes. Sadly none of these have permitted investment or re-investment in businesses by the owner-managers, or their lineal antecedents or descendants. There are a number of barriers to small firms attracting external funds. Any scheme which ignores these and restricts equity investment incentives to third parties will be constrained to having limited application.

The experience of the past three years, in which banks have made significant provisions against their small business loan portfolios, provides evidence of the extent to which lenders are exposed to risk as a result of their commercial debt contracts. In the absence of agreements which provide higher than average returns on loans to successful businesses, it is inevitable that these institutions will continue to focus on avoiding losses. Occasionally the result of such risk aversion will be the rejection of potentially viable proposals.

Collaboration between TECs, banks and high prospect firms could reduce the extent of information asymmetry between parties to the debt contract, and enable lenders to support some businesses which would otherwise have financing proposals rejected. The propositions would also be enhanced by the prospect of ongoing management support from the TEC adviser.

The major area of investment for many small businesses is working capital. Originally trade credit was intended to support stockholding by customers as goods pass down the supply chain. The practice of paying suppliers periodically instead of at the time of delivery also reduces administrative burdens. However, analysis shows that the value of credit taken by firms is now more closely associated with the level of accounts owed to the business by its customers. This practice results in a credit spiral, with ever increasing levels of debtors constraining cash-flows resulting in further delay in settling suppliers' accounts in order to 'balance the books'.

An increasing number of representative bodies and institutions support the calls for government to introduce legislation and provide a statutory right to interest on accounts paid late. Whilst this action would not be a panacea it is a logical first step. Everything possible should be done to improve payment practices in the UK, as the economy as a whole would benefit from shorter credit periods.

Mature SMEs require distinctive patterns of support usually beyond the skills required for new and micro-businesses. In particular, advisers must quickly gain the respect of client companies and specialist sectoral expertise is particularly valuable. Sector-based support and advice has not merely a higher chance of being acceptable to clients, thus encouraging take-up, but also of making more of a real impact on the business.

The traditional modus operandi of consultants conducting quick in and out studies reduces the beneficial impact on firms. Longer term relationships contribute to the learning of owner/managers far more effectively. The most obvious role model of an effective business advisory service is the Rural Development Commission. This organisation offers a mixture of ongoing advice and financial support and is widely appreciated by its customers.

Asian SMEs do have particular needs for advice not necessarily typical of other sectors. In particular racial discrimination is found to influence the ways in which ethnic business owners approach potential markets and specialist marketing support is required to mitigate some of these difficulties.

NOTES

1. In the last Spring budget speech Norman Lamont, who was then Chancellor, acknowledged the vital role of small firms: 'small firms play a crucial role in our economy. Small businesses do not follow the economy — they lead it. That has been demonstrated time and time again.'

   This is a most interesting assertion, presumably based upon the fact that even in recession between 1/4 and 1/3 of small businesses have continued to expand (see for example Forum of Private Business 1992). However this is not necessarily the same as the small business sector 'leading the economy out of recession' and as yet no rigorous evidence of this leadership role has been produced.

   If research were to confirm that small firms do indeed occupy such a pivotal function the impact on macro-economic policy could be profound.
2. Storey has found that 4% of small firms create 50% of all jobs and other studies reach similar conclusions (Gallagher and Miller 1991, Smallbone et al 1992). For example Gallagher and Miller's work indicates that 92% of new employment was created by 18% of small businesses.
3. For a further discussion of these issues see Hall (1992).
4. For example, when the assets of a failed firm are purchased from a liquidator at below economic value and then used in competition with established firms who are subsequently driven out of business.
5. Such as the commercial application of new technology and other 'new combinations of economic resources' as identified by Schumpeter (1934).
6. Problems of asymmetric information result from differences in information available to owners of entrepreneurial firms in comparison to outsiders. Smaller firms generally have higher levels of asymmetric information since the length of their trading record is shorter, there will be greater variability in the level of profits and sales (Storey et al 1987) and the quality of their financial statements may vary (Coker and Hayes 1992). This final problem is likely to become more widespread if the statutory audit is abolished in the UK.
7. An agency problem arises when decision-makers (owners) have incentives to take decisions that are not necessarily in the interests of other stakeholders. As a result of information asymmetries such decisions cannot be perfectly monitored (Barnea et al 1981).
8. Research by Brennan and McHugh (1992) investigated the impact of recession on small business owners and concludes that even when facing severe personal and financial pressures many proprietors remain reluctant to seek professional advice.
9. Source: Budget Statement 1990/1.

REFERENCES

ACOST (1990) The Enterprise Challenge: Overcoming Barriers to Growth in Small Firms, HMSO, London.

Barnea A., Haugen R. and Senbet L. (1981) Market imperfections, agency problems and capital structure: a review, Financial Management, Summer.

Bartlett D. (1992) Strategy for established small businesses, paper presented to the 15th National Small Firms Policy & Research Conference, Southampton, November.

Binks M. and Vale P. (1990) Entrepreneurship and economic change, McGraw Hill, London, p. 93.

Bolton J.E. (1971) Report of the Committee of Enquiry on Small Firms, Cmnd 4811, HMSO, November, p. 192.

Brennan C.V. and McHugh M.L. (1992) Coping with recession: are entrepreneurial strengths being eroded?, Paper presented to the 15th National Small Firms Policy and Research Conference, Southampton, November.

Camp M. and Sexton D.L. (1992) Trends in venture capital investment: implications for high technology firms, Journal of Small Business Management, Vol. 30, No. 3, July.

Carswell M. (1990) Small Firm Networking and Business Performance, Paper presented to the 13th UK Small Firms Policy & Research Conference, Harrogate, November.

Chittenden F. (1991) Business Legal Structures, Forum of Private Business, Knutsford, pp. 33–35.

Chittenden F., Kennon A., Mahindru S. and Bragg R. (1993) Payment Practices, Legislation and Their Effect on S.M.Es: A Comparative Study, National Westminster Bank, May.

Churchill N. and Lewis V. (1983) The Five Stages of Business Growth, Harvard Business Review, May–June.

Coker J.W. and Hayes R.D. (1992) Lenders' perceptions of income tax basis reporting by small businesses, Journal of Small Business Management, July, Vol. 30, No. 3.

Department of Employment (1992) Small Business in Britain, HMSO, London.

Forum of Private Business (1992) Action for Recovery, FPB, Knutsford, Quarter 4.

Fuller T. and Heslop J. (1992) Encouraging growth orientation in SMEs by simulating advisers' viewpoints, paper presented to the 15th National Small Firms Policy & Research Conference, Southampton, November.

Gallagher G.G. and Miller P. (1991) New fast growing companies create jobs, Long range planning, Vol. 24, No. 1.

Gray C. (1990) Business independence – impediment or enhancement to growth in the 1990's?, Paper presented to 13th National Small Firms' Policy and Research Conference, Harrogate, November.

Gray C. (1992) Growth orientation and the small firm, in Small Enterprise Development: Policy and Practice in Action, eds Caley K., Chell E., Chittenden F. and Mason C., Paul Chapman Publishing, London, pp. 59–71.

Hall P.J. (1992) Small business portfolios: a study of their patterns related to small business owners' managerial abilities and entrepreneurial inclinations, paper presented to the 15th National Small Firms Policy & Research Conference, Southampton, November.

Holliday R. (1992) Cutting new patterns for small firms research, in Small Enterprise Development: Policy and Practice in Action, eds Caley K., Chell E., Chittenden F. and Mason C., Paul Chapman Publishing, London, pp. 166–177.

Keeble D., Bryson J. and Wood P. (1992) Entrepreneurship and flexibility in business services, in Small Enterprise Development: Policy and Practice in Action, eds Caley K., Chell E., Chittenden F. and Mason C., Paul Chapman Publishing, London, pp. 43–58.

Leigh R., North D. and Smallbone D. (1991) Adjustment processes in high growth small and medium sized enterprises: a study of mature manufacturing firms in London in the 1980's, Working paper No 2, ESRC Small Business Research Initiative, Middlesex University Project.

Macnabb A. and McCoy J. (1992) Growth orientation and control issues from the small firm owners' perspective, paper presented to the 15th National Small Firms' Policy & Research Conference, Southampton, November.

Mason C. and Harrison R. (1992) A strategy for closing the small firms finance gap, in Small Enterprise Development: Policy and Practice in Action, eds Caley K., Chell E., Chittenden F. and Mason C., Paul Chapman Publishing, London, pp. 132–150.

Morrison A. (1992) The small firm within the UK hotel industry: routes to survival, paper presented to the 15th National Small Firms' Policy & Research Conference, Southampton, November.

NERA (1990) An evaluation of the loan guarantee scheme, National Economic Research Association, Research Paper 74, Department of Employment.

North D., Leigh R. and Smallbone D. (1991) A comparison of surviving and non-surviving small and medium sized manufacturing firms in London during the 1980's, Working paper No 1, ESRC Small Business Research Initiative, Middlesex University Project.

Oakey R. (1984) High Technology Small Firms, Frances Pinter, London.

Peterson R. and Shulman J. (1987) Capital structure of growing small firms: a 12 country study on becoming bankable, International Small Business Journal, Summer, Vol. 5, No. 4.

Pyke F., Beccatini G. and Sengenberger W. eds (1990) Industrial Districts and Interfirm Co-operation, International Labour Organisation, Geneva.

Schumpeter J.A. (1934) The Theory of Economic Development, Harvard University Press, Cambridge, Massachusetts.

Smallbone D., North D. and Leigh R. (1992) Managing change for growth and survival: a study of mature manufacturing firms in London during the 1980's, Working Paper No 3, Middlesex University Project.

Stanworth J. and Curran J. (1973) Management Motivation in the Smaller Business, Gower Publishing, Aldershot.

Stockport G. and Kakabadse A. (1992) Using ethnography in small firms research, in Small Enterprise Development: Policy and Practice in Action, eds Caley K., Chell E., Chittenden F. and Mason C., Paul Chapman Publishing, London, pp. 178−191.

Storey D. and Johnson S. (1987) Job Generation and Labour Market Change, Macmillan, London.

Storey D., Keasey K., Watson R. and Wynarczyk P. (1987) The Performance of Small Firms, Croom Helm, London.

Welsh J.A. and White J.F. (1981) A small business is not a little big business, Harvard Business Review, July/August.

Westhead P. and Birley S. (1992) Environments for business deregistrations in the United Kingdom 1987−1990, paper presented to the 15th National Small Firms Policy & Research Conference, Southampton, November.

2.

SHOULD WE ABANDON SUPPORT TO START-UP BUSINESSES?

David Storey

INTRODUCTION

During the 1980s the UK government was concerned to promote an 'Enterprise Culture'. A key component of this was the encouragement given to individuals to start their own businesses. This encouragement included the creation of the Enterprise Allowance Scheme (EAS), the provision of free and subsidised advice to people wishing to start, the provision of training programmes such as Firmstart, the provision in some parts of the country of subsidised accommodation for new and small businesses, and more general attempts to encourage particular groups of individuals to consider the option of becoming self-employed – such as the Graduate Enterprise Programme.

This paper argues that, at the present time, policies intended to increase the formation rate of new firms are unlikely to be as cost effective with public funds as policies to enable growing businesses to grow somewhat faster. It argues that, particularly in current conditions, a shift of resources away from the encouragement of start-up businesses and towards growing businesses is entirely appropriate.

Section 2 provides a review of some key research findings in this area. It argues that the impact of public policies encouraging start ups is extremely diffuse, primarily because of the high proportion of new businesses which fail in their early years and the fact that job creation amongst surviving firms is heavily concentrated amongst a few. The problem for policy makers is that, at start up, it is extremely difficult to distinguish between those businesses which will succeed, in the sense of creating significant numbers of jobs, compared with those which will fail. In short, assistance to start-up businesses is a lottery in which the odds of winning are not good.[1]

Section 3 then discusses current research on 'growth' businesses, i.e. those businesses which are small and independent but which experience significant employment growth over a short time. The section argues that many of the constraints on these growth businesses have been identified in prior research, although these are likely to vary in severity from one firm to another.

Section 4 provides evidence that, in terms of international comparisons, the UK currently has relatively high rates of new firm formation. It also shows that countries with high increases in self-employment – which may reflect high rates of new firm formation – are those with high increases in rates of unemployment. Most significantly it shows that despite a huge increase in self-employment in the UK in the 1980s, the UK's employment growth was virtually identical to that in the 1970s.

The fifth section of the paper discusses how, in practice, a policy of targeting public assistance towards growth businesses might be implemented in the current UK context.

It argues that Training and Enterprise Councils (TECs) would be well advised to shift a proportion of their enterprise budgets away from the promotion of start ups and towards 'growth' small businesses. The paper then provides a blueprint for the operation of procedures needed.

THE SURVIVAL AND PERFORMANCE OF NEW FIRMS

The single most important fact to be borne in mind by policy makers when implementing measures for smaller firms is the high death rate of such businesses. Ganguly (1985) showed that the deregistration rate for Value Added Tax (VAT) of the smallest size of firms (those with less than a turnover of £14,000 in 1980) was more than six times as high as that of the deregistration rates for businesses with a turnover of £2 million or more. Ceasing to trade is therefore endemic and central to the small firm sector.

The second clear finding from the analysis of VAT-based data is that deregistration rates are very much higher for new small businesses than for longer established small businesses. For example, 36% of new businesses cease to trade within three years, whereas only a further 37% cease to trade in the following seven years (DoE 1992).

The third key research finding is that small firms exhibit considerably greater year to year fluctuations in both their profitability and their sales than is the case for larger firms (Storey et al 1987). This reflects the fact that small firms are much more likely to have a single product and a single customer than larger firms (Cambridge Small Business Research Centre 1992) and that they are therefore much more strongly influenced by changes in demand, by either that one customer or for that one product.

The fourth key research finding is that employment growth in small firms is heavily concentrated amongst a few. My own research has been pointing to this since 1985 (Storey 1985), but it is interesting to note that the contribution of fast-growing firms is now increasingly widely recognised (Gallagher and Miller 1991, Smallbone et al 1992). For example, Gallagher and Miller in their study of firms in South East England which started between 1980 and 1982, found that 18% of all firms accounted for 92% of the jobs created. The figure which has consistently emerged from my own work is that, over a decade, 4% of the businesses which start will end up providing 50% of the jobs. The clear message is that the small firms which Gallagher and Miller refer to as 'flyers' are the main source of new job creation amongst smaller firms.

In short, the evidence is that the small firm population may usefully be separated into three categories: short-life businesses which are unlikely to trade for more than three years ('turnover' firms or 'failures'), businesses likely to survive for a considerable period of time, but which are unlikely to create significant numbers of jobs ('trundlers'), and thirdly a tiny proportion of small firms which are disproportionately important in terms of job creation ('flyers' or 'gazelles').

Hence when politicians and others make statements about the extent to which 'the small firm sector' is a source of new job creation, this might be thought to imply that job creation occurs in the 'typical' small firm. It does not. Significant job creation occurs amongst very few small firms (the 'flyers'), yet it is these firms which are disproportionately important to the economy.

We now turn to a very brief review of research which has examined the factors which influence the survival of new and small businesses. This is shown in Table 1.

The Table makes two distinctions: it distinguishes between research on small firm survival in the UK and in the USA. It also makes a distinction between macro-economic factors which influence survival and what are referred to as 'internal' factors. It identifies three categories of response: the first where a fairly consistent relationship has been identified in several studies, the second where no relationship has been identified, and the third where either the picture is inconsistent or where the subject has been inadequately examined.

Taking the macro-economic factors first, the work by Robson (1991) and that by

Table 1: Factors influencing the survival of small firms

	United Kingdom	United States
Macro		
Interest rates	?	×
Output growth	?	×
Youth/age	×	√
Internal		
Employment growth	?	√
Education	?	√
Gender	?	?
Experience	?	?

Key: √ = clear relationship; × = no relationship; ? = 'mixed' results or not tested.

Cuthbertson and Hudson (1990) and Hudson and Cuthbertson (1993) on the UK suggests that the failure rate of small firms or the number of personal bankruptcies rises when interest rates are high and when output growth is low. The VAT deregistration data, however, seem to tell a different story. For the UK as a whole deregistration rates were 11% of the stock of businesses in every year between 1980 and 1990 except for 1981 when they were only 9% — probably because of a Civil Servants' dispute in that year. This is despite widely varying macro-economic conditions (Daly 1991). It is for this reason that Table 1 shows the symbol ? as reflecting an uncertain outcome of macro-economic variables. The youth/age variable has not been fully incorporated in these studies.

The results from the USA study on business failures by Lane and Schary (1990) suggest that the business cycle has only a very modest impact upon small business failure rates. Their key conclusion is that business failure rates in year t are primarily influenced by the number of businesses started three years previously, in year $t-3$ — so that a high number of business starts in a particular year lead to more deaths three years later, irrespective of current macro-economic conditions.

A second, and almost unrelated, area of research into small business survival has attempted to relate the characteristics of the entrepreneur or business owner to whether or not the business survives. These we refer to as 'internal' factors — distinguishing them from the macro-economic conditions discussed above. Table 1 identifies four 'internal' factors which have been the subject of some discussion amongst researchers.

There is no comprehensive UK study which has attempted to relate these personal characteristics of the individual to the survival or non-survival of the business. The problem with undertaking such work is that of obtaining a comprehensive record of all start-up businesses, together with data on the personal characteristics of the individuals. The second problem is that of conducting analyses of a large enough sample to enable all the variables to be held constant.

There have been a number of useful studies of businesses which have ceased to trade, such as that by Hall (1992), but the work of Cressy (1992) now seems likely to satisfy the conditions set out above. His work, looking at 2000 individuals who started business with National Westminster Bank in 1988 and a further 700 who started in 1991, can provide some useful insights but the precise implications are likely to be commercialised by the sponsor of the research, rather than being available to public authorities.

To some extent these problems have been overcome in the USA where more comprehensive and accessible data bases exist and have been the subject of analysis for longer periods of time. Probably the key finding in this area is that by Phillips and Kirchhoff (1988). They find:

Within the first two years of a new firm's life, the firm which generates any jobs has about a 20% higher chance of lasting two years than a firm which does not create any jobs ... After only four years the firm which generates jobs has a 40% higher chance of survival ... If the new firm has created between 1 and 4 jobs during its first four years its chances of survival rise to 80% ... Clearly the ability to generate jobs allows a firm the ability to adjust to the business cycle as it increases its cash flow and is a dramatic correlation of the firms' ability to survive ... When a new firm goes to 10 or more employees within the first six years of life it is close to a guarantee of survival for at least ten years.

The USA data also shows that education of the entrepreneur is associated with the survival of the firm. Work by Bates (1990) shows there is a broadly positive association between the level of education of the entrepreneur and the survival of the firm. Kalleberg and Leicht (1991) show there is no evidence that gender influences survival.

Overall the interpretation of these research results for policy makers in the UK is that our understanding of the human capital characteristics of individuals who are likely to have businesses which survive is weak. It is also highly probable that, even if much more extensive efforts were directed towards a better understanding of these factors, results would not be forthcoming for a number of years. Even then perhaps, our ability to 'explain' would only be modest. In short, we have to recognise that currently there is very little basis in research for predicting those businesses, at start up, which are likely to survive for any period of time. There is certainly no basis in research for believing that public monies devoted to encouraging the start up of new businesses could usefully be targeted towards certain types of groups or individuals.

If this is the case it means one of two things: either that start-up assistance has to be available to all, on the grounds that we cannot discriminate between individuals (this is current policy), or that uses could be found for resources currently focused upon 'start ups'. One of these alternative uses could be to provide greater encouragement to established 'growth' businesses.

MORE 'GROWTH' BUSINESSES?

There have been a number of surveys and studies of the growth constraints experienced by smaller firms. Probably the five most frequently identified constraints are shown in Table 2. A number of studies such as those by Aston Business School for the Department of Trade and Industry (1991) and the Cambridge Small Business Centre (1992) have indicated that firms which wish to grow are frequently constrained by an inability to recruit and develop suitable types of labour. A similar point is made by Atkinson and Meager (1992). The difference between the Cambridge and the DTI study however is that the latter placed a much greater emphasis upon labour issues than the former. Thus the Cambridge study argued that the availability and cost of finance for expansion was the key constraint, and this was particularly binding for fast growth and newer firms. It was significantly more important than the inability to recruit skilled labour. The Aston study however, which was conducted one year previously, at a time when bank finance

Table 2: Constraints upon growing small firms

Problem area	Comments
1. Labour force	Consistent problems
2. Premises	Not now in general
3. Finance	In general, not a constraint but problems with high-tech firms, small sums of venture capital, and over banking relationships
4. Owners	Motivation
5. Management teams	Skill in developing teams is important for those wishing to grow

was probably more easy to obtain and the labour market was tighter, chose to place the emphasis upon labour market issues.

A number of studies in the early 1980s identified a shortage of premises as a key constraint upon the development of the small business sector (Jurue 1980, Coopers & Lybrand 1980). This has led to an extensive programme of primarily public provision of new and converted premises for smaller businesses. It is probably fair to say that this is one aspect in which there has been a clear improvement in the position of small firms over the last decade or so, although almost certainly there are local instances where this general improvement is not apparent.

Despite these differences of emphasis between the surveys, labour force and finance problems are consistently identified as important constraints upon the growth of small firms. These problems do vary from one geographical area to another, they vary from one business type to another and they clearly vary according to the nature of macro-economic conditions.

For example, the work of Moore and Sedaghat (1991) on high technology firms in the Cambridge area, together with the Advisory Council on Science and Technology (ACOST) study (1990), suggests that high technology firms may have particular difficulties in financing, reflecting the uncertainty associated with innovation.

It is important to make a distinction between the provision of debt and equity capital. For many small firms wishing to grow, irrespective of sector, Mason and Harrison (1991) point to the difficulties of obtaining small sums of equity capital. They show that a number of smaller firms have responded to this problem by forming an association with 'business angels' — wealthy individuals making a personal equity investment in a small business. Despite these developments it remains the view amongst observers of small business such as Mason and Harrison that it is difficult to obtain equity sums of less than £100,000.

The work by Curran et al (1991) addresses the key question of the motivations and aspirations of business owners. They point out that business owners come from a wide variety of backgrounds and establish a business for a variety of different motivations. Amongst these motivations, the maximisation of income and a desire to grow a business is paramount in only a few cases. Indeed many individuals establish a small business for the sole purpose of avoiding working in a large organisation, and would see growth as one of the least important of their objectives. These business owners are more concerned to generate a particular lifestyle, for the business to survive, and possibly to be passed on to the next generation. For this group the key growth 'constraint' is actually the people who run the businesses themselves. They are unlikely to be changed by the provision of financial or other incentives to grow the business more rapidly. Indeed, if the results of the work by Rees and Shah (1992) on the self-employed apply to the small-business-owning population more generally, the provision of financial assistance to this sector would simply result in these individuals committing less effort to their business, rather than more.

Finally Table 2 points to the problems of assembling management teams. It emphasises that whilst some businesses may wish to grow, the individual or individuals who own them are unable to recruit suitable managerial staff, delegate responsibilities, or be capable of owning and managing a slightly larger firm. The differences in the way in which managerial teams are assembled is addressed by Wynarczyk et al (1993) and by ACOST (1990).

Overall Table 2 demonstrates there is no single constraint which operates on all small firms. Many do not wish to grow, and those which do may be constrained by a shortage of skilled labour, an inability to recruit suitable management, financial constraints in the form of shortages of equity or bank finance, or a shortage of suitable premises or any combination thereof. Finally the particular configuration of constraints is likely to vary from one geographical area to another.

It means that policies to overcome growth constraints are best implemented at a local level and will have to vary according to the firm concerned. It therefore means that TECs are in a strong position to develop such policies.

INTERNATIONAL COMPARISONS OF BUSINESS STARTS AND SELF-EMPLOYMENT

The Bolton Committee Report (1971) argued in 1968, the most recent year for which data were available, that 0.4 new companies were registered in Britain per 1000 population compared with 1.4 per 1000 in the USA. On the basis of this it was inferred that the UK had a relatively low rate of new firm formation, compared certainly with the USA. Storey (1982) challenged this data comparison on the basis that 1968 was a uniquely low year for new company incorporations in the UK and that the comparison with the USA was therefore exaggerated. Nevertheless, as in many other instances, the stylised fact which drove small firm policies was that the UK had low rates of new firm formation, compared with more 'enterprising' economies, most notably the USA. Policy makers very unwisely embraced the view that this needed to be rectified by stimulating new firm formation on the grounds that this would lead to greater wealth and job creation.

The error of this view is illustrated in Figures 1 and 2. They show changes in both self-employment and total civilian employment amongst OECD countries in the 1973—1979 period in Figure 2. Comparable data for 1979—1990 are shown in Figure 1. The position of the UK shows that during the 1973—79 period the annual increase in employment was virtually identical to that between 1979—1990, i.e. about 1%. However, comparing Figures 1 and 2 shows that the UK had a massive increase in the numbers of self-employed during the 1980s, of about 6% annually, with this being considerably out of line with virtually all other OECD countries. The two graphs suggest that, although the UK did experience a major increase in self-employment (and increases in self-

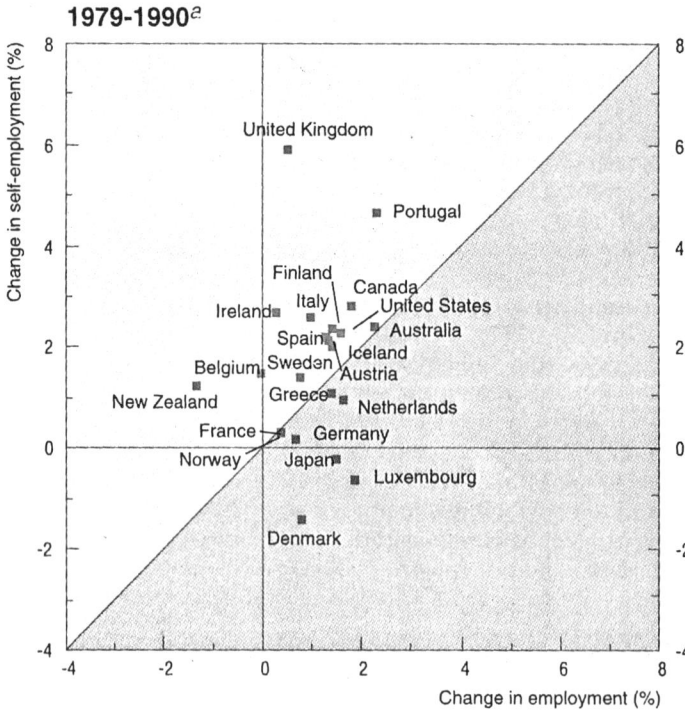

Figure 1: Growth of self-employment and total civilian employment (annual averages) 1979—1990. (Greece 1979—1989, Iceland 1979—1988, New Zealand 1986—1990). Source: *OECD Labour Force Statistics 1970—1990*, Paris, 1992.

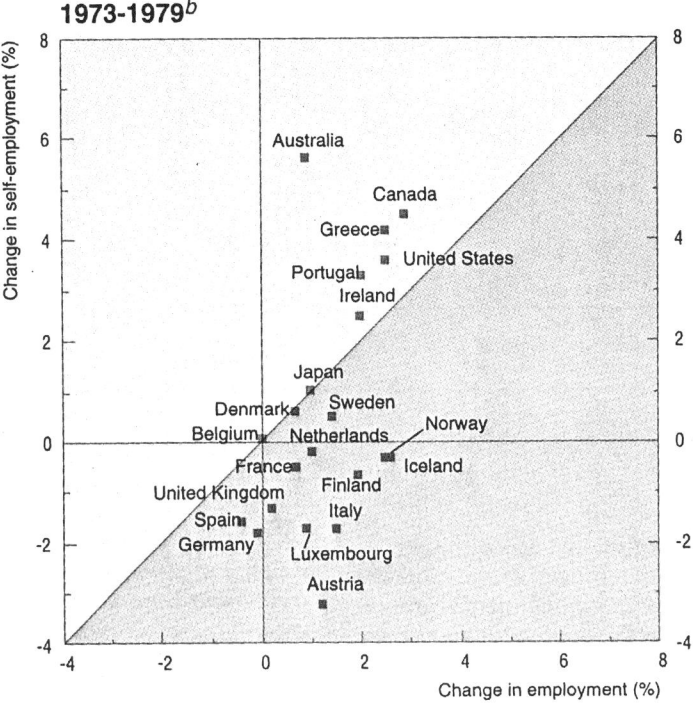

Figure 2: Growth of self-employment and total civilian population (annual averages) 1973–1979. (Greece 1977–1979, The Netherlands 1975–1979). Source: *OECD Labour Force Statistics 1970–1990*, Paris, 1992.

employment are likely to broadly reflect new firm formation), there was little evidence that this impacted upon changes in total employment.[2]

The value of OECD time series data is that it also enables a test to be made of the implicit assumption underlying UK small firm policy that increases in self-employment or entrepreneurship/enterprise lead to, or are associated with, lower rates of unemployment. This is examined in Figures 3 and 4, where again a distinction is made between the 1979–90 period in Figure 3 and 1973–1979 in Figure 4.

Taking Figure 4, covering the 1973–1979 period, the general pattern observed was precisely the opposite to that which has been articulated by UK policy-makers. The countries which experienced a large increase in self-employment were those countries which experienced a large increase in unemployment. Nevertheless the pattern across countries is extremely diverse during this period.

During 1979–1990 it is difficult to decipher any relationship between the change in self-employment and the change in unemployment. The only clear point is that the UK is strikingly out of line with other countries in terms of its increase in self-employment rates, yet its changes in unemployment appear close to the OECD average.[3]

Finally Table 3 presents data, reproduced by Van der Horst (1992), which attempts to generate cross-country comparisons of business start-up rates in Europe. It is clear that, with the exception of Denmark where the data appear not to be comparable with elsewhere, the UK had, in 1989, the highest rates of business start ups in Europe.

These international comparisons have made three important points. The first is that, even if it was the case 20 years ago, the UK currently does not now have low rates of firm formation. For whatever reason the last two decades have seen a major increase in these rates. The second is that, despite this much faster growth in self-employment in

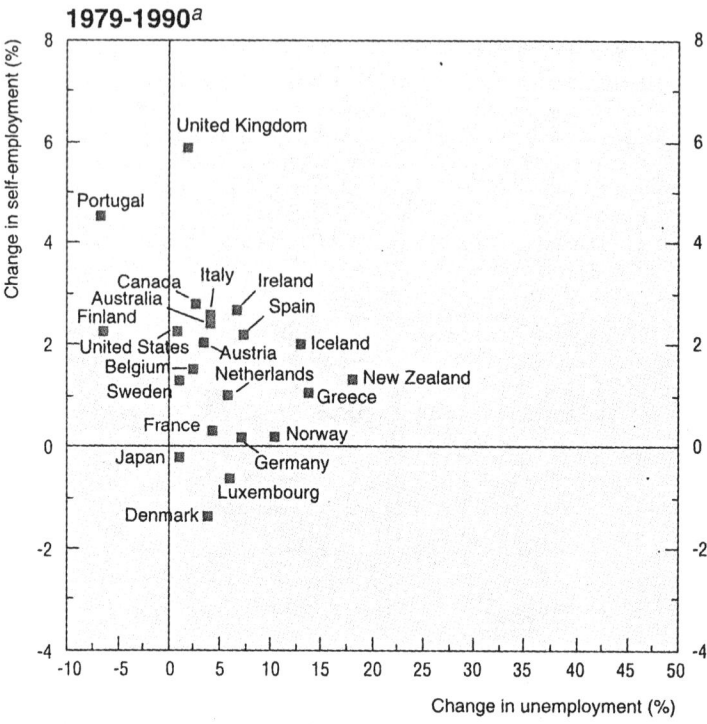

Figure 3: Growth of unemployment and self-employment (annual averages) 1979–1990. (Greece 1979–1989, Iceland 1979–1988, New Zealand 1986–1990). Source: *OECD Labour Force Statistics 1970–1990*, Paris, 1992.

the 1980s in the UK, there is no evidence that it has had a major impact upon inducing either increased employment or reduced unemployment, compared with other OECD countries which did not experience this scale of shift. The third point is that, whatever the UK economy needs, it does not require further incentives to stimulate new firm formation, for two reasons. The first is because our rates are higher than almost all of

Table 3: Start-ups as a percentage of the active labour force, 1989

Country	Percentage
Denmark	(5.4)*
United Kingdom	1.59
Luxembourg	1.46
Ireland	1.25
Italy	1.20
Germany	1.13
France	1.12
Spain	0.64
Belgium	0.62
Portugal	0.34
The Netherlands	0.33
Greece	NA
EC	0.97

Sources: Eurostat (Luxembourg) and Institut ANCE (Paris) OECD Employment Outlook.
* Data in respect of Denmark are not fully comparable with other countries due to the large number of start-ups for fiscal reasons and a special category of female entrepreneurship.
NA, not available.

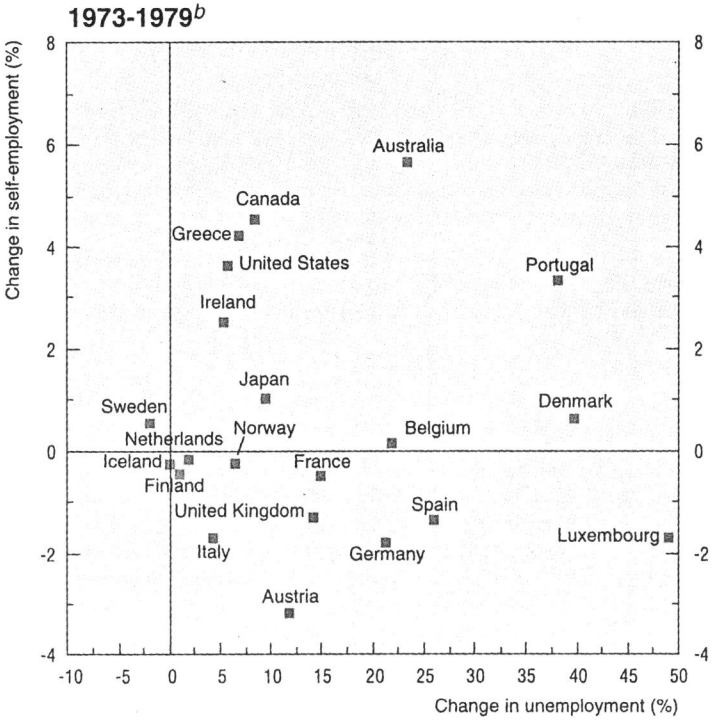

1973-1979[b]

Figure 4: Growth of unemployment and self-employment (annual averages) 1973–1979. (Greece 1977–1979, The Netherlands 1975–1979). Source: *OECD Labour Force Statistics 1970–1990*, Paris, 1992.

our competitors, and the second is because the impact which incentives have upon employment creation is negligible, since they primarily lead to 'churning' (more births and more deaths) rather than to net employment gains.

Instead it is the recommendation of this paper that resources should be shifted away from increasing the number of start-up firms, towards encouraging the growth of a small proportion of existing firms.

TOWARDS A POLICY OF TARGETING GROWTH BUSINESSES

It is assumed that any policy which focuses upon 'growth' businesses would be implemented through TECs. This section provides practical advice to TECs on how to operationalise a policy focusing upon growing SMEs.

The first stage is to identify a list of fast-growing young firms in the TEC area. Here it would be possible to use a commercial data base to initially identify firms according to four criteria. The criteria are that the firms should be between three and five years old, cover all sectors, have at least 20 employees and be independent businesses in the sense of not being owned by any other firm.[4]

Once this list had been compiled for a given TEC area, the firms could be contacted to find whether they were seeking further expansion. If so, they would be invited to discuss these expansion plans with the relevant TEC officials, who would offer to visit the firm at their own premises. In many cases the firms themselves would either indicate that they were not interested in expansion, or that they were not interested in discussing these with TEC officials. Nevertheless a proportion of firms might be interested in further dialogue.

When the TEC official visited the firm the purpose would be to clarify the nature of any constraints upon growth which the firm might be experiencing. As we have observed above, these might be financial in the sense of being unable to obtain a suitable combination of term loans/overdrafts/equity etc.; they might be problems over obtaining suitable premises; they might be problems of obtaining suitable skilled or managerial labour, or they might be basic information about exporting, insurance, etc.

The key point of these visits would be to determine whether there was some way in which the TEC could provide managerial assistance to the firm over a short time to enable a specific constraint to be overcome. The difference between what is being proposed, and what is in operation currently, is that the purpose of the TEC officer would be to find out what problems the firm had, rather than to inform the firm about what assistance is available. In this sense the provision of advice services has to be demand, rather than supply, led.[5]

The key theme of these proposals is a recognition that SME problems vary markedly from one firm to another, and probably from one TEC to another. They also recognise that the key constraint upon the growth of SMEs is likely to be managerial. Hence the TEC is likely to have to provide temporary managerial assistance to expanding firms to enable them to overcome short-term problems. It may be likened to someone running down a hill very quickly and observing a brick wall in front. The purpose, in this context, is that the TEC provides the rope ladder to enable the wall to be scaled and the individual to continue running down the slope the other side.

Once the constraints for the individual firm have been diagnosed the assistance which the TEC would provide would be managerial. It might be to provide a finance professional to work with the firm for a period of time to negotiate a suitable package of finance for expansion; it might be to provide an individual who specialises in assisting firms to both find new premises and to help the firm move to those premises; it might be an individual who is able to identify and recruit a Marketing Director.

The point of these illustrations is threefold. The first is that they demonstrate that these are not short-term assignments. They will require TEC involvement with the firms for a considerable period of time. The second is that this means that relatively few firms can be helped, so that TECs cannot 'play the numbers game'. The third is that the TEC is becoming closer to the consultancy services which could be provided by the private sector.

SOME CONCLUDING REFLECTIONS

It is appropriate to conclude with some reflections upon this proposal for a fundamental refocusing of small firm policy. The first is that the types of skills which the expanding firm requires are not those likely to be available amongst TEC staff, many of whom were formerly Civil Servants. This expertise will only be available amongst former or current business owners or senior managers with operational experience. Hence there may be a problem for the TEC in obtaining access to those skills. It may indeed be the case that the TEC has to undertake some training itself in order to meet these needs — 'physician heal thyself'.

Nevertheless the central point is that the criteria by which the 'success' of an initiative is judged is not the number of leaflets that were handed out, nor the number of visits made to an Enterprise Agency, nor the number of businesses established in the locality, etc. Instead the criteria for success is the ability to stay with only a small number of firms for a significant period of time, perhaps up to six months, and to enable that firm, as a result of the assistance provided, to overcome a particular growth hurdle.

Finally it is appropriate to introduce two important caveats to the scheme. The first is that it is not suggested that only young firms would be included. Our suggestion of perhaps initially focusing upon firms which are three to five years old could be considered to be an appropriate starting point; it would not necessarily exclude the possibility that, at a later stage, firms of different ages would be included for assistance.

The second caveat is that TECs may still choose to provide some resources to facilitate the start up of some types of businesses. They may well wish to be seen to be providing assistance to certain groups of ethnic minorities or handicapped individuals. Nevertheless the main focus has to be to shift away from encouraging the start up of a business, towards enabling growing businesses to reach their full potential.

Despite these caveats, the prime purpose of the proposal is to demonstrate that there is clear evidence of a need to move resources away from a focus upon start ups and towards growing businesses. It also demonstrates that practical and operational procedures to enable this to be successful can now be devised.

NOTES

1. To continue the analogy, some may find the comparison between horse-racing and small firms policy helpful. I see an analogy being that government policy in the 1980s is comparable to an unwise bookmaker, who takes bets and gives the same odds whether the horses are at the starting-gate or whether they have jumped a significant number of hurdles in the race. In effect, despite the risk of falling/failure, government still persists in putting its (or 'our') money on the horses at the start of the race, when it would be much better advised to study their 'form' in the early stages of the race.
2. It is appropriate to be cautious in moving from micro- to macro-economic changes. On the one hand it can be argued that without the rise in self-employment in the 1980s, the level of unemployment would have been even higher. On the other hand the shift in policy towards self-employment and enterprise clearly had no net observable effect.
3. It is appropriate to point out that whilst the UK experienced an annual average increase in unemployment which was similar to the OECD average in both time periods, the absolute rates are much lower in the 1980s (around 2%), than in the 1970s (around 15%).
4. It is not suggested that these are the only growing firms in an area. For example some long-established firms may currently be undergoing rapid growth because of changed market conditions, a new owner, etc. However the current definitions have the advantage of identifying the bulk of growing firms whilst being very convenient to administer.
5. Again we can liken the proposal to the difference between sitting down in a restaurant and being presented with a menu or being asked what you would like to eat. Currently public policy 'tells' small firms that, subject to a number of restrictions, they can choose items from the menu. If what they want is not on the menu then that is unfortunate. The proposals presented here are different. They are asking the firm what it would like to eat, and on the basis of the responses received the TEC formulates the services/assistance which it provides.

REFERENCES

ACOST (1990) The Enterprise Challenge: Overcoming Barriers to Growth in Small Firms, HMSO, London.

Aston Business School (1991) Constraints on the Growth of Small Firms, Department of Trade and Industry, HMSO, London.

Atkinson J. and Meager N. (1992) Running to Stand Still: Small Business in the Labour Market, Paper presented at ESRC Workshop, University of Warwick, September.

Bates T. (1990) Entrepreneurial human capital inputs and small business longevity, Review of Economics and Statistics, November, Vol. 72, No. 4, pp. 551–559.

Bolton J.E. (1971) Small Firms: Report of the Committee of Inquiry on Small Firms, Cmnd 4811, HMSO, London.

Cambridge Small Business Research Centre (1992) The State of British Enterprise, University of Cambridge.

Coopers and Lybrand (1980) Provision of Small Industrial Premises, Department of Industry:

Small Firms Division, London.

Cressy R. (1992) Small Firm Debt Re-scheduling versus Insolvency, The Banks Decision Problem, Working Paper No 9, SME Centre, Warwick Business School.

Curran J., Blackburn R. and Woods A. (1991) Profiles of the Small Enterprise in the Service Sector, Kingston University, May.

Cuthbertson K. and Hudson J. (1990) The Determination of Compulsory Liquidations in the UK: 1972–1988, University of Newcastle upon Tyne (mimeo).

Daly M. (1991) VAT registrations and de-registrations in 1990, Employment Gazette, November, pp. 579–588.

Department of Employment (1992) Small Firms in Britain Report, HMSO, London.

Gallagher G.G. and Miller P. (1991) New fast-growing companies create jobs, Long Range Planning, Vol. 24, No. 1, pp. 96–101.

Ganguly P. (1985) UK Small Business Statistics and International Comparisons, Paul Chapman, London.

Hall G. (1992) Reasons for insolvency amongst small firms – a review and fresh evidence, Small Business Economics, Vol. 4, No. 3, September, pp. 237–250.

Hudson J. and Cuthbertson K. (1993) The determinants of bankruptcies in the UK, 1971–1988, Manchester School, Col 61, No 1, pp. 65–81.

Jurue (1980) Industrial Renewal in the Inner City, University of Aston, Birmingham.

Kalleberg A.L. and Leicht K. (1991) Gender and organisational performance: determinants of small business survival and success, Academy of Management Journal, Vol. 34, No. 1, pp. 136–161.

Lane S. and Schary M. (1990) The Determinants of Business Failures, 1956–1988, Working Paper 90–62. School of Management, Boston University.

Mason C. and Harrison R. (1991) A Strategy for Closing the Small Firms' Finance Gap, Venture Finance Research Project, Working Paper No. 3, May, University of Southampton.

Moore B. and Sedaghat N. (1991) Factors constraining the growth of small high technology companies: a case study of the Cambridge sub-region, Paper presented to 18th Annual Conference of the European Association for Research on Industrial Economics, Ferrara, Italy.

OECD (1992) Recent developments in self employment, Chapter 4, in Employment Outlook, OECD, Paris, pp. 155–194.

Phillips B.D. and Kirchhoff B.A. (1988) The survival and quality of jobs generated by entrepreneurial firms, Paper presented to Annual Babson Conference on Entrepreneurship, Calgary, Canada.

Rees H. and Shah A. (1992) The characteristics of the self employed: the supply of labour, Paper presented to ESRC Workshop, University of Warwick, September.

Robson M.T. (1991) A Survey of Recent Time Series Studies of Business Formations and Dissolutions in the United Kingdom, University of Newcastle upon Tyne (mimeo).

Smallbone D., North D. and Leigh R. (1992) Managing change for growth and survival: a study of mature manufacturing firms in London during the 1980s, Working Paper No. 3, Middlesex Polytechnic.

Storey D.J. (1982) Entrepreneurship and the New Firm, Croom Helm, London.

Storey D.J. (1985) Manufacturing employment change in northern England, in D.J. Storey (ed) Small Firms in Regional Economic Development: Britain, Ireland and the United States, Cambridge University Press, London.

Storey D.J., Keasey K., Watson R. and Wynarczyk P. (1987) The Performance of Small Firms, Croom Helm, London.

Van Der Horst R. (1992) The volatility of the small business sector in the Netherlands, Paper presented at the International Conference on Small Business, OECD, Montreal.

Wynarczyk P., Watson R., Storey D.J., Short H. and Keasey K. (1993) 'The People Gap': Managerial Labour Markets in the Small Firm Sector, Routledge, London (forthcoming).

3.

FROM UNEMPLOYMENT TO SELF-EMPLOYMENT IN THE EUROPEAN COMMUNITY

Nigel Meager

INTRODUCTION

The 1980s saw self-employment increase across the EC, both absolutely and as a proportion of total employment, although the experience of individual countries was variable, with the UK experiencing by far the greatest increase, and others (such as France and Germany) experiencing little growth, and still others (Denmark and Luxembourg) where it continued to decline. This variety occurred against the background of government policy stances broadly and increasingly supportive of self-employment in all EC countries, given the general trend towards industrial and labour market deregulation and the belief that small businesses were an engine of job creation. Without exception, EC countries introduced schemes to encourage members of the labour force (particularly unemployed members) to become self-employed.

The chapter presents comparable data on EC countries and briefly examines recent self-employment trends, and the explanations which have been put forward for such trends. I present, in particular, some new empirical evidence on inflows to and outflows from self-employment, arguing that such flow data play a useful role in comparative evaluations of policy measures. Finally I look in more detail at these policy initiatives, and the comparative evaluation issues they pose. The chapter draws on research conducted by the author at the Wissenschaftszentrum Berlin (WZB) on behalf of the Commission of the European Communities (DGV), under the MISEP[1] programme.

DEFINITION

We define the self-employed as those who work on their own account rather than for an employer in a conventional (dependent) employment relationship. The conceptual issues associated with this and other definitions of self-employment are discussed in Meager (1993), but the data used here derive from the European Labour Force Survey (ELFS), which uses a concept of self-employment based on respondents' self-definition. This raises some difficulties of comparison, since the ways individuals define themselves may vary between countries, partly because different social norms affect the 'value' attached to self-employment, and individuals' willingness to define themselves as self-employed. These may also vary within a country over time. In the UK, for example, it is argued that the Thatcher government's emphasis on the 'enterprise culture' generated a more positive climate of opinion towards self-employment (Hakim 1988), and hence some workers whose activities lie close to the border between employment and self-employment may have become more willing to identify themselves as self-employed.[2]

In the light of these difficulties, and the limitations of available data, there is little point in imposing *ab initio* a more precise definition of self-employment than that above. Rather, as with all international comparisons, we need to take account of complexities of definition and meaning, and exercise due caution when interpreting data. In attempting to explain differences between countries we must always ask how far the data indicate real differences or changes, and how far they simply reflect definitional differences or changes.

Finally, we should note that a key feature of almost all previous studies of self-employment is that however defined, the self-employed are an extremely diverse category in terms of their individual characteristics, their skill levels, and their degree of 'independence'. The 'typical' self-employed person does not exist. Self-employment covers a wide range of individuals with little in common other than the fact of their self-employment; and the influences of policy and economic forces may be very different between the different 'segments' of self-employment.

FACTORS INFLUENCING SELF-EMPLOYMENT

In addressing the causes of recent self-employment trends, the theoretical social science literature does not help us much. As Meager (1993) shows, self-employment has not, until recently, attracted significant attention from social scientists. In the absence of an adequate theoretical framework, the research strategy adopted here was not to attempt to develop one, but rather to draw in an eclectic fashion on existing theoretical and empirical work in labour and industrial economics and sociology, to identify the main factors influencing self-employment at an aggregate level. In place of a single theoretical framework, therefore, a looser, analytical schema was used, tracing the links and relationships between these factors, to construct a coherent account of recent changes, and inter-country differences, consistent with available evidence. This schema is presented elsewhere (Meager 1993), but the essential point for the present chapter is that any attempt to isolate the impact of public policies for self-employment cannot consider these policies in isolation. Rather, they are but one of a set of inter-related influences on self-employment, of which others include:

1. Macro-economic forces (issues of 'unemployment push' and 'prosperity pull' are relevant here);
2. Structural change, in particular the shift from manufacturing to service employment in most advanced nations;
3. Changes in the organisational structure and behaviour of employers (e.g. the shift to 'contracting out' of service functions, the growth of franchising, etc.);
4. Changing demographic structures, given the different self-employment propensities of different sections of the workforce (a growing female activity rate, and an ageing labour force is relevant here).

We argue, further, that the combined influence of these factors is mediated by a constellation of legal and institutional factors, which are crucial in explaining different self-employment patterns. Two of the most important of these factors are:

1. the institutional/regulatory framework governing business start-up and occupational entry;
2. the structure, regulation and functioning of capital markets facing potential entrepreneurs.

The role of these factors can be illustrated through a comparison of the UK and Germany (see Meager et al 1992). Institutional differences between these countries led, in the 1980s, to UK self-employment being more 'dynamic' and more unstable, with higher rates of both entry and exit, than its German counterpart. Taking the first of the two factors, it appears that despite deregulation in both countries during the 1980s, regulation over entry to certain occupations and over business start-up in general, remained higher in Germany than in the UK. This is particularly true in Handwerk (crafts), which covers a wide range of activities (from bakers and hairdressers to dispensing opticians) — see Doran (1984). To set up in self-employment in Handwerk one must be a Meister in the occupation concerned (or to employ such a Meister), which means having served an apprenticeship, and having acquired certain post-apprenticeship experience and training. There is no such requirement in the UK. Thus, to a greater extent in Germany than in the UK, entry into self-employment in many occupations is dependent on prior, long-term career choices, and in so far as entry to self-employment responds to short-term macro-economic fluctuations, such responsiveness tends to be less in the more regulated German environment.

Turning to the second factor, it was generally easier for entrepreneurs to obtain start-up finance in the UK than in Germany in the 1980s. Financial deregulation in the UK led to a credit boom, with financial institutions keen to lend directly to potential entrepreneurs, or indirectly through loans for consumption or house purchase, which could be recycled for other purposes. This contrasts with a tighter credit environment in Germany and was reinforced in the UK by the large and growing rate of home ownership which, coupled with house price inflation, led to growing personal housing wealth which could be used as collateral for business start-up (further, capital gains from housing often leaked into other areas via 'equity withdrawal'). There is also evidence (Danish Technological Institute, 1991), that the venture capital industry specialising in high risk financing of new business is more developed in the UK than in Germany, and expanded in the 1980s.

Thus a lower degree of regulation in the UK over many occupations and businesses, as well as a looser lending environment than in Germany, is consistent with our evidence below of lower inflow rates to self-employment in Germany than in the UK. It seems, further, that new German entrepreneurs in this period were better placed to survive in business than their UK counterparts because: (a) German self-employed were more likely to be qualified in the relevant occupation; (b) they were more likely to have their proposed business scrutinised by a lending institution; and (c) those entering regulated sectors (e.g. Handwerk) enjoyed relatively protected markets. Further, having set up in business, self-employed Germans face a wider array of central and local government-funded support and advice (Bannock and Albach 1991); thus Anglo-German differences in small business policy stance reinforce the institutional differences. As a result, new entrants to self-employment in Germany are more likely to come from dependent employment than from unemployment or economic inactivity (as confirmed by the ELFS data below), since the former are better endowed than the latter in terms of both financial and relevant human capital. A further consequence is that self-employment outflows run at a lower rate, and are less responsive to recent inflows in Germany than in the UK (again confirmed by the ELFS). Hence international comparisons of self-employment trends must take account of the way different institutional and legislative contexts condition the response of self-employment to economic variables. We now turn to examine these recent trends in EC self-employment.

RECENT SELF-EMPLOYMENT TRENDS

Across the nine EC members of 1975[3], self-employment grew by nearly a quarter between 1975 and 1989, from 12.7 million, to over 15.5 million (whilst total employment grew by only 8.9%). An important, and as yet unresolved question (OECD 1992), is how far this is merely a short-term deviation from the long-term downwards trend, due to cyclical or one-off factors, and how far it represents a more permanent shift towards smaller units of employment (see Sengenberger et al 1990).

Beneath this overall picture of self-employment growth, however, lies considerable inter-country variation. Figure 1 shows that trends in the four countries (Denmark,

Total self-employment (1975=100)

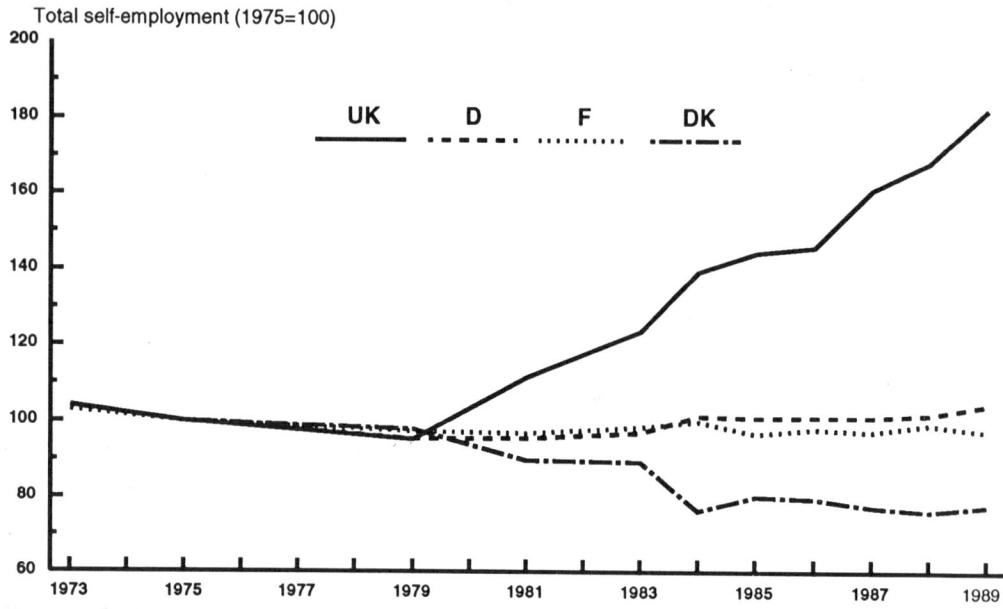

Figure 1: EC self-employment trends 1973–1989 (all sectors). Source: European Labour Force Surveys.

France, Germany and the UK) selected for detailed study in this research, diverged sharply after 1979, with self-employment taking off into strong and sustained growth in the UK at one extreme, and continuing to fall in Denmark, at the other.

As well as differences in the rates of growth of self-employment, however, there are significant differences in the relative importance of self-employment in comparison with wage employment. As Figure 2 shows, self-employment rates are generally higher in the southern EC countries (which only partly reflects the greater role of agriculture in these countries' economies – see Meager (1993)). It also shows that there is no clear relationship across EC countries between the extent of self-employment and its rate of growth. It is not the case that countries with relatively high self-employment rates have also experienced fast growth in self-employment, or vice versa.

One explanation links inter-country differences in self-employment rates to differences in the level of overall economic development (Acs et al 1992).

Figure 3 plots self-employment rates against GDP per capita in 12 EC countries, apparently confirming the existence of such a relationship. One problem with this argument, however, is that it implies an inexorably falling self-employment trend as national incomes grow. This may be valid when comparing developing with developed economies (International Labour Office (ILO) 1990), but is less clear within EC countries, which are all relatively 'high income'. Thus in Figure 2, within the EC, among both the richer northern countries, and the poorer southern countries, we can find countries that exhibit self-employment growth and others that decline. An argument based on income levels is an insufficient explanation for recent trends in EC countries, and an alternative analysis of the short-term dynamics of self-employment is required.

CYCLICAL FLUCTUATIONS IN SELF-EMPLOYMENT

The relationship between self-employment and the economic cycle has been extensively explored elsewhere, and the literature is reviewed in Meager (1992a, b). Much recent research (Bögenhold and Staber 1990, 1991) argues that labour market pressure in general, and mass unemployment in particular, played crucial roles in reversing the

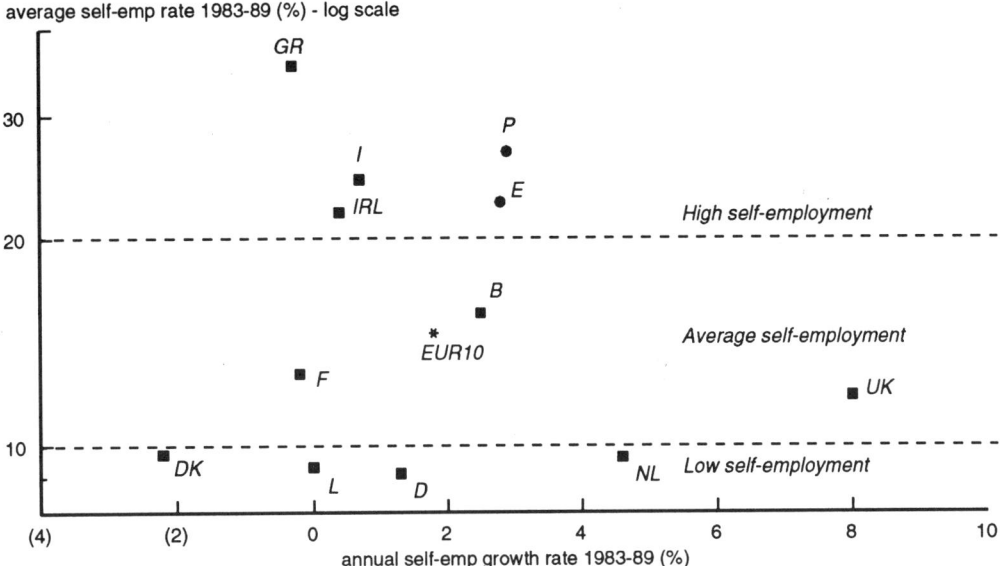

Figure 2: EC self-employment rates and growth rates 1983–1989 (all sectors); Spain and Portugal 1986–1989 only. Source: European Labour Force Surveys.

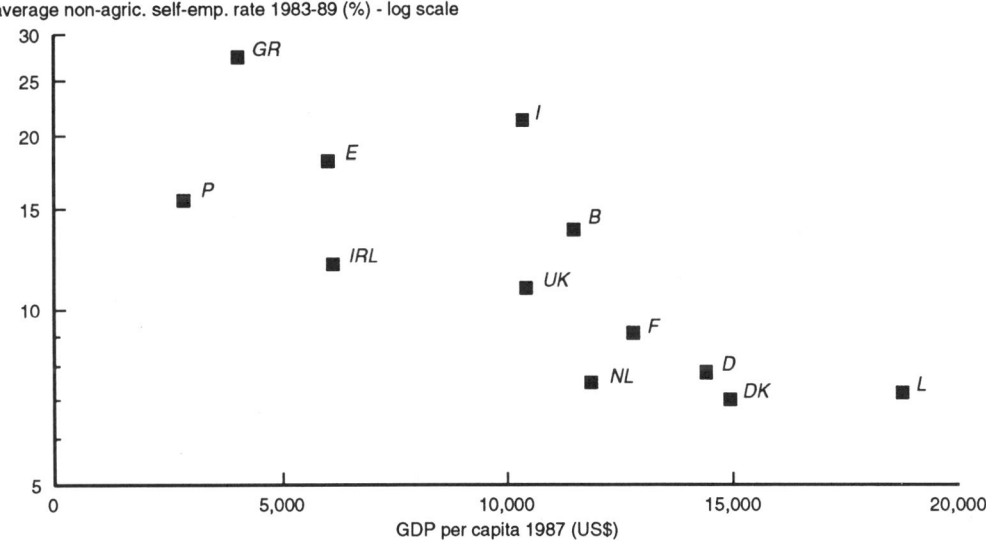

Figure 3: EC self-employment rates and GDP; Spain and Portugal 1986–1989 only. Source: European Labour Force Surveys/ILO.

previous decline in self-employment. This perspective sees growing self-employment as a response to lack of wage employment opportunities. As I have argued elsewhere, however (Meager 1992a, b), whilst 'unemployment push' is likely to have played some role, self-employment dynamics are more complex than this. There is, for example, also a relationship between unemployment and the economic cycle in the opposite direction, with high unemployment dampening self-employment growth, due to poorer market opportunities and higher risk of business failure in recession.

There are, furthermore, major methodological problems associated with previous authors' time-series correlations between self-employment stocks and unemployment and/or GDP. Such analyses cannot test for, or discriminate between, the various hypotheses for the cyclical behaviour of self-employment (see Meager 1992b). Meager (1992a) presents evidence for 10 EC countries, that when the level rather than the rate of self-employment is used, there is in most countries no clear positive relationship between self-employment and unemployment. Indeed, for several countries the relationship is negative. This does not invalidate the unemployment push hypothesis, but implies that flow data are required to examine it adequately. In the next section we consider such flow data.

THE DYNAMICS OF SELF-EMPLOYMENT

It is possible to construct 'quasi-flow' data from the ELFS using information on respondents' employment status one year prior to the survey. Whilst there are deficiencies in these data, it is likely that they will pick up major changes in the dynamics of self-employment flows (see OECD 1992). Aggregate self-employment inflows and outflows for a number of EC countries are presented in Meager (1993), for 1983–1989. Inflows exceed outflows in most countries throughout the period, consistent with the general upward trend in EC self-employment levels (the main exception is Denmark, where outflows exceed inflows by a considerable margin). The excess of inflows over outflows is particularly marked in the UK, where as we have seen, self-employment grew faster than elsewhere. Meager (1993) also relates inflows and outflows to aggregate unemployment trends in each country over the period. The observed pattern is very mixed. In Germany, for example, there is some relationship (in the direction predicted by 'unemployment push'), but in the UK inflows to self-employment increased when unemployment fell, and vice versa. Overall, the patterns observed do not provide evidence for a push relationship between unemployment and the flow into self-employment. One possibility, however, is that the push hypothesis holds not for the aggregate inflow, but for one or more of its sub-component inflows (from unemployment, employment or economic activity – see Meager (1992a)), and we might expect each of these flows to respond rather differently to the economic cycle. Given such differences in the way in which the economic cycle influences different types of inflow to self-employment, it is not surprising if no clear 'push' effect is evident in the aggregate inflows, and there is a strong case for disaggregation – a task attempted below.

Meager (1993) also examines the relationship between self-employment outflows and unemployment, again with mixed results, although in Germany and Ireland there does appear to be a positive relationship between the two variables with the outflow from self-employment increasing as unemployment increases, and vice versa. It must also be recognised, however, that the two sets of flows are unlikely to be independent of each other, and outflows from self-employment may themselves be a lagged function of earlier inflows, in line with evidence in the literature of a certain amount of 'churning' in the small firms sector, largely independent of the overall economic climate. As shown in Meager (1992a), and confirmed with more recent data (Campbell and Daly 1992) this effect is visible in national data from the British LFS with a lag of about two years.

So far we have discussed absolute self-employment flows. To compare inflows and outflows between countries, however, we need to express them in proportion to self-employment stocks, and this is done for inflows in Figure 4. The ranking of inflow rates is similar to the ranking of self-employment growth rates shown earlier. The UK has by far the highest rate (around 18% p.a. for most of the period), followed by France and Germany, with inflow rates of about 10%, and finally Denmark, with much lower inflow rates than the other countries (averaging 2–3%).[4]

Looking at outflows (the data are presented in Meager (1993)), Denmark still records the lowest rate (around 6%), and Danish self-employment is unambiguously 'less

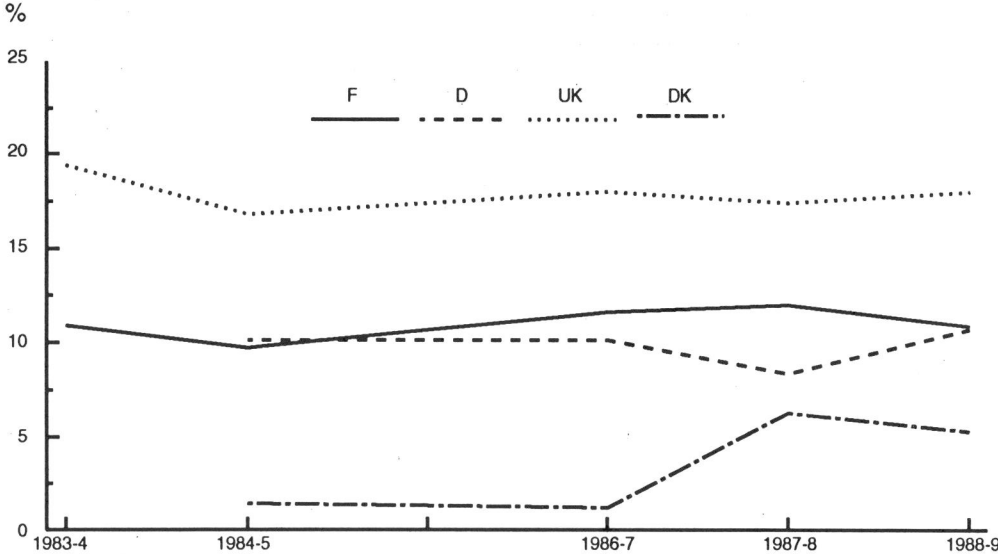

Figure 4: Self-employment inflows over year as per cent of start of year's stock; data for individual years for Denmark may be unreliable due to small cell sizes. Source: ELFS.

dynamic' than in the other countries. The low exit rate is a consequence of the low entry rate (the Danish self-employed stock is 'older' and more stable than in the other countries). Danish self-employment is declining not because of a high failure rate, but because the number of new entrants is insufficient to match even the small outflow rate. The outflow rates of the other three countries are more similar than the inflows, with France and the UK recording the highest rates (around 9%), and the German rate lying slightly below these. The fast growth in UK self-employment results from this difference between inflow and outflow rates, with the former nearly twice the latter. The greater 'dynamism' of UK self-employment compared with France and Germany is predominantly associated with this very high inflow. Differential trends in self-employment stocks arise, therefore, from differences between stable inflow and outflow rates in individual countries, rather than from increases or decreases in those rates of flow themselves, although this may have been a phenomenon of economic growth in the 1980s. The UK pattern, for example, appears to have changed drastically since 1989 with a sharp increase in outflow rates, and an even sharper fall in inflows (Campbell and Daly 1992).

So far we have looked at aggregate flows. To obtain a fuller picture of self-employment dynamics, however, we must examine the composition of those flows, in terms of their sources and destinations. Meager (1993) summarises this information for nine EC countries, showing for example, that wage employment is the largest source of entrants to self-employment in all countries, although its relative importance varies considerably from 31% of inflows (Spain, 1987–88) to 75% (Germany 1988–89). Flows between unemployment and self-employment are of particular interest, because of the role which unemployment is often hypothesised to play in leading to greater self-employment, and because of the emergence in the 1980s of policies encouraging the unemployed to enter self-employment. The largest proportions of the inflow to self-employment originating in unemployment are found in Ireland (28.2–31.7%), Spain (22.4–30.0%), Denmark (16.9–28.7%), the UK (17.0–23.3%) and Belgium (18.4–22.7%). The corresponding proportions are somewhat lower in Greece, Portugal and France, whilst the smallest share of inflows from unemployment is found in Germany. Germany is again an extreme case, and we have outlined above some possible reasons for this, notably the greater degree of regulation facing the newly self-employed in Germany, which is likely to favour entrants with previous employment experience, over groups such as the unemployed.

In looking at different sources of self-employment inflows, we need to take account of the relative size of the stock from which the inflows come. Meager (1993) presents rates of inflow to self-employment, showing the relative probabilities of unemployed people, employees, family workers and the economically inactive becoming self-employed during a year. A key finding is that with the occasional exception of Germany, the average probability of an unemployed person entering self-employment is always greater than that of an employed or economically inactive person. Germany is again unusual in having both a low rate of inflow from unemployment and a high rate of inflow from employment, such that in some years the latter is as high as or even slightly higher than the former. Figure 5 charts the rate of entry from unemployment to self-employment and the UK again stands out, with the rate more than doubling during the 1980s. Trends are generally less marked in other countries. How can we explain these patterns? In particular, does the 'unemployment push' hypothesis provide any explanation? Meager (1993) examines for the five EC countries for which we have sufficient observations during the period in question, trends in the flow rates from unemployment to self-employment against trends in the unemployment rate itself. The pattern is mixed − in Belgium and France there is a relationship (albeit not a perfect one), in the predicted direction. In Germany and the UK, by contrast, the relationship is in the opposite direction, with falling unemployment associated with an increasing inflow rate from unemployment to self-employment, and vice versa (which is more indicative of discouragement, associated with a worsening economic climate, than of unemployment push). Unemployment push is, therefore, on the evidence available, inadequate as a general explanation of inflows to self-employment. A fuller explanation, across the range of EC countries, however, clearly needs to consider other major influences on the flow, obvious candidates being the policies introduced in all EC countries during the 1980s, aimed at encouraging the unemployed to become self-employed, which we consider in the rest of the chapter.

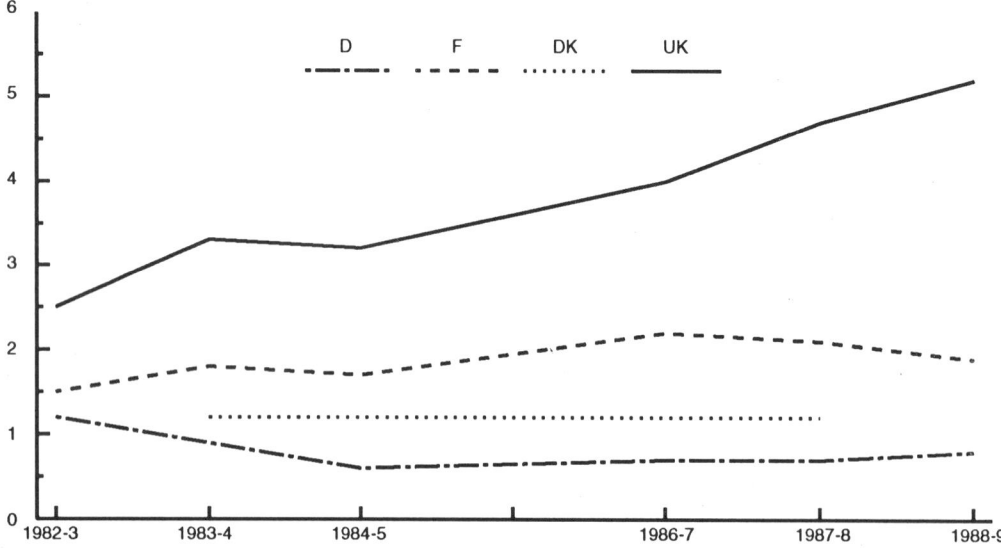

Figure 5: Entry rate to self-employment from unemployment. Source: ELFS.

LABOUR MARKET POLICIES FOR SELF-EMPLOYMENT IN EC COUNTRIES

During the 1980s, EC countries introduced a wide range of publicly-funded schemes to stimulate or support the expansion of self-employment. Of particular interest, given their size and universality, and our interest in flows from unemployment to self-employment, are those schemes aimed at promoting self-employment among the unemployed. Such schemes exist in all the member states, although in our research we excluded the main Italian scheme which is confined to unemployed youth resident in the Mezzogiorno region. Meager (1993) shows that such schemes constitute a small component of overall labour market policy expenditure (1.6% of total 1988 expenditure on labour market schemes in nine EC countries). Although small, however, it is growing – doubling in proportionate terms over 1985–1988 alone. There is also some diversity between the countries (in Spain the scheme accounted for close to 7% of labour market policy expenditure).

Clearly there are other ways of documenting the importance of expenditure on such schemes. Table 1 standardises each country's expenditure relative to the size of the target group for such schemes in that country (the unemployed). On this criterion Spain has clearly the largest scheme, spending more than $250 per unemployed person, whilst the UK, France and Denmark spend between $100 and $150 per head, and the other countries all spend less than $100. The table also confirms the general upward trend in such expenditures.

These schemes are generally incorporated within the unemployment compensation system of the countries concerned,[5] with payments to the unemployed who set up a business being in lieu of the benefits or insurance payments they would have received whilst unemployed. This implies, as others have noted, that these schemes are 'cheap' in exchequer cost terms compared with other labour market policies. Thus, even if the effect of such policies in terms of reduced unemployment or job creation is small, after allowing for deadweight and displacement,[6] the net exchequer cost per job created is also likely to be small given the negligible gross cost.

COMPARATIVE EVALUATION: SOME RESEARCH QUESTIONS

The main issues to be faced in comparative evaluation of such schemes are at least fourfold:

Table 1: Expenditure on self-employment schemes for the unemployed, per head of unemployment

Country	Per capita expenditure in US $[†]			
	1985	1986	1987	1988
Spain	30.2	142.0	192.8	256.1
UK	42.0	64.9	110.2	150.5
France	93.8	130.8	129.9	123.2
Denmark	*	54.6	91.4	114.3
Greece	0.0	0.0	0.0	81.6
Ireland	63.6	85.1	66.7	51.4
Germany	0.0	5.2	12.7	45.7
Belgium	0.0	0.0	51.2	44.3
Portugal		6.2	18.3	26.1

* Data not available.
† Scheme expenditure and unemployment data are derived from OECD statistics, and expenditure data have been converted into US $ at the prevailing annual average of national exchange rates against the $ for each year.

Identifying scheme objectives

A key difficulty in defining evaluation criteria, is identifying the underlying objectives of the scheme. Is success measured in terms of reduced unemployment (and if so, is this a short-term 'register effect' or a more indirect, job-creation impact)? Is the creation of enterprises an aim of the scheme in its own right? Are there other less clearly measurable objectives (e.g. impacts on labour supply quality or on aggregate earnings levels)? An important initial decision, therefore, is whether to concentrate on the scheme's unemployment impact or on its impact on self-employment. In national evaluation studies, these two questions have been treated as equivalent. Clearly in the short-term, they are, but over time, more complex dynamic effects may also need to be considered. For example, do scheme beneficiaries whose businesses fail return to unemployment, or do they get jobs, perhaps because the experience of self-employment has improved their position in the labour market? Or, are the existing businesses displaced by the subsidised self-employed, businesses which otherwise had better survival chances than those displacing them?

Our research concentrated on the effects of such schemes on self-employment rather than their unemployment impact, but in explaining differences between schemes, we take account, where possible, of differences in the underlying objectives of the policy-makers. These differences may be subtle ones which become clear only on detailed reading of official texts. A good example emerges when we compare the UK's Enterprise Allowance Scheme (EAS), with its German counterpart, Überbrückungsgeld. The schemes are ostensibly similar in design and objectives. In both cases the prime objective is the reduction of unemployment, although the German scheme is cast in a traditional labour market policy framework, whilst the literature on the UK scheme includes significant objectives associated with promoting the 'enterprise culture'. More interestingly, however, the German scheme has an explicit objective which is the 'avoidance of undervalued/underpaid employment'. Thus, it is an explicit requirement of the scheme that the participant must show that their business can generate a minimum level of income (in 1988 this was set at a level of 3400 DM per month). The position taken by UK policy-makers was rather different: many studies of EAS recipients note the extremely low earnings generated by the subsidised businesses. This is, however, seen as a supply side 'benefit', of the EAS, namely a contribution to reduced wage pressure in the economy.[7] The EAS has often been criticised for encouraging unemployed participants to enter low-margin competitive activities, in which they have poor survival chances or tend to displace existing businesses. It should be recognised, however, that such effects can be seen as consistent with one of the stated objectives of the scheme.

Controlling for differences in the environment

This is the most serious difficulty faced in comparative evaluation, which must make allowance for the different economic and institutional environments into which the various schemes are introduced, since these differences may constrain or support the flow from unemployment to self-employment in the absence of policy. We have set out the issues involved here in the earlier part of this chapter, which looked at the nature and composition of self-employment, together with recent self-employment trends in EC countries.

Deadweight and displacement

These effects (measuring the extent to which scheme participants would have entered self-employment anyway, and to which subsidised businesses displace unsubsidised ones) are the traditional meat and drink of policy evaluation, and are clearly important in any analysis of self-employment schemes for the unemployed.

Differences in scheme design and implementation

Differences in individual scheme performance (e.g. with regard to deadweight, displace-ment and survival rates) depend not just on the environment into which the scheme is introduced, but also on differences in the design and implementation of individual schemes. The most important of these are:

1. Eligibility

This has two aspects: firstly, whether the scheme is open or targeted to specific groups; and secondly, if targeted, the question of who is targeted. All the schemes are designed to increase the flow from unemployment to self-employment, and eligibility is normally confined to the unemployed. In most countries, eligibility is widely defined to cover all those entitled to unemployment compensation. Some countries (Germany, the UK and Ireland) exclude the very short-term unemployed, whilst two countries − Portugal and Denmark[8] − confine eligibility to the long-term unemployed (while Denmark also imposes an age criterion).

In evaluation terms a contrast needs to be made between schemes with limited eligibility and those with wide eligibility. Within the latter category, there is a need to examine the extent to which those who benefit from the scheme are representative of the eligible group. Evidence from several countries suggests that they tend not to be − with those entering the scheme being concentrated amongst the more advantaged unemployed (better qualified, male, with shorter durations of unemployment, etc.). *A priori*, it is not clear which kind of scheme design is more effective. On one hand a scheme with wide eligibility and self-selected participants risks high deadweight, whilst on the other a scheme targeted at disadvantaged groups may have lower deadweight, but poorer survival rates.

2. Whether the scheme involves a lump sum or an allowance

Although the schemes are similar in their ultimate funding source, they differ with regard to the disbursement of those funds to scheme participants. The key difference is between: countries (e.g. France and Spain) which provide funds in advance in the form of a grant (which in Spain is a simple capitalisation of the unemployment benefits the participant would have received); and the others, which provide an allowance over time, analogously to the payment of unemployment benefit.

Whilst there is little difference between these funding modes from an exchequer viewpoint, they may have rather different outcomes in practice, and an important evaluative element should therefore be a comparison of the performance of the two types.[9] Economic theory suggests that the impacts of two schemes identical in total budgets, but one reducing the capital constraint on business entry, and the other increasing the income stream during the initial period of self-employment, may be very different. Under perfect capital markets, of course, the two approaches would be equivalent,[10] but one feature commonly characterising the capital markets faced by would-be entrepreneurs, is their lack of perfection.

Evaluation must consider how the funding mode influences the numbers entering the scheme, the type of people entering (is a lump sum better at attracting disadvantaged groups, who would not otherwise enter self-employment?), and the types of activity they enter. The latter may be particularly important in influencing survival rates. We noted above that a common criticism of the UK scheme (an allowance) has been that it encourages a high rate of entry to markets with low entry barriers, low added value, and low returns. In these crowded, largely service sector markets, survival rates are low and displacement high. A key question, therefore, is whether a lump sum grant helps to avoid this and achieve a 'better' sectoral distribution of scheme participants.

3. Support and training

Is ongoing support and training provided for scheme participants, and if so, what? Are such mechanisms voluntary or compulsory; how are they administered; and how do they link in with other small business support and advisory networks in the countries concerned? The existence of appropriate support may weaken the trade-off between deadweight and survival identified above.

4. The scale and duration of payments
This concerns the inter-related questions of the size of the payments to scheme participants, the duration of payments, and the number of participants. To take extreme cases, is it more effective to spend a given budget on a small number of participants receiving a relatively large payment for a long time, or to spread it more thinly, with more participants, smaller payments and shorter durations of payment?

Space precludes discussion of all four features in the present chapter, where we concentrate on eligibility and funding modes. Meager (1993), however, considers the other scheme design features in more detail.

EVALUATION METHODOLOGIES

Ideally, evaluation would involve control-group experiments as in the USA. Typically, however, these have been ruled out in EC countries on grounds of cost, ethical objections to experimental evaluations, or because political expediency required rapid scheme implementation. In so far as evaluation must be *ex post facto*, there are three options:

Scheme administrative data/follow up surveys
This is the commonest approach in most countries, and involves use of administrative data to identify the participants' characteristics, and/or surveys to identify their perceptions, experiences, survival rates, etc. Its main drawback, apart from cost, is that without comparisons of non-scheme entrants to self-employment, it is difficult to draw strong conclusions. Equally, reliance on participants' perceptions to identify deadweight and displacement, is fraught with difficulties (Elias and Whitfield 1987). For comparative evaluation, the validity of such data is limited, since they are inevitably not comparable between countries. We have nevertheless reviewed the findings from such studies (see Meager 1993), and argue that there is some scope for using such data in conjunction with ELFS data (see below).

Aggregate impact studies
These look for scheme impact in aggregate data, controlling for the effects of other economic and environmental factors. We discuss such approaches below, and present some preliminary aggregate evaluations of our own, but such approaches are hindered by the lack of a robust theory of self-employment flows, and the absence, in most countries, of adequate time series flow data.

Inference through comparisons with micro-data
Such approaches involve the use of flow data (for comparative purposes the ELFS is ideal) to examine the characteristics of the newly self-employed, and the characteristics of those entering self-employment from unemployment. Similarly one can examine outflows and their characteristics. Comparisons of these patterns with the characteristics of scheme participants can provide some insights on scheme performance. We present below some of our own findings in this regard.

Each approach has advantages and disadvantages for international comparisons, and my research strategy has been to use elements of all three, and attempt through 'triangulation' to arrive at a better knowledge of the relative scheme performance. My approach aims to throw some light both on the schemes themselves, and on the possibilities of comparative evaluation offered by the availability of flow data, from the ELFS and other sources.

AGGREGATE EVALUATION OF SCHEME IMPACT

The simplest question which can be posed in evaluating self-employment policies of the kind discussed above is whether self-employment is higher than it would have been without the policy, and if so, by how much. Despite the considerable sums spent on such schemes, and the considerable effort spent in 'evaluating' them, this question remains largely unanswered (as confirmed by OECD (1990)). This partly results from the inevitable deficiencies of an approach that relies on the following up of scheme participants. In principle, such surveys can obtain some estimate of deadweight — by asking participants whether they would have entered self-employment without the scheme. A range of deadweight estimates, for example, has been derived from surveys of participants of the UK scheme (EAS) (see PA Cambridge Economic Consultants (PACEC) 1990). By definition, however, this approach cannot estimate displacement (it is difficult to attach credence to the approach made by several UK evaluation studies of asking participants how much business they have taken from existing firms). Elias and Whitfield (1987) provide a comprehensive account of the methodological difficulties of measuring displacement and conclude that intensive, costly, local labour market studies are the best solution. To date, only one such study has been undertaken (again of the UK's EAS) — Hasluck (1990), which considered EAS impact in two sectors ('hairdressing and beauty' and 'other business services') in a local labour market. In hairdressing, displacement was found to be close to 100%, whilst in the business services it was much lower. These results simply reinforce the difficulties in generalising from particular localities and sectors to estimate an overall scheme displacement effect.

Alternative approaches to assessing overall scheme impact (Elias and Whitfield 1987) involve aggregate macro-level analysis. One of the few examples of such an approach is Johnson et al (1988), who estimate a time-series aggregate model for the UK with self-employment levels as the dependent variable, and an independent policy variable for the EAS, alongside variables for unemployment, structural change and other factors. The results were, however, inconclusive, providing only weak evidence for a positive EAS effect on aggregate self-employment. A key problem with such analyses, moreover, is their reliance on the stock of self-employment as a dependent variable. The immediate objective of such schemes is to increase the inflow from unemployment to self-employment, and only aggregate modelling of the relationship between the scheme and the self-employment inflows can indicate whether there is such an effect (net of deadweight). Similarly the combined effects of non-survival scheme participants and displacement of non-participants can, in principle, be picked up only by modelling self-employment outflows.

Unfortunately our ELFS flow data offer too few observations for time-series modelling, but we can at least examine the possibility (see below) of using them in cross-country comparisons of scheme impact, before going on to illustrate a methodology for time-series impact analysis using a unique German flow dataset (see below).

AGGREGATE SCHEME IMPACT: CROSS-SECTION ANALYSIS

Is there any relationship across EC countries between the numbers entering self-employment from unemployment and the numbers of participants in self-employment schemes for the unemployed? If deadweight is generally high we would not expect a relationship, since the scheme would make little difference to the flow from unemployment to self-employment. To examine this, we express scheme participation as a percentage of the unemployed stock. Figure 6 plots the rates of entry from unemployment to self-employment over 1987–88 from the ELFS (see above 'The dynamics of self-employment'), against these rates of scheme participation.

This suggests a strong positive relationship between the two variables across EC countries (correlation 0.7). There is, however, no reason to assume that such schemes are the only, or the most important, variables influencing entry from unemployment to self-employment. As discussed above, there is a considerable literature arguing that unemployment itself will be an influence on self-employment inflows. As a crude test of this Table 2 presents a cross-section regression analysis for the nine countries, with the

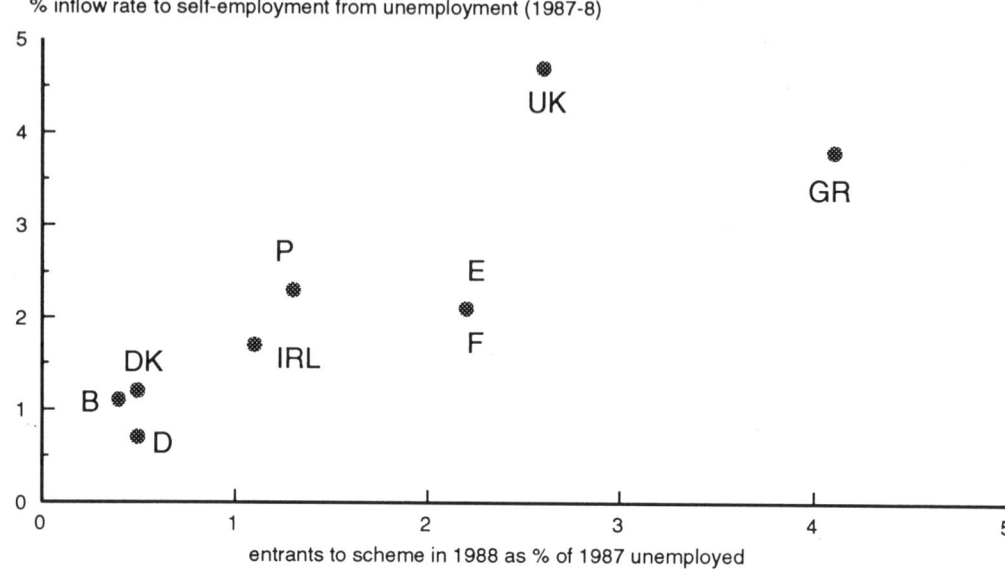

Figure 6: Self-employment schemes and inflows from unemployment 1987–1988. Source: ELFS and OECD 1990.

Table 2: Regression results – dependent variable = % of unemployed entering self-employment over 1987–88

	Coefficient	*t*-statistic
Constant	0.89	
% of 1987 unemployed entering scheme in 1988	0.88	3.71
1987 unemployment rate	−0.01	0.25
R^2	0.69	

rate of inflow to self-employment from unemployment (1987–88) as the dependent variable, and the rate of scheme participation (as defined above), together with the (1987) unemployment rate, as independent variables. It can be seen that the positive relationship between the scheme variable and the self-employment inflow persists when unemployment is included as an explanatory variable. The unemployment variable itself, however, has no significant impact, again suggesting that the evidence for 'unemployment push' is relatively weak.

The strong relationship between the scheme variable and the unemployment/self-employment inflow is nevertheless striking. Countries with larger schemes have higher overall rates of entry from unemployment to self-employment. Indeed, the regression results suggest that such schemes generally have very low deadweight elements – of the order of 12%, and that in the absence of the schemes just under one in every 100 unemployed people would enter self-employment over a year. We cannot, given the data inadequacies, interpret the results in such a strong form, but the fact that the relationship is both positive and significant suggests at least that the schemes have some effect (or deadweight is less than 100%).

AGGREGATE SCHEME IMPACT: TIME SERIES ANALYSIS – A GERMAN ILLUSTRATION

Aggregate time-series on self-employment flows are scarce in most countries. Germany is, however, unusual in having for the years since 1970, a consistent set of labour market flow data, the Arbeitskräfte-Gesamtrechnung (AGR). There are a number of deficiencies in this data set (e.g. its self-employment data include unpaid family workers), which should be used with caution (see Reyher and Bach 1988). We have, nevertheless, used AGR flow data to illustrate the potential such data offer for modelling self-employment flows, and the aggregate impact of self-employment schemes. We examine a time-series equivalent of the cross-section relationship presented above, with unemployment/self-employment as the dependent variable, and an unemployment measure, a measure of scheme intensity, and a time trend as independent variables (see Johnson et al (1988) for a justification of the time trend).

Before setting out the model itself, however, it is worth briefly describing the main features of the German scheme which involves a bridging allowance (Überbrückungsgeld) to unemployed people who set up in self-employment. The allowance, introduced in 1986, was initially payable for up to 3 months and (from 1988) for up to 6 months, its value being equivalent to the level of unemployment benefit/allowance received by the participant, subject to a ceiling (see Kaiser and Otto 1990).

Incorporation of a variable for Überbrückungsgeld into a model of self-employment inflows allows for a test of the short-term impact of the scheme itself, and the extent of likely deadweight. Although the scheme itself is relatively small (in 1988, scheme entry peaked, with about 18,000 participants), and accounts for only a small proportion of the overall inflow into self-employment, it is by no means negligible as a proportion of the (sub-)flow into self-employment from unemployment. Thus according to the AGR data, in 1988 about a fifth of those entering self-employment from unemployment were Überbrückungsgeld recipients. Despite its short life, then, the scheme is sufficiently large such that any influence it may have on the inflow ought to be detectable in statistical terms.

Turning now to the empirical examination, we estimate the model:

$$I_t = f(U_t, \; t, \; \ddot{U}_t)$$
$$\quad + \quad ? \quad +$$

where:
I_t = inflow from unemployment to self-employment in year t;
U_t = the unemployment level at the beginning of year t;
$\ddot{U}_t$ = some measure of the existence/intensity of Überbrückungsgeld in year t;
t = a time trend variable.

We have no theoretical basis for a particular functional form, but a preliminary data plot suggested non-linearity, and that a log-linear or semi-log estimating equation might be appropriate. Annual observations for I_t and U_t are obtainable from the AGR data set for 1970–1989 (with I_t calculated as a residual from these data). $\ddot{U}_t$ is the number of scheme participants in year t.

Table 3 shows ordinary least squares estimates of a semi-logarithmic model of this relationship. Four versions of this model are estimated. In version 1, I_t is simply regressed against $\ln(U_t)$. Whilst this yields a clear positive and statistically significant coefficient on $\ln(U_t)$, the Durbin–Watson statistic lies below the lower bound of acceptance, indicating a strong possibility of (first order) autocorrelation.

In version 2 which includes a time trend, the overall fit is improved slightly, and $\ln(U_t)$ retains its significance. Interestingly, the time trend has a significant coefficient, but with a *negative* sign suggesting not that the initial bivariate relationship between I_t and $\ln(U_t)$ was spurious due to both variables being subject to similar time trends, but rather that I_t is subject to an underlying downward trend, modified by the strong

Table 3: Regression estimates

Model	1 (1970–1989)	2 (1970–1989)	3 (1970–1985)	4 (1970–1989)
Dependent variable	I_t	I_t	I_t	I_t
Constant	−42.662	−83.516	−121.936	−108.796
	(4.034)*	(4.660)*	(8.538)*	(6.605)*
$\ln(U_t)$	17.112	24.981	32.890	30.214
	(11.254)*	(7.695)*	(12.193)*	(9.786)*
t		−1.282	−3.104	−2.513
		(2.652)**	(6.292)*	(4.583)*
$\ddot{U}_t$				0.927
				(3.191)*
R^2	0.88	0.91	0.96	0.95
D−W	0.55	0.60	1.70	1.64
F-statistic	126.66*	88.06*	166.14*	93.81*

Units of measurement are thousands.
Absolute values of t-statistics are given in parentheses: * significance at 1%; ** significance at 5% (2-tailed tests for t-statistics).

upward influence of growing unemployment. Again however, the Durbin−Watson statistic suggests autocorrelation, and possible omitted variables. Versions 3 and 4 of the model, therefore, explore the possibility that the key omitted variable is the labour market policy variable $\ddot{U}_t$. Version 3 is identical to version 2, but estimated over 1970−1985, excluding the period in which Überbrückungsgeld operated. If Überbrückungsgeld is the key omitted variable, we would expect version 3 to perform better than version 2. The results confirm this expectation, with the model fitting slightly better than before, but more importantly, it now shows no evidence of autocorrelation. The coefficients retain their significance and signs. Finally, version 4 covers the whole estimation period 1970−1989, including the Überbrückungsgeld variable $\ddot{U}_t$. This equation performs rather well. The overall fit is good, there is no evidence of autocorrelation, and the coefficients on all three variables are highly significant, with the coefficient on $\ddot{U}_t$ having the expected positive sign, and the other two retaining their signs from previous versions of the model. Given the lack of theoretical basis, further examination of the models' sensitivity to changes in the functional form seemed worthwhile, and further versions are estimated in Meager (1993). In each case, however, the pattern of results is broadly unchanged, and the results appear robust to several alternative functional forms.

These findings apparently confirm that all three independent variables play an important role in the development of inflows into self-employment. As far as 'unemployment push' is concerned, the evidence supports it only in its weak form, that is to say in the form which concerns only the sub-flow from unemployment to self-employment, which increases in response to an increase in unemployment. The stronger version, however, which argues that the probability of an unemployed person becoming self-employed increases as the unemployment level increases, is not supported by the evidence. Indeed the estimated equations show that the flow rate (I_t/U_t) tends to decrease with increasing unemployment.

Turning to the time trend, our results suggest that but for the influence of unemployment and policy, the flow from unemployment to self-employment is on a downward trend in Germany, falling by 2−3,000 per year. Some caution should be exercised, however, given that the AGR data include unpaid family workers, which in Germany as elsewhere, are subject to a long-term historical decline. It is possible, therefore, that the negative time trend may simply reflect the inclusion of this group.

The significant results for the scheme variable are of particular interest. Taking the coefficient on $\ddot{U}_t$ in version 4 at face value, it seems not only that Überbrückungsgeld has a significant effect on self-employment inflows, but that in line with our earlier multi-country analysis, the scheme's deadweight is small (around 7%). It is sensible also to exercise caution in interpreting this finding, and it is again possible that the inclusion of unpaid family workers in the data has affected this result. Further caution is suggested by the fact that these data indicate that the scheme performs rather better in deadweight terms than, for example, its UK equivalent, where survey evidence suggests that short-term deadweight may be as high as 30–40% of scheme participants (PACEC 1990). *A priori* we might expect the German scheme to have higher deadweight than the UK one, since the subsidy, although larger than in the UK, is payable for a shorter period, whilst the eligibility criteria for the German scheme are stricter (requiring evidence of the proposed business's viability). Against this, it is arguable that the threshold arrangements in the German scheme, whereby the allowance paid increases with previous unemployment duration, tips the balance of the scheme in favour of more 'disadvantaged' participants, unlikely to become self-employed without the subsidy. It is unfortunate that official follow-up surveys of Überbrückungsgeld recipients have not included a direct question on deadweight, although such surveys have suggested that the subsidy played an important support role for more than 2/3 of the scheme participants (and possibly for more than 85% of them), which is consistent with a relatively low deadweight element. Even if the AGR data are unreliable, however, this analysis serves to demonstrate the potential for using such labour market accounting systems to track labour market dynamics, providing a better empirical handle on the impact of such policy initiatives.

EXAMINATION OF SCHEME IMPACT THROUGH COMPARISON WITH REPRESENTATIVE MICRO-DATA

In this final section we consider the possibilities of ELFS flow data comparing scheme performance across countries. To illustrate the approach, some working hypotheses might be:

- the more the schemes are targeted (at disadvantaged groups, and people with characteristics not normally found among the self-employed), the less will be initial deadweight, but the lower the long-term survival rates of participants. Such targeting involves a trade-off between deadweight and survival, and it is unclear *a priori*, where the optimal balance lies. Using the ELFS we can build a profile of the personal characteristics of people who enter self-employment anyway. By comparing this with the characteristics of scheme participants, we can assess whether deadweight is likely to be high or low. Similarly, in so far as we can assess the survival chances of people with 'atypical' characteristics for self-employment, it may also be possible to provide some indications of the likely increased failure rates associated with targeted schemes.
- schemes providing a lump sum grant are more likely to encourage start-ups in markets with higher initial entry barriers but with long-term income and survival prospects, whilst allowance-based schemes are more likely to encourage entry to crowded markets with low entry barriers and capital requirements. It is likely that displacement will be smaller in the former case as new entrants reduce the (protected) profits of existing businesses rather than drive them out of business. Again ELFS data can indicate the typical business activities of the newly self-employed. This can then be compared with the sectoral profile of scheme participants, to assess whether the scheme is shifting the profile, and whether grant-based schemes shift it in a different way from allowance-based schemes.

Thus we use ELFS data to examine the personal characteristics of scheme participants (for reasons of space we confine ourselves in this chapter to analysing gender), and the characteristics of the businesses they set up (as indicated by industrial sector). Previous evaluations have compared the characteristics of the scheme participants with those of the self-employed as a whole.

The important advantages offered by ELFS data are twofold. Firstly they enable us to compare the characteristics of scheme participants with those of other entrants to self-employment from unemployment. Without such comparisons, it is impossible to conclude that the schemes are influencing the types of unemployed people who would otherwise become self-employed. Secondly they enable us to compare scheme performance across countries, taking account of the underlying structure of self-employment flows. Thus, if, for example, the proportion of participants in manufacturing is higher in Germany than France, this does not necessarily imply that the German scheme is more successful than the French in supporting manufacturing start-ups, since we also need to take account of the proportions of the overall flow from unemployment to self-employment entering manufacturing in the two countries.

Before setting out the results of these comparisons, however, I briefly summarise the schemes themselves in Table 4 (see also Meager 1993, Barker 1989, OECD 1990). Key differences are the relatively large scale of the UK and French schemes; the fact that the French scheme is a lump sum grant, and the others are allowances; the initial targeting of the Danish scheme on the long-term unemployed (subsequently widened); the wide eligibility of the UK scheme and (until 1987) the French scheme, as against the German scheme which requires greater scrutiny of the proposed businesses. Of the allowance-

Table 4: Summary of self-employment schemes for the unemployed in four EC member states

	Germany	France	UK	Denmark
Name of scheme	Uberbrückungsgeld	Aide aux chômeurs créateurs d'entreprises	Enterprise Allowance Scheme	Iværksætterydelsen
Date introduced	1986	1979/80	1983	1985
Eligibility	Registered unemployed (after 11 weeks: reduced to 4 weeks in 1988). No legal entitlement (*Bundesanstalt für Arbeit* can operate budgetary ceiling for scheme)	All receiving or entitled to unemployment benefits (recently extended to include recipients of other welfare benefits)	Unemployed for at least 8 weeks and receiving unemployment or supplementary benefit (family credit). From 1991 limit reduced to 6 weeks, and local Training and Enterprise Councils (TECs) have discretion to waive 6 week rule for certain categories of unemployed	Long-term unemployed over 25 (unemployed for at least 21 months and had at least one statutory 'job offer'). Revised 1989 to include LTU under 25 (with 12 months unemployment and one 'job offer'), and other 'interested' unemployed with at least 5 months unemployment
Form of support	Monthly allowance	Capital grant	Weekly allowance	Monthly allowance
Rate of payment	Equivalent to previous benefit entitlement (ceilings introduced and progressively reduced after revision of scheme in 1988), and contributions to some social security costs	Between FF.10,750 and 43,000 (*diminishes* with length of previous unemployment); plus exemptions from some social security payments (extra grant if new enterprise creates jobs)	Flat rate of £40 per week. From 1991, individual TECs have discretion to vary payments (from £20–£90 per week)	50% of maximum unemployment benefit (up to a ceiling of DKr.54,000 p.a.)

Table 4: Contd.

	Germany	France	UK	Denmark
Duration of payments	Up to 3 months. Increased to 6 months in 1988, and thresholds introduced, whereby duration of payments increase with duration of previous unemployment	One-off payment	Up to 52 weeks. From 1991 TECs have discretion to vary payment period (from 26 to 66 weeks)	Up to 3.5 years
Conditions for receipt of payment	Must have proposal approved by competent authority (bank, chamber of commerce, professional assoc. etc); business must guarantee likely minimum income of DM3,400 p.m.	No restrictions initially. Since 1987, applicants must fill in detailed questionnaire, and are vetted on the likely viability of their proposed business	Must have £1,000 initial own capital. Must work in new business for at least 36 hours per week. New business must be the whole investment. Certain types of 'unsuitable' business activities excluded. From 1991 TECs have discretion to vary requirements – many now require business plans to be vetted prior to entry	No specific restrictions on applicants, or type of business. No own capital requirements
Support mechanisms	None tied to scheme, but participants eligible for wide range of advice/support through chambers of commerce, etc.	None tied to scheme, but participants eligible for normal state-funded business advice, etc.	Must attend initial 'awareness day' prior to entry. Participants visited at least once by officials during year. Option of 3 free business counselling sessions during year	Recipients have option of participating in special courses for new entrepreneurs at technical or commercial schools
Number of participants	1986: 5,728 1987: 9,996 1988: 17,985 1989: 11,242	1979: 9,200 1986: 71,577 (peak) 1990: 49,316	1983/4: 27,600 1987/8: 106,300 (peak) 1990/1: 60,300	1985: 409 1987: 1,008 1989: 5,508 1990: 5,641
Survival rates	Not available, but of scheme participants in calendar year 1987, some 8% were again unemployed by May 1988. The corresponding figure for 1988 participants was 6%	Aggregate figures are: after one year about 85% are still trading. After two years about 75%. Highest survival rates in construction and manufacturing, lowest in commercial services	Of those who complete 12 months on the scheme, about 3/4 survive a further 6 months, and about 2/3 survive a further 2 years	About 76% of starters in 1989 were in business 2 years later. Earlier studies show that about 29% of participants do not survive the 3.5 years of eligibility

based schemes, the UK is the smallest (the maximum an individual could receive under the scheme was 3016 ECU in 1988) and the Danish the largest (the maximum was 23,800 ECU in 1988); whilst the German scheme although involving a larger monthly payment than the UK scheme, had considerably shorter duration (maximum 6 months). The maximum grant available under the French scheme was 5,800 ECU.

Table 5 compares the gender distributions of scheme participants with those of the self-employment stock and the inflows to self-employment. The UK scheme shows strong growth in the proportion of female participants (from 15% to 36% by 1989). This partly results from a deliberate policy to encourage women to participate in the scheme, following a perception that they were 'under-represented' (although, as Table 5 shows, when the comparison is made with the aggregate inflow from unemployment rather than the self-employment stock, this perception is probably wrong). This approach,

Table 5: Gender composition of self-employment, self-employment flows, and scheme participants

	% female share of:			
	Self-employed stock	Inflow to self-employment	Inflow to self-employment from unemployment	Participants in self-employment scheme for the unemployed*
UK				*Enterprise Allowance Scheme*
1982−3	23.6	32.7	11.8	7.0
1983−4	24.0	34.0	17.7	14.6
1984−5	25.0	35.8	19.2	19.1
1985−6				22.5
1986−7	25.1	34.8	20.8	24.7
1987−8	24.8	32.8	18.5	30.3
1988−9	26.7	33.1	21.3	35.8
Germany				*Überbrückungsgeld*
1982−3	22.5	31.6		
1983−4	23.2		Average (1982−5): 39.5	
1984−5	22.6	34.7		
				19.2
1986−7	23.5	36.2		21.0
1987−8	23.9	34.6	Average (1986−9): 29.1	22.4
1988−9	24.1	37.0		22.3
France				*L'aide aux chômeurs créateurs d'entreprises*
1982−3	21.1	39.1		19.1
1983−4	21.0	34.4	Average (1982−4): 19.3	
1984−5	21.2	39.1	30.1	
1985−6				21.0
1986−7	22.3	37.1	21.2	21.7
1987−8	22.8	34.6	16.5	23.0
1988−9	24.0	40.8	22.0	24.0
Denmark				*Iværksætterydelsen*
1982−3	12.4			
1983−4	15.9	Avge (85−5): 35.4		
1984−5	14.9			50
1985−6			Avge (82−9): 33.8	55
1986−7	14.8			58
1987−8	12.9	Avge (86−9): 29.2		63
1988−9	14.8			46

* Data on the composition of scheme participants are derived from administrative records, and in some cases follow-up surveys of participants (in the UK's case they are average estimates from several data sources for each year).
Sources: ELFS for aggregate stock and flow data.
For scheme participants, data are taken from administrative data and follow-up surveys of scheme participants in individual countries − see Meager (1993) for detailed references.

whilst successful in targeting a group disadvantaged in terms of access to the means of setting up a business, and therefore reducing likely deadweight, does not seem to have been at the expense of survival rates (although EAS evaluation studies show that survival rates of women were lower than those of men — partly because they set up different types of business than men — overall survival rates rose over the period, due to the improving economic situation in the late 1980s).

The Danish scheme also exhibits over-representation of women compared with the aggregate inflow to self-employment. This results from their over-representation in the scheme's long-term unemployed target group, and the proportion of women in the scheme fell significantly following the widening of the eligibility criteria in 1989. Women are under-represented among the self-employed to a far greater extent in Denmark than in the other countries (only 15% of Danish self-employed are women), and it seems, therefore, that this initial targeting of the Danish scheme on disadvantaged groups involved relatively low deadweight. This is confirmed by survey data (Rosdahl and Mærkedahl 1987) which show that at least 44% of participants would definitely not have set up in self-employment without the scheme, a much higher proportion than is found in UK surveys (between 14 and 34% — PACEC (1990)).

Of the other two schemes, the proportion of female French scheme participants is generally similar to the overall female share in self-employment entrants. The German scheme, however, exhibits a considerable under-representation of women, reflecting its more stringent entry criteria: business viability must be assessed by a 'competent authority', and must generate a specified initial monthly income. This latter criterion, in particular, discriminates against female applicants; UK surveys show that female EAS participants are much more likely than males to enter low-margin competitive service sector activities such as hairdressing and other personal services. Such activities are often ruled out in the German case by the income requirements. *A priori*, we would expect these restrictions to result in the German scheme having high levels of deadweight but also high survival rates. In practice, as discussed above, the evidence does not suggest that the German scheme has higher deadweight than in other countries (it seems to be lower than in the UK, and closer to the Danish levels), although low post-scheme re-entry to unemployment (about 6–8%) is consistent with high survival rates. It is unclear why the German scheme has such low deadweight, but one explanation may lie in the tapering payment eligibility according to unemployment duration. If the unemployed most likely to set up in business without a subsidy are more likely to do so in the early months of unemployment, such tapering may deadweight. Thus it would seem that the German scheme's design, giving greater weight to longer-term unemployed, whilst imposing strict criteria for the viability and income potential of the proposed business, may increase survival (and possibly also reduce displacement — see below), without increasing deadweight unduly, albeit at the cost of discouraging female participation.

Finally, in Table 6, we compare businesses set up by scheme participants with the activities of the newly self-employed in general. In the UK, the features which stand out are the over-representation of certain service activities — especially 'other services' and, to a lesser extent, distribution, hotels and catering. This is consistent with the expectation that the EAS, as an allowance, with a small weekly payment, and few eligibility conditions, would have a high proportion of participants entering small-scale service sector activities, with few entry barriers and requiring little financial or human capital. It is interesting to note that service activities where such barriers may have been higher (business services, and transport and communications) were not over-represented among EAS participants.

The sector most under-represented among EAS participants is construction. Self-employment grew strongly in UK construction in the 1980s, and this finding is con-sistent with the argument put forward elsewhere (Meager 1991), that much of this was 'disguised employment', reflecting the growth of 'labour only' subcontracting, and the

Table 6: Sectoral composition of self-employment, self-employment flows, and scheme participants (%)

Sector (NACE)	Self-employed stock		Inflow to self-employment		Inflow to self-employment from unemployment		Participants in self-employment scheme for the unemployed			
Germany	1983	1989	1983–5	1987–9	1983–5	1987–9	1986	1987	1988	1989
Agriculture (00)	22.2	15.4	11.2	10.4	8.5	7.6	2.3	2.4	2.6	2.4
Production (10–40)	13.0	13.6	20.9	21.8	12.7	8.9	15.9	15.9	14.0	14.1
Construction (50)	7.6	7.7	8.4	7.0	5.7	8.3	10.0	9.0	8.5	8.3
Distribution, hotels, catering (60)	31.1	28.5	30.3	25.8	32.8	31.2	35.3	36.2	35.6	34.0
Transport, comm. (70)	3.4	4.1	3.8	4.3	4.7	5.1	4.0	4.1	4.1	4.3
Finance, bus. servs.(80)	10.1	15.1	11.9	14.5	19.7	17.2	32.5	32.4	35.2	36.9
Other services (90)	12.7	15.4	13.4	16.1	15.7	21.7				
France	1983	1989	1983–5	1987–9	1983–5	1987–9	1987	1988	1989	
Agriculture	35.3	32.3	29.8	26.6	8.6	9.7	(1.8)			
Production (10–40)	8.0	7.9	8.9	8.3	12.2	9.1	18.0	23	21	
Transport, comm. (70)	1.9	2.3	2.3	2.5	2.1	2.3	4.1			
Construction (50)	11.2	11.4	9.0	9.7	16.1	17.3	18.5	18	19	
Commerce & services (60, 80, 90)	43.5	46.0	50.0	52.9	61.0	61.6	57.8	59	60	

UK	1983	1989	1983-5	1987-9	1983-5	1987-9	1983-5*	1987-9*
Agriculture (00)	11.8	8.6	4.3	3.2	3.2	4.9	4.7	3.2
Energy, water (10)	0.1	0.2	1.7	1.2	(1.3)	1.3	0.1	0.0
Minerals, chemicals (20)	0.7	0.7					0.8	0.8
Metals, engineering (30)	2.6	3.1	2.7	3.5	3.7	3.1	4.4	1.6
Other manuf. (40)	4.7	6.0	6.7	6.8	5.7	8.0	10.4	9.0
Construction (50)	20.3	24.1	19.3	22.2	29.1	25.6	14.9	15.7
Distribution, hotels, catering (60)	31.1	24.6	28.1	23.5	29.6	21.9	30.1	25.9
Transport, comm. (70)	4.3	5.0	4.2	5.5	5.1	8.5	4.6	4.3
Finance, bus. servs. (80)	9.7	11.4	10.7	12.8	6.2	8.8	8.2	10.8
Other services (90)	14.6	16.3	22.4	21.3	15.9	17.8	22.0	27.4

Denmark	1983	1989	1983-5	1987-9	1983-89	1989
Agric., production, construction (00-50)	52.5	49.6	18.0	30.3	12.7	23
Distrib., hotels, catering (60)	23.7	22.5	49.3	31.3	49.0	35
Other services (70-90)	23.8	27.9	32.6	38.4	38.3	41

* Note that the UK data are averages of the sectoral structure of participants over the period in question, derived from several data sources.
Sources: as Table 5.

convenience of the self-employed label for tax purposes. This growth would not be reflected among EAS participants, since such self-employment would not meet the eligibility conditions of the scheme (see Evans and Lewis 1989).

The German scheme, similar in conception to the EAS, but with more stringent entry requirements, yields a different picture. Service and agricultural activities are under-represented and manufacturing over-represented, in comparison with the aggregate inflow to self-employment from unemployment. Table 6 shows (see also Meager 1993) that manufacturing accounts for a much higher proportion of self-employment stocks, and of inflows to self-employment in Germany than in other EC countries. Table 6 also shows that the unemployed may be disadvantaged in entering such activities, since the representation of manufacturing in the flow from unemployment is rather lower (this is consistent with the German institutional environment discussed above). It seems, there-fore, that Überbrückungsgeld may go some way to redress that imbalance, with its relatively generous support, coupled with stricter scrutiny of eligible businesses. It is likely, for example, that manufacturing and Handwerk activities are more likely to satisfy the income conditions of Überbrückungsgeld, than their counterparts in services (Gout and Bùchtemann 1987) confirm that service sectors contain higher proportions of self-employed with very low incomes than do production sectors).

Our earlier hypothesis, however, was that among self-employment schemes, those based on a lump sum grant might be most effective in shifting the sectoral composition of supported businesses away from marginal, low-earning, service activities, since relaxation of the capital constraint may help overcome initial entry barriers to capital intensive activities in higher margin, more protected markets. The data from the French scheme are consistent with this hypothesis, since participants exhibit the greatest over-representation of production activities among the schemes examined (the proportion of participants in production sectors is twice as high as the proportion of the aggregate inflow from unemployment to self-employment which is in these sectors).

None of these findings are conclusive, and confirmation requires more detailed exam-ination of the characteristics and performance of individual schemes, and a consideration of a wider range of characteristics of scheme participants than is possible here. They do, nevertheless, illustrate the potential of flow data in evaluating the impact of different policy designs.

CONCLUDING REMARKS

I have ranged widely over recent self-employment trends in EC countries, their nature and causes, and the role of the self-employment policies in contributing to these trends. Given this range, the treatment has necessarily been superficial in parts. I have never-theless illustrated a strategy for comparing developments across countries and evaluating such schemes, using comparative flow data from labour force surveys.

I have discussed the major issues involved in explaining recent trends in self-employ-ment, and stressed the importance of institutional variations when comparing different countries' experiences. I have considered the difficult issue of separating out cyclical fluctuations in self-employment from underlying trends, and argued that much previous research on cyclical influences on self-employment is inconclusive because of its reliance on stock rather than flow measures of self-employment. The argument that recent self-employment growth reflects 'unemployment push' is particularly vulnerable to such a critique, and I present new empirical evidence for this using flow data from the ELFS.

These data reinforce the role of institutional differences (indicating a much more 'dynamic' picture of self-employment in the UK than in Germany for example), as well as providing a new dimension to comparative evaluation of the self-employment schemes for the unemployed introduced in EC countries in recent years. I have, more generally, identified the main methodological issues in such evaluations, and begun to tackle them. I conclude, *inter alia*, that the existence of such schemes does make a difference: they are not purely 'deadweight'. Both cross-section comparisons between countries, and our time-series example for Germany suggest that more unemployed people enter self-employment as a result of these schemes than would otherwise be the case. This does not imply that all scheme designs are equally effective, and that the self-employment thereby generated is necessarily sustainable (the fall in UK self-employment in the post-1989 recession is evidence of this). Scheme design also makes a difference, therefore, and our evidence is consistent with the notion that more selective eligibility criteria and/or a lump sum grant rather than an allowance-based subsidy may help to shift such schemes towards the development of sustainable self-employment with significant earnings potential (and perhaps subsequent employment generation potential).

Many questions remain unanswered, and require further research — I have, for example, been unable to develop a convincing explanation for why Denmark has not shared in the recent growth in self-employment experienced elsewhere. Promising avenues of explanation, however, involve a mixture of cyclical, structural and institutional factors. Danish self-employment shares many of the features of German self-employment which distinguish the latter from the UK — including a policy emphasis on existing small businesses rather than start-ups, and a relatively small scale and selective self-employment scheme for the unemployed. In addition Danish self-employment contains a relatively large agricultural component, and it is further possible that relatively high unemployment/welfare benefits in Denmark act as a dampening factor on any 'unemployment push' element contributing to self-employment growth in recent decades.[11] A further factor is that the Danish labour market is relatively unregulated (Denmark ranks lowest of our four countries on the 'job security' index calculated by Bertola (1990)). Some have argued (see OECD 1992) that a high degree of employment protection adds to the impetus for self-employment to increase, especially during times of economic downswing, by providing an incentive for employers to subcontract to small enterprises. Such a hypothesis, is of course, difficult to square with the UK experience of rapid self-employment growth despite labour market deregulation from already relatively low levels of employment protection.

Institutionally-based international comparisons do, however, offer the most scope for improving our understanding of the causes and implications of the historically unprecedented recent developments in self-employment, as well as for evaluating the new range of policies aimed at stimulating self-employment, and drawing conclusions about scheme design and impact which can be transferred across countries.

NOTES

1. Mutual Information System on Employment Policies.
2. In practice, however, there is little hard evidence of attitudinal change to self-employment in the UK during the 1980s (Blanchflower and Oswald 1990, Blackburn et al 1991).
3. Belgium, Denmark, France, Germany, Ireland, Italy, Luxembourg, the Netherlands, and the UK.
4. Given small sample sizes, little significance can be attached to the increase in Danish inflow rates over the period.
5. See also Barker (1989).
6. The concepts of 'deadweight' and 'displacement' are explored further below.
7. See Owens (1989) p. 6.
8. In Denmark eligibility was widened to include short-term unemployed in 1989.
9. An experimental evaluation of the two approaches is under way in the USA. It is unfortunate that no such evaluation exists in Europe, and that the US results are not yet available (Wandner and Messenger 1991).
10. Except that under an allowance, even participants could borrow against the guaranteed income stream, and they would pay interest, whilst under a lump sum grant, the subsidy is usually interest free.

11. Denmark has the most generous unemployment compensation system in the EC (see Commission of the European Communities 1992, Chapter 7).

REFERENCES

Acs Z., Audretsch D. and Evans D. (1992) The determinants of variations in self-employment rates across countries and over time, Wissenschaftszentrum Berlin für Sozialforschung, discussion paper, FS IV 92−3.

Bannock G. and Albach H. (1991) Small Business Policy in Europe: Britain, Germany and the European Commission, Anglo-German Foundation for the Study of Industrial Society, London.

Barker P. (1989) Self employment schemes for the unemployed, Local Initiatives for Employment Creation, Cahier No. 10, OECD, Paris.

Bertola B. (1990) Job security, employment and wages, European Economic Review, Vol. 34, pp. 851−886.

Blackburn R., Curran J. and Woods A. (1991) Exploring Enterprise Cultures: Small Service Sector Enterprise Owners and their Views, Kingston Business School, Kingston upon Thames (mimeo).

Blanchflower D. and Oswald A. (1990) Self-employment and Mrs Thatcher's Enterprise Culture in British Social Attitudes: The 1990 Report, Gower, Aldershot.

Bögenhold D. and Staber U. (1990) Selbständigkeit als ein Reflex aus Arbeitslosigkeit, Kölner Zeitschrift für Soziologie und Psychologie, Vol. 42, No. 2.

Bögenhold D. and Staber U. (1991) The decline and rise of self-employment, Work, Employment and Society, Vol. 5, pp. 223−239.

Campbell M. and Daly M. (1992) Self-employment: into the 1990s, Employment Gazette, June, pp. 269−292.

Commission of the European Communities (1992) Employment in Europe 1992, Directorate-General for Employment, Industrial Relations and Social Affairs, Brussels/Luxembourg.

Danish Technological Institute (1991) Survey of initiatives in Sweden, Great Britain, Schleswig-Holstein and within the EEC which aim at reducing the problems and financing of SMEs and new companies, Dansk Teknologisk Institut, Taastrup.

Doran A. (1984) Craft Enterprises in Britain and Germany: A Sectoral Study, Anglo-German Foundation for the Study of Industrial Society, London.

Elias P. and Whitfield K. (1987) The Economic Impact of the Enterprise Allowance Scheme: Theory and Measurement of Displacement Effects, Report to MSC, Institute for Employment Research, Coventry, University of Warwick.

Evans S. and Lewis R. (1989) Destructuring and deregulation in the construction industry, in Manufacturing Change: Industrial Relations and Restructuring, eds Tailby S. and Whitston C. Basil Blackwell, Oxford.

Gout M. and Büchtemann C. (1987) Développement et structure du travail 'indépendant' en R.F.A, Wissenschaftszentrum, Berlin (mimeo).

Hakim C. (1988) Self-employment in Britain: a review of recent trends and current issues, Work, Employment and Society, Vol. 2, No. 4, December.

Hasluck C. (1990) The displacement effects of the Enterprise Allowance Scheme: a Local Labour Market Study, DE Programme 1989/90: Project Report, Institute of Employment Research, University of Warwick.

International Labour Office (1990) The Promotion of Self-Employment, International Labour Conference, 77th Session 1990, Report VII, Geneva, International Labour Office.

Johnson S. Lindley R. and Bourlakis C. (1988) Modelling Aggregate Self-Employment: A Preliminary Analysis, Department of Employment Programme 1988/89 Project Report, University of Warwick, Institute for Employment Research, December.

Kaiser M. and Otto M. (1990) Übergang von Arbeitslosigkeit in berufliche Selbständigkeit', Mitteilungen aus der Arbeitsmarkt- und Berufsforschung, Vol. 22, No. 2.

Meager N. (1991) Self-Employment in the United Kingdom, IMS Report No. 205, Brighton, Institute of Manpower Studies.

Meager N. (1992a) Does unemployment lead to self-employment?, Small Business Economics, Vol. 4, pp. 87−103.

Meager N. (1992b) The fall and rise of self-employment (again): A comment on Bögenhold and Staber, Work, Employment and Society, Vol. 6, No. 1, pp. 127−134.

Meager N. (1993) Self-employment and labour market policy in the European Community, Discussion Paper, Research Area 1 (Labour Market and Employment), Berlin, Wissenschaftszentrum Berlin für Sozialforschung.

Meager N., Kaiser M. and Dietrich H. (1992) Self-Employment in the United Kingdom and Germany, Anglo-German Foundation for the Study of Industrial Society, London/Bonn.

OECD (1990) Report by OECD Evaluation Panel No. 11, Organisation for Economic Co-operation and Development, Paris (mimeo).

OECD (1992) Employment Outlook July (1992), Organisation for Economic Co-operation and Development, Paris.

Owens A. (1989) Enterprise Allowance Scheme Evaluation: Sixth 6-month National Survey, Sheffield, Employment Service, Research and Evaluation Branch, August.

PA Cambridge Economic Consultants (1990) Evaluation of Jobclubs and the Enterprise Allowance Scheme in Great Britain, Cambridge.

Reyher L. and Bach H-U. (1988) Arbeitskräfte-Gesamtrechnung: Bestände und Bewegung am Arbeitsmarkt, Beiträge zur Arbeitsmarkt- und Berufsforschung, No. 70.

Rosdahl A. and Mærkedahl I. (1987) Uddannelses og iværksætterydelsen til langtidsledige, Socialforskningsinstituttet, København.

Sengenberger W., Loveman G. and Piore M. (1990) The re-emergence of small enterprises: industrial restructuring in industrialised countries, International Institute for Labour Studies, Geneva.

Wandner S. and Messenger J. (1991) From unemployed to self-employed: self-employment as a re-employment option in the United States, US Department of Labor, Employment and Training Administration, Washington DC (mimeo).

4.

SMALL FIRMS IN RECESSION IN BRITAIN

*John Stanworth, David Purdy, Nick Zafiris, Peter Wilson, Adrian Woods
and David Kirby*

INTRODUCTION

The current recession in Britain continues to have a profound effect upon the small firms sector as well as the economy as a whole. Following on directly from the 'Lawson Boom' budget of 1988, it is the longest and deepest recession of the post-war era. Given the sheer length of the recession, few research studies will have been fortunate enough to possess the longitudinal span to record its full breadth. The two pieces of research reported in this paper both possess data covering a period spanning pre-recessionary times up to the present day. Both are still on-going and will be able to observe our subsequent economic recovery.

The current recession appears something more than a downturn in a traditional post-war pattern of economic 'stop-go's. By way of illustration of its severity, Clive Woodcock, editor of the New Business page in the *Guardian* newspaper, commented on 3 August 1992:

> ... with the Federation of Small Businesses, the largest of the lobby groups, anticipating a further 60,000 firms to go out of business this year to add to last year's 50,000, the place to find entrepreneurs seems more likely to be in the bankruptcy courts or the dole queue than in the still growing number of business parks.

There is also evidence to suggest that the British recession is more severe than that of most of our European competitors. For instance, at the 22nd European Small Business seminar held in September 1992, in Amsterdam, an eight-nation study funded by the European Commission (DGXXIII) showed Britain at the foot of the table where small firm job losses over the last three years are concerned (Research Institute for Small and Medium-Sized Businesses 1992). Britain's performance was inferior to even that of the Republic of Ireland and Finland.

THE SMALL BUSINESS RESEARCH TRUST/NATWEST QUARTERLY SURVEY OF SMALL BUSINESS IN BRITAIN

The above survey has been in existence since the final quarter of 1984 and typically yields over 1,000 responses from a larger sample of firms drawn from an SBRT Volunteer database (including members of the National Chamber of Trade, the Federation of Small Businesses and firms contacted through Business in the Community). Between the period 1984/Quarter 4 and 1992/Quarter 3, the survey has followed the well-established CBI practice, in its Industrial Trends Survey, of generating an economic summary statistic – termed the balance – to monitor changes in sales and employment.

The balance is the percentage of respondents replying 'up', minus the percentage replying 'down' (ignoring for this purpose the percentage replying 'same'), in response to questions on the direction of changes in sales and employment over a given period.

Figure 1 presents 'actual' changes over time as opposed to the often more optimistic 'expected' changes sometimes used as a barometer of 'business confidence'. It should be remembered that such surveys are essentially surveys of surviving firms, since firms which have failed no longer respond to questionnaires.

Figure 1 shows the relative seriousness of the current recession following a dip into negative balance figure for both sales and employment from late 1990 onwards.

Figure 2 plots responses from responding firms to quarterly requests to identify their main single business problem. The frequency of two factors in particular appears to reflect degrees of economic buoyancy. The first of these, low turnover or lack of business dipped into single figures in 1988/89 at a period when the second factor, lack of skilled employees, rose to double figures. In the third quarter of 1992, the proportion claiming low turnover or lack of business as their major problem rose to an all-time high of 43.7% whilst lack of skilled employees was selected by only 2.8%.

Figure 3 records major problems separated out by business sector and, as might be expected, shows low turnover or lack of business as a particularly severe problem for firms in the construction industry but somewhat less so for other sectors, particularly agriculture. Figure 4 records major problems against size of firm. Differences here do not appear to be large, though those which do occur are probably fairly predictable, e.g. smaller firms being more concerned with issues of premises/rent/rates and larger firms being more concerned with access to finance.

LONGITUDINAL SMALL FIRMS 'GROWTH CORRIDOR' PROJECT

This project (Stanworth et al 1992) tracked 120 small manufacturing and business services firms between 1989 and 1992 but also collected retrospective data relating back to 1986. The firms were situated in three geographical areas — the North, East Midlands and South East.

Figures 5, 6 and 7 record growth in employment by size, sector and region for the periods 1986—1989 and 1989—1992. Some interesting observations emerge here. Firstly, the dramatic reversal in job creation effectiveness during the two periods. In fact, fortunes during the two respective periods are almost a mirror image of each other in that the principal job creators of the 1986—1989 period were the main job losers of the 1989—1992 period, i.e. firms in the 1—4 size category, firms in the business services sector and firms in the Northern region particularly. It would appear that the 'soft' growth generated under the greenhouse conditions of 1986—1989 tended to be particularly exposed to the economic frosts that lay ahead. The size influence at the bottom end of the size-scale observed here has recently been similarly reported elsewhere (Curran and Blackburn 1992) in a sample heavily concentrated at the smaller end of the current size-range.

Figures 8, 9 and 10 relate to measures of year-on-year reported financial turnover, based on a May 1991 and May 1992 comparison (but with adjustments made in cases where either May figure appeared to be wholly untypical of a more general trend). However, these recent turnover figures do not always correlate comfortably with trends expressed in terms of job losses. For instance, looking at Figure 8 which breaks down results by size, the weakest performance emerges from firms in the 5—9 band (job loss figures recorded show the reverse picture). In Figure 9, the differences between manufacturing and business services appear fairly negligible yet differences in job loss figures are quite marked. Finally, in Figure 10, firms in the East Midlands appear to be markedly under-achieving those in the North, yet their job retention record appears noticeably superior.

Many different factors may be at work here, some not always immediately apparent. For instance, we know that even where firms were not reducing their absolute workforce sizes, they were often cutting or eliminating overtime and freezing (or even reducing) wages. On occasions, jobs were even still counted as existing but 'not filled'. Also, even where financial turnover levels were being maintained, prices were often being frozen, and customers reducing order sizes but increasing order frequency (approximating to a 'just-in-time' system of supply). This involved increased handling and invoicing costs. Payment times often extended out from 30 days to 60 or 90 and the firms themselves were obliged to match 'just-in-time' sales to their own customers with 'just-in-time' buying from their own suppliers – once again increasing levels of administrative burden.

There were indications from the job loss/financial turnover level figures that the manufacturing firms may have been making greater efforts to retain staff, for fear of not being able to replace them in the event of an upturn, than was the case in business services sector firms. Also, the particularly high job loss rates in the North (appearing to more than fully reflect losses in financial turnover levels) could possibly reflect greater levels of historical turbulence in Northern labour markets and less reluctance to shed staff.

To these factors of course, we could add that of problems with obtaining reliable research data when studying small firms. We shall be delving below into the issue of soliciting financial data from small firms at times of recession, but, even when it came to the issue of workforce size, a surprising number of firms were not as immediately aware of their exact workforce size as researchers might expect – particularly once workforce sizes had climbed into double figures. We might ask the question here, why in any case they should be expected to carry such information around in their heads – after all they are not labour market researchers.

The point to be made overall here is that the relationship between levels of business turnover and workforce size appears a fairly complex one, and it involves a number of factors in addition to the most obvious one of holding on to staff in the early days of a recession in hopes of an economic upturn, and then later absorbing the early stages of recovery by use of overtime, etc., until the upturn appears likely to be sustained.

FORECASTING: FUTURE WORKFORCE SIZE

Figures 11, 12 and 13 illustrate the variation between the forecasts of workforce size for 1992, made in 1989, compared to actual levels prevailing in 1992. Setting aside the 'don't knows', the distribution displays two clusters of firms and is arguably bimodal. One group (accounting for approximately 40% of the original sample), offered forecasts which fell within −25% and +75% of the actual Full Time Equivalents (FTE) workforce size, i.e. the estimates fell within a range spanning an underestimation of 25% and an overestimation of 75%. The second group (approximately 30% of the sample), overestimated their expected workforce size for 1992 by 100% or more. This group includes the vast majority of firms that had ceased trading by 1992.

Given that the original sample, overall, experienced a 41% increase in workforce over the previous three-year period, i.e. from 1986 to 1989, it appears that many owner-managers were simply expecting 'more of the same'.

Accepting that the forecasts were obtained without prior notice, there are significant implications for investment in plant and equipment, premises and training, not to mention future profitability, if workforce projections in smaller businesses can be subject to overestimations of these magnitudes. Moreover, these investment issues apply, in varying degrees, to firms operating in either of the manufacturing or business services sectors.

OBSERVATIONS ON SMALL FIRMS' REPORTING OF FINANCIAL PERFORMANCE IN RESEARCH SURVEYS

The recession has brought to light a curious phenomenon: that declared results and forecasts by small firms do not always square with actual outcomes. Firms responding to research surveys appear typically optimistic, report better than actual profitability, do not easily reveal losses and generally demonstrate how the power of ignorance and self-deception can subvert reality and lead to misleading conclusions.

In an expanding market, reactive business strategies are likely to achieve positive results since, even with new competitors entering the market, sales are relatively easy to achieve and with a minimum of controls, help the net profit line. Thus the owner-manager has to understand only the sales function reasonably well to be in a fairly strong position to report on profits, or the trend in profits.

In a contracting market, however, the reporting situation becomes more complicated. In the early stages of demand stagnation, as soon as the level of future sales starts to become unpredictable, the owner's confidence about the currency of business information is undermined. As the decline in profits and availability of cash to fund fixed and working capital becomes more invasive, the owner responds by starting to cut down (out) investment expenditure, since there is no reliable method to predict future streams of income and profit from any such investment and, more relevantly, no proactive marketing to squeeze profitable sales out of a declining market.

The one possible exception to this general rule is where price discounting is used to generate sales at lower gross margins. But in this case, since there is no reliable or up-to-date information about contribution levels for different kinds of products and markets, the owner is susceptible to the conclusion that increasing sales must again lead to continuing profits. It often comes as a shock when this is not the case.

In a prolonged recession, with the realisation that a reactive strategy no longer works and when sales have already started to fall away, profits can be eroded completely and losses quickly follow, leading to a progressive deterioration of the capital base of the firm. Without tight controls, monthly cash flows rapidly become negative and the business overdrawn. Sales tend to plateau early in the cycle and the business attempts to stabilise its cash position by cutting capacity to match sales.

At this point the business may be operating below its full profit break-even, but just about at its cash break-even, largely because the owner has decided to reduce his own salary as well as cut out all forms of capital expenditure (not only is there no new cash expenditure on capital, but also the impact of depreciation is eliminated). To an ill-informed owner, the business appears to have weathered the storm — to change metaphors, at this point it is bumping along the bottom.

There is considerable evidence that hundreds of thousands of small firms in the UK right now are just surviving, waiting for demand to improve and carry them in a sales-led bubble back towards relative prosperity. Moreover, it is quite clear that there is nowhere for the business to go except upwards — in other words, to improve sales and overall performance. To admit otherwise would be tacitly to accept defeat, which no self-respecting entrepreneur would care to do. There is no category of unemployment called 'out of work entrepreneurs'. The socio-psychological pressures to 'hang in there' are immense.

Thus, when the researcher asks questions about current performance of, and future prospects for, the firm, responses may be governed not only by lack of information about sales and profits year-on-year, but also by psychological pressures to deny that things could get worse. Many small firms will be tempted to report optimistically on their financial status and profit performance (current and future), since to do otherwise would force them to confront their own business mortality.

Unfortunately, the solution does not lie simply in getting sight of actual figures because these are often not usually available at all, or are out-of-date or meaningless because of the way in which small firm profit and loss accounts and balance sheets are compiled.

Clues to real performance are perhaps best found in the way an organisation functions and its management manages, in its sales and marketing activities and its concern for quality and effectiveness (as revealed in the behaviour of its people and the appearance and age of its physical assets). The tell-tale signs of corporate good or bad health are generally there for all to see — if the researcher knows what to look for.

In summary, what are the underlying possible causes of financial misrepresentation by owner-managers? They can be grouped into the following five areas:

No proper understanding of the profit concept

The accounting concept of net profit has a very different meaning (and thus relevance) to the owner-manager compared to the large firm manager or accountant. The former is concerned more with actual physical cash transactions than with net profit. But the concern is deeper than this. Profit is at best a notional concept devoid of real meaning when it comes to calculating whether bills can be paid at the end of the month and whether sufficient funds exist to fund future expenditures. This is because of the uncertainties that surround the timing of cash receipts from sales and the corresponding certainty of payroll and rent costs having to be met (by far the largest cost items in most businesses). Other creditors, too, will not be deterred from making their demands on time.

The reasons are also to do with the nature and timing of costs. A first example is depreciation. Although recognised by the owner as a cost, many firms do not regard the necessity to account for the using up of capital items over their useful life as a constraint on their thinking. This typically affects the outcomes of the costing, estimating and pricing processes in many firms, which may be arbitrary at best. In a recession, there is every incentive not to include depreciation in a costing.

Another example concerns the costs of marketing activities. In many small firms there are very few explicit marketing costs, the main exceptions being motor, travel, subsistence, some entertaining, possibly advertising and a little printing. Therefore marketing costs are typically understated – a great deal of the marketing and selling is done by the owner or people who have other roles to perform. Moreover, proactive marketing would normally include expenditure on publicity and public relations, literature, telephone, salaries, etc. Real costs may differ from recorded costs because some are hidden; and if these were to be made explicit in the accounts, the firm's real profit situation may be infinitely worse than that currently perceived by the owner.

No perceived need for recording and reporting of profit

A second possible cause of misinformation in the small firm is that the owner has no obviously revealed need for accurate and up-to-date recording and reporting of profit, beyond that of having to meet legal requirements. Bookkeeping and reporting requirements to meet the demands of the Inland Revenue are not very strenuous and there is no practical way that the small firm can be forced to keep books and summary accounts in a way that would permit the instant production of a full set of accounts.

Obligatory disclosure requirements aside, net profit is often too imprecise a figure to concern the owner. For example, the allocation of costs to different sales periods through the year, to align expenditure to the relevant sales transactions, has little practical import to the owner. The accrual concept is meaningless for all practical purposes since most people tend to consider costs only when they actually happen, rather than when the benefits with which they are associated accrue. This is probably because people prefer to think of costs in terms of cash payments, rather than promises to pay.

Nor is net profit an accurate guide to the payment of corporate or income taxes. The adjustments that take place before corporations and individuals are assessed for tax, are frequently not revealed to business owners by their accountants. Thus the mystique that accompanies the production of annual accounts tends to work against an understanding of the profit concept. In a recession, with losses more likely, the chances of paying tax are much reduced anyway, which tends further to reinforce the view that accurate and up-to-date recording of sales revenues and costs is not a priority for the owner.

A fixation for cash

There is a powerful cash nexus that drives the small firm, causing an imbalance in the owner's perceived need for information about profit performance. Cash is clearly the lifeblood, for without it there are no salaries, bills cannot get paid and no investment can be made in the long-term.

Borrowing to achieve any of the above outcomes is unlikely to appeal to the owner with a cash fixation. The discomfort experienced by not having cash will be so strong in a recession that the owner will eschew borrowing (negative cash) in the face of uncertain repayment prospects.

This quite rational view and set of responses has its basis in the under-capitalisation of the small firm (and its antecedent, the relative impecuniousness of the owner). A common motivation for going into business is the need for personal achievement; the most explicit demonstration of this achievement is the conspicuous consumption achieved with the use of cash. Nor is there any fiscal incentive to accumulate and build reserves for a rainy day (this is especially so for the unincorporated business which is assessed to tax on profits before owner's drawings).

The cash fixation means that small firms have little impetus to give due consideration to profit as a measure of performance. Cash is collected from customers and monies are paid to landlords, suppliers, staff and other creditors (including the tax man). The balance is available to the owners to distribute as they please. In this context, the recording of profit has little immediate relevance.

No concept of competitive performance

The small firm tends to set financial performance standards according to internal consi-derations (such as how much the owner wants to take out of the business, how much capacity is available and how well the firm performed last year). Competitors' performance tends not to enter into the frame.

This is not only because information is not readily available about competitors, but rather it reflects the absence of an overt competitive strategy. This in turn is because the owner-manager tends not to think of the firm in competition with others − the thought that customers have choices which might conceivably change their buying loyalties does not find favour with small business owners. For example, when asked to reveal their firm's competitive advantage, most owners tend not to have a clear idea of why their customers buy from them. Without an overtly competition-based view of the marketplace, financial performance standards will tend to be internally driven. And if they are, in the absence of adequate recording and reporting procedures, they are unlikely to be articulated frequently, with the results that owners will find it difficult to recall them accurately.

Short-term planning horizons

A final cause of mis-reporting of financial performance by the owners of small firms lies in their short-term thinking. Reactive responses to market and other stimuli are the result partly of poorly developed business skills and partly of their lack of power in the markets for products, capital, labour and other resources. Disempowerment has a rational legacy of short-term thinking and lack of planning since, when the firm is subject to the vagaries of its markets, there are no strong incentives to invest in the future. The 'receding horizons' syndrome negates planning as a philosophy − the belief that everything will come good at some unspecified time in the future and the ability to push back this time as one wishes. With such a philosophy, there is every likelihood that the long-term future will be viewed with relative uninterest by the owner. The result is a tendency to eschew medium and long-term planning and the collection of data to inform the planning process. In turn, this has the effect of diminishing the need for data capture and accurate recall of performance measures.

The prolonged recession would appear to have accentuated a phenomenon in small firms research which, although previously known to exist, now needs to be considered more carefully when analysing research findings and drawing conclusions. Historical performance and future prospects data on small firms need to be interpreted with care. The recession has exacerbated the economic and psychological conditions that cause mis-reporting.

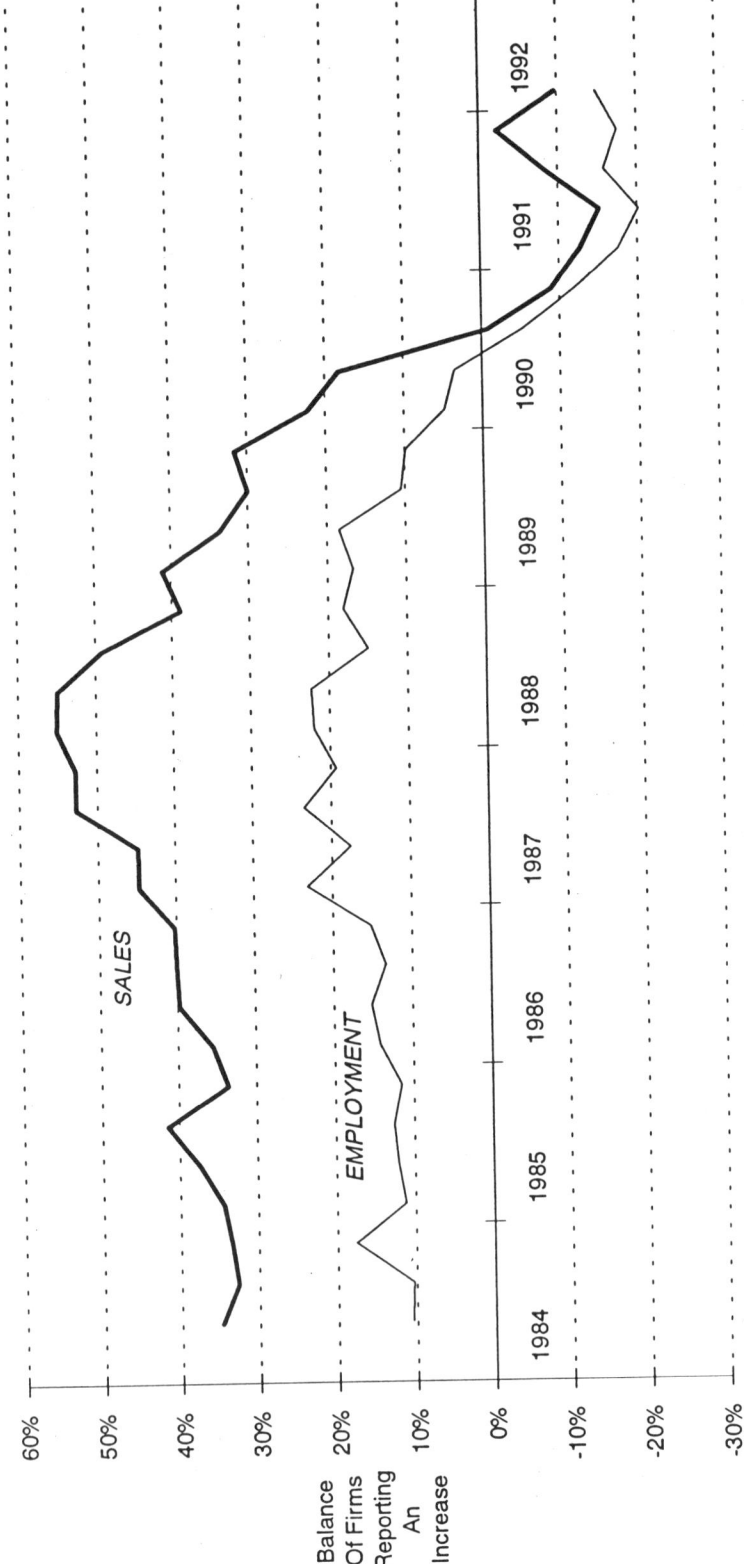

Figure 1: Change in sales and employment for small businesses, year on year for comparable quarters. Source: SBRT/NatWest Quarterly Survey of Small Businesses in Britain, August 1992.

Survey Date	Inflation	Interest Rates	Access to Finance	Lack of Skilled Employees	Total Tax Burden	Low T/over Or Lack of Business	Competition From Big Business	Govt Regs and Paperwork	High Rates of Pay	Shortage of Material & Supplies	Internal Management Difficulties	Cashflow & Payments	Premises, Rents & Rates	Other	No Response	Number of Replies Analysed
1984/4	3.5%	17.1%	-	5.4%	15.9%	15.3%	12.0%	12.6%	4.2%	1.1%	-	-	-	10.9%	1.4%	3,056
1985/1	3.8%	19.4%	-	4.4%	15.9%	14.5%	10.0%	15.7%	3.4%	1.3%	-	-	-	9.5%	1.5%	1,795
1985/2	5.0%	22.1%	-	4.3%	16.1%	14.3%	10.8%	12.5%	2.4%	1.3%	-	-	-	9.1%	1.5%	1,181
1985/3	2.0%	23.6%	-	4.9%	12.8%	13.8%	11.2%	13.1%	3.7%	1.9%	-	-	-	8.6%	3.8%	1,090
1985/4	2.2%	24.0%	-	5.6%	16.6%	15.7%	11.0%	10.2%	2.0%	0.9%	-	-	-	9.2%	2.0%	1,072
1986/1	3.0%	21.4%	-	7.2%	17.1%	14.4%	11.7%	9.6%	2.0%	1.8%	-	-	-	9.9%	1.3%	1,326
1986/2	1.7%	29.9%	-	7.3%	16.3%	12.6%	9.1%	9.9%	2.2%	1.2%	-	-	-	9.4%	0.6%	1,052
1986/3	0.9%	21.3%	-	7.3%	16.6%	17.0%	11.5%	7.3%	1.4%	0.9%	-	-	-	13.7%	2.0%	1,285
1986/4	1.1%	25.0%	-	7.2%	17.7%	14.7%	11.8%	6.8%	1.3%	1.3%	-	-	-	10.0%	3.1%	1,435
1987/1	0.9%	26.4%	-	8.0%	16.0%	13.0%	12.0%	7.4%	1.6%	1.3%	-	-	-	9.1%	4.2%	1,166
1987/2	1.0%	23.7%	-	9.6%	17.7%	12.0%	10.7%	7.6%	2.6%	1.5%	-	-	-	10.3%	3.3%	1,746
1987/3	1.1%	20.3%	-	11.8%	17.9%	12.9%	11.5%	6.6%	1.9%	2.2%	-	-	-	10.5%	3.5%	1,113
1987/4	1.1%	18.0%	-	11.1%	21.3%	13.0%	12.5%	6.3%	1.3%	1.3%	-	-	-	9.6%	4.5%	977
1988/1	0.7%	21.6%	-	11.1%	20.1%	9.6%	11.4%	6.1%	2.3%	1.9%	-	-	-	14.9%	0.3%	1,042
1988/2	1.0%	19.4%	-	12.7%	15.5%	10.2%	14.4%	8.0%	1.8%	2.3%	-	-	-	13.7%	1.4%	933
1988/3	0.9%	17.6%	-	17.7%	13.7%	11.3%	11.4%	8.3%	2.4%	2.7%	-	-	-	11.4%	2.4%	983
1988/4	2.8%	25.5%	-	16.9%	12.5%	8.7%	10.4%	6.0%	1.3%	3.3%	-	-	-	10.6%	1.9%	950
1989/1	5.3%	23.4%	-	16.4%	11.1%	5.7%	5.9%	7.1%	1.4%	0.3%	-	-	-	19.0%	4.3%	1,523
1989/2	6.3%	28.4%	-	14.0%	12.2%	7.1%	5.9%	5.2%	1.0%	0.8%	-	-	-	14.5%	4.7%	947
1989/3	6.1%	32.9%	-	13.3%	7.1%	13.1%	5.9%	5.9%	1.5%	0.5%	-	-	-	12.1%	1.6%	2,274
1989/4	6.9%	39.2%	-	10.4%	5.4%	12.9%	4.7%	5.1%	1.1%	0.6%	-	-	-	12.2%	1.4%	795
1990/1	4.2%	31.3%	3.1%	6.7%	5.3%	13.3%	-	5.5%	2.5%	0.7%	0.6%	11.5%	8.4%	5.3%	1.7%	1,091
1990/2	6.7%	27.9%	3.3%	7.8%	2.9%	14.6%	-	5.6%	1.5%	0.3%	1.6%	11.6%	6.6%	8.2%	1.4%	1,384
1990/3	4.3%	30.0%	3.6%	6.4%	3.7%	14.7%	3.1%	4.3%	1.6%	0.0%	1.9%	13.7%	4.8%	5.5%	2.5%	1,043
1990/4	7.5%	26.6%	2.3%	5.7%	4.4%	18.9%	3.8%	6.3%	0.2%	0.3%	0.8%	8.6%	4.7%	7.9%	1.9%	1,250
1991/1	6.0%	29.6%	2.6%	3.4%	4.2%	21.1%	2.6%	5.6%	0.9%	0.5%	0.8%	11.4%	4.2%	5.4%	1.9%	1,239
1991/2	4.0%	21.3%	4.3%	2.8%	5.1%	25.3%	2.9%	4.0%	0.4%	0.4%	0.6%	14.9%	7.1%	5.9%	1.0%	984
1991/3	3.2%	15.1%	3.0%	2.3%	4.7%	37.6%	2.4%	6.6%	1.2%	0.3%	1.2%	10.9%	3.3%	6.6%	1.5%	1,718
1991/4	1.2%	7.5%	4.6%	4.5%	4.1%	38.2%	3.4%	3.8%	0.7%	0.3%	1.3%	13.2%	5.7%	10.7%	0.8%	835
1992/1	1.9%	9.2%	5.2%	2.1%	5.6%	36.3%	3.3%	5.5%	0.5%	0.4%	1.2%	15.9%	4.0%	7.0%	1.8%	1,684
1992/2	2.2%	11.7%	4.3%	3.4%	5.4%	34.6%	4.4%	5.2%	0.4%	0.3%	1.0%	13.4%	5.0%	7.3%	1.3%	1,359
1992/3	1.6%	7.6%	3.9%	2.8%	5.1%	43.7%	2.1%	8.0%	0.3%	0.9%	0.8%	13.6%	3.0%	5.8%	0.8%	1,527

Note: From 1989/1, all figures shown in this table have been weighted to the VAT sectoral distribution.

Fig. 2: Problems experienced by respondents. Source: SBRT/NatWest Quarterly Survey of Small Business in Britain, Vol. 8, No. 3, 1992.

PROBLEM	Agriculture	Manufacturing	Transport	Construction	Wholesale	Retail	Catering	Business Services	Other Services	Other	All
Inflation	0%	0.6%	2.9%	0%	0.6%	1.4%	5.1%	1.2%	2.1%	8.0%	1.2%
Interest Rates	7.4%	6.1%	2.9%	5.9%	5.0%	7.1%	20.5%	5.1%	8.5%	8.0%	6.4%
Access to Finance	7.4%	3.9%	2.9%	0.8%	5.6%	3.3%	2.6%	3.9%	4.3%	8.0%	3.9%
Lack of Skill	7.4%	3.3%	0%	2.5%	3.1%	1.4%	0%	3.2%	2.8%	4.0%	2.8%
Total Tax Burden	11.1%	6.1%	5.9%	3.4%	5.6%	3.3%	5.1%	4.6%	2.8%	12.0%	4.9%
Low Turnover	25.9%	44.0%	52.9%	59.7%	48.4%	48.8%	41.0%	40.6%	36.9%	24.0%	44.3%
Competition from Big Business	0%	1.9%	8.8%	0%	4.3%	4.7%	0%	1.2%	1.4%	4.0%	2.3%
Government Regulations	18.5%	5.5%	0%	3.4%	2.5%	5.7%	10.3%	6.6%	13.5%	8.0%	6.4%
High Pay	0%	0.8%	0%	0%	0%	0.9%	0%	0.5%	0%	0%	0.5%
Shortages of Materials	3.7%	0.3%	0%	0%	3.1%	1.9%	0%	0.2%	0%	0%	0.8%
Internal Difficulties	0%	2.2%	0%	0%	0.6%	1.9%	0%	1.2%	0.7%	0%	1.2%
Cashflow/Payments/Debtors	7.4%	15.5%	17.6%	20.2%	15.5%	7.6%	5.1%	18.6%	15.6%	8.0%	15.1%
Premises/Rent/Rates	3.7%	4.2%	2.9%	0%	1.9%	7.6%	5.1%	2.2%	0.7%	4.0%	3.2%
Other	7.4%	4.4%	2.9%	4.2%	3.7%	3.8%	5.1%	9.3%	7.8%	12.0%	6.0%
N/R	0%	1.1%	0%	0%	0%	0.5%	0%	1.5%	2.8%	0%	1.0%
Base	27	361	34	119	161	211	39	409	141	25	1,527
Check	100.0%	100.0%	100.0%	100.0%	100.0%	100.0%	100.0%	100.0%	100.0%	100.0%	100.0%

Unweighted data

Figure 3: Most important problem by business activity. Source: SBRT/NatWest Quarterly Survey of Small Business in Britain, Vol. 8, No. 3, 1992.

MOST IMPORTANT PROBLEM BY EMPLOYMENT SIZE BAND

PROBLEM	1	2	3 - 4	5 - 9	10 - 14	15 - 24	25 - 49	50+	All
Inflation	2.0%	4.0%	2.9%	3.0%	4.4%	2.5%	1.6%	4.0%	3.1%
Interest Rates	9.9%	11.3%	15.1%	17.2%	16.4%	10.2%	14.5%	12.0%	13.8%
Access to Finance	2.0%	3.0%	2.9%	3.0%	2.5%	5.1%	4.0%	4.0%	3.0%
Lack of Skill	1.6%	1.3%	3.4%	3.3%	5.0%	3.4%	4.0%	2.0%	2.9%
Total Tax Burden	5.5%	3.7%	2.3%	5.0%	4.4%	5.9%	3.2%	6.0%	4.2%
Low Turnover	47.8%	37.3%	32.6%	36.0%	35.2%	39.8%	35.5%	36.0%	37.3%
Competition from Big Business	2.4%	2.3%	2.9%	2.2%	1.9%	2.5%	4.0%	2.0%	2.5%
Government Regulations	2.4%	7.3%	5.4%	5.0%	4.4%	10.2%	8.1%	10.0%	5.8%
High Pay	0%	0%	1.1%	1.1%	0.6%	0%	2.4%	2.0%	0.8%
Shortages of Materials	1.6%	0%	0%	0.3%	0%	0%	0%	2.0%	0.3%
Internal Difficulties	0.4%	0.3%	0.9%	1.4%	1.9%	1.7%	1.6%	2.0%	1.0%
Cashflow/Payments/Debtors	9.9%	14.0%	16.0%	12.2%	13.2%	11.9%	11.3%	14.0%	13.0%
Premises/Rent/Rates	4.3%	4.7%	4.3%	3.9%	1.9%	2.5%	1.6%	2.0%	3.7%
Other	7.1%	8.0%	9.1%	6.1%	6.9%	4.2%	6.5%	0%	7.0%
N/R	3.2%	2.7%	1.1%	0.3%	1.3%	0%	1.6%	2.0%	1.6%
Base	253	300	350	361	159	118	124	50	1,719
Check	100.0%	100.0%	100.0%	100.0%	100.0%	100.0%	100.0%	100.0%	100.0%

Figure 4: Most important problem by employment size band. Source: SBRT/NatWest Quarterly Survey of Small Business in Britain, Vol. 7, No. 3, 1991.

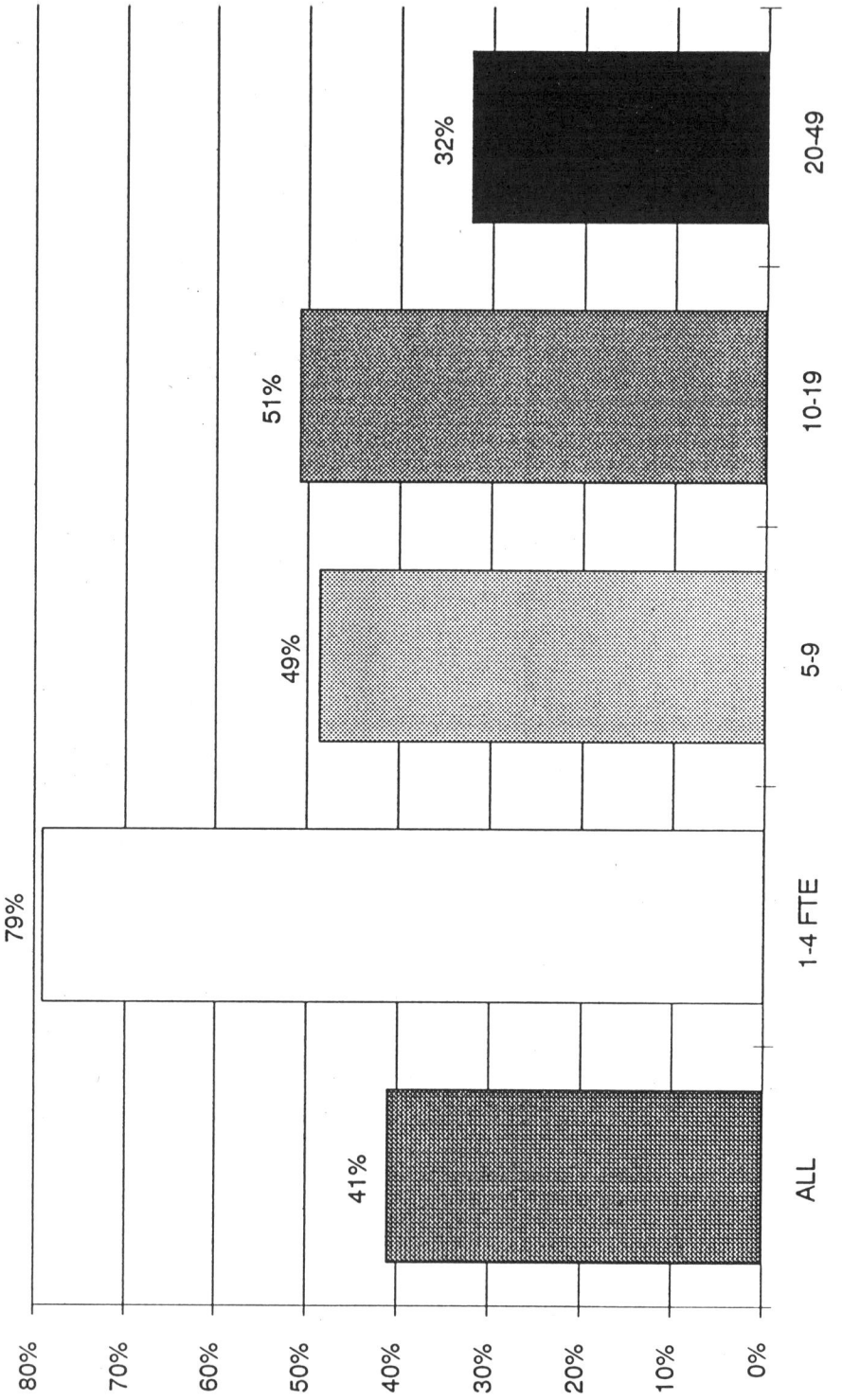

Figure 5: (a) Growth in FTE employees 1986–1989, by FTE employment.

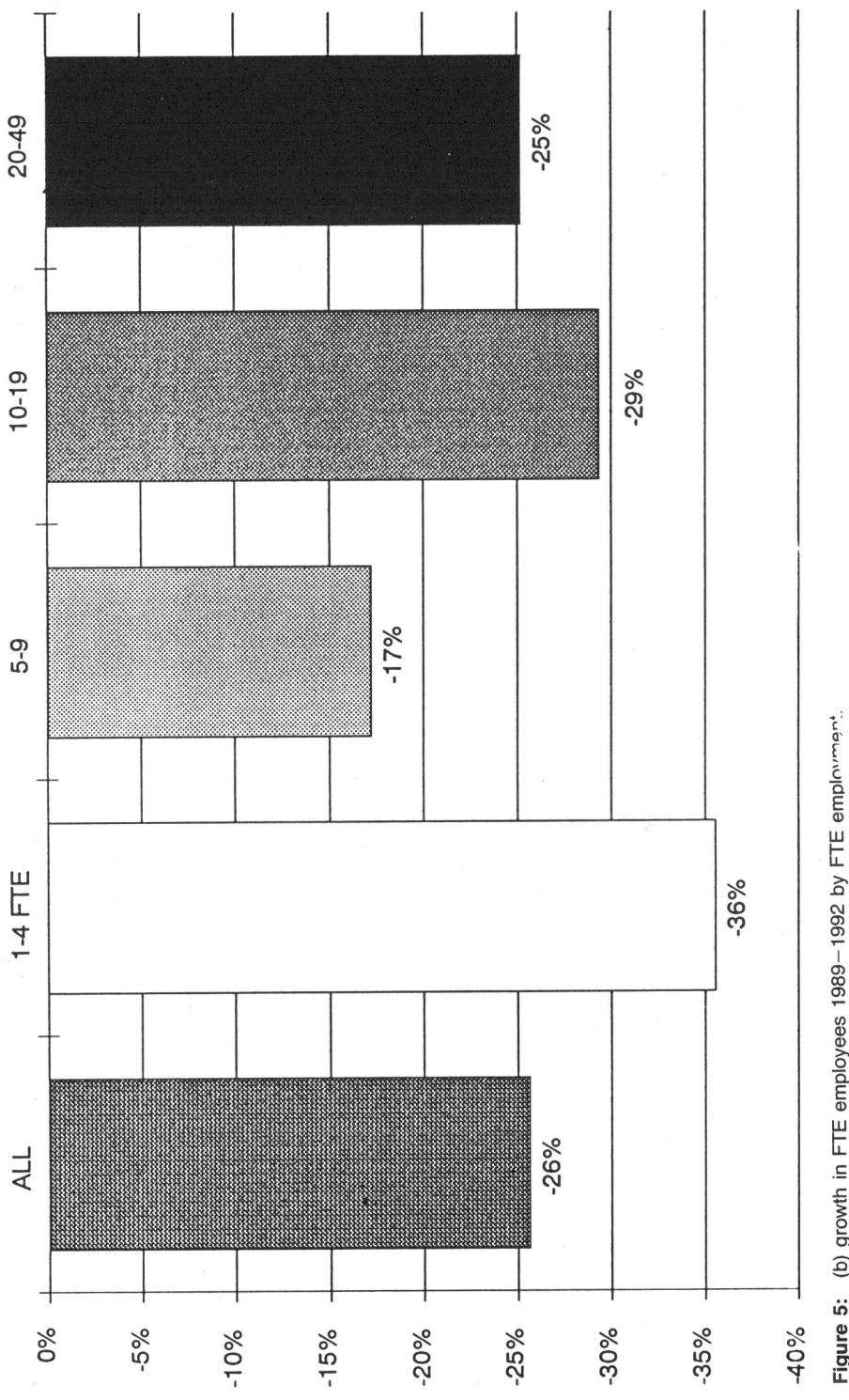

Figure 5: (b) growth in FTE employees 1989–1992 by FTE employment.

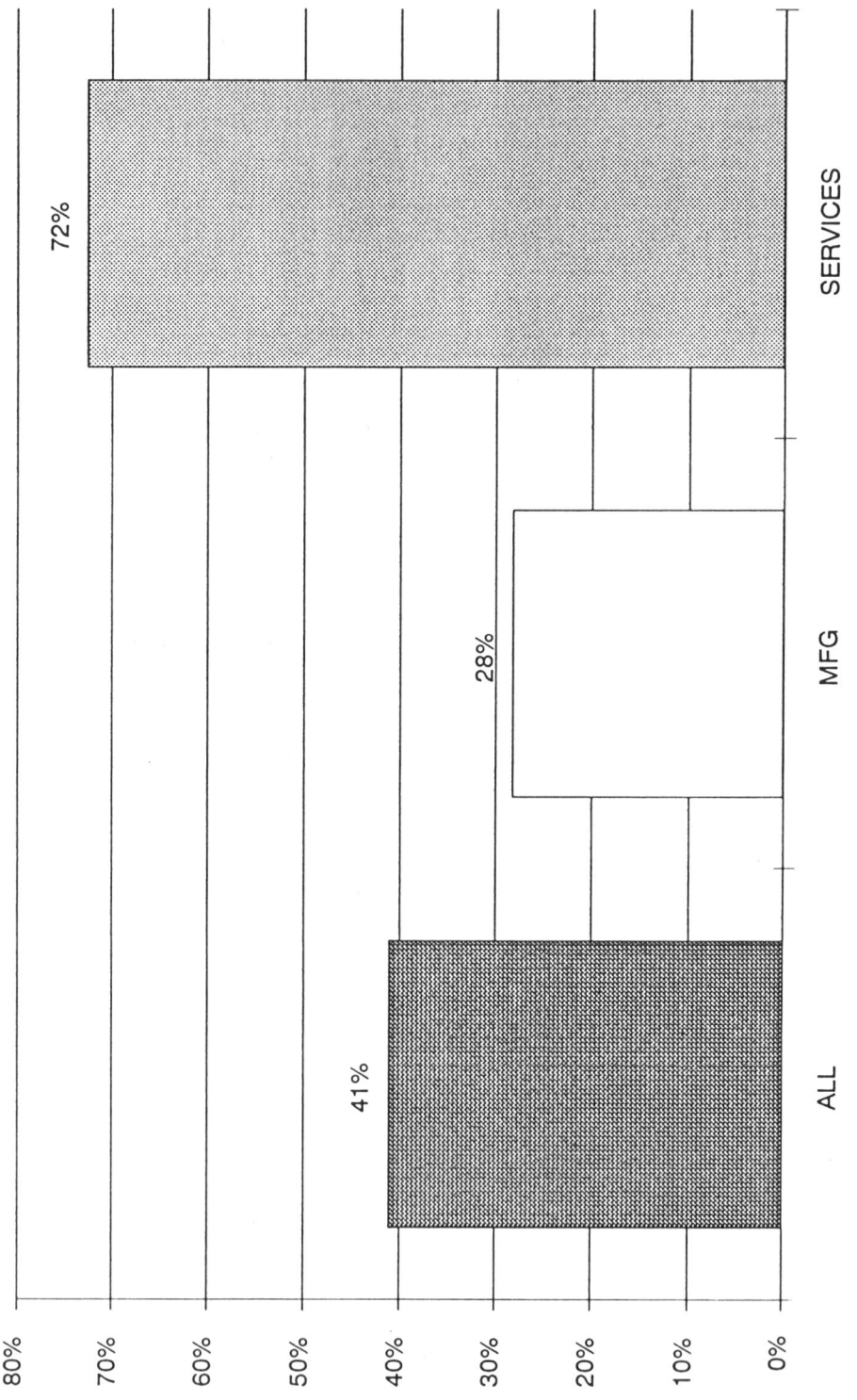

Figure 6: (a) Growth in FTE employees 1986–1989 by sector.

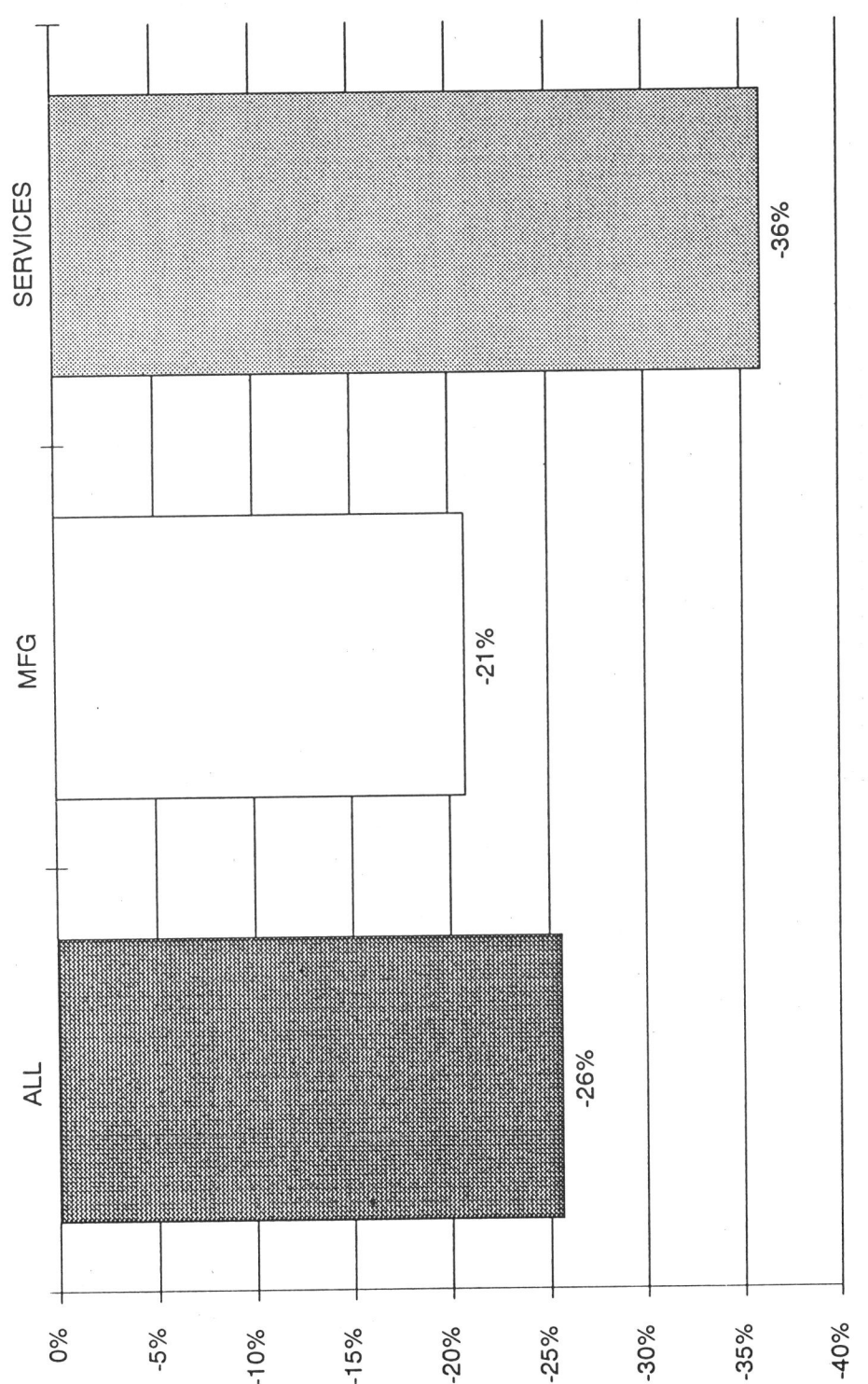

Figure 6: (b) growth in FTE employees 1989–1992 by sector.

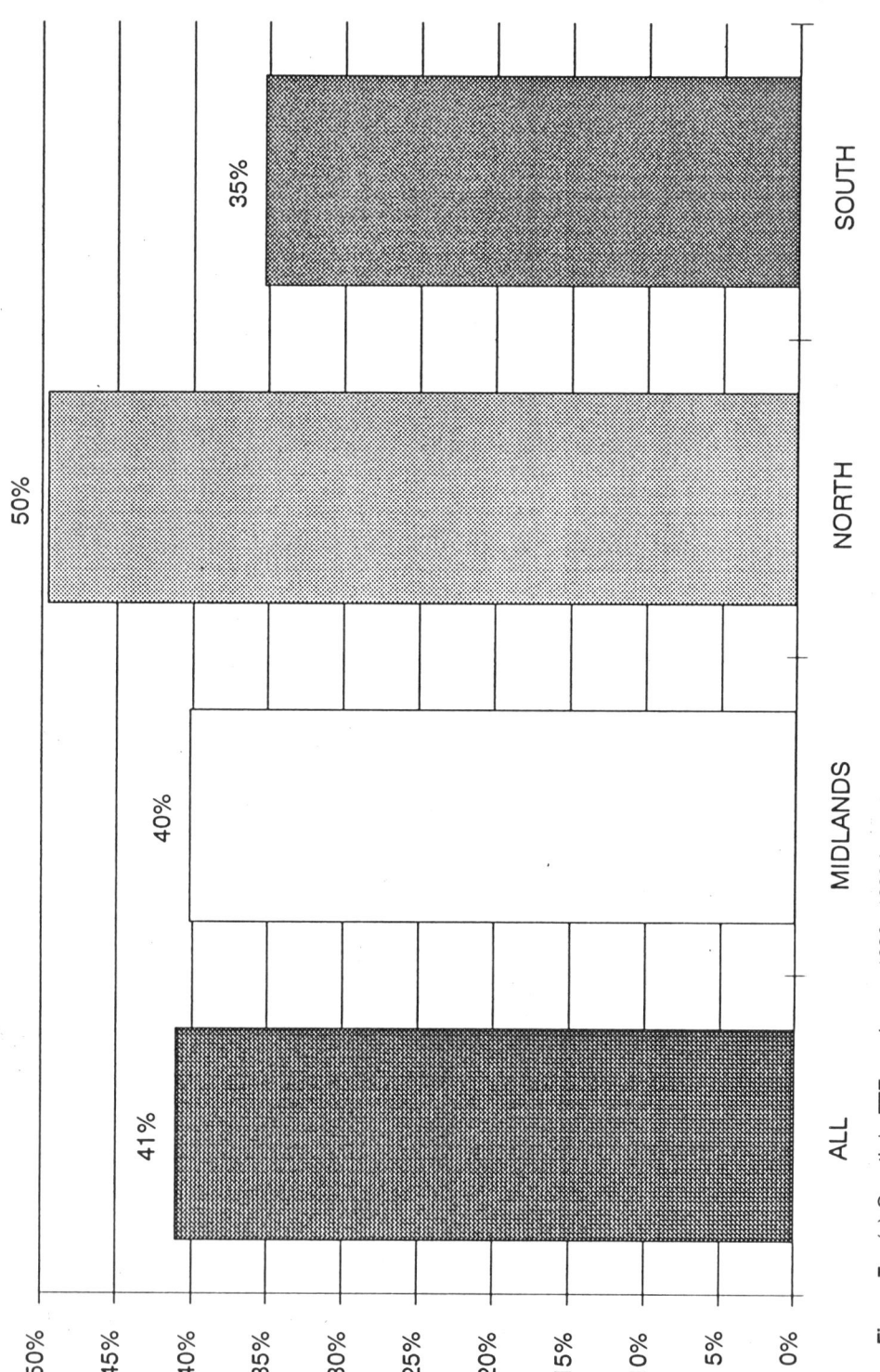

Figure 7: (a) Growth in FTE employees 1986–1989 by region.

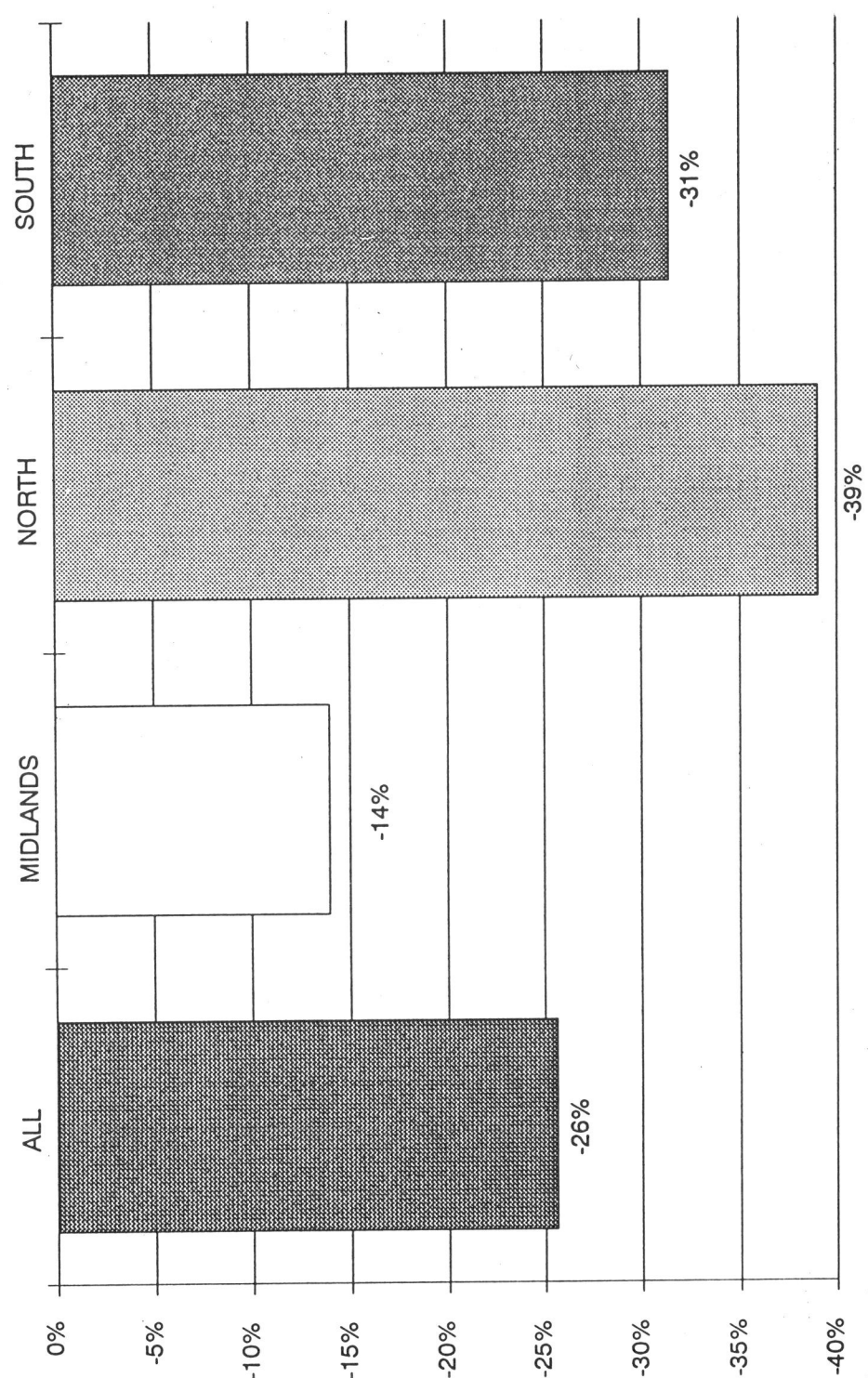

Figure 7: (b) growth in FTE employees 1989–1992 by region.

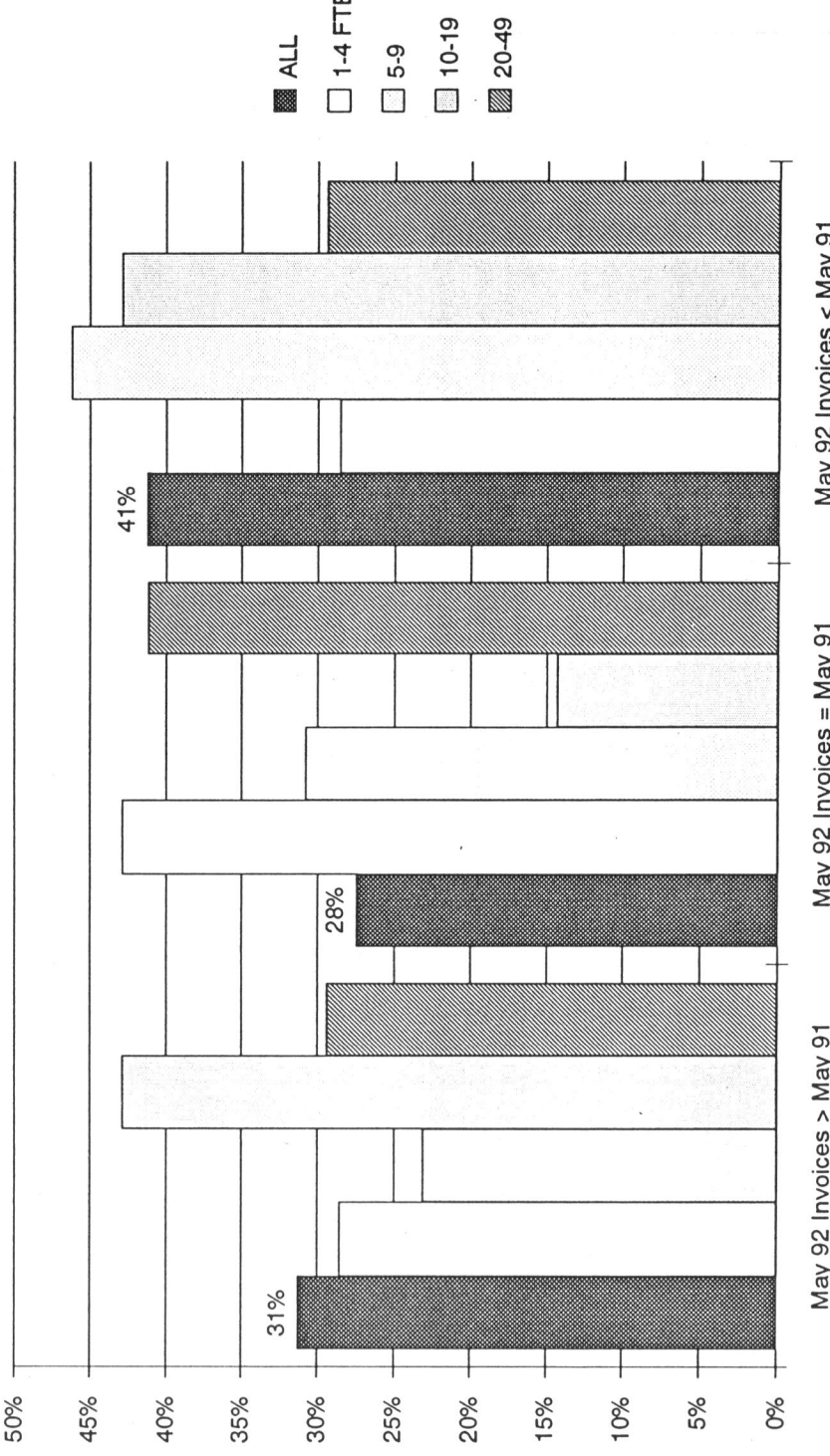

Figure 8: Turnover comparison 1992 cf 1991 by FTE employment.

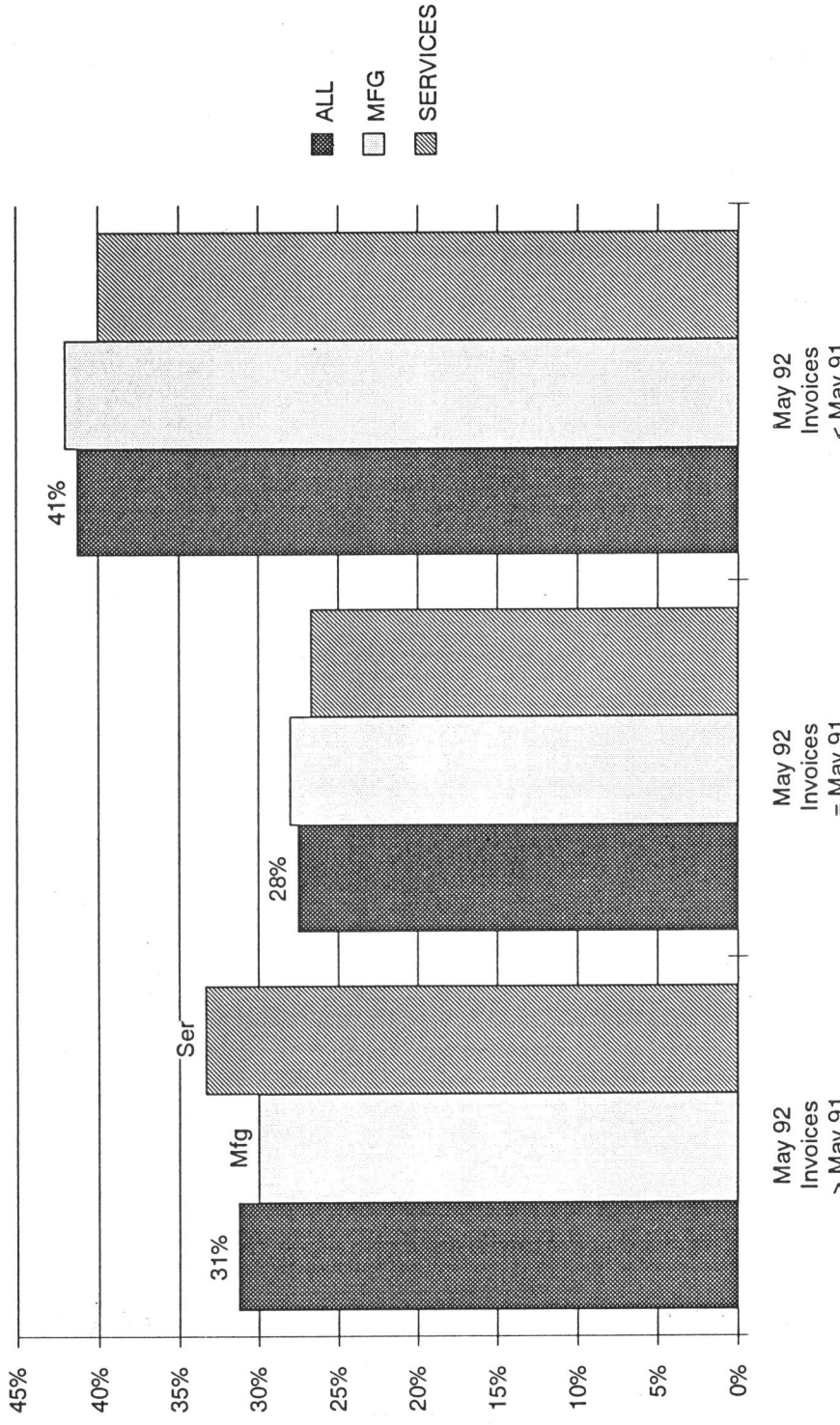

Figure 9: Turnover comparison 1992 cf 1991 by sector.

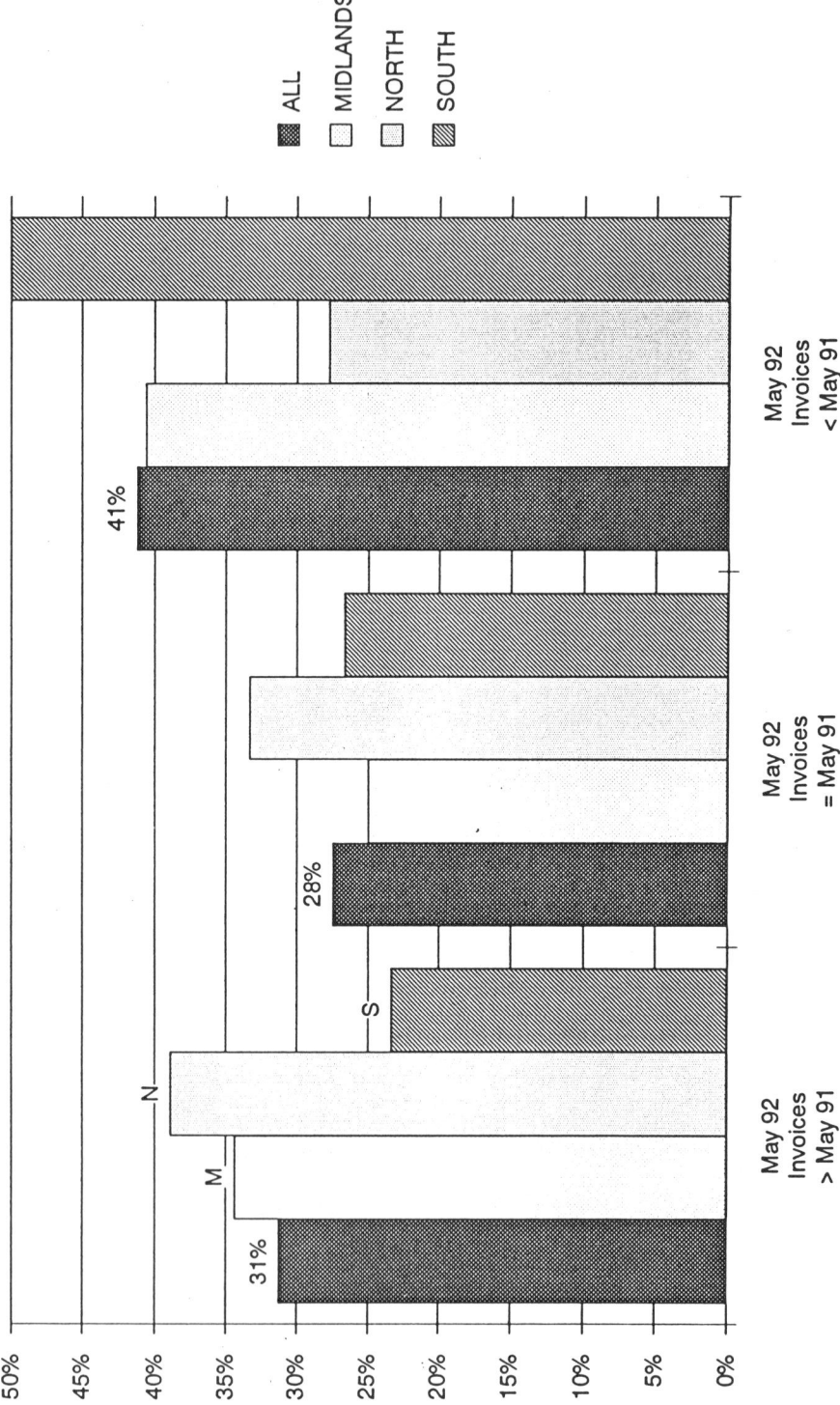

Figure 10: Turnover comparison 1992 cf 1991 by region.

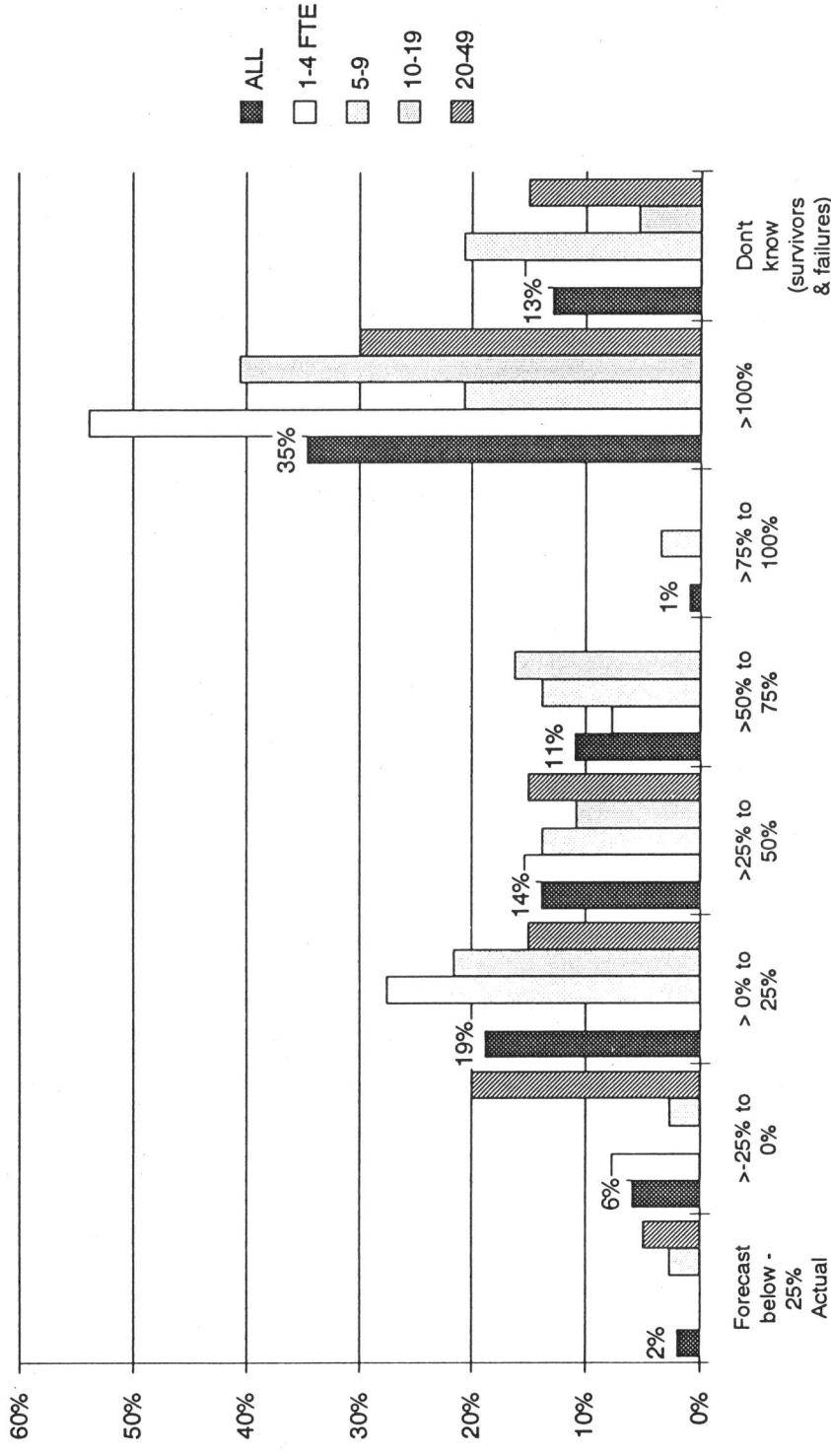

Figure 11: Employment levels 1992, forecast in 1989 vs actual, by FTE employment.

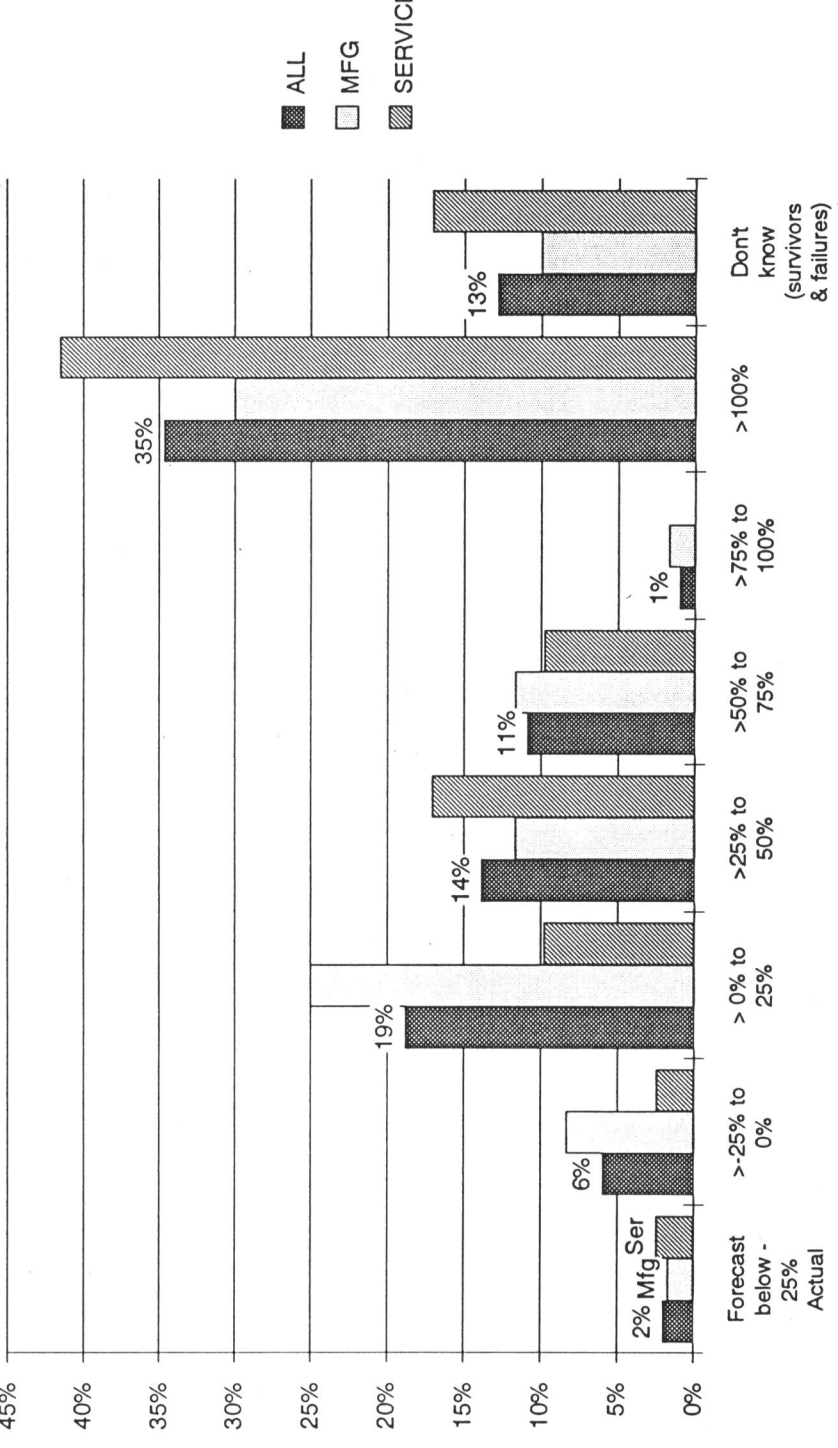

Figure 12: Employment levels 1992, forecast in 1989 vs actual, by sector.

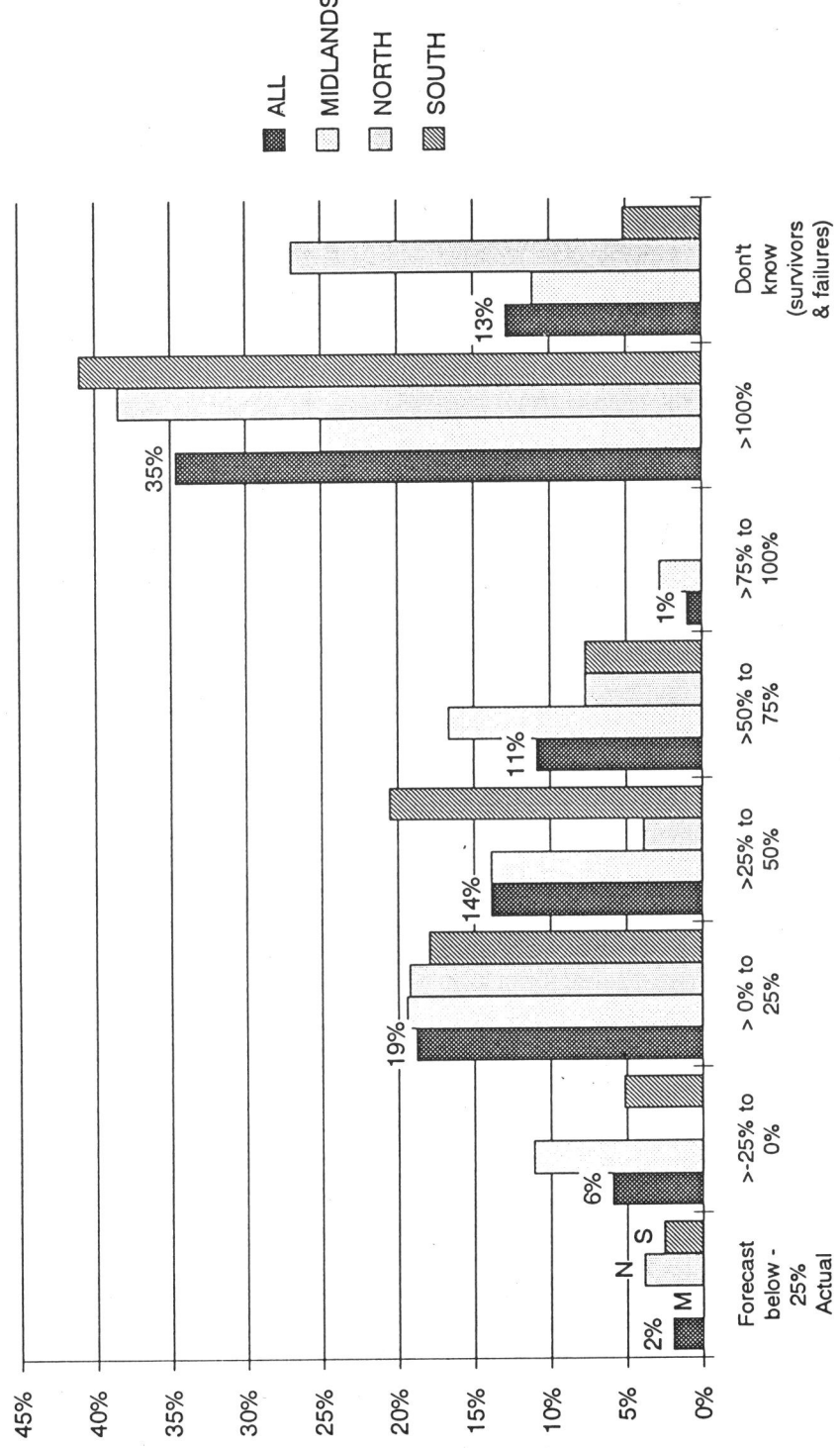

Figure 13: Employment levels 1992, forecast in 1989 vs actual, by region.

REFERENCES

Curran J. and Blackburn R. (1992) Small Business Survey, Kingston University, Kingston upon Thames.

Research Institute for Small & Medium-Sized Businesses (1992) Competitiveness, Autonomy and Business Relationships – An International Comparative Study in 8 European Countries, 22nd European Small Business Seminar, Amsterdam.

Small Business Research Trust/NatWest (1991, 1992) Quarterly Survey of Small Business in Britain, Volumes 7 and 8.

Stanworth J., Purdy D. and Kirby D. (1992) The Management of Success in 'Growth Corridor' Small Firms, Small Business Research Trust.

Woodcock C. (1992) A vision that could be just an illusion, New Business, Guardian, 3 August.

5.

Regional Variations in the Population of Small and Medium-Sized Enterprises in Britain

Colin Gallagher, Geoff Robson and John Kerr

INTRODUCTION

The results are given here of a detailed empirical study of firm change in terms of births, deaths, expansions and contractions in Britain over the 1987–1989 period, by small and medium-sized firms (SMEs) of between one and 499 employees. Firm population change is analysed in terms of the 10 major UK regions. It has been found in earlier studies of Britain in total, that in general it is the smallest firms which make the largest contribution to job creation (Gallagher et al 1991, Daly et al 1991, 1992). However, it has not been possible in the past to determine the effects which variations in regional firm size distributions would be likely to have on the nature and extent of job creation at the regional level. It is this aspect which is explored in this study. While some validation work has been carried out on these results, they are preliminary, and require further work.

The most recent national job generation study estimated the job creation performance of all sizes of firms over the years 1987–1989 (Daly et al 1991). Its major conclusions were:

1. Those firms which employed fewer than 10 people had created roughly half the net total growth, despite employing less than 1/5 of all people.
2. All size groups of firms made a net contribution to job creation (this was not a time of recession).
3. The overall job creation of small firms is less affected by the economic cycle than that of large firms.

The data used in this regional study is drawn from the very large private sector database of Dun and Bradstreet, the credit rating and marketing organisation, which has been evaluated in detail for research purposes in a previous report (Robson and Gallagher 1992). Using a sample of over 100,000 records, it has been possible to extract considerable detail on a number of aspects of regional change in SMEs.

For reasons described in the appendix, firms in this analysis were limited to having less than 500 employees. This range of up to 500 is also the definition of SMEs used by the EEC. The analysis was carried out using 13 narrowly defined detailed employee cohorts, but for the purposes of presentation, the results have been summarised into six cohorts.

All holding companies, subsidiaries and branch plants were removed from the database. The data was then validated and grossed up (to reflect population results) as in the national study (Daly et al 1991).

A comparison was made of the regional coverage of the D and B grossed results, with the value added tax (VAT) database for companies only (*Employment Gazette*, November

1991). The main divergence of coverage occurred in the South East, where the D and B based data used in this study had 43% of records, compared to 46% on the VAT database. The overall implication was that the grossed results provided a reasonable reflection of the distribution of firms between the regions.

THE DISTRIBUTION OF FIRMS ACROSS THE REGIONS

The distribution of firms by region and cohort size

Table 1 shows the distribution of firms between the regions, and Table 2, the relative percentage distribution by region and cohort size. A skew is apparent in the distribution of firms in that the North, Scotland, East Midlands and Yorkshire have a relatively low proportion of firms in the 1–4 cohort. For comparison purposes, the percentage

Table 1: Distribution of firms in 1987 by region and cohort

	1 to 4	5 to 9	10 to 19	20 to 49	50 to 99	100 to 499	Total
South East	198,942	101,574	60,210	16,924	6,458	4,227	388,334
North West	51,063	26,285	16,980	5,284	1,894	1,055	102,562
West Midlands	40,729	21,648	15,065	4,486	1,844	1,000	84,772
Yorkshire	32,016	17,973	12,746	3,864	1,540	900	69,039
South West	31,292	16,418	10,875	3,020	1,086	642	63,332
East Midlands	28,690	15,611	10,715	3,504	1,346	835	60,700
Scotland	20,118	10,892	8,535	2,570	1,250	828	44,194
East Anglia	15,421	8,528	5,532	1,708	652	421	32,263
Wales	15,480	8,345	5,555	1,532	606	318	31,836
North	11,844	6,806	4,943	1,632	660	427	26,313
Totals	445,596	234,079	151,156	44,524	17,336	10,653	903,344

Table 2: Percentage distribution of firms in 1987 by cohort and region

	1 to 4	5 to 9	10 to 19	20 to 49	50 to 99	100 to 499	Total
Cohort							
South East	51.2	26.2	15.5	4.4	1.7	1.1	100.0
North West	49.8	25.6	16.6	5.2	1.8	1.0	100.0
West Midlands	48.0	25.5	17.8	5.3	2.2	1.2	100.0
Yorkshire	46.4	26.0	18.5	5.6	2.2	1.3	100.0
South West	49.4	25.9	17.2	4.8	1.7	1.0	100.0
East Midlands	47.3	25.7	17.7	5.8	2.2	1.4	100.0
Scotland	45.5	24.6	19.3	5.8	2.8	1.9	100.0
East Anglia	47.8	26.4	17.1	5.3	2.0	1.3	100.0
Wales	48.6	26.2	17.4	4.8	1.9	1.0	100.0
North	45.0	25.9	18.8	6.2	2.5	1.6	100.0
Totals	49.3	25.9	16.7	4.9	1.9	1.2	100.0
Region							
South East	44.6	43.4	39.8	38.0	37.3	39.7	43.0
North West	11.5	11.2	11.2	11.9	10.9	9.9	11.4
West Midlands	9.1	9.2	10.0	10.1	10.6	9.4	9.4
Yorkshire	7.2	7.7	8.4	8.7	8.9	8.4	7.6
South West	7.0	7.0	7.2	6.8	6.3	6.0	7.0
East Midlands	6.4	6.7	7.1	7.9	7.8	7.8	6.7
Scotland	4.5	4.7	5.6	5.8	7.2	7.8	4.9
East Anglia	3.5	3.6	3.7	3.8	3.8	4.0	3.6
Wales	3.5	3.6	3.7	3.4	3.5	3.0	3.5
North	2.7	2.9	3.3	3.7	3.8	4.0	2.9
Totals	100.0	100.0	100.0	100.0	100.0	100.0	100.0

distribution of firms with less than 20, and with between 100 and 499 employees, is given in Table 3, ranked by size.

In Britain as a whole, 92% of SME firms had less than 20 employees. In the 1−19 cohort, while the South East, the South West, and Wales, had around 92.5%, in this category, the North and Scotland had less than 90%. For the larger SME cohort of 100 to 499, the reverse emerged, in that Scotland and the North had around 1.7%, while Wales, the South West, and the North West had only 1.0%. According to the findings of all recent job generation studies, it is likely that those regions with the lower percentage of the smallest firms will have a more restricted job-creation ability.

The distribution of firms per million of population

Table 4 and Figure 1 show the regional distribution of firms per million of population.

Table 3: The percentage distribution of SME firms (1−499 employees) by size

Region	Percent
Less than 20 employees	
South East	92.9
South West	92.5
Wales	92.3
North West	92.0
East Anglia	91.4
West Midlands	91.4
Yorkshire	90.9
East Midlands	90.6
North	89.7
Scotland	89.5
Total	92.0
100−499 employees	
Scotland	1.9
North	1.6
East Midlands	1.4
East Anglia	1.3
Yorkshire	1.3
West Midlands	1.2
South East	1.1
North West	1.0
South West	1.0
Wales	1.0
Total	1.2

Table 4: The distribution of firms in 1987 per million of population

	Population (millions)	1 to 4	5 to 9	10 to 19	20 to 49	50 to 99	100 to 499	Total
South East	17.46	11,395	5,818	3,449	969	370	242	22,244
West Midlands	5.22	7,803	4,147	2,886	859	353	191	16,240
North West	6.39	7,991	4,114	2,657	827	296	165	16,050
East Anglia	2.06	7,486	4,140	2,686	829	317	205	15,662
East Midlands	4.02	7,137	3,883	2,665	872	335	208	15,100
Yorkshire	4.95	6,468	3,631	2,575	781	311	182	13,947
South West	4.67	6,701	3,516	2,329	647	233	137	13,561
Wales	2.88	5,375	2,898	1,929	532	210	110	11,054
Scotland	5.10	3,945	2,136	1,674	504	245	162	8,666
North	3.08	3,845	2,210	1,605	530	214	139	8,543
Total	55.83	7,982	4,193	2,708	798	311	191	16,181

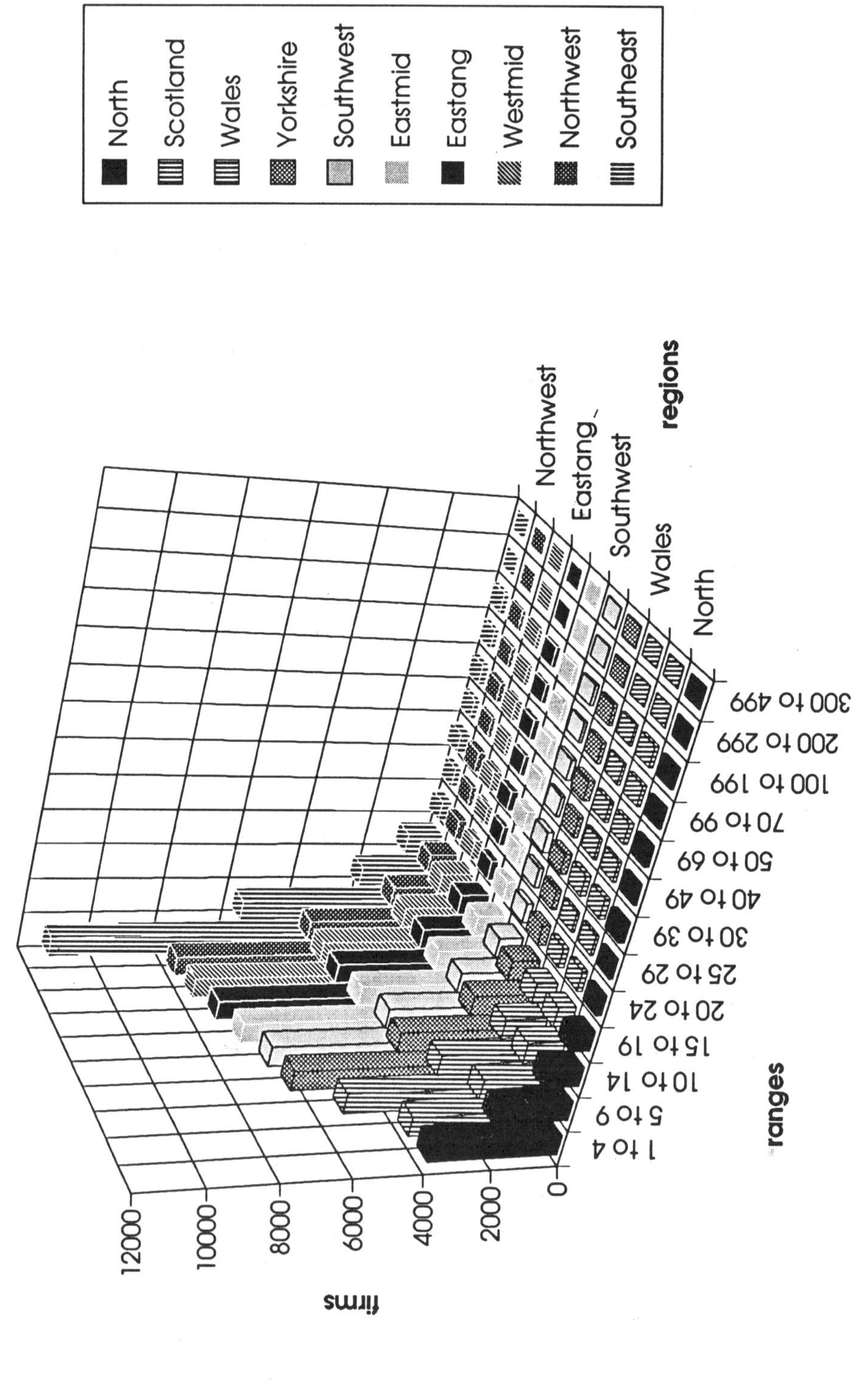

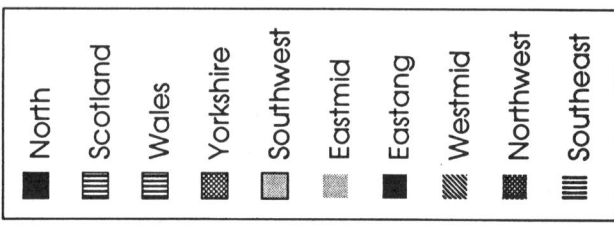

Figure 1: Firms/M by region.

Significant differences in firm density are apparent in Table 4. In particular, the almost 3 to 1 ratio in firm density between the South East and the North is to be noted. Small-firm density falls into three broad groupings. One group with the lowest levels is made up of the North, Scotland, and Wales. The South East can be looked upon as a separate group, with a uniquely high level. The remaining regions then form a broad middle group. In general, these proportions can be seen to hold for all size cohorts. As would be expected, there is a slight but definite tendency for those regions with a higher density of firms to have a higher percentage of the very small (1 to 4) small firms.

A partial explanation for the very high proportion of small firms in the South East may lie in sectoral differences. There are, for example, fewer service firms in the North and Scotland compared to the South East.

The distribution of employees per firm

The regional distribution of the number of employees per firm is shown in Table 5, and the respective distribution of employment across both the regions and the size ranges is given in Table 6. The overall picture is one of consistency, with little variation between either region or cohort size. This is slightly surprising, given the variation in sectoral makeup of the different regions.

Changes to the 1987 stock of firms

Table 7 gives in percentage terms, the results of the detailed changes which took place over the 1987–1989 period to the total stock of firms in the regions. The regions have also been ranked by firm density from highest to lowest. While there are significant differences in firm densities across regions, it is apparent that the relative changes which have taken place over the period have not varied markedly between regions. In other words, a region such as the North, with a firm density which is only 1/3 that of the South East, nevertheless very closely mirrors both the South East and the national average in terms of the proportions of firms which either expanded, contracted, remained at a constant employment level, were born or died over the 1987–1989 period.

The proportion of firms which did not change

There was very little variation in the number of firms which did not change their employment, nor did the proportions vary significantly by cohort size. The variation seen in Table 7 occurred around a national average of 53%, with a minimum of 49% (East Anglia), and a maximum of 55% (North West, Yorkshire, Wales, and Scotland). Thus in the SMEs in all regions, less than 50% of all firms experienced any employment change, and the majority remained at constant employment.

Table 5: The distribution of employees per firm by region and firm size

Cohorts	1 to 4	5 to 9	10 to 19	20 to 49	50 to 99	100 to 499	Total
South East	2.8	6.6	13.0	29.6	66.5	188.2	9.6
North West	2.7	6.6	13.0	29.3	66.3	180.0	9.8
West Midlands	2.7	6.7	13.2	29.6	66.3	178.8	10.5
Yorkshire	2.7	6.7	13.1	29.3	65.8	185.6	10.9
South West	2.7	6.7	13.0	29.8	65.9	185.0	9.7
East Midlands	2.7	6.7	13.1	29.8	65.9	184.0	11.0
Scotland	2.8	6.7	13.0	30.4	67.9	184.2	12.6
East Anglia	2.7	6.6	13.1	29.8	66.4	181.2	10.5
Wales	2.8	6.7	13.1	29.4	64.8	180.1	9.8
North	2.7	6.8	13.3	29.7	67.3	178.1	11.9
UK total	2.7	6.6	13.1	29.6	66.4	184.5	10.2

Table 6: Percentage distribution of employment across ranges and regions

Cohorts	1 to 4	5 to 9	10 to 19	20 to 49	50 to 99	100 to 499	Total
South East	14.70	18.00	21.00	13.44	11.52	21.35	100.00
North West	13.55	17.41	22.11	15.44	12.54	18.96	100.00
West Midlands	12.51	16.31	22.36	14.94	13.76	20.12	100.00
Yorkshire	11.44	15.91	22.07	15.02	13.42	22.13	100.00
South West	11.52	15.60	21.00	15.61	13.28	22.98	100.00
East Midlands	13.56	17.81	23.01	14.64	11.65	19.34	100.00
Scotland	10.05	13.12	20.00	14.06	15.29	27.49	100.00
East Anglia	12.08	16.51	21.29	14.95	12.73	22.44	100.00
Wales	13.64	17.87	23.31	14.37	12.53	18.27	100.00
North	10.20	14.74	20.97	15.52	14.21	24.37	100.00
UK total	13.22	16.95	21.50	14.37	12.54	21.43	100.00
South East	45.18	43.15	39.68	38.00	37.31	40.47	40.62
North West	11.19	11.21	11.22	11.73	10.92	9.66	10.92
West Midlands	9.16	9.32	10.06	10.06	10.62	9.09	9.68
Yorkshire	7.12	7.73	8.44	8.60	8.81	8.50	8.23
South West	6.86	7.03	7.16	6.82	6.22	6.04	6.69
East Midlands	6.35	6.70	7.11	7.92	7.71	7.81	7.28
Scotland	4.60	4.68	5.62	5.92	7.38	7.76	6.05
East Anglia	3.39	3.61	3.67	3.86	3.77	3.88	3.71
Wales	3.52	3.60	3.70	3.41	3.41	2.91	3.41
North	2.63	2.96	3.32	3.68	3.86	3.87	3.41
UK total	100.00	100.00	100.00	100.00	100.00	100.00	100.00

Variations within the 1−4 cohort across regions
The 1−4 cohort accounted for around 50% of all SMEs in this study, and their distribution is shown separately in Table 8 and Figure 2. In very broad terms, considerable similarity is apparent across the regions.

Table 7: Percentage regional firm change 1987−1989 by cohort size

	1 to 4	5 to 9	10 to 19	20 to 49	50 to 99	100 to 499	Total
South East							
Firms expanding	20	21	23	28	35	43	22
Firms stable	55	52	50	45	35	25	52
Firms declining	5	13	17	18	23	27	10
Firms deaths	19	14	10	8	7	5	16
Total	100	100	100	100	100	100	100
Firms births	29	15	7	5	2	2	20
North West							
Firms expanding	20	21	22	26	34	39	21
Firms stable	56	55	56	52	42	30	55
Firms declining	5	8	12	14	18	25	8
Firms deaths	19	15	10	8	6	6	16
Total	100	100	100	100	100	100	100
Firms births	28	13	7	5	3	2	19
West Midlands							
Firms expanding	22	22	22	25	36	42	23
Firms stable	54	54	56	57	43	30	54
Firms declining	3	8	12	11	17	24	7
Firms deaths	21	16	10	7	4	4	17
Total	100	100	100	100	100	100	100
Firms births	27	12	6	3	2	2	17

Table 7: Contd.

	1 to 4	5 to 9	10 to 19	20 to 49	50 to 99	100 to 499	Total
East Anglia							
Firms expanding	25	28	26	30	42	43	27
Firms stable	50	50	50	46	33	21	49
Firms declining	5	10	15	16	23	33	10
Firms deaths	20	12	10	7	2	3	15
Total	100	100	100	100	100	100	100
Firms births	32	10	4	3	1	1	19
East Midlands							
Firms expanding	21	22	24	27	36	43	23
Firms stable	55	56	55	52	43	30	54
Firms declining	4	8	11	14	16	23	7
Firms deaths	21	14	10	7	5	4	16
Total	100	100	100	100	100	100	100
Firms births	29	14	6	3	2	1	18
South West							
Firms expanding	22	22	26	28	37	39	24
Firms stable	52	51	52	45	34	25	51
Firms declining	6	12	14	18	23	30	10
Firms deaths	20	15	9	8	6	6	16
Total	100	100	100	100	100	100	100
Firms births	36	16	8	4	4	2	24
Yorkshire							
Firms expanding	20	23	23	29	34	44	23
Firms stable	57	55	56	52	45	29	55
Firms declining	3	9	12	13	16	24	7
Firms deaths	20	13	9	7	5	3	15
Total	100	100	100	100	100	100	100
Firms births	29	12	7	4	2	2	18
Wales							
Firms expanding	21	23	23	27	40	42	23
Firms stable	57	57	54	51	38	29	55
Firms declining	4	7	13	12	17	24	7
Firms deaths	19	14	10	10	6	5	15
Total	100	100	100	100	100	100	100
Firms births	32	17	10	5	3	2	22
Scotland							
Firms expanding	20	22	21	25	38	38	22
Firms stable	57	55	56	53	41	33	55
Firms declining	4	9	12	15	17	27	8
Firms deaths	19	14	11	8	4	2	15
Total	100	100	100	100	100	100	100
Firms births	42	22	9	7	5	2	27
North							
Firms expanding	24	26	26	25	40	44	25
Firms stable	57	53	52	53	38	28	54
Firms declining	3	8	12	15	16	23	8
Firms deaths	16	14	9	7	6	5	13
Total	100	100	100	100	100	100	100
Firms births	36	15	9	5	5	2	22
UK total							
Firms expanding	21	22	23	27	36	42	22
Firms stable	55	53	53	49	39	28	53
Firms declining	5	10	14	15	20	26	9
Firms deaths	20	14	10	8	6	5	16
Total	100	100	100	100	100	100	100
Firms births	30	14	7	4	3	2	20

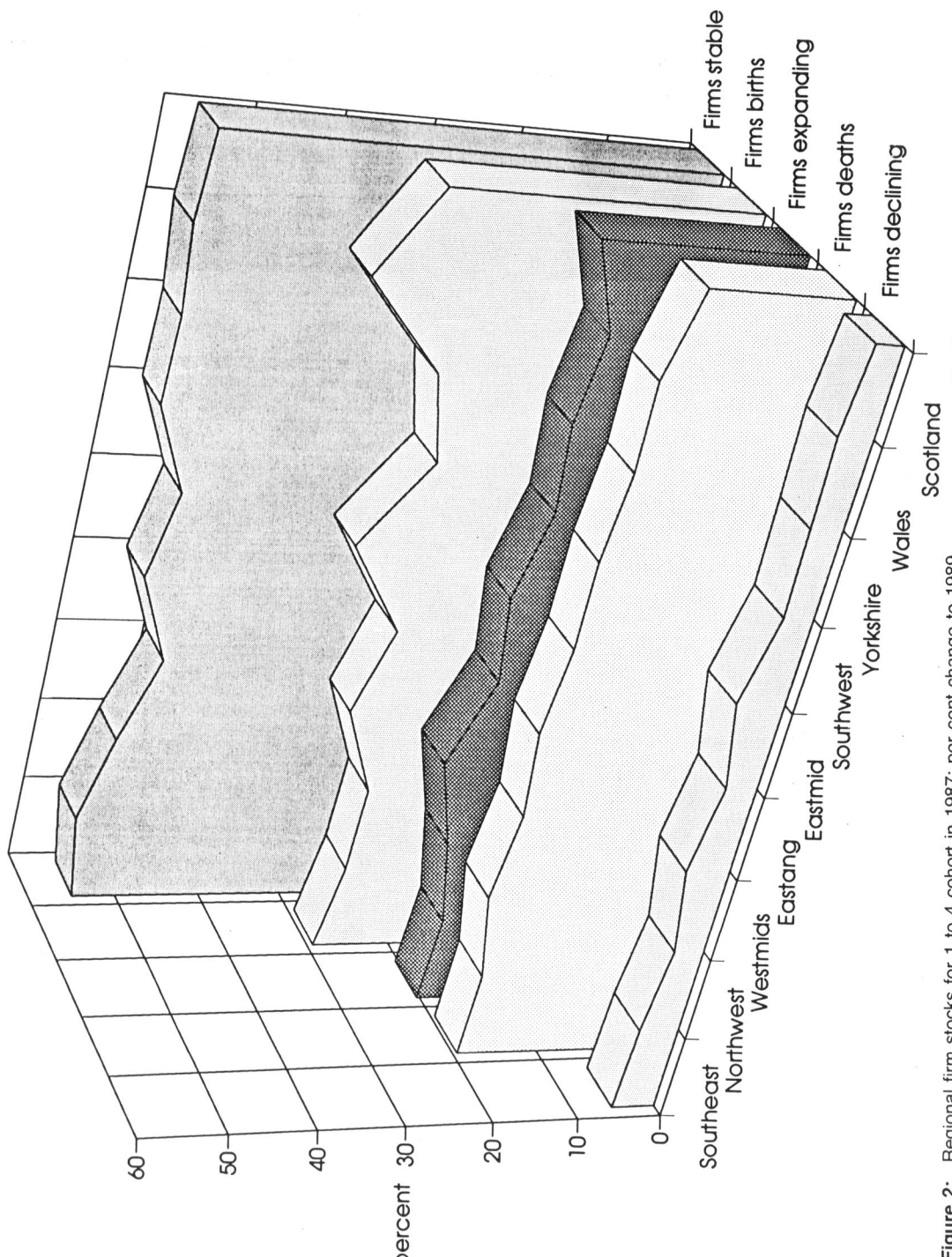

Figure 2: Regional firm stocks for 1 to 4 cohort in 1987: per cent change to 1989.

Table 8: Percent change by region for 1–4 cohort

	South East	North West	West Midlands	East Anglia	East Midlands	South West	Yorkshire	Wales	Scotland	North
Firms declining	5	5	3	5	4	6	3	4	4	3
Firms deaths	19	19	21	20	21	20	20	19	19	16
Firms expanding	20	20	22	25	21	22	20	21	20	24
Firms births	29	28	27	32	29	36	29	32	42	36
Firms stable	55	56	54	50	55	52	57	57	57	57
Total	100	100	100	100	100	100	100	100	100	100

VARIATION IN FIRM BIRTHS, DEATHS AND CHURNING

Variation in firm births

Table 9 shows the number of births for each region, and births as a percentage of initial stock, arranged in descending order of regional firm density. Within the 1−4 cohort (in Table 9 and Figure 3), a modest but definite tendency is apparent, that a higher rate of firm births occurred in those regions with the lowest firm densities. It must be noted that the ratio of births which take place into a cohort, to initial firms in that cohort, can be misleading, in that it is unlikely to be the direct actions of the incumbent small firms in a cohort which cause new births. Recent research for example, has found that in manufacturing, new small firms are predominantly founded by entrepreneurs who emerge from existing small firms, while in financial services, they emerge from large firms (Small Business Research Centre, Cambridge 1992).

It can be speculated that the observed variation in firm birth rates across region is due to:

1. variations in the sectoral make-up of regions;
2. differing regional attitudes to new formation;
3. the result of a natural concentration phenomenon;
4. the effect of new firm regional employment policy.

Point 3 argues that regions with low small-firm density will tend to perform better than those with higher concentrations, because the lower density will leave more room for new firm birth and expansion. Point 4 suggests that we may be observing the effects of regional employment policies on new firm formation.

Variation in firm death rates

The number of firm deaths, and percentage of deaths to the initial stock of firms in each region arranged in descending order of regional firm numbers, is shown in Table 10. It was anticipated that firm deaths (relative to the initial stock) in a given size cohort

Table 9: Firm births 1987−1989 for 10 regions and as a percentage of 1987 stock

	1 to 4	5 to 9	10 to 19	20 to 49	50 to 99	100 to 499	Total
South East	58,220	14,840	4,482	778	148	88	78,556
North West	14,100	3,520	1,140	260	48	19	19,087
West Midlands	11,100	2,630	840	136	38	19	14,763
Yorkshire	9,420	2,090	912	150	26	18	12,616
South West	11,320	2,700	822	128	42	12	15,024
East Midlands	8,280	2,110	678	112	30	7	11,217
Scotland	8,380	2,410	762	168	60	14	11,794
East Anglia	4,920	870	216	54	6	4	6,070
Wales	4,940	1,380	552	84	16	7	6,979
North	4,240	1,000	468	80	32	9	5,829
Totals	134,920	33,550	10,872	1,950	446	196	181,934
South East	29.3	14.6	7.4	4.6	2.3	2.1	20.2
North West	27.6	13.4	6.7	4.9	2.5	1.8	18.6
West Midlands	27.3	12.1	5.6	3.0	2.1	1.9	17.4
Yorkshire	29.4	11.6	7.2	3.9	1.7	2.0	18.3
South West	36.2	16.4	7.6	4.2	3.9	1.9	23.7
East Midlands	28.9	13.5	6.3	3.2	2.2	0.8	18.5
Scotland	41.7	22.1	8.9	6.5	4.8	1.7	26.7
East Anglia	31.9	10.2	3.9	3.2	0.9	0.9	18.8
Wales	31.9	16.5	9.9	5.5	2.6	2.1	21.9
North	35.8	14.7	9.5	4.9	4.8	2.1	22.2
Totals	30.3	14.3	7.2	4.4	2.6	1.8	20.1

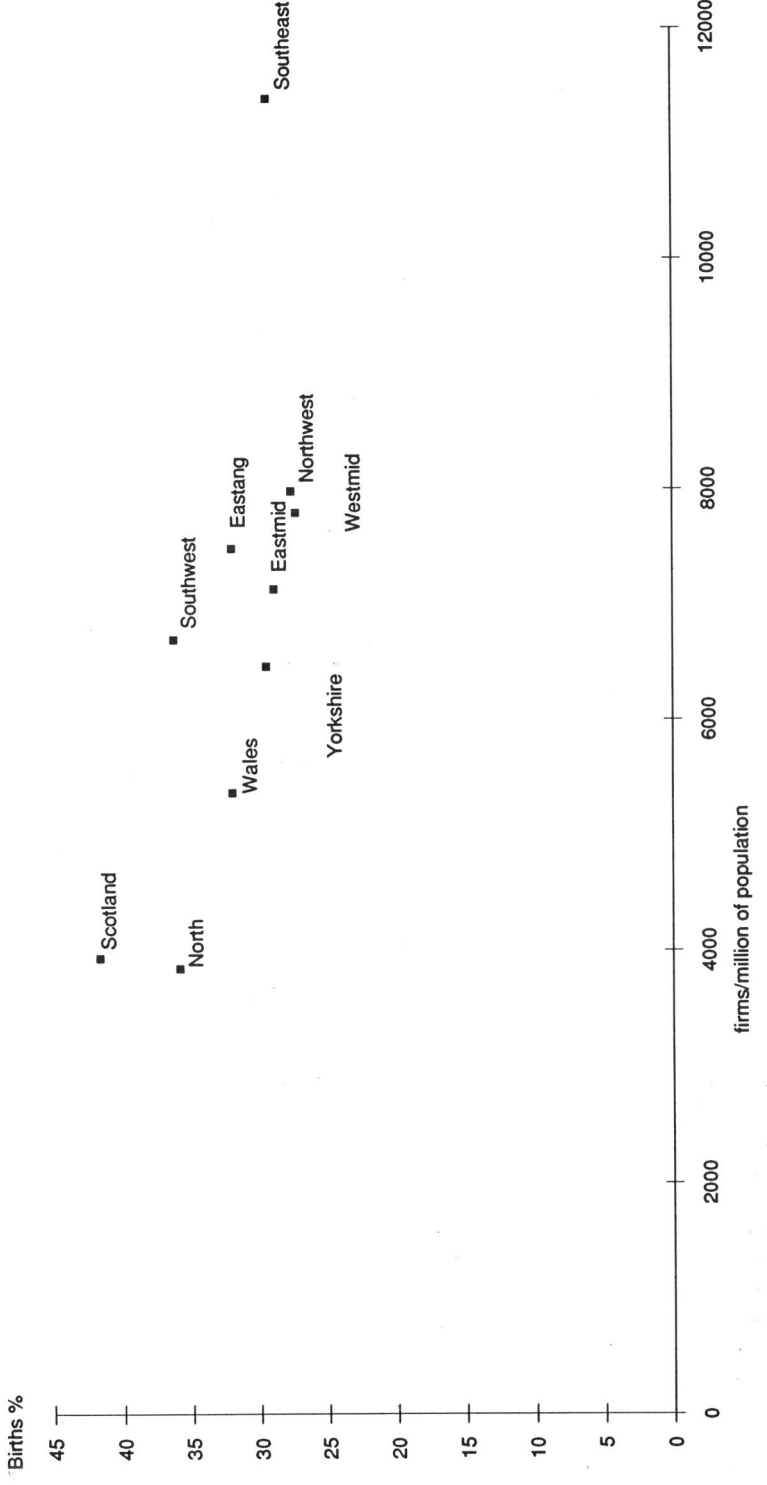

Figure 3: Firm stock and birth rate 1987–1989 for 1 to 4 cohort.

Table 10: Firm deaths 1987–1989 for 10 regions and as a percentage of 1987 stock

	1 to 4	5 to 9	10 to 19	20 to 49	50 to 99	100 to 499	Total
South East	38,780	14,230	6,012	1,404	436	218	61,080
North West	9,760	4,030	1,758	440	116	64	16,168
West Midlands	8,560	3,500	1,530	296	74	36	13,996
Yorkshire	6,260	2,300	1,104	270	76	28	10,038
South West	6,120	2,510	954	246	60	37	9,927
East Midlands	5,940	2,180	1,098	258	62	35	9,573
Scotland	3,780	1,530	900	202	54	17	6,483
East Anglia	3,040	1,010	546	120	16	12	4,744
Wales	2,880	1,160	540	148	36	17	4,781
North	1,940	940	462	116	40	22	3,520
Totals	87,060	33,390	14,904	3,500	970	484	140,308
South East	19.5	14.0	10.0	8.3	6.8	5.2	15.7
North West	19.1	15.3	10.4	8.3	6.1	6.0	15.8
West Midlands	21.0	16.2	10.2	6.6	4.0	3.6	16.5
Yorkshire	19.6	12.8	8.7	7.0	4.9	3.2	14.5
South West	19.6	15.3	8.8	8.1	5.5	5.7	15.7
East Midlands	20.7	14.0	10.2	7.4	4.6	4.1	15.8
Scotland	18.8	14.0	10.5	7.9	4.3	2.0	14.7
East Anglia	19.7	11.8	9.9	7.0	2.5	2.8	14.7
Wales	18.6	13.9	9.7	9.7	5.9	5.4	15.0
North	16.4	13.8	9.3	7.1	6.1	5.1	13.4
Totals	19.5	14.3	9.9	7.9	5.6	4.5	15.5

would not vary significantly across regions, and this does appear to be the case. The smallest variation across regions is in the bands covering the 1–19 range, with the exception of the low figure for the 1–4 cohort for the North. Past analyses of the VAT data have shown that a high correlation exists between birth and death rates, which appears to be a result of the constant relative proportion of firms which fail within fixed time periods.

The effects of firm churning at a regional level

The extent of change which takes place when firms expand, contract, are born, and die, has been described as 'churning'. It is of considerable interest to know whether there is any relationship between the level of churning which is taking place in a region, and its ability to create net new jobs and firms. A churning index was therefore calculated for firm change for each region, which has been arbitrarily defined as the ratio of the sum of all firms in the region which changed in some way, to the number which remained stable.

The results, ranked by overall index, are shown in Table 11 and Figure 4, and some consistency in the extent of churning among the regions can be observed. Nevertheless, it is apparent that in the South West and East Anglia, for every 100 firms which did not change, there were 160 which did, while in Wales, the North West, and Yorkshire, only 130 changed in some way. The reasons for this variation may lie in differences between the regions in firm density, size distribution, sector composition, and level of economic activity.

As cohort size increases, there is a tendency for the variation in the degree of churning between regions to increase, so that there is significant variation in the index for the 100 to 499 cohort, where the highest (East Anglia at 3.8) is almost double that of the lowest (Scotland, 2.1). Thus for this cohort in East Anglia, for every firm which did not change, there were four which did, while in Scotland, only two changed in some way. The indices for the smaller cohort sizes in general vary in the same direction as the largest cohort, but with a very much smaller range.

In general, the results show that for any regional cohort, higher than average birth

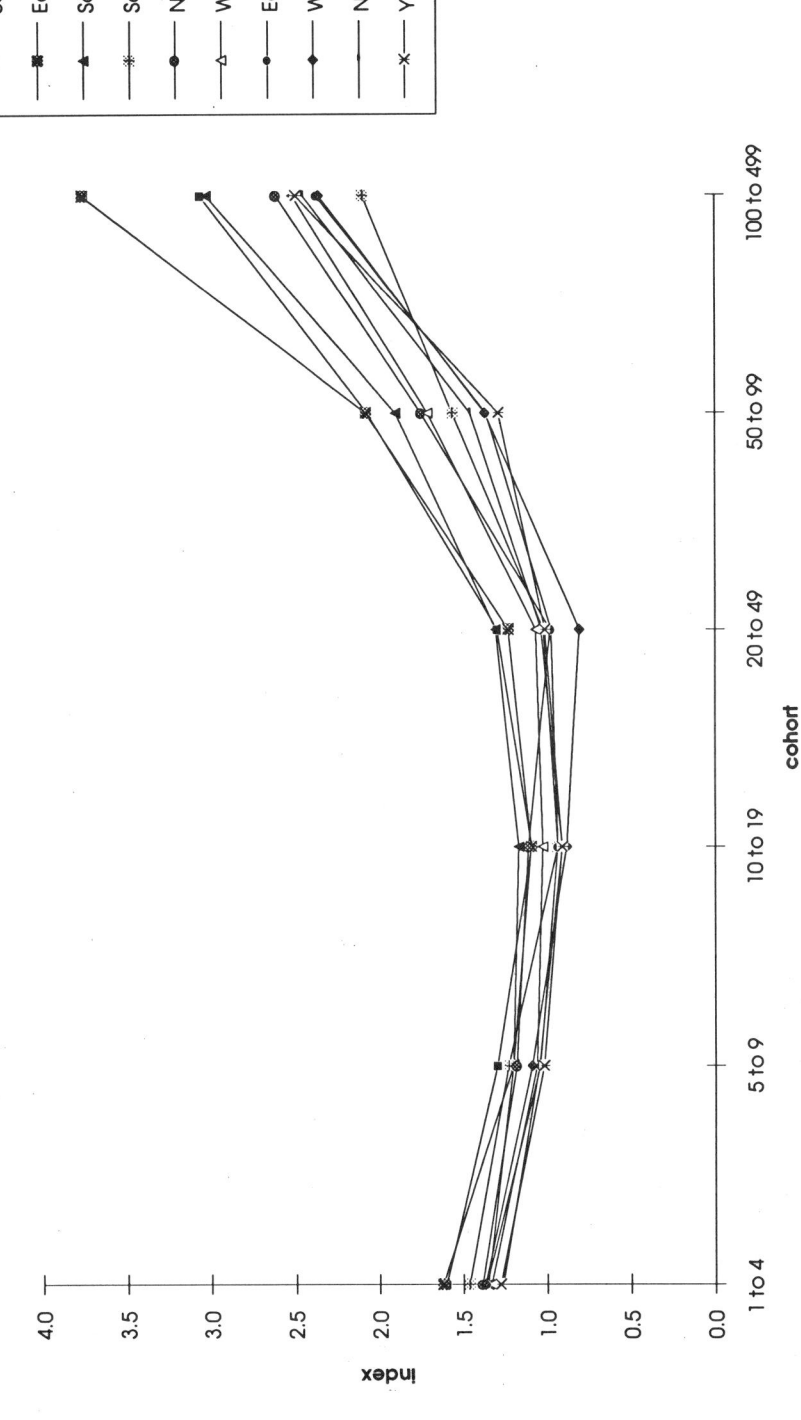

Figure 4:   Churning index by region and cohort.

Table 11: A churning index for SMEs for each region and cohort

	1 to 4	5 to 9	10 to 19	20 to 49	50 to 99	100 to 499	Total
South West	1.6	1.3	1.1	1.3	2.1	3.1	1.4
East Anglia	1.6	1.2	1.1	1.2	2.1	3.8	1.4
South East	1.4	1.2	1.2	1.3	1.9	3.0	1.3
Scotland	1.5	1.2	0.9	1.0	1.6	2.1	1.3
North	1.4	1.2	1.1	1.0	1.7	2.6	1.3
Wales	1.3	1.1	1.0	1.1	1.7	2.5	1.2
East Midlands	1.4	1.0	0.9	1.0	1.4	2.4	1.2
West Midlands	1.4	1.1	0.9	0.8	1.4	2.4	1.2
North West	1.3	1.0	0.9	1.0	1.5	2.4	1.1
Yorkshire	1.3	1.0	0.9	1.0	1.3	2.5	1.1
UK total	1.4	1.1	1.0	1.1	1.6	2.7	1.3

The ratio of all firms which changed, to the number of stable firms, i.e. the ratio of the total of firms which expanded, contracted, and died, to unchanged firms.

rates (in comparison with those of other regions into the same cohort) are accompanied by higher than average death rates. In a similar way, higher than average expansion rates are accompanied by higher than average contraction rates.

It can also be seen that churning is at a minimum for the 10–19 cohort. This phenomenon may contribute to an explanation of the long observed very low net job creation performance of this cohort, if the level of churning is linked to job creation performance in some way.

FIRM DENSITY AND GDP PER CAPITA

Table 12 and Figure 5 show the regional distribution of firm density and GDP per capita (*Regional Trends* 1992). Three groups of regions become apparent in Figure 5. First, the South East is in a group of its own with a firm density and GDP per capita which is significantly higher than that of any of the other regions. A second group is made up of Wales, the North, and Scotland at the opposite extreme, with the lowest firm density and GDP per capita. A final mid-group contains the remaining regions, and forms an intermediate cluster. It would appear that some relationship exists between firm density and GDP per capita at the regional level, although clearly other important factors such as level of economic activity, sectoral composition and skill levels will influence this relationship.

Table 12: Small firm density and GDP in the UK regions

Region	GDP £/head UK = 100	Firms (1 to 4 employees) per million
South East	117.7	11,395
North West	92.1	7,994
West Midlands	92.0	7,804
East Anglia	99.4	7,490
East Midlands	97.5	7,139
South West	94.3	6,705
Yorkshire	92.4	6,465
Wales	86.1	5,373
Scotland	93.9	3,943
North	89.2	3,852
Total	100.00	7,983

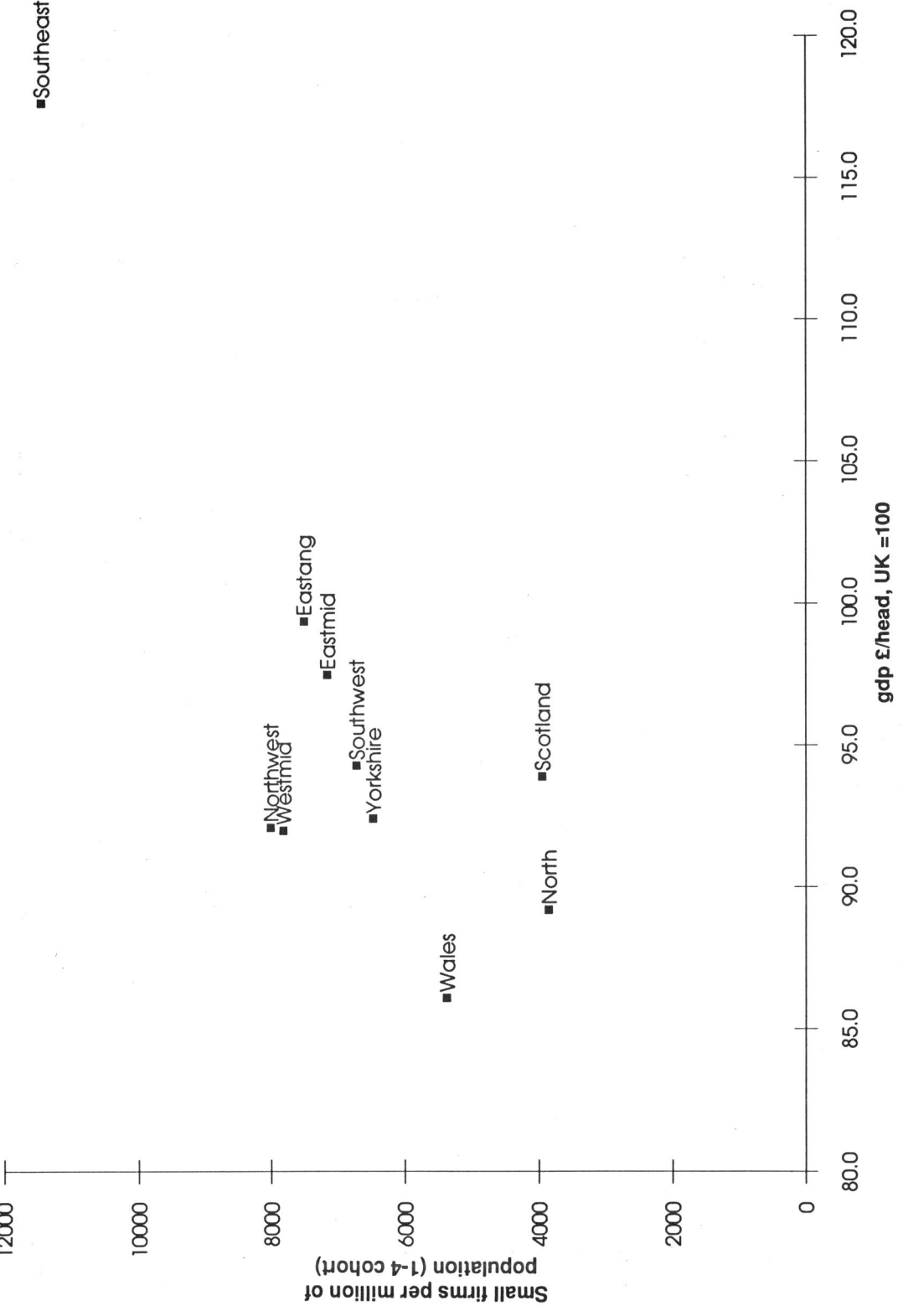

Figure 5: 1987 small firm density (1 to 4 cohort) and GDP in the UK regions.

GENERAL DISCUSSION AND CONCLUSIONS

The births, deaths, and 'no changes'
In all regions, there was considerable consistency in the proportion of SME firms which did not change their employment in any way. In general, less than 50% of firms experienced any change. There was a modest but definite tendency for a higher rate of firm births to occur in those regions with the lowest firm density per million of population. This could be due to different sector structures, differing regional attitudes to new firm formation, or the result of some form of natural concentration type phenomenon.

Regional variations in firm density
Very significant differences in firm density per million of population exist between the regions, and in particular, between the South East, and the North (a 3 to 1 ratio). The variation in small-firm density appears to fall into three broad groups. First the North, Scotland, and Wales, with the lowest levels, next the South East with the highest, and finally a broad middle group made up of the remaining regions. In spite of this regional variation in firm density in expansions, contractions, births, deaths, and no change, the distribution of employment by cohort size in the regions closely mirrored national averages.

The proportions of firms and employment based in micro-firms
There is a variation in the proportions of employment and firms based in the 1−4 size band between the regions. The North, Scotland, East Midlands and Yorkshire, all have a relatively low proportion of firms in this cohort. If it is indeed this cohort which is the principal source of job creation, then these regions will need a higher formation rate of such firms, if they are to improve their overall job creation performance.

Regional firm density and GDP per capita
As a result of the analysis of regional firm density and GDP per capita, three loose groupings of the regions emerged which in descending order of both variables were;

1. the South East in a rank on its own;
2. an intermediate group made up of East Anglia, the East Midlands, the North West, the South West, the West Midlands, and Yorkshire;
3. the North, Scotland, and Wales.

These results suggest that some form of relationship may exist between firm density, and GDP per capita, at the regional level. The extent of this relationship can be used as one measure of the extent of differences between the regions. It also suggests that if overall economic variations between the regions are to be reduced it will only occur by addressing the more fundamental underlying problems, such as that of differences in firm density.

APPENDIX

Introduction
D and B have over recent years made significant improvements to the quality and accuracy of their data, and new techniques have been employed in the validation and grossing-up procedures used with the data.

On the database, employment in branch plants and the subsidiaries of large firms is 'allocated' to the head office location. This database structure therefore, could lead to a significant distortion of the distribution of employment in large firms by region. By restricting the study to the smaller firm size range of firms with one to 499 employees, any problems which would arise from this method of recording employment data have been alleviated. Because branch plant and UK subsidiary employment in large firms is allocated to its holding company, it is also difficult to assess the effect of a subsidiary on job creation in a region.

It could be argued that it may be sectoral rather than regional factors which have made the biggest contribution to our observed differences in regional performance, but it is likely that regional and sectoral factors are so interwoven that they cannot be meaningfully separated. A shift-share type of analysis would enable the relative influence of these factors to be examined in more detail.

Possible biases in the data

There is some bias in the database by sector in that there are more small firms on the database in the service sector than there are in the population. It is also possible that the database may be slightly biased by region, both in terms of density of coverage, and the variation of the sectoral structure of firms across regions. However in this study these factors are not of critical importance because the major focus is on relative performance.

No measures of a simple form were used to take account of (a) employment present on the database which is based in overseas subsidiaries, and (b) merger and acquisition activity which does not result in actual net job creation.

REFERENCES

Daly M.J., Campbell M., Robson G.B. and Gallagher C.C. (1991) Job creation 1987–89: The contribution of small and large firms, Employment Gazette, November, pp. 589–596.

Daly M.J., Campbell M., Robson G.B. and Gallagher C.C. (1992) Job creation 1987–89: preliminary analysis by sector, Employment Gazette, August, pp. 387–392.

Gallagher C.C., Daly M.J. and Thomason J.C. (1991) The growth of companies 1985–87 and their contribution to job generation, International Journal of Small Business Economics, Vol. 3, pp. 269–286.

Regional Trends (1992) Central Statistical Office Publications, Cardiff.

Robson G.B. and Gallagher C.C. (1992) The use of the Dun and Bradstreet database for job generation research. An evaluation of the 1988 database, Newcastle University School of Business Management Discussion Paper 92–7, May.

Small Business Research Centre (1992) The State of British Enterprise: Growth, Innovation and Competitive Advantage in Small and Medium Sized Firms, Cambridge.

6.

LOCAL ECONOMIES AND SMALL FIRMS:
A View from the Ground

James Curran and Robert A. Blackburn

INTRODUCTION

Small firms and local economies are perceived as being inextricably linked in a number of ways. For instance, small firms are often assumed to be principally or almost exclusively, concerned with serving the needs of local markets. Undoubtedly, in any delimited geographical area which might be labelled a 'local economy', the vast majority of businesses will be what most would term 'small'. In policy terms, both government (that of the UK and the EC) and especially local authorities, have seen the small firm as a key element in the sustaining and regeneration of local economies (Bannock and Albach 1991, Stanworth and Gray 1991, Ch. 2, Coulson 1990). In economic geography the link between the local economy and the small firm occurs in a number of ways illustrated most clearly recently in the debates on industrial districts (Pyke et al 1990) and in several examples of the analysis of spatial aspects of economic structure (Hudson 1988, Mason 1991).

During the 1980s, a revival of interest in small-scale economic activities and the spatial aspects of social and economic activities coincided. Both were previously dismissed largely as of declining or lost importance in the development of industrial economies and societies (Curran 1990, Urry 1990). As a result of these renewed interests, there has been the sharpening of controversies concerning the role and character of small-scale enterprise in Britain's economy and controversy on the conceptualisation of 'local economies' and the significance of the local and the spatial in understanding contemporary economic, social and political processes (Massey and Allen 1988, Cooke 1989, Curran 1990, Harloe et al 1990). While the two sets of issues are often linked in the literature, the conceptual debates they have engendered have, despite superficial indications to the contrary, remained curiously unrelated.

Small-business researchers, for instance, have, with some exceptions,[1] been very inward looking in discussing the small enterprise and its revival in the UK economy. The vast majority of studies have focused on owner-managers and the enterprise but have rarely attempted to systematically link these with the wider economy and society. The proliferating literature on local economies and the spatial dimensions of economic restructuring often talks a great deal about the key role of the small firm in these processes but, again, nearly always fails to treat the small enterprise as a set of economic and social relations. This weakness is most apparent in the industrial districts debate where the small firm is so central to the thesis offered by those who regard such districts as crucial to economic restructuring (Piore and Sabel 1984, Hirst and Zeitlin 1989). None of these proponents appear to have had much contact with small firms, preferring instead to deal in generalities or idealisations (Amin 1989, Curran 1990).

More basically, debates on the significance of spatial aspects of economic activities and the role of small firms in the economy have raised deep conceptual issues over what the 'local economy' is and how small firms articulate with local economies. One distinction basic to these concerns is whether local economies are seen as constituted through formal or substantial social relations (Sayer 1984, Burrows and Curran 1989). Local economies are most often defined administratively as, for example, 'travel to work areas' or by local government boundaries. Although at an implicit level these categories are glossed into other notions such as 'the local community' to suggest that they refer to relations of contact and interaction between people and groups supposedly part of 'the local economy', more strictly such conceptual approaches beg all kinds of questions about such real relations. To what extent do people running businesses actually interact or share a sense of identification with, or belonging to, local economies defined formally?; or to put it another way, to what extent do they have substantial relations with each and what is the character of any such relations?

Of course, the above questions are by no means new or unaddressed. A long-standing debate exists, for example, on the theme of whether locality matters in contemporary British society (see Hammett et al 1989). Yet this debate rarely focuses on the business or economic units directly. Other debates are concerned with economic issues such as the economic strategies of local authorities (Cooke 1989, Goodwin 1989, Cochrane 1990) but are conducted at a general level, at what might be termed the 'macro-local level'.[2] Even where attempts at detailed analyses of specific local economies have been made such as the group of localities studied under the ESRC initiative, The Changing Urban and Regional System of the UK (Cooke 1989, Harloe et al 1990) the interpretations offered remain very general. The businesses mentioned in any detail are larger enterprises and there is rarely any mention of the role of smaller enterprises, even though they constitute the bulk of the businesses in any given locality.

A GROUND LEVEL VIEW OF LOCALITY AND ECONOMIC ACTIVITIES

The present paper analyses issues relevant to several of the above debates from a different, 'ground level' perspective, that is, from the point of view of those who own and operate businesses or are otherwise involved in economic activities in localities. It draws on data collected in three research projects over the period 1990–1991 carried out in seven geographically contrasting areas. The data is used to explore three main issues:

1. the indications from the data on the extent to which it is relevant to talk of a 'local' economy in the sense of a coherent and integrated set of economic activities which can be 'mapped' by tracing the actual linkages and real relations between businesses, large and small, in the designated area;
2. the ways in which those involved in economic activities, particularly owners of small businesses, in a geographical area articulate with other businesses in that area and the character of such relations. This concerns not only the frequency of these connections but the consciousness of locality in economic actors' deliberations;
3. the trends suggested by the data on the increasing or decreasing importance of the 'local' in economic activities in the UK and the implications of the finding for the wider debate on these issues.

BACKGROUND AND METHODOLOGICAL CONSIDERATIONS

Two of the research projects from which data is reported are derived from part of a large-scale research programme on the small enterprise in the services sector while the third was a separate project carried out by the same researchers. Project One consisted of interviews with 350 owner-managers of small service-sector firms from seven areas of services:

1. computer services;
2. garage repairs and servicing;
3. employment, secretarial, and training agencies;
4. plant and equipment hire;
5. advertising, marketing and design agencies;
6. video hire, health, beauty and leisure clubs;
7. free houses, wine bars and licensed restaurants.

This particular mix of sectors was selected for a number of reasons. First, the emphasis on services reflects the fact that the great majority of small businesses are in services (Curran and Burrows 1988, p. 55) even though much previous research on the small business has neglected this point and given much more attention to the small business in manufacturing. Second, the particular activities were chosen to ensure that small businesses from both older, long-established forms of service-sector enterprises, such as garages and free houses, were represented together with emerging sectors such as computer services and leisure sectors. Third, it was also felt necessary to balance small businesses in producer services, meeting mainly the requirements of other businesses, with small businesses serving the needs of individual consumers or with a mixed clientele of business and private customers.

The businesses were located in five strongly contrasting localities: Nottingham, Guildford, North East Suffolk, Doncaster and Islington in London. The localities were selected to provide indicators of the experiences of small service-sector businesses in a wide range of localities. Thus they include examples of localities with high levels of economic activity and employment in a highly affluent region (Guildford), a locality representing an area with older industries, lower levels of activity and high unemployment (Doncaster), an inner-city economy (Islington), a midland economy (Nottingham), and a mainly rural locality (North East Suffolk).[3]

The second project from which data is analysed in the paper was based on a sub-sample of owner-managers interviewed in the above project. In Project Two, 45 of the original owner-managers were re-interviewed using a 'critical incident' approach to explore how they dealt with crises or other important events which had an impact on the running of the firm. The firms were in three economic activities: computer services; employment, secretarial and training agencies; and garage and vehicle repairing; but were drawn from all five local areas.

Project Three from which data is presented was a study of large-firm—small-firm relations among firms in two localities. The 60 small firms were in two industries: printing and electronics. Printing was chosen because although it is often grouped in manufacturing in official statistics, it provides a service to virtually all other firms in the economy (British Printing Industries Federation 1991). It is an industry composed largely of small firms whose activities should illustrate well how small firms link with other large and small firms. Electronics is an area of manufacturing where both small and large enterprises are well represented and there are well developed vertical links between the two (National Economic Development Council 1988, 1990, 1991). This study also included findings from interviews with representatives of 16 large private and public sector organisations, designed to gather data on their links with small firms and especially within the two localities. The organisations were either based solely in the locality or the local branch was big enough to make it one of the largest dozen or so employers in the locality.

The two localities from which the small firms and large organisations were recruited for Project Three were Sheffield, and Kingston-upon-Thames on the South West London—Surrey borders. These were again selected for the contrasts they offer. Sheffield is a locality, like Doncaster, where long-established heavy industry, particularly steel making, and traditional manufacturing have declined, only being partly replaced by newer forms of economic activities in the services and high tech sectors. Kingston-upon-Thames is part of the affluent outer-London area of the highly dynamic South East region which has enjoyed high levels of economic prosperity over a prolonged period (Martin 1988). Its main economic activities are in aerospace and the defence industries with a strong representation of high tech firms in electronics, and in services, particularly in business and professional services.[4]

In all three projects, interviews were face-to-face and tape-recorded. Projects One and Three used semi-structured questionnaires while Project Two used a more open approach based on an introduction of each of the critical incidents and probes. In the large organisations in Project Three, respondents were executives responsible for purchasing and/or purchasing policy strategies.

In all seven localities, further interviews with a wide variety of others representing economic development units, enterprise agencies, chambers of commerce and similar bodies were carried out and a substantial amount of secondary analysis of official and other data on each of the localities was also completed. While each project had its own specific aims, all produced data on links between firms in the localities, attitudes to participation in local economic and other networks, with the projects cumulatively producing both data and methodological triangulation to add considerably to the robustness of the analysis.

Overall, therefore, the three projects offer findings from interviews with 410 owners of small enterprises in seven localities, and representatives of 16 large organisations in two of the localities. The small firms are from both services and manufacturing with the proportions from each broadly representative of the sectoral make-up of the UK small business population: 15% of the businesses are in manufacturing and 85% in services.[5] The fact that, for five of the localities considered, all the small firms are from the services sector with no representatives of large organisations included, and that for two of the localities all the small firms were drawn from manufacturing, while less than ideal, is held not to detract from the value of the analysis for the aims of the paper.[6]

TRADING PATTERNS AND LOCALITIES

Conventional views have long stressed the close links between small firms and their immediate localities (Bolton Report 1971, p. 26). Small firms, it is argued, serve local markets and through their abilities to respond quickly to local demands, their close knowledge of local conditions and their ability to exploit the economic advantages of being close to the local market, can often operate more effectively than larger enterprises based inside or outside the locality. These strengths are most clearly seen in the provision of services for private consumers, for example, in catering. In addition, small firms are also frequently portrayed as a support army for larger firms and organisations particularly through subcontracting arrangements of various kinds in both manufacturing and services (Rainnie 1989).[7]

In fact, the data from the projects in this study show that the trading patterns of small and large firms are extremely varied and cut across most accepted notions of 'locality'.[8] The major finding reiterated again and again throughout the data was of the importance of economic sector rather than locality in understanding firms' links with their wider environment.

Firms in consumer services (video hire, health studios and clubs, free houses, wine bars and small restaurants) were tied closely to local markets but a 'local market' in this context is still far from a simple notion. For instance, a video hire outlet's 'local market' in an area such as a suburb of Nottingham might be confined to a few streets over a mile or less: beyond this limited area, consumers may find other, competing outlets more convenient, unless the video hire outlet specialises in some way such as meeting the needs of an ethnic minority.

A free house might also be a 'local' in the traditional sense with the majority of customers coming from roughly the same-sized area as that served by most of the video hire outlets. But a city centre free house or wine bar might display very different trading patterns. For example, one of the Nottingham city centre free houses in the ESRC sample had a predominantly younger clientele and the owner claimed that, at weekends, young people came from as far as 50 miles away because Nottingham's city centre had acquired a reputation as a place for 'a good night out', overshadowing areas, including other nearby urban centres such as Derby and Loughborough.

In short, small firms serving consumers can have a predominantly local clientele but nevertheless still draw their customers from a whole variety of different 'local' markets related to the kinds of activities in which they are engaged. What the data shows clearly is the differing ways in which small firms, ostensibly offering the same service, created a niche through the combination of management strategies and local circumstances.

Small firms in business services displayed a similar or even greater range of ways of articulating with the wider economy. Employment, secretarial and training agencies, for example, might reasonably be assumed to concentrate on meeting the needs of other firms within a relatively small geographical area. Yet of the 50 small businesses of this kind in Project One, just over one in five claimed that 75% or more of their business was with customers outside the locality. These were mainly agencies specialising in the supply of particular forms of labour, for example, for the electronics or computing industries where a local market would be unlikely to offer sufficient demand for their services.[9]

The firms showing the least likelihood of doing business in their immediate locality were those in the advertising, marketing and design sector. For this sector, over half (53.5%) of the 52 owner-managers interviewed reported that over 75% of their business was with clients outside the locality. This confirms a study by Keeble et al (1991) of small management consultancy and market research firms (whose activities appear closely related to those of the advertising, marketing and design businesses interviewed) which found that over 70% of sales were outside the locality (that is, more than 20 miles away).

As Keeble et al (1991) point out, it has been in the area of business services and especially information-based services, that the greatest amount of small business growth has occurred since 1980. The implications of the findings on trading patterns in this sector from these studies are important in relation to the discussion of the significance of locality in the analysis of the relations between small firms and local economies. For small firms in services, even those most likely to be trading over a relatively limited geographical area the geographical 'shape' of their markets may vary substantially even where they are engaged in very similar kinds of endeavour. There is no specifiable market they share which can be delimited geographically without becoming an arbitrary category virtually devoid of shared realities of economic action and inter-relations amongst those supposedly inhabiting such a 'local economy'. But further, if the sectors in which small service firms are most likely to be expanding are those in which trading patterns extend over wider, more varied geographical areas, than could be encompassed in any reasonable definition of a 'the local economy', then again the link between small scale economic activities and locality becomes further attenuated.[10]

SMALL FIRMS IN MANUFACTURING AND RELATIONS WITH LOCALITY

The great bulk of small business research to date has focused on manufacturing firms. Small firms in manufacturing have also conventionally been seen as linked closely with local economies and, indeed, much of the recent debate on the role of the small firm in economic restructuring has concentrated on the small manufacturing firm, linking it with the development of industrial districts or Japanese influenced industrial patterns of large enterprises served on a 'just-in-time' basis by a host of geographically close small firms.

The trading patterns of the 60 small manufacturing firms studied in Project Three throw light on the above assumptions and also show, as for the small services firms, considerable variations. The printing firms operated over much more limited geographical areas than the firms in electronics with over 80% of their trade occurring with customers within 10 miles. Just over a quarter of the small electronics firms reported that over 75% of their business was with firms within a 10 mile radius.

There was also a difference between the two localities in the study. The small electronics firms in the Kingston local economy had markedly more geographically extensive trading patterns. The explanation for this difference appeared to be related to differences in the development and age of the electronic firms in the two localities. Those in Kingston, an area where the electronics industry has a longer history, seem to have developed higher levels of specialisation and market confidence than those in Sheffield where the industry has a shorter history and such firms are smaller measured by employment and turnover.

The distinction between 'specialists' and 'generalists' (Keeble et al 1991, p. 5) to analyse the strategies of the business services firms is helpful in analysing the strategies of the owner-managers of the manufacturing firms in this study. 'Specialists' attempt to create a market niche for the firm by concentrating on a narrow range of services or products: 'generalists' take the view that a firm has to take whatever orders come along if they are to survive. Printing firms were much more likely than electronics firms to be generalists. In the main, this is not so much a choice of owner-managers as a reflection of the character of the industry and its market. Historically, most printers have been jobbing or general printers and owner-managers were often proud that they could handle any job likely to come their way. However, there may well be more specialisation emerging in the industry as a result of changes in technology and capital costs as well as labour skills. There has been some deskilling but the decline of the traditional apprenticeship has also accompanied a need for more employees with up-to-date specialist skills.[11]

The electronics small firms, on the other hand, contained a substantial proportion of 'specialists', firms who have deliberately created a product range which gives them a market niche allowing them to compete even with large firms on similar terms. As Keeble et al point out, the extent to which a firm achieves such specialisation is likely to be inversely related to the geographical area of its markets: the more a firm specialises, the less likely the local market can provide adequate demand for its output, other things being equal.

SMALL FIRM–LARGE FIRM RELATIONS IN TWO LOCALITIES

The study of small manufacturing firms investigated their relations with larger enterprises in their localities and looked at larger local enterprises on their policies on dealing with local small firms. Such relations can be regarded as a key element in the level of economic integration in any locality. Most localities will contain a very large number of small enterprises and a handful of large firms and organisations who are very prominent in any analysis of the way the local economy functions.

Daly and McCann (1992, p. 48), for example, have recently estimated that almost nine out of 10 of all businesses in the UK employ five or fewer people, but in 1990 in Sheffield, for instance, the five largest employers had almost 85,000 employees (Curran and Blackburn 1991, p. 29). Put another way, if it is assumed that the typical small business employs five people, then these five organisations were the equivalent of about 17,000 small businesses in employment terms.[12] So while there may be only a handful of large enterprises in a local economy, it can be argued that their impact is potentially large. But although it is possible to estimate the impact of larger organisations in employment or production value terms over some defined geographical area, this may say very little about their connections with other firms in the locality.

Over two out of three small firms in Kingston and Sheffield reported doing business with organisations on a list containing the largest private and public enterprises in their localities. However, closer analysis indicated that many of these links were indirect, that is, the small firms carried out work for customers who were the direct suppliers of the larger enterprises. Most of the links, whether direct or indirect, were one-offs with very few contractually based continuing relationships between the small firms and larger customers. Sectorally, the printing firms reported more trading contacts with local large enterprises than the small electronics firms, a finding consistent with the more general data on small firm trading patterns in the two industries presented above.

There was a particularly wide difference between the electronics firms in the two localities in their links with their local larger enterprises. Small electronics firms in Kingston were much less likely to trade with local larger enterprises than their counterparts in Sheffield. The explanation for this difference appeared to be related to the maturity of the electronics sector in Kingston. The industry's small firms in this part of Britain have developed a wider regional and even national significance in terms of their markets. Their equivalents in Sheffield are less well established and have not gained footholds in markets outside the locality to anything like the same extent. The result is they appear to be much more dependent on each other and on larger, geographically nearby firms.

The qualitative data collected also clearly shows an ambiguity on the part of small-business owners in both printing and electronics about whether they wanted to do business with large enterprises. One major reason was the complaint that large organisations were slow to pay — a much voiced complaint of small business owners in the UK (CBI 1991). Another reason was the fear of becoming over-dependent on a large customer. A small business might receive what, for the larger enterprise, is a small order but which for the small firm could be risky to accept if it meant problems in meeting the needs of other customers or other strains on the firm's resources. More serious still, a small firm could come to rely on orders from the larger firm which, were they to cease for any reason, could again threaten the firm. As several small-business owner respondents pointed out, when they dealt with a large organisation such as British Telecom, they dealt not with the organisation itself but with a particular person. If that person left or was moved or promoted, their links with the organisation could be severed overnight since there was no guarantee that their contact's successor would want to continue the links.

On the other hand, some small-business owners were much more confident about the possibilities of dealing with larger organisations. Small print-firm owners often stressed the personal character of the service they offered: many other small print firms could produce work of as high quality but they also offered person-to-person contact between the owner and the customer. Every order, they claimed, was tailored closely to the customer's wants and they were willing to go to great lengths to meet those wants, often above and beyond what most competitors would or could provide.

Some of the electronics small firm owners also showed confidence in dealing with larger customers but this was often based on more than their belief in the quality service they could provide, though again, like the small print-firm owners, they felt this was a key reason why they were able to survive in the market. They also often stressed the technical expertise embodied in their products which some claimed could not be matched by other firms whatever their size, either because of sheer technological superiority or because it was not worth the while of larger firms to compete in such specialised areas.

Few of the printing or electronics small firms advertised or actively sought customers as a marketing strategy. Instead, most had a fairly stable customer base built up over time which they tried hard to maintain by personalising relations with their contacts in customer firms. Lost customers were more or less balanced by acquiring new customers through word of mouth. This included recommendations of existing customers, suppliers or others in their sector, even competitors perhaps unable to handle a particular order. In effect, what might be called a 'latent network' existed. Businesses were known to each other through everyday transactions but without any special investment of resources by owners. A latent network of this kind has no necessary coincidence with any particular geographical area: modern communications allow a wide variety of geographical 'shapes' to such networks depending on factors such as type of product, market needs and technology.

Proactive marketing strategies, as other research has reported (e.g. Hankinson 1985), such as advertising were thought to be expensive and ineffective and although 'cold calling' might be used where the firm was going through a particularly difficult time or during a recession, owner-managers disliked such strategies because they hinted that the business was not doing well and were impersonal. Thus, the marketing strategies of the small firms were not of the kind which would allow them to easily make contact with larger enterprises whose customer relations are constructed much more on the formal, bureaucratic bases of modern marketing.[13]

What these findings show is that small-firm−large-firm relations can be potentially unstable from the small-firm owners' viewpoint. Clearly, not all business owners find the idea of trading with larger organisations attractive and levels of continuing business links with larger enterprises among these small firms were not anything like as high as the recent literature on subcontracting and its assumed increased importance in the UK economy might imply (Pollert 1991, Blackburn 1992). Most of the manufacturing small businesses in this study did most of their business with other small to medium-sized businesses. Nor should this be surprising once the extreme skewness of the size distribution of businesses in the UK and the vast majority of localities is recalled (Daly and McCann 1991, Hughes 1991).

POLICIES AND STRATEGIES OF LARGE ORGANISATIONS

The above analyses of small-firm−large-firm relations is from the point of view of the small-firm owners but what of the attitudes of large enterprises? The interviews with large organisation representatives in Kingston and Sheffield responsible for purchasing or purchasing policies for their organisations, offered both important insights into dealings with small firms, attitudes to localities and their role in purchasing strategies.

Although a few of the large organisation representatives mentioned that their organisations favoured supporting local industry where possible (these were representatives mainly of public sector organisations), what emerged very strongly and clearly from the interviews was the overriding importance of price, quality and delivery in dealings with suppliers. Policies of purchasing from smaller businesses were almost entirely absent and, indeed, several respondents offered reasons why their organisation would be unlikely to purchase from smaller firms.

Much of the purchasing of large organisations with branches in particular localities is either carried out directly from head office located elsewhere or local purchasing is very strongly influenced by head office policies and procedures. Often these procedures are very bureaucratic with lists of 'preferred suppliers' which, in effect, discriminate against small firms and take little account of locality. There were, of course, exceptions to the above: in all large organisations some proportion of minor purchases are left to the discretion of individual heads of department or lower level managers but whether such purchases go to smaller firms depends on the kinds of purchases. For example, small scale purchases of stationery items are as likely to go to a large stationery supplier as small local suppliers.

Of the three criteria of overriding importance (price, quality and delivery) in large-organisation purchasing behaviour, it might be thought that delivery gave local suppliers some edge in competing with other more distant suppliers. However, delivery followed price and quality and given the efficiency of UK distribution and transport systems, the advantage of geographical proximity though still present, should not be exaggerated.

One problem faced by small electronics firms was the reluctance of larger firms, particularly those involved in defence production, to deal with them because of the importance of 'traceability', that is, the need to have a fully documented, high quality and assured source of supply over a potentially long period. Large firm purchasing representatives felt that small firms could not be relied on in this context and that their customers, the military and other large customers, would have less confidence in them if they used small firms as subcontractors. There was also the administrative problems of dealing with large numbers of suppliers. Several of the large organisations were reducing the number of 'preferred suppliers' and insisting on some form of formal quality assurance which the small firm owner-managers were not enthusiastic about adopting.

For both kinds of small firms in Project Three, large firms were sometimes reluctant to consider them as suppliers because it was felt that a small firm could not cope with the size or complexity of the kind of order the large firm would normally want fulfilled. As one purchasing executive of a large retailer in Kingston put it, if what was wanted was a four-colour print job with a 50,000 print run, there were not, in the respondent's view, many small local printers who could handle an order of this kind.

Small firms did work for the large organisations in the survey but it was often as second-order suppliers, that is, they carried out work for a larger, often medium-sized firms who were the prime contractors. However, the large firm for whom the work was ultimately intended was not 'local'.

The other major way in which small firms might carry out work for larger organisations was as an emergency or overflow order supplier, when a larger organisation, due to some unplanned occurrence, was forced to seek a way of obtaining supplies or services and used Yellow Pages or a similar guide to find a supplier. Here local firms stood a better chance of receiving the order. Sometimes this led to a longer relationship between the small and large firms and several large-firm purchasing officers expressed satisfaction at how well a small firm had carried out an order at short notice. Yet, this did not necessarily lead to repeat orders, or a contract, or convince large-organisation representatives that they ought to revise their views or policies on dealing with small firms in general. Responses indicated an appreciation of the widely accepted strengths of small firms such as their responsiveness, attention to quality and the ability to talk to the person responsible for supervising the order, but this did not go with any real enthusiasm for placing work with small firms.

Overall, therefore, the responses of large-organisation representatives on their dealings with local small firms might be summed up as not very extensive, with small businesses equalling small, often intermittent, purchases. Locality had little overall influence on large organisation purchasing against the criteria of price, quality and delivery. While there was a generalised appreciation of the advantages of dealing with small firms, this did not apparently increase the likelihood of using local small firms as suppliers. In fact, there were several indications that such links might well become even less in the future. For example, as national distribution systems become ever more effective and real levels of distribution costs fall, the advantages of being local decline. The adoption of formal quality standards such as BS 5750 and the rationalisation of supplier lists, will almost certainly work against small firms generally as suppliers in the future.[14]

OWNER-MANAGER LINKAGES WITH LOCAL INSTITUTIONS

Links between firms in localities are not only directly business to business. Other, third parties may perform important functions in promoting higher levels of economic activity by bringing business owners and executives together for business-related and social activities. The obvious examples of such third party institutions are chambers of commerce, enterprise agencies, local educational institutions, local authorities and, more recently, training and enterprise councils. In addition, providers of professional services, banks, accountants and solicitors, for instance, may also help promote links between businesses.

In both the studies of services and manufacturing firms, information was sought on their connections with third party institutions. Data on two of the non-professional service institutions – chambers of commerce and enterprise agencies – showed that, overall, a quarter of the small firms belonged to a chamber of commerce and fewer than one in five had ever sought advice from their local enterprise agency. There were variations between the types of firms and the different localities. For instance, while only 8% of the owners of small garage and vehicle repairers belonged to a chamber of commerce, among the employment, secretarial and training agencies the level was almost 45%. Customers of small garage owners are predominantly private individuals and it might be that garage owners see little advantage to their business in belonging to a forum of other business owners. The employment, secretarial and training agency owners, in contrast, might well see a clear advantage in joining a local organisation of businesses who are the market for their services. Among owners of small manufacturing firms, chamber of commerce membership at an average of 35% was substantially higher than among the services firms overall, although the reasons for this higher level were not immediately apparent.

Localities also showed variations in chamber of commerce membership. For example, in North East Suffolk, just under 19% of firms were members, while in Guildford the level was almost twice as high at 37.5%. Some of the reasons for these locality variations were fairly obvious: some chambers of commerce are much more energetically run than others and in areas such as North East Suffolk the problems of building and maintaining voluntary organisations are much greater where businesses and people are geographically dispersed.

Other locally based institutions which might act to bring together businesses had lower levels of small-business owner membership or use. For instance, rotary clubs and similar bodies attracted less than 5% of all the small business respondents in the two studies. Less than 15% of the owner-managers had ever approached a local educational institution in connection with their business and among the manufacturing firm owner-managers, only 10% had ever approached their local authority on a business-related matter.[15]

These contacts with local institutions can be contrasted with contacts with non-local business-related institutions such as trade associations. Overall, 27.3% of the small business owners were members of trade associations, slightly higher than membership of chambers of commerce but substantially higher than any other local body such as a rotary club or round table. On the other hand, membership of national bodies claiming to represent the interests of small business owners such as the National Federation of Self-Employed and Small Businesses was also low at under 10% overall. In other words, local institutions did no better than national bodies in winning the membership of the small business owners, illustrating the relative weakness of local institutions to provide much of a forum for mutual support and business links.

PROFESSIONAL SERVICES AND LOCAL ECONOMIC INTEGRATION

Providers of professional services – banks, accountants, solicitors, management consultants – are another possible means through which businesses in a locality might be linked to each other. However, evidence that these providers of professional services might also function as a means of bringing businesses together or increasing levels of local economic integration was not strong.

While virtually all the small firms had a bank account and used an accountant, these relations were often narrowly and strictly functional. For instance, only around a third (33.7%) of the small services businesses reported ever seeking advice or help from their bank manager.[16] Among the firms in manufacturing the level was higher: 50% had sought advice from their bank at some time.[17] Conversely, however, a rather higher proportion of the services small firms had sought advice on a business problem from their accountant compared with the small manufacturing firms (76.3% and 63.3% respectively).

Just why such differences occurred is difficult to say but, very speculatively, it might be that the manufacturing firms had larger capital bases (particularly in the form of working capital) and hence maintained closer relations with their banks. This might require their owners to be rather more skilled at managing finance than the owners of the services firms and this greater familiarity with the financial aspects of the business meant they did not find it as necessary to use accountants as a source of advice so frequently.

One clear finding was that providers of professional services such as banks, accountants and solicitors[18] were not seen as particularly knowledgeable about the respondents' industries or businesses and, hence, they were regarded as of limited use as sources of advice. Further, respondents judged the fees charged for professional services as 'high' and as a result often said they thought twice about using such services. While a handful of respondents reported that they had made links with new customers or other businesses through their accountant or other providers of professional services, the evidence did not suggest this was common.

CRITICAL INCIDENTS AND LOCAL ECONOMY AND COMMUNITY LINKS

One criticism which can be levelled against the kind of data presented above is that it over-concentrates on routine links with others such as customers, providers of professional services and memberships of chambers of commerce. Small businesses are, however, not always or even perhaps commonly, based on routine economic behaviours. Often they are beset by insecurities resulting from the kind of role they occupy in an economy, that is, as marginal providers of goods and services, easily made unstable by the loss of a customer and with much less ability to control their environment or plan their futures, than larger enterprises.

A further criticism of the emphasis on business-related links in the above data might be that it ignores the potential of non-business institutions such as social and community associations, kinship and friendship groupings as means by which businesses and their owners may be bonded with the local economy. The golf club, for example, is often stereotyped as a common venue for doing business locally. In short, the links constituted by the community as a social framework need to be examined for the role they might play in linking businesses in a local economy.

In Project Two, 45 of the 350 owner-managers of small services firms interviewed in 1990 were re-interviewed in 1991 using a critical incident approach. This approach, as the label implies, suggests that most areas of social behaviour, whatever their context, will offer examples of 'critical incidents' or unanticipated, non-routine events which have the potential to disrupt the normal day-to-day patterns of the business. Research based on critical incidents or analogous notions has been used widely in social research ranging from the study of helicopter crashes to the growth process of the small enterprise (Flanagan 1954, Gibb and Davis 1990, Easterby-Smith et al 1991, p. 83).[19] Focusing on such incidents, it is argued, can produce evidence of behaviour, interactions and attitudes not revealed by other research methods and can investigate linkages between the business and the wider environment and/or can add substantially to the interpretations generated by more conventional research on such linkages.

In this project, owner-managers were asked if any of five possible critical incidents had occurred to them or their businesses over the previous two years. The incidents were: losing or gaining a major customer; an event in the owner's family or personal life which had a serious impact on the business (such as the birth of a child, the break-up of a marriage or the serious illness of a spouse or partner); losing or gaining a partner or fellow director in the business; making a major investment in the business (such as the purchase of capital equipment); or any contacts with the local authority which had potentially serious implications for the business.

A large proportion of the respondents had experienced one or more examples of critical incidents of the above kind and were willing to talk through their experiences.

The interviewer encouraged the respondent to talk as freely as they wished in relating the incident but used probes at appropriate points to ensure that information was offered on the kind and extent of external contacts used by the owner-manager in their attempts to cope with the problems associated with the incident.[20]

What emerged very clearly from owner-manager narratives of the incidents and their attempts at resolving the problems associated with them, was the lack of resorting to external contacts. Even where the incident involved finance or other aspects, where talking to a professional advisor would appear obvious in attempting to resolve the problems connected with the incident, there was often a surprising failure to use such sources of help. Kinship and friendship links were mentioned but usually only as limited sources of emotional support rather than as sources of practical help or advice. Other social groupings such as those based on leisure activities or religion or charitable activities, also played very little part in incident resolution.

A careful analysis of the tape recorded accounts of the critical incidents offered by owner-managers suggested several reasons for the lack of resort to any extensive links with others in business, kinship or social groupings outside the enterprise. First, as so much previous research has indicated (Stanworth and Gray 1991, Ch. 7, passim) a dominant psychological characteristic frequently displayed by small enterprise owner-managers is a strong emphasis on independence and autonomy: running the business is a key way of exemplifying these values and often the prime motivation for their starting or buying the business in the first place. To go outside the enterprise, therefore, for help or advice in resolving a problem, even a major problem, might be interpreted by both the owner-manager and outsiders as showing an over-dependence on others. The data from the study offered several examples of owner-managers withstanding high levels of stress rather than going to others outside the business for help. Spouses or partners, close relatives or friends might be told about the problems associated with the incident, not in order to seek advice, but to allow them to act as stress relievers and to reward the respondent for the independence and fortitude they were displaying in solving their problems.

Second, business contacts, owners of other businesses, customers and suppliers, employees, etc. were also often kept at a distance in attempts at resolving the incident. In some instances, the reasons for this were as expected. For example, if a major customer had been lost, the owner-manager might feel that this reflected badly on the way the business was being run or might suggest the business was in trouble and risk losing other customers or supplier credit. Professional advisers were often seen as not knowledgeable enough to be sources of sound advice and their fees were sometimes regarded as offering poor value for the advice they were likely to offer.

Third, the owner-managers often led rather limited social lives. A major reason for this was the sheer number of hours they devoted to their businesses. Among the 350 service sector small-business owners, for example, almost two out of three (63.3%) reported working more than 50 hours a week. Most were married or in stable personal relationships and a high proportion had children still living at home. In short, work and family commitments made it very unlikely they would have the time or energy to spend a lot of time socialising with others outside the family even if there was some chance that contacts of this kind might have a pay-off for the business.

Overall, what came across very strongly in the analysis of the data collected from this third project was the way in which so many of the owner-managers appeared to adopt a kind of 'fortress enterprise' mentality in relation to their businesses. The business was their major form of personal expression outside, or even above, their non-economic lives. It was a demonstration of their autonomy, of their ability to stand on their own two feet and show that they controlled their own destinies. Thus it would not be surprising if their links with the locality in economic and community terms were attenuated. Such links exist, of course, since every business has to have suppliers, customers and connections with institutions such as banks, accountants and government departments such as the Inland Revenue, but the levels, the intensiveness and the extensiveness of such links can vary greatly. What the evidence from the critical incidents project shows, in agreement with the evidence from the other two projects reported in this paper, is that small businesses and their owners have restricted, as well as widely differently shaped, patterns of connections with the wider economy. But whether we are examining routine, day-to-day contacts, or those associated with a critical incident, the varying connections of small business owners do not indicate approximations to the closely integrated local economy which is the implicit foundation of so many discussions both of how small firms articulate with the wider economy and of patterns of economic linkages in geographical areas.

CONCLUSIONS

In this paper, data from three research projects has been marshalled to examine the ways in which small and large firms participate in local economies. The main issues which the analysis addresses are: to what extent it is useful to talk of a 'local economy' in the late 20th century; what are the ways in which businesses — small and large — link with each other within their immediate geographical vicinity; and what might be the trends in the development of local economic patterns?

On the first of the issues, the extent to which it is sensible or useful to talk of a 'local economy', the question is how does the economy in the kind of specified geographical area such as a local authority area or a city such as Sheffield approximate to a conceptualisation in which

> ...it should be conceived as a social and economic whole. That is to say, there are close inter-relationships between the different social, political and economic spheres, and the functioning of one, say the economic, is shaped by the functioning and organisation of the others

> (Pyke et al 1990, p. 2)[21]

Emphases of the above kind were common in studies in the pre-1980s (See e.g. Dennis et al 1956, Stacey 1960, Frankenberg 1966)[22] but have received a considerable boost recently by the return to seeing spatial elements as important in understanding the economy. The view has been that a local economy should not be seen as an aggregate of geographically proximate economic units but as an organic whole drawing on social and other local networks to function effectively in ways which mark it off clearly from other, similar geographically coherent economic groupings.

None of the seven local economies, on the evidence from the studies, resembles or even approximates at all closely to such an ideal type. Rather, these economies show a range of fragmented, ill-defined economic patterns contingent upon particular types of economic activities and the management strategies of the small-business owners and large enterprises in their relations with the wider environment. Among the small businesses (the most numerous economic units in any 'local economy') owner-managers' values, self-definitions and attitudes to the wider environment add up to a kind of self-imposed distancing of the enterprise from the wider economy. Even for those types of business anchored in the local economy by the market for their product or service, the focus was on a set of functional relationships with customers, suppliers and professional services while their involvements in the business and social community through institutions such as chambers of commerce was limited. For many of the small businesses, even their core market relations did not impose any real need for a local focus to their activities since a good part of their trading relations extended well beyond what might be seen as a local market.

In other words the findings from the three projects suggest that the patterns of substantial relations in which the small firms and their owners are involved are extremely variable and do not coincide at all closely with notions of the 'local economy' constituted as formal relations in a wide range of theorising and research. A similar point can be made about the findings on the large organisations' relations with the wider environment.

For the larger enterprises, even those most closely connected with the locality (such as those whose headquarters were in the local economy studied), locality appeared to be relatively unimportant in their decision-making on relations with other businesses. For them the strict economic criteria of the market − price, quality and delivery − dictated attitudes and links with the wider economy. Loyalty to locality emerged only faintly, if at all, after the impact of these criteria. Links with local small firms were not strong not only because economic constraints of these kinds dictated against such links but also because the large enterprises demonstrated mixed attitudes concerning the capabilities of small firms in meeting their needs. These doubts were matched, on the other side of these potential small-firm−large-firm relationships, by small-firm owner-managers' doubts about doing business with larger enterprises. So while links between businesses in the locality existed and many small firms' markets were overwhelmingly within the locality, it would go against the evidence to suggest that such links and markets indicate a highly integrated local economy with a clear identity in the minds of those involved which overlapped with other non-economic social, community and political networks.[23] The notion that any of the localities investigated might resemble anything approaching an 'industrial district' as described by proponents of the revival of integrated local economies, appeared unlikely in the extreme.

On the final issue addressed by the paper, the trends revealed by the results from the three projects on the likely future of the local economy, the data suggested that the decline of the local economy is continuing and even accelerating. Historically, the case for well-developed integrated local economies has been made in many studies of towns and areas dominated by a single industry or business − the engineering industry in the Black Country and its links with the car industry in the West Midlands and clothing manufacturing in places such as Nottingham, Leicester and the East End of London. Similarly, the dominance of places such as St Helens by Pilkington Glass or Teesside by ICI have also been offered as examples of the ways in which a local community could be integrated economically and socially (Cooke 1989, Harloe et al 1990). All these examples have lost their force as arguments for the existence of such well-defined local economies in the 1970s and 1980s, as restructuring and the internationalisation of the economy has diluted these former sharply delineated, local patterns of economic integration.

The services firms in two of the projects exemplify small firms in what is now the core of the UK economy, the services sector (Graham et al 1989, Coates 1991, Ch. 2, passim). It might be broadly argued that even allowing for exceptions, it is in those areas such as health and education and financial and business services, the least tied to local economies, that have seen the most rapid expansion while many of the more locality-bound services such as small scale retailing, have shown either negative or much slower rates of growth (Coates 1991, p. 65, Howe et al, 1992, p. 42). It might be surmised, then, that these trends in the core sector of the economy do not indicate much of a prospect of a strengthening of levels of local economic integration or more clearly defined local economies through the activities of small firms.

The small manufacturing firms show a similar trend. To the extent that manufacturing based on traditional technologies is declining, to be replaced by firms employing more recent forms of technology, locality links might well again become weaker. The small electronics firms in one of the studies reported in this paper appear to support this conjecture. The longer established, more confident small electronics firms were the most likely to trade outside their local areas: as more firms approximate to this pattern this trend is likely to continue. Even among the small printing firms, traditionally one of the types of economic activities most closely tied to locality, there were indications that new technology, increased capital costs and new skills specialisation would lead to firms producing a narrower range of products and, hence, having to seek wider geographical markets.

The larger enterprises in two of the localities examined offered little indication that their activities would become more locally focused. Indeed, changes in corporate practices such as centralisation of procurement and preferred supplier lists coupled with a greater emphasis on formal quality standards, appeared to work against greater integration into the local economy. Counter views which have received a lot of attention in recent years such as the suggestion that more and more firms will turn to just-in-time and local sourcing along the lines practised by Japanese companies, received little support from the data presented. Of course, this might reflect the types of activities covered and other limitations of the research designs but just-in-time arguments are most closely associated with manufacturing and, as pointed out above, manufacturing is now only a relatively small part of the UK economy. Some of the large organisations interviewed for the research were in manufacturing and others were in services, but in neither was there anything but the most limited indications of policies emphasising local sourcing. Overall, therefore, these large firms' strategies do not offer much confidence for a suggestion that local economies are likely to become more integrated.

This paper and the three projects upon whose findings it is based, can only offer limited answers to the above questions. It would take a much more comprehensive study, covering a much wider range of localities and sectors of the economy to offer a more confident analysis. But in taking a ground level view of small and large businesses' economic activities and their relations with locality, it tenders a contrasting view to the great majority of discussion and research on these topics which adopts a macro, top down perspective. Interestingly, this ground level view makes many of the fashionable spatial arguments on the significance of the local economy in the UK economy look questionable and suggests that many of the heady debates they have engendered need a similar bringing down to earth.

NOTES

1. Rainnie (1989) is a notable exception since he attempts to combine an analysis of the internal workings of the small enterprise with a theory of its relations with the economy at the macro-level. Others have been interested in the role of the small enterprise at the macro-level but have not been very concerned with the small enterprise itself and have treated it as a kind of unopened 'black box' unit of analysis.
2. The references cited suggest that local authority economic policies in the UK have not been particularly effective overall. But these sources and others often offer examples of local authorities which have allegedly been effective, such as the former Greater London Council and Sheffield City Council, but from the vantage point of 1992 it is difficult to see how much real impact these authorities had on their local economies especially taking into account central government strategies which have reduced the power of local authorities to fund local economic strategies on any scale.
3. Further details of the reasoning behind the selection of the types of enterprise, the localities, the methods of sample construction and response rates are given in the Appendix in Curran et al (1991b).
4. Further details of both the sample, its construction, response rates and the industries and the localities are provided in Curran and Blackburn (1991).
5. The 15–85% division of small businesses between manufacturing and services is based on the calculations drawn from the secondary analysis of data on the owners of small businesses (employing between 1–24 people) in the general household by Curran and Burrows (1988). Printing is usually classed as 'manufacturing' in official statistics such as the Census of Production although it is quite possible to argue that it might also be seen as part of the business services sector.
6. Further findings from the projects are reported more fully in Curran and Blackburn (1991), Curran et al (1991a, b).
7. The industrial districts thesis is one variant on this argument but the links between small firms and large in localities is a long-standing theme more generally, particularly

historically. It is one of the arguments of this paper to suggest that such historically established links of these kinds are disappearing in the UK.

8. The definition of 'local' which emerged in the interviews with the owner-managers is, as the examples here show, somewhat variable. Interviewers were instructed to use ten miles from the place of business as a definition of 'local' where asked or where this appeared to be useful as a guide to respondents in forming answers to questions on trading patterns. But many respondents' answers indicated that arbitrary definitions of this kind did not fit their notions of the markets their businesses served. However, for the purposes of calculating the proportions of businesses carried out locally and over wider areas, the arbitrary definition was used.

9. Some of the employment agencies in the sample had an international market for their services, having built a business supplying labour to the construction industry in the Middle East, and did relatively little business within their locality.

10. It is not simply that small businesses in services and the services sector as a whole are expanding and especially in newer areas such as information-based activities, but small businesses in older areas of services are also in decline. This is most obvious in small scale retailing. The number of single outlet retailers declined by more than a third over the 16 year period from 1971 to 1987. In 1971, single outlet retailers were responsible for almost 43% of retail trade turnover: by 1987 this had fallen to 28.3% (Howe 1992, p. 107–108). Small retailers are a traditional small business of the kind most likely to be linked to local markets and it is these which are declining while many of the newer kinds of small services businesses are less likely to have a geographically restricted market.

11. Further details and statistics on the printing industry are provided in Appendix 1 of Curran and Blackburn (1991).

12. In fact, this assumption is very conservative since businesses employing up to five people accounted for 87.7% of all businesses in the UK in 1989 (Daly and McCann 1991, p. 48). Given the extreme skewness of the size distribution of businesses measured by employment, the average size of a business in employment terms is well below five people.

13. There were differences between the printing and electronics firms in marketing behaviour. The electronics firms, for example, relied more on information being transmitted through trade magazines and on trade exhibitions as ways of showing their products to prospective customers. But neither of these methods were major marketing tools or mentioned by all owner-managers when asked how they sought customers.

14. A clear example of the patterns that may well become much more widespread is reported in Curran and Blackburn (1991, p. 87) where a large firm is quoted as having reduced its supplier list from 3,500 to 1,500 firms in a drive to cutting costs, using long-term contracts to a greater extent and emphasising quality. Another respondent pointed out that one major reason for reductions was changes in industrial relations. In the early 1970s it was normal to dual and even triple source supplies to assure continued supplies to avoid disruptions due to disputes but this was no longer necessary.

15. This question was not put to the owner-managers of the small service sector firms in the same form but there were indications that the level of contact with local authority economic development units or other departments on business-related matters was as low as among small manufacturing firms.

16. Since the question asked respondents if they had ever sought advice or help from their bank manager, this might have been a single occasion which had occurred some time ago, perhaps even several years prior to the interviews.

17. Data is also available on the frequency of small manufacturing firm owner-managers' contacts with their banks. Almost a quarter had not had any contact with their bank manager over the previous year, 38.9% had seen the bank manager once or twice and a further 37.4% had visited the bank manager three or more times. It should be added, however, that not all the visits were initiated by the owner-managers: in

several instances, respondents made it clear that the contacts were made by the bank to monitor the performance of the business.

18. The level of using solicitors as sources of business advice was slightly lower than using accountants for this reason (67.6% and 74.4% respectively). Again, the question was in the form of whether the respondent had ever used a solicitor for business advice and the qualitative data indicated that while most had used a solicitor in this way at some time, they had done so only very infrequently.

19. The phrase 'critical incident' may suggest that the event is usually of a 'negative' kind, but although critical incidents are often unforeseen crises they may also be much more positive events such as the purchase of new equipment for expansion or a move to larger premises. What is 'critical' here is that the event is likely to produce the need for decisions and strategies not employed previously in the business.

20. A fuller account of this project is provided in *Small Firms and Networks: Constructs, Methodological Strategies and Some Preliminary Findings*, ESRC Centre for Research on Small Service Sector Enterprises, Kingston Polytechnic, 1991.

21. These authors are here offering a conceptualisation of the most recent radical invocation of the integrated local economy, the industrial district but it may be taken to offer an ideal type of a more general integrated local economy.

22. It should be stressed, however, that the notion of the integrated social, economic and political community clearly demarcated from the wider society was a matter of considerable debate even in this early period (see e.g. the summary of this debate in Lee and Newby (1983, Ch. 4, passim).

23. While the extent of such non-economic networks was not investigated by the present research projects, there is clearly a parallel debate in the literature on whether it is sensible to talk of 'a local community' in many parts of Britain (see e.g. Cooke 1989). The background data collected for the present studies did not indicate any strong community networks which inter-related with the economic relations investigated though there were often hints of a definite, if ill-defined, cultural identification with the area in some of the localities such as Sheffield. In others, on the other hand, such as Islington in London, the absence of any sense of local identity among the small business owners was very apparent.

ACKNOWLEDGEMENTS

Part of the data reported in this paper is derived from research carried out as part of the Economic and Social Research Council's Small Business Research Initiative. We wish to acknowledge the financial contributions from the Economic and Social Research Council, Barclays Bank, Commission of the European Communities (DG XXIII), Department of Employment and the Rural Development Commission. Any views expressed do not necessarily reflect those of the sponsoring organisations. Other data is taken from a research project carried out for the Midland Bank and the authors would like to acknowledge the financial support of the Bank for the project. Again, the authors are solely responsible for the interpretation of the data collected.

REFERENCES

Amin A. (1989) Flexible specialisation and small firms in Italy: myths and realities, Antipode, Vol. 21, No. 1, pp. 13–34.
Bannock G. and Albach H. (1991) Small Business Policy in Europe, Anglo-German Foundation for the Study of Industrial Society, London.
Blackburn R.A. (1992) Subcontracting, What is it and Where? in The New Entrepreneurs, eds Felstead A. and Leighton P., Kogan Page, London.
Bolton Report (1971) Report of the Committee of Inquiry on Small Firms, Cmnd 4811, HMSO, London.
British Printing Industries Federation (1991) Notes on the Printing Industries, May, British Printing Industries Federation, London.

Burrows R. and Curran J. (1989) Sociological research on service sector small businesses: Some Conceptual Considerations, Work, Employment and Society, Vol. 3, No. 4, pp. 527–539.

CBI (1991) Late Payment of Trade Debts, A Survey of Small and Medium Sized Businesses, Confederation of British Industry, London.

Coates D. (1991) Running the Country, Hodder and Stoughton in association with the Open University, London.

Cochrane A. (1990) Recent Developments in Local Authority Economic Policy in Local Economic Policy, ed Campbell M., Cassell Educational, London.

Cooke P. (Ed) (1989) Localities, the Changing Face of Urban Britain, Unwin Hyman, London.

Coulson A. (1990) Evaluating Local Economic Policy, in Local Economic Policy, ed Campbell M. Cassell Educational, London.

Curran J. (1990) Rethinking economic structure: exploring the role of the small firm and self-employment in the British economy, Work, Employment and Society, special issue, May, pp. 125–146.

Curran J. and Blackburn R.A. (1991) Small Firms and Local Economic Networks, Relations Between Small and Large Firms in Two Localities, Small Business Research Centre, Kingston Polytechnic, Kingston-upon-Thames.

Curran J., Blackburn R.A. and Woods A. (1991) Profiles of the Small Enterprise in the Service Sector, ESRC Centre for Research on Small Service Sector Enterprises, Kingston Polytechnic, Kingston upon Thames.

Curran J. and Burrows R. (1988) Enterprise in Britain: A National Profile of Small Business Owners and the Self-Employed, Small Business Research Trust, London.

Curran J., Jarvis R., Blackburn R.A. and Black S. (1991) Small Firms and Networks: Constructs, Methodological Strategies and Some Preliminary Findings, Paper presented at the 14th National Small Firms' Policy and Research Conference, Blackpool, November.

Daly M. and McCann A. (1992) How Many Small Firms?, Employment Gazette, February, pp. 47–51.

Dennis N. Henriques F. and Slaughter C. (1956) Coal is Our Life, Eyre and Spottiswoode, London.

Easterby-Smith M., Thorpe R. and Lowe A. (1991) Management Research, An Introduction, Sage, London.

Flanagan J.C. (1954) The critical incident technique, Psychological Bulletin, Vol. 54, No. 4, pp. 327–356.

Frankenberg R. (1966) Communities in Britain, Penguin Books, Harmondsworth.

Gibb A.A. and Davies L. (1990) In pursuit of frameworks for the development of the small business, International Small Business Journal, Vol. 9, No. 1, pp. 15–31.

Goodwin M. (1989) The politics of locality in Politics in Transition, eds Cochrane A. and Anderson J. Sage with the Open University, London.

Graham N., Beatson M. and Wells W. (1989) 1977 to 1987: A decade of service, Employment Gazette, January, pp. 45–54.

Hankinson A. (1985) Pricing Behaviour, A Study of Pricing Behaviour of Dorset-Hampshire Small Engineering Firms, 1983–1985, ICMA and Dorset Institute of Higher Education, London and Poole.

Hammett C., McDowell L. and Sarre P. (1989) Restructuring Britain, The Changing Social Structure, Sage in association with the Open University, London.

Harloe M., Pickvance C. and Urry J. (Eds) (1990) Place, Policy and Politics, Do Localities Matter, Unwin Hyman, London.

Hirst P. and Zeitlin J. (1989) Reversing Industrial Decline? Industrial Structure and Policy in Britain and Her Competitors, Berg, Oxford.

Howe W.S. (1992) Retailing Management, Macmillan Educational, London.

Hudson R. (1988) Labour market changes and new forms of work in 'old' industrial regions, in Restructuring Britain, Uneven Development: Cities and Regions in Transition, A Reader, eds Massey D. and Allen J. Hodder and Stoughton, London.

Hughes A. (1991) UK Small Businesses in the 1980s: Continuity and Change, Regional Studies, Vol. 25, No. 5, pp. 471–479.

Keeble D., Bryson J. and Wood P. (1991) Entrepreneurship and Flexibility in Business Services: the Rise of Small Management Consultancy and Market Research Firms in the United Kingdom, Paper presented to the National Small Firms' Policy and Research Conference, Blackpool, November.

Lee D. and Newby H. (1983) The Problem of Sociology, Hutchinson, London.

Martin R. (1988) Industrial capitalism in transition: the contemporary reorganisation of the British space-economy, in Uneven Development, Cities and Regions in Transition, eds Massey D. and Allen J. Hodder and Stoughton with the Open University, London.

Mason C. (1991) Spatial Variations in Enterprise: the geography of new firm formation in Deciphering the Enterprise Culture, Entrepreneurship, Petty Capitalism and the Restructuring of Britain, ed Burrows R., Routledge, London.

Massey D. and Allen J. (Eds) (1988) Uneven Development, Cities and Regions in Transition, Hodder and Stoughton with the Open University, London.

National Economic Development Council (1988) Electronics Industry Sector, London, NEDO, June.

National Economic Development Council (1990) Electronics for Growth and Competitiveness, London, NEDO, March.

National Economic Development Council (1991) Electronics: Strengthening the United Kingdom's Technological Base, London, NEDO, May.

Piore M. and Sabel C. (1984) The Second Industrial Divide, Basic Books, New York.

Pollert A. (Ed) (1991) Farewell to Flexibility? Blackwell, Oxford.

Pyke F., Beccattini G. and Sengenberger W. (eds) (1990) Industrial Districts and Inter-Firm Co-Operation, International Labour Organisation, Geneva.

Rainnie A. (1989) Industrial Relations in Small Firms, Small Isn't Beautiful, Routledge, London.

Sayer A. (1984) Method in Social Science: A Realist Approach, Hutchinson, London.

Stacey M. (1960) Tradition and Change, A Study of Banbury, Oxford University Press, Oxford.

Stanworth J. and Gray C. (Eds) (1991) Bolton Twenty Years On, The Small Firm in the 1990s, Paul Chapman, London.

Urry J. (1990) Conclusion: Places and Policies, in Place, Policy and Politics, Do Localities Matter?, eds Harloe M. Pickvance C. and Urry J., Unwin and Hyman, London.

7.

THE INDUSTRIAL DIVIDE in SERVICES:
Technological Innovation, Co-operation and Competition in Small Employment, Design, Plant Hire Firms and Garages

Stephen Lloyd-Smith, Keith Dickson and Adrian Woods

INTRODUCTION

It is apparent to the casual observer that small advertising and design companies differ from small garages in obvious ways, and that small Plant Hire firms are clearly different to small employment and training agencies. Differences between the fixing of vehicles and the training of employees are easily grasped.

However beneath the readily apparent contrasts are a set of major contrasts which are much less obvious, though of greater theoretical and even practical importance. These have to do with contrasting levels of trust, reciprocity and individualised competitiveness. Although there have been parallel findings in the study of changing farming economies and societies, we suspect that our research may be the first to have identified a pattern in our four selected industries. Part of the reason that the pattern does not appear to have been spotted earlier may be because it cannot be dealt with adequately through conventional competitive economic models of the behaviour of the firm. Had garages and plant hire fallen within a rural industrial classification, then their high trust and therefore somewhat rural qualities might have been picked up by models in rural sociology. As we will show later, none of our sectors really conform to Fordist and post-Fordist models either. For the most part then, existing models seem to be just as blind as common sense to the features which are the central focus of this paper.

A new theoretical framework will therefore be put forward which enables a set of fundamental comparisons to be made. This will be developed to explain the sharp 'Industrial Divide in Services', found between distinct high trust, and low trust sectors and their markets. This paper thus offers explanations for the very different social forms which private, nominally 'free' markets can take. Some are normatively self-regulated by collective consent among producers; other equally private and equally free markets operate without customary rules and standards of behaviour; they are anomic, that is, thoroughly individualised. A case will thus be presented for looking at markets from outside the discipline of economics, not as the net outcome of individual needs and preferences, but primarily as social systems. A new classification of managerial strategy is also put forward.

We began our research by posing five linked questions: (1) What does it mean to be 'technologically innovative' in the service sector and what determines the use of new technologies among small service enterprises? (2) How do selected, contrasting service sectors, operate in practice; what is the social organisation of their markets? (3) What is the relationship between different forms of market organisation, and the owners' ideologies and idioms? (4) What norms constrain and regulate their relations with other firms in and beyond their trade? (5) Is there any relationship between the psychological disposition of individual design, employment agency, garage and plant hire company owners, and the way these firms do business?

These questions were posed in order to make some evaluation of the relative importance and research power of a number of rather different kinds of model, including individual and psychological, sociological, and technologically-determined models. On the whole it is the second of these which this paper concentrates on. Although further analysis of the data continues, the sociological approach has proved successful, and may contribute towards a synthetic and formal account of petit-capitalism in Britain in the 1990s. What emerges is an industrial great divide separating two very different kinds of petit-capitalism. The psychological pre-dispositions of the owners explain only a small part of the contrast.

What does it mean to be 'technologically innovative' in the service sector? 'Generic' information technologies, such as fax, PCs, photocopiers, ansaphone machines, standard software, have spread throughout the four sectors selected for this study: advertising and design, employment agencies, plant hire, and garages. So in both 'blue collar' and 'white collar' industries, conventional office IT is now commonplace and familiar. Generic IT is no longer novel. On the other hand, sector specific technologies, for example CAD and PC-linked 'smart' photocopiers in advertising and design; computerised engine tuning and diagnostic equipment in garages; interactive disc training in employment agencies, and high technology construction equipment in plant hire, have spread much more unevenly within each sector. Many confident users of generic IT have not bought specialist technologies.

There is however a sharp distinction between, on the one side of an industrial divide, most advertising and design firms and employment agencies, and on the other, virtually all garage and plant hire firms. The first group operate in a competitive, low-trust, or isolated idiom and the second group operate in a co-operative, high-trust or solidary idiom. Moreover there are further important differences which distinguish firms within each sector. Differences here help to explain the fate of specialist technologies.

The term 'idiom' has been chosen carefully, because the ideology which an owner-manager may use to describe the way she or he conducts business may not correspond directly with what happens in practice.

Some classification of the way small firms operate is nevertheless useful. A basic distinction is drawn between those 'high-trust' companies which welcome, and those 'low-trust' companies which are wary of, links with other companies. In the sector descriptions which are given later, 'Type A' companies are those which operate in a competitive, low-trust and isolated idiom and 'Type B' operate in a co-operative, high-trust and socially solidary idiom.

There is a case for further dividing these into sub-categories, A1, A2, B1, B2 etc., largely according to the level of specialisation involved in each firm, and according to corresponding difference in the nuances given by the operator to the respective dominant industrial idioms.

Throughout the project we have thus focused on the social organisation of small firms' economies. A major gain has been a growing appreciation that in order to understand small business in practice, it is important to look at the detail which orthodox economic modelling of competitive behaviour may be missing. For example, as Curran has consistently argued, not all small firms have competitors in any case; so being small need not mean being vulnerable to intense price competition. This runs against the convention that only large firms have monopolies.

It should also be noted that small companies such as repair garages, which have scores of very close competitors, invariably co-operate with them. So while economic theory dictates that the more homogeneous firms are, the more fiercely competitive they ought to be, this is not the case with garages, which are generally embedded in a network of mutual favours and obligations. We therefore question the adequacy of conventional economic models.

But by adopting the Type A and Type B distinction, our analysis also highlights some problems in another theoretical approach. A re-classification of business activity has been attempted by industrial sociologists like Piore and Sable (1986), and Abernathy (1982). Debate has ranged around 'Fordist' versus 'post-Fordist' and 'post-modern' organisational structures, and on 'mass production', versus 'flexible specialisation' and the 'unit of one'. Unfortunately, the debate has concentrated mainly on manufacturing firms. Our sectors do not readily fit into this scheme. For example, if you are prepared to accept, qua Sable, that a firm with many intricate horizontal links is 'post-Fordist' (and that an isolated subjugated and competitive producer is working within a 'Fordist' setting), then our garages and plant hire firms − which have self-evidently not been considered exciting enough to attract much academic attention − far from being old-fashioned and dull, would have to be defined as 'highly post-Fordist', (or even 'pre-Fordist'). They have many links. They are highly flexible: any car, any hire-job can be accommodated by utilising links in a garage's or a plant hirer's 'industrial district'. One Garage in Nottingham could name forty competitors within a couple of square miles. Above, all garages carry virtually no inventories which makes them a classic case of just-in-time production. The variation in the product is so extreme that they could not possibly hold spares for all the varied makes, models and repair tasks which they are required to do.

Under Sabel's classification, the treatment of design and employment 'agencies' (*sic*) is also somewhat paradoxical. These companies at least partly owe their existence to the respective breakdown of old Fordist, integrated (that is in-house) design offices and of centrally bargained, national (that is unionised) labour markets. By this token, design agencies and employment agencies ought to welcome or seek out post-Fordist horizontal links in profusion. Yet while these firms have unavoidable links with suppliers, they are untrusting and fiercely competitive in their stance towards other designers. In other words, though apparently 'post-Fordist', it is difficult to distinguish their business ideologies from those of old 'hard-nosed' component suppliers within the 'old' car industry of the 1960s and 1970s.

In short, these features cannot be made to fit any of the familiar economic and socio-logical theories. New, grounded theories of the social organisation of the economy must be developed.

Simmel

Type A/ Type B distinction can be modelled by using Georg Simmel's formal theory of groups, developed at the turn of the century. We can derive a conclusion from Simmel to the effect that A-Type companies are forced to act in the competitive idiom because most of their links are dyadic − simple, specific relationships between pairs. Type Bs exhibit high trust because their linkages are multiplex, multipurpose relationships, among many. A longer discussion of reciprocity and competition already appears in an earlier working paper. However as our evidence shows a high degree of fit with Simmel's predictions, it is worth recalling Simmel's approach here.

Simmel's thinking is purely formal and ahistoric: stripped of any reference to the persons or other entities involved in a relationship; regardless of the subject matter of the relationship, and regardless of historical period.

This ahistorical quality is both a source of strength and of weakness. It should apply to our firms formally quite regardless of the technology, sector, size, locality, personality and so on. But it takes no account of historically specific conditions. For example, Simmel cannot be used to explain why different industrial linkages take dyadic, triadic or larger forms in particular circumstances. Casson (1991) makes a similar concession. (Casson also freely admits that economics has lagged behind other disciplines, by cling-ing to the concept of individual economic agency. However, he claims that because economics is the 'imperial social science', by building sociality into new models, econo-mists stand the best chance of successfully popularising the concept that markets have a social basis.)

The pathways taken by different industries deserve an historically specific treatment, and this may prove to be complementary to a formal treatment of it. Nevertheless Simmel would not have welcomed this as he was distinctly anti-historical in much of his writing.

Coser (1971) offers a concise description of Simmel's approach, explaining that,

> [Simmel] uncovers the new properties that emerge from the forms of association among individuals, properties that cannot be derived from characteristics of the individuals involved.
>
> Because [dyads depend] on only two participants, the withdrawal of one would destroy the whole: 'A dyad depends on each of its two elements alone — in its death though not in its life: for its life it needs both, but for its death, only one.
>
> Hence the dyad does not attain the superpersonal life which, in all other groups creates among its members a sense of constraint ... The dependence of the whole on each partner is obvious; in all other groups duties and responsibilities can be delegated, but not in the dyad, where each participant is immediately and directly responsible for any collective action ...

The source of instability is explained formally, thus:

> When a dyad is transformed into a triad, the apparently insignificant fact that one member has been added actually brings about a major qualitative change ...

And the source of stability?

> The dyad relies on immediate reciprocity, but the triad can impose its will upon one member through the formation of a coalition between the two others ...
>
> (Coser 1971, pp. 184–185, see also Wolf 1950)

In other words, from a simple, but elegant, formal perspective, triads and larger groups are firstly more resistant to destructive behaviour by a single member — they are comparatively immune, purely on the basis of numbers; and secondly, by implication, the transgression of a social norm within a triad can be censured through the mobilisation of the majority in defence of that norm. Deviants can be controlled in larger groups in a way that is just not possible within the dyad.

What is interesting about this argument is firstly that it sensitises us to the relative intensities and instabilities of different kinds of inter-firm links. A contrast exists between the dyad (narrow, deep and intensive) and the triad and larger groups (exhibiting 'superpersonal' constraints and the power to ostracise). The greatest instabilities occur in the dyad, which, in Simmel's memorable words, 'for its life it needs both, but for its death, only one' (Wolf 1950) than to the triad with its 'super-personal' constraints on the actions of each member.

As we will see later, Simmel's analysis of groups can be used to explain the contrast between Type A firms on one side of the industrial divide, and type B firms on the other. Ample quantitative and qualitative evidence of this divide is given later.

Research design

First a note on research design. 'Sector' was expected to be significant for the rather obvious reason that some techniques and technologies would be specific to each sector. But we also wanted to look at the interaction between technology and the kind of market which each sector inhabits, the predominance of small or large firms within particular sectors, and sector-specific industrial cultures, customs and practices.

On the basis of some of our earlier work in high technology manufacturing, we expected that firms might develop inter-firm links and networks, as a means of minimizing uncertainty, and maximising access to various resources. This drew on Hakansson (1987) and others. Firms which had links were expected to be better off for a number of reasons. Links among users (i.e. with colleagues and competitors) help raise awareness of market tendencies and opportunities. User/supplier, and user/user links should enhance technological awareness. Extensive communal links, and more specific dyadic linkages, might provide respectively, a rough and ready source of tacit knowledge and assistance, or highly valuable, if comparatively less stable specific gains to collaborators.

It was also expected that the small firm was likely to reflect the owner's personality and disposition. The extent to which small service sector enterprises (SSSEs) had adopted new technology, and formed links should partly reflect the psychological disposition of owners towards technical novelty and his or her disposition towards others.

However if each sector turned out to be decisive when accounting for what firms did, then the relative importance of owners' personalities would be measurably less. The research design accommodated this. The design also enabled us to gauge the importance of urban−rural differences which might cut across sector and psychological features.

Forty-five from an original sample of 350 SSSEs were selected, in three localities (N.E. Suffolk, Guildford, Nottingham), and four sectors (plant hire, advertising and design, employment agencies, garages). Each locality and sector was represented by almost equal numbers of firms. Face-to-face interviews with the owner-manager using a semi-structured questionnaire were conducted, whilst a complementary attitude survey was also completed. Secondary interviews with selected suppliers and associated firms within two sectors (advertising and design, and garages) in two localities (Guildford and N.E. Suffolk) provided background sectoral information and further evidence regarding inter-firm linkages.

The themes generated a number of hypotheses grounded and grand, and while some of our original conjectures (as outlined in the position paper, 'Innovation and Co-operation in Small Service Sector Enterprises', CRSSSE Position Paper 91/3) have been confirmed, others have generated surprising results.

After some general findings on technology, sections follow covering strong sector contrasts, weak or non-existent locality effects and weak or mild personality effects.

GENERAL FINDINGS

Many firms were clearly experiencing recessionary effects; employment agencies, advertising and design firms and plant hire are vulnerable to economic crisis; repair garages more immune. Recruitment and capital works are the first to go in a slump; people hang on to their cars at all costs. Although all firms were clearly concerned with survival, Type As and Type Bs appear to be using quite different strategies. The Type As are pursuing competitive retrenchment. The Type Bs are drawing on the goodwill built into their trade links. Although generic information technologies had spread to most companies, current conditions were clearly inhibiting new specialist equipment purchases among all firms. As one respondent put it, 'It is harder to get rid of new technology than people.' Most had become wary of inflexible leasing arrangements.

Even convinced users of generic technologies remain sceptical of these sector-specific applications. Many designers were satisfied with drawing boards, and the subcontracting of the 'technological' stages of the job; this was regarded as safer than combining all functions on expensive CAD and DTP when demand could collapse at any time leaving the company exposed to large debts. Garage owners, who readily acknowledged the value of generic PCs and software, nevertheless insisted that computerised testing and tuning only worked on new or fairly new vehicles. When re-tuning old engines, careful allowances had to be made for the interplay of relatively worn parts, and there is no computerised substitute for this skill and experience, they insisted. An engine 'could look just right from the display [read out] and still sound rough'.

There are good, specific reasons for using or eschewing specialist IT. IT does not appear to be determining the fate of businesses, though IT can damage the business if owners allow this.

Strong evidence, both qualitative and statistical, indicates that the market organisation of each 'sector' was by far the most powerful determinant of firm behaviour. It also appears to be a good indication of 'the level of awareness of technological change in your industry'. Within sectors there are major differences between different types of firm, in terms of the geographical spread of its customers and suppliers, the degree of specialisation, the form of its integration into the market and in terms of 'reputable' Type B, and 'competitive loner' Type A owner strategies.

There were perhaps too few examples of major product and process changes to excite the mechanical and electrical engineer. A notable and rare exception was one Nottingham plant hire firm which had developed an entirely new service as a result of new waste recycling equipment. Another 'technophile' plant hirer was re-writing software to create a bespoke product.

Most technical change was limited to numerous minor product and process innovations. None of the effects of these changes could be described as revolutionary. The effects on the organisation were mostly small. A specific exception was that the common use of fax machines was associated with growing pressures on designers from customers. Fax users seem to regard faxed material as having priority over other media, and therefore expect more or less instantaneous responses to it. Fax (and the portable phone) represent an unusual form of 'control' technology. As one designer put it, 'Pictorial images at speed; that's vital to our business. "In the Post" is an out-of-date excuse.'

It appears that the initial justification for new technologies was usually couched in terms of quantitative efficiency gains – productivity. Like manufacturing firms, qualitative benefits, such as new or enhanced services, tended to manifest themselves to SSSEs only later, if at all. (Further analysis of our data on technical changes will continue.)

There were some contrasts between sectors in the way information was gathered on new technologies. Advertising and design firms mainly gathered such information formally from exhibitions, publications and equipment suppliers, whereas Garages or Plant Hire firms relied more on casual visits and enquiries from suppliers and friendly competitors for information.

However, on the data we have looked at so far, our hypothesis that 'links among users, and between users and suppliers would raise technological awareness' was not supported by the quantitative evidence. Although Table 1 suggests a mild positive association between 'co-operation between others in the trade' and its 'importance in foreseeing technical change', its significance is too low (0.44843) to reject the null-hypothesis that there is no such link.

Table 1: The level of trade co-operation and the importance of links in foreseeing technical change compared

Extent of co-operation	None	A little	A fair amount	A lot
Very important	2	1	1	4
Quite important	1	1	4	3
Not important	3	6	4	2
Unnecessary	1	0	1	0

10 non-responses.

Was there the relationship we had expected between having links and gaining technical awareness on a sector-by-sector basis? No. Table 2 reveals no such relationship at this sample size (significance, 0.87237). In each sector, respondents were about as likely to answer 'yes' as to say 'no'.

Table 2: The unimportance of links in foreseeing technical change by sector

	Advert. & design	Employ. & training	Garages	Plant hire	All
Important	3	3	6	5	17
Not important	5	3	5	4	17
Totals	8	6	11	9	34

Here we are dependent on respondents' own awareness of whether or not links had contributed to their knowledge of technical change. What remains to be checked further is whether or not there was a difference in the take up of technology between high- and low-link firms, that is, in their behaviour.

CO-OPERATE OR COMPETE

Advertising and Design

Not all designers are the same, but most are reluctant to co-operate with other designers. Major new technologies are available to this sector which can reduce a designer's dependence on other firms, such as DTP, CAD, photocomposition systems, printing, 'intelligent' photocopiers directly linked to a network of PCs, etc.). These also improve the designer's scope. Given the competitive idiom adopted by nearly all designers interviewed, they might be expected to be very eager to buy. But many designers do without all of these. The adoption and use of these depends on the designers' strategies, and the work they undertake, with a clear contrast between, on the one hand, Type A1 'jobbing' designers undertaking varied, labour-intensive, short-term work, and Type A2 designers doing 'high specification' work for large corporate clients on a long-term basis, using advanced equipment whose costs have in effect, been paid for by the client.

Some design agencies, Type A3, do not design at all. They find clients and create a specification, and then subcontract all functions to different firms. (Even the buying and selling of newspaper advertising space is generally a subcontracted function.) A3s are co-ordinators and brokers, and have little or no skills as designers. Their skill rests in impressions management: creating an image, striking a posture in commercial relations with others; a careful use of language and mannerism, which would madden the average plant hire operator, or garage owner. There is an industrial–cultural divide within the small bourgeoisie!

Compared with our other sectors, advertising and design firms have a markedly more national distribution of clients, in remote contact by 'phone, telex, fax and modem, though much of the industry is concentrated on London. There appeared to be very little social, informal interaction within their sector. Contacts between designers were definitely eschewed. This may be tied to the notion of the autonomous, creative professional. Design partnerships are often loose associations between individuals who are cultivating their own clients, and whose intention is to leave to form a new business. There is a similarity with garages here in that most young garage mechanics also cultivate their own private circle of clients (in this case locally – down their home street, among relatives and friends). Yet when mechanics break away and establish their own business, they exhibit none of the wariness and distrust characteristic of designers. The industrial culture is markedly different.

The research found no Type Bs in design; no self-professed collaborators. But most designers use many subcontractors. They are vitally dependent on other specific kinds of designers (for colour, graphic design, photography, layout, etc.). The puzzle is that industrial interdependence is as great as it could be. Yet independence is the prized value. As seen later, garages are also interdependent, but cherish good links, and social solidarity among competitors. Why is this true? The solution may lie in the 'geometry' (Simmel) of the links involved. The designer's dependence on another designer is specific: a particular service, from a particular designer, at a particular moment. In other words, each link formed is dyadic. In these cases, to recall Simmel (above):

> The dependence of the whole on each partner is obvious; [But] ... the dyad does not attain the superpersonal life which, in all other groups creates among its members a sense of constraint ...

This absence of constraint means that business 'rip-offs' and disappointments are likely. It follows that designers are bound to prize their 'independence', because there is good reason, within the dyad, for one to be wary of dependence on the other.

It does indeed appear that there is a major, corresponding cultural divide between designers and garages that does not relate in any simple way to their market or class position. While designers have specific, 'high gain' links with other designers, garages have 'low gain', generalised links with most other local garages. Garages' (and plant hire firms') links bring them a myriad of *ad hoc* small, diverse gains from a large, common pool of contacts. These relationships are, like triadic and larger sets, much more stable because they are regulated by 'supra-individual constraint'. We will detail the kinds of links which garages have later; suffice to say that garages and designers approach their links differently, because they are different kinds of links.

The strong qualitative data on the cultural differences between sectors is borne out quantitatively: Table 3 shows that there is a highly significant (0.00669) difference between the sectors in terms of their expressed willingness to 'co-operate with others in the trade'. This is in keeping with an analysis based on Simmel.

On the face of it, small garages everywhere have a 'rural' quality, reminiscent of reciprocal networks among farmers. Designers everywhere are urbanites. To paraphrase from another of Simmel's essays, in his account of the 'metropolitan psyche', designers have 'a matter of fact attitude in dealing with men and with things; and in this attitude a formal justice ... often coupled with an inconsiderate hardness ... an unmerciful matter of factness'. And like the metropolitan individual, designers also show social relationships that distinctly exhibit 'repulsion', 'aversion' and 'atrophy' (Simmel 1903).

Here are typical comments from designers on the questions of co-operation, the industry, their own strategies and on some of the industry's inherent contradictions. An industrial culture begins to show through clearly.

Respondent (a) was Type A3 (a design broker). Commenting on an impromptu visit to his competitor when he found himself in the area by chance:

> I tried once − but he slammed the door in my face, though I think perhaps we ought to [co-operate] with a company ... [so] similar to us. [Yet] I don't ever see the time when I'd want to lay off business to a competitor as an option rather than expanding, becoming more selective or raising our prices and making a bit more out of it. The next stage would be to recruit another consultant ... [But] I am very wary

Table 3: The level of co-operation within each trade

	Advert. & design	Employ. & training	Garage	Plant hire	Total
Co-operate a lot or a fair amount	2	3	8	9	22
Co-operate a little	4	2	4	2	12
Do not co-operate	6	4	0	0	10
Totals	12	9	12	11	44

of attracting any further fixed overheads ... Would need an extra £25—30K [of annual business] to justify it. Collapsed order books have caught a lot of people out ...

This is different to the Garage's strategy. Here the interviewee appears to have ruled out the possibilities of growth by insisting on keeping all growth to himself, while some farming out to other designers might at least have enabled him to capture the tasks that he was able to do without increasing his overheads. As will be seen later, garages spread work and thereby directly minimise the overheads that each garage has to carry. They have lower expectation of gain, but more certainty of realising it.

q. Did he 'withhold advantageous information'?
Yes [Confidential information] is worth its weight in gold. It is very important to know when a [client] is becoming ripe for a new [job].

Respondent (b) was Type A1 (a jobbing designer).

q. How has trade been?
Getting more cut throat!
q. Discuss with others?
We don't want other people to know what our business is ... We don't talk direct. It is as simple as that! It is very, very competitive. We don't want other people to know who we are dealing with. It is not just us being unfriendly ... With customers of course [links] are very important ... because they know their business.
q. Discuss with competitors?
The sad thing about not talking to each other is that knock ups[2] cost everybody more — £1—200 [each time]. So it's cutting off your own nose if you don't talk to each other. We [i.e. all designers] spend 20 hours on it [a specification] but we [can] only charge for 10! Business is very much cut throat at the moment. Trust went out the window because customers want the lowest price. This is happening more and more.
q. Were 'any changes planned'?
It is just so much hassle now. The enjoyment's gone out of it ... We have ... decided that it is just not worth trying to push for the money ... It is not so much the economic climate on its own, as the attitude of other people. So many big companies ... have got financial constraints, they don't care who they tread on. That is not how I work.

Respondent (c) was also Type A1.

q. Sources of suggestions?
... Just don't talk to each other. We are all out to kill each other rather than speak to each other ... [Yet] We are now more uncertain about future growth, and we can't grow much more from internal resources. The ideal is to offer even more services, perhaps linked in with a printer [*sic*] or another design group. We would welcome any such approach, not to sell out, but to realise a special type of service.

Respondent (d), Type A2 (specialist, high specification).

q. Discuss industry?
Discuss with friends ... not very close ... I don't go out of my way to talk.

Respondent (e), Type A2.

q. Co-operate with Designers?
No! they are the enemy!

The adoption of high-technology design tools remains risky because the necessary turnover cannot be guaranteed. But it could bring greater independence. Continued respondent (c):

New technology is throwing everything into turmoil ... There are two ways to go ... You can either not bother with it, and be trapped in a safe trading position, probably losing 20% of your staff, not invest in the new technology and have a fairly comfortable life style, or we can expand and take on board the new technology. It is the latter we have done ... It is affecting relationships with suppliers because it means that more of the business is being done [without] outside suppliers.

Respondent (e) thought:

Over the next five to 10 years, studios are going to install computers that will take design through from conception straight through to making films, taking a whole stage out – reprographics.

To the extent that designers like to act alone, then all inclusive technologies which cut out subcontractors are bound to be attractive. Yet the threshold level of business required to pay for it is difficult to reach, precisely because Designers are loath to pool customers, and have thereby debarred themselves from maintaining high asset utilisation. To go for high technology would require co-operation with other Designers who might pass on jobs they cannot handle themselves. (Plant Hire firms do cross-hire, see below.)

Alternatively, high tech Designers could seek out a large stream of contracts from one or two large customers, though this might also offend their sense of independence.

To paraphrase Marx, the relations of production seem to be fettering the forces of production in design.

Employment and training agencies

Both Type A1, general white and blue collar Employment Agencies, and Type A2, specialist professional recruitment agencies (dealing in legal, computer, management, and accountancy skills), tended to adopt a competitive and independent-minded stance to their competitors. Horizontal linkages (i.e. with similar organisations) were non-existent for Type A2 firms and minimal for Type A1. No large A2s (the specialist agencies) appeared to exist. We found one case of a Type B strategy, a general training agency. It is significant that it was a workers' co-operative (B1), with many co-operative linkages in the co-ops movement (below).

Type A1 secretarial agencies made much use of 'an army' of roving, self-employed, freelance trainers and instructors. Companies seem to form when, as in design, one or two freelancers were able to corner a large enough contract to justify finding other independent trainers to join them on a semi-permanent basis.

Respondent (a), Type A2.

q. Talk with competitors?
I haven't got one!

Links were deliberately avoided, except for 'clients or friends of clients'.

Respondent (b), Type A2.

I've only got one, indirect, competitor. Sometimes [we] talk very generally about business and about the industry.

Respondent (c), Type A1.

There is a lot of competition in the recruitment business. The industry has got a bad name and has got worse. We are trying to distance ourselves from the tarnished image of recruitment ...

q. Passing on information?
Only to clients. Never to competitors!

Respondent (d), Type A1.

Links can be useful, but whether or not they are telling the truth ... hiding the facts? ...

Respondent (e), Type B1.

This case is an exception-that-proves-the-rule. Most employment agencies have little or no co-operation with others in the trade (see also Table 5). Unique among our final sample of employment and training agencies,[3] she co-operated a very great deal, acting within the Type B idiom. Why was this?

The company provides secretarial, WP, assertiveness and awareness training, and acts as a consultant in personnel management. Because her company is a workers' co-operative, and because it holds many public contracts, the respondent stressed that she likes to operate in a public, transparent and reputable way. For these reasons it has developed many links.

> We get help from BBBB. They are likely to help — so we are affiliated to them ... Colleagues in the Co-op movement. We talk to them quite a lot; a lot comes from that.
> q. Importance of business links?
> Links are crucial. We have quite a few formal and informal links. It is crucial to keep them up to date with any changes — not so much technological changes as what's wanted with the product. We have almost no links at all with the private sector. We see them, and recruit from there on Women's Courses — we ... wouldn't really get into a dialogue with them. We do have links with the FE college. We also have good links with Community Business Network. So we take up links where they are going to be of use to the business ... the federation for workers' co-ops.
> q. Quality of links with local businesses?
> The people we are in competition with ... they would be quite similar organisations to us and we feel we have quite friendly arrangements. And if it was something that we knew we couldn't do, either by date or by content, we would just pass that on its way. There is usually no mileage in hiding anything. The competition really doesn't work that way. The competition happens within the tender if you like. The co-or-dinator is actually choosing what would be most suitable for them, rather than we providing exactly the same service as everybody else.
> We have a different style. We tend to do a lot of sharing of information. If it is not really for us, we say why not try X?

Plant hire

Four types of businesses were identifiable in our sample of construction equipment plant hire firms. Each appeared to exhibit various distinctive levels of co-operation. The whole sector depends on the fact that construction companies choose not to own much of the equipment they use. The construction industry thus has an unusual industrial structure. It does not own its means of production.

Type B1 firms, the established generalist Plant Hire operators, carry considerable overheads in the form of a large range of hire equipment (trucks, mixers, skips, excavators, space heaters, etc.).

The evidence suggests that their survival depends on a remarkable system which maximises the utilisation of their equipment via contract referrals, subcontracting and participation in resilient networks, in which there appears to be some well-established, unwritten rules (especially over maintained prices). Sharing of equipment, and exchange of business and technical information seem commonplace amongst firms at this level.

In the current recession, few can be worse hit than Plant Hire operators in the building industry. Their current strategy is, at the very least, to participate in parts of those contracts that are on offer. For example, the winner of a contract from a builder charges the customer the market rate — say £13 per hour for a lorry of a given tonnage — for a vehicle which they might not even have available at that time. The Type B1 contractor then 'phones around the trade re-offering the same contract only fractionally under the charge which he has agreed with the builder. (Just £1 per hour under the market rate would not be unusual.) This cuts down the first contractor's profit on the work he is passing on almost to zero.

The benefits are wholly long term; the reputable Type B1 trader will eventually become the recipient of other B1s' re-circulated contracts in return. In other words reciprocity is developed and the net effect is that all participants make the maximum possible use of all their assets. It is a way of maximising the utilisation of capital in the long run.

It is a testament to the strength of normative regulation within the Plant Hire industry that this culture of co-operation was surviving in the face of the worst recession in construction since the 1930s.

In contrast, Type A1 'one man' businesses operate perhaps just one or two trucks. They were seen as very cost competitive, ruthless and opportunistic loners, often having broken away from larger reputable Type B1 firms. Type As were not part of the trade network and were viewed with disdain as 'cowboys' by the Type B1s. The way they work was reported as follows. Plant Hire firms make extensive use of a commercial two-way radio network. Lorry movements are instructed over the air and builders may even offer contracts in this way. The cowboy operator listens into the transmissions and if he judges that he can get his truck to a site faster than anybody else, will literally cut corners to get there fast. On arrival he will under-cut the market rate without compunction, and steal the business from underneath the Type Bs. Type A1 plant hire firms have something in common with Type A1 designers (above).

The reason why Type A plant hirers act differently now becomes clearer. They, like most designers, have low overheads, therefore they do not need to co-operate in order to maximise the use of their equipment. They are not under an economic compunction to act reputably. They are free to choose a different market morality.

Of course if they are successful as mavericks and expand to take on other drivers and equipment, then their overheads grow, and they are compelled to cultivate the reputable, co-operative disposition of the mature firm. This is confirmed by looking at the history of some 'reputable' Type B1s which indicates that they had been cowboys once. That is, they grew into the regulated network. They grew a new market morality.

Plant Hire included two other permutations. First, specialist firms with large overheads including crane hire firms, designated Type B2s. They often use very sophisticated state-of-the-art lifting equipment. These firms behave somewhat like Type B1 firms within their region, with two provisos. Firstly, because they are specialists, their networks with other similar companies are thinner. There will only be three or four other 'independent' crane hire firms in a region. They will behave responsibly towards each other, and this includes passing subcontracts around the regional network. But some comments suggest that these Type B2s revert to Type A (predatory) behaviour when winning contracts outside their own customarily regulated patch, where they are not known, and do not therefore have a reputation to damage.

Finally Type B3 general tool hirers appeared moderately co-operative.

No small plant hire firm will have anything to do with the one or two large national operators. They will not subcontract to or from them, and regard them as 'the major threat to all independents'.

In short there is a specific logic to each competitive/co-operative dynamic in each specific sub-sector in plant hire.

Looking at the civil engineering industry as a whole, but what is confusing to social science, it is interesting that large construction companies — firms that are big enough to act monopolistically — were reported to be very competitive towards each other in practice; while small plant hirers, which orthodox models would treat as competitive (by virtue of their size, and large numbers), practise co-operation.

Plant Hirers' typical comments on co-operation follow.

Respondent (a) is a Type B2 (a specialist), and therefore arguably only a moderate collaborator. Did he 'pass on information'?

> Some, relating to our four similar companies in the region. But [I] do not pass on 'valuable' information. We have contacts if we are desperate for a machine to do a job.
> q. Discuss industry?
> If a job is in London, or Scotland [i.e. far from here] then [our] company will locally subcontract the plant hire.

q. Quality of relations, and q. Foreseeing technical change?
Two or three of us will get together . . . it does help get the word around on the quality of new machines.
q. Links with suppliers?
They will pull the stops out if I'm desperate.
q. And customers?
We are at their beck and call at all times – that personal touch like that telephone call that just came in. Whatever advice I give, he'll take my word for it because he trusts me.

Respondent (b) is a Type B3 (tool hire).

I try and involve other people . . . keep in touch, find out what is going on. We warn each other [competitors] if there are thefts or frauds [going on].

Respondent (c) is Type B1. He is involved in

lots of cross-hiring.

Respondent (d) is Type B2.

[It is] very important to keep friends. The competition all use each other, especially ZZZ and YYY. No poaching. There is a naughty boy who is undercutting. Was a driver [with us] until two years ago. I helped to get him started. Now he's got two or three cranes, and he's the naughty boy.

Respondent (e) is Type B1. He will

cross-hire with competitors for regular customers . . . [but] you have to be careful who you deal with.

Respondent (f) has a virtually unique business and has no effective competition at all. There are some other similar firms a long way off, and he is a member of the relevant national association. He has few informal links and declares himself to be 'very secretive about new developments' he is making. He could make no comment on q. 'Making contacts in the industry?'

Garages
This sector provided a good deal of evidence of long-standing, co-operative links. Informal networks abounded in this sector. Numerous examples were given where garages assisted each other, either with technical or trade information, or through borrowing of parts and equipment. There was a significant amount of subcontracting taking place, in a manner comparable to Type B1 plant hire, that is, the re-circulation of customers. (A non-MOT garage would accept a job from a customer which entailed an MOT, and drive down the road to get this done elsewhere.) Body repairs, fitting helicoils, resprays, etc. could all be farmed (*sic*) out. Reciprocity and trust thus appeared to be common features within a web of inter-garage links. Links are integral to business, and the reliability of these links has allowed them to be treated as friendship links.

For example, one garage owner was involved in a near fatal boating accident. Because of his injuries he was off work for several months, leaving the business without the cash to pay its creditors. Because of his high reputation, numerous creditors were prepared to 'wait as long as it took' before payment. Without this support, this business would almost certainly have collapsed.

It is difficult to imagine how a business could totally avoid any amount of discussion within its industry. Even so, garages and plant hire firms appear to be significantly more open to discussion than designers or employment agencies. Table 4 demonstrates that garages and plant hire firms regularly discuss their industry with their own competitors. All 12 garages and all eight plant hire firms said that they had regular discussions with their competitors. In contrast, Employment Agencies were evenly split (significance 0.01407).

Table 4: Discussing the industry with competitors by sector

	Advert. & design	Employ. & training	Garage	Plant hire	All
Discuss industry with competitors	8	4	12	8	32
Do not discuss with competitors	3	4	0	0	7
Totals	11	8	12	8	39

Only now did Designers admit links; eight out of 11.

Beyond 'discussion', the next step would be practical co-operation with competitors. The industrial divide becomes even clearer when we look at 'co-operation with others in the trade', sector-by-sector. Table 3 revealed a very highly significant pattern. Eight out of 12 garages said they co-operated 'a fair amount, or a lot'. Not one garage owner said they did not co-operate with the trade at all. Nor did a single plant hire firm. On this side of the industrial divide, co-operation is dominant. Table 3 also shows that on the other side of the divide, co-operation is much rarer. The majority of designers and employment agencies said they do not co-operate; on their side of the divide, links are fewer and weaker.

For garages, a complementary network involving suppliers also existed, although these supplier/user links were, by their very nature, more specific, and thus dyadic – and less personal. These included motor factors (who supply garages with most of their spare parts) and sales reps (from the large component and equipment manufacturers).

Most small Type B2 specialist garages, such as vintage and classic car restorers, also had extensive networks of suppliers. This makes specialist garages distinctly like specialist Type B2 crane hire firms.

As an alternative to specialisation, some garages diversify into car hire, car sales, roadside cafe, breakdown recovery. They too maintained an extensive set of business links but the impression is that the informality and reciprocity of these links was lower. For example a very congenial local garage owner also ran very formalised relationships with the AA and a national vehicle recovery association when it came to his breakdown service.

Here is what garage owners typically said about co-operation:

Respondent (a)

> You've got to share to survive! We have all got bits and pieces we can share off each other. There are four or five garages around that if I've got something I'll tell them and if they've got something they'll tell me. [It] saves us each going out to buy it. Basically we've got a little co-op here. We share info[rmation] as well.

Respondent (b)

> q. Basis for lending?
> I expect them to put trade my way [and I] send passing trade elsewhere, regularly.

Respondent (c)

> In restoring [cars], other garages are colleagues you see. We help each other out if we can – certain things I can do which other restorers cannot, and vice versa ... delicate measuring equipment, staff that [one] wouldn't use very often, heavy pulling and lifting gear; swap things around as it were. [Nor do] modern garages see me as a threat and are more than happy to send me the odd things they don't want to do.

Respondent (d)

> You must have the respect of colleagues to survive.

q. Advantageous information ever withheld?
I can't think that at the end of the day it would work to your advantage.

(Interview constantly interrupted by a stream of 'phone calls and visits, leg-pulling and banter.)

Garage (e) is an exception-which-proves-the-rule: his technology is all supplied by the franchiser, who tightly controls the way he works. Thus:

q. Passing on information?
Yes, to others in the XXXXX service network. But we don't go shouting it around ... that is giving our blood away ... our reserve away, ... and ... certainly, I won't tell another garage who is not in the XXXXX network about [ideas] ... except those in another town!

URBAN—RURAL DIFFERENCES?

In terms of innovative activities and co-operative linkages, few, and probably no, differences could be detected between rural firms (based in N.E. Suffolk) and those in more urban settings. Some differences are conceivable.

It is conceivable that the physical distance between firms might affect supply links and service offered, making them more tenuous over greater distances. However there was little evidence of this. Motor factors in all the locations were located such that all their customers were within a 20 or 25 mile radius — this being about the maximum range that permitted an hourly service to all customers. One motor factor based in Diss has dealings with approximately 100 garages (or at least 100 people who are paid to repair cars) within 20 miles of the town. Motor factors in Guildford were however similarly spaced in travel time. One hour delivery seems a universal requirement in the vehicle repair industry, which is as we stressed above, an excellent example of just-in-time production!

Whilst small garages in such localities still had extensive informal networks, the frequency of interaction would be lower than in urban networks where garages were sometimes neighbours or just down the road. While the frequency of contact was lower, the interactions were less hurried and probably richer in terms of information exchange and social intercourse.

This difference is easy to overplay. For example in a similar vein, a major office equipment supplier considered that small rural firms were likely to be less aware of new technological developments because of their relative geographical isolation. This supplier had permanent exhibition sites in the large cities but only organised yearly, travelling 'road shows' in rural areas. Yet our analysis of the very large sample of firms in the Lead Project clearly showed that there was no difference between urban and rural firms' awareness of technical change in their industry.

Table 5 reinforces the case against ruralism. Seven out of 13 firms in Nottingham, exactly half the firms in Guildford, and exactly half the firms in N.E. Suffolk exhibited 'a lot', or 'a fair amount' of co-operation with others. Co-operation may be the quintessential theoretical characteristic of rural life. But there was no evidence that it was any greater in 'rural' Suffolk than in 'urban' Nottingham, nor 'suburban' Guildford.

Table 5: Level of trade co-operation by locality

	Co-operate a lot	Do not co-operate	Co-operate a little	Co-operate fair amount	Total
Nottingham	2	3	3	5	13
Guildford	4	2	6	4	16
N.E. Suffolk	5	5	2	2	14
Totals	11	10	11	11	43

Comparing our regions further, no significant relationships could be found between locality and a large range of features which would indicate communalism, and therefore be a critical test of urban–rural differences. Not 'lending to others' (significance = 0.71050), nor 'borrowing instead of buying' (0.85201), 'contacts counted as friends' (0.56287), 'long or short term relationships' (0.25140), 'friendly relations' (0.56287), 'formality of relations' (0.48322), or 'the quality of relations between local businesses' (0.51900). Nor was there any significant variation in the 'amount of subcontracting' (significance = 0.92305, virtually pure random chance).

The quantitative data no more than suggest that businesses are less prepared to trade information in Guildford (13 out of 16 would not) than in Nottingham (eight out of 13 would not) and N.E. Suffolk (where only half would withhold advantageous information (significance = 0.22089).

But to build a case for urbanism and ruralism in business, a researcher would have to obtain significant results in most or all of these kinds of features. There are not any, not even one. Clearly the case for urban–rural differences has failed the test.

INDUSTRIAL DISTRICTS, SPACE AND PLACE

Although none of the firms in our sample exported their services, it would be simplistic to think of small firms as being typically 'local' suppliers and users (for a discussion, see Curran 1986). As we have argued, most small garages and plant hire firms can be classified as truly local firms; but employment agencies, and design agencies are more likely to operate at a regional or national level. (Generally the greater the specialisation, the more national are the user and supplier links.) Small firms may share the same street, but their market structures and operating idioms differ according to sector and sub-sector. The local high street need not represent the face of a local economy, but an access point to several very different spaces and places. One main local attribute of a locality is the more or less unique permutation of sectors represented there.

While no two localities are the same, the way a sector operates in one place is similar to the way it operates elsewhere. Thus the idiom, the market structure, the relative permanence of user and supplier links and the scope for a garage in Nottingham is very similar to that of a garage in Guildford or N.E. Suffolk. So too with plant hire, employment and even design. Better therefore to think of the 'district' in which a SSSE is located, not in terms of locality, but as an amalgam of market, technical, spatial, and non-spatial features.

We asked firms what proportion of their links were 'mostly or all local', 'mostly national' or 'evenly split'. Table 6 suggests that local links predominate, but that employment agencies are the least localised, and garages the most.

Table 6: The proportion of local business links by sector

Sector	All local	Most local	Even split	Most national
Employment & training	1	2	1	1
Advertising & design	1	5	1	2
Plant hire	5	2	2	0
Garages	4	7	0	0
Totals	11	16	4	3

10 non-responses.

Because both user and supplier links are included together, the full picture is being obscured. (The significance level of Table 6 is low at 0.1688.) But we have already shown that the sectors differ significantly in terms of their expressed willingness to co-operate with others in the trade, to discuss their industry with their competitors, and to co-operate with others in their trade. Regardless of location, it was the two most localised sectors – garages, plant hire – that were most willing to co-operate.

The industrial divide in services shows up more clearly by condensing Table 6, as shown in Table 7.

Table 7: The proportion of local business links across the divide

Sector	Most or all local	Most national or evenly split
Employment & training, advertising & design	9	2
Plant hire, garages	18	2
Totals	27	4

What other measures of localisation could be used? Table 8 shows how firms in different sectors felt about the 'quality of relations between local businesses'. It might be assumed that the higher the expressed quality of local business links, the more solidly local that sector's economy.

Table 8: The quality of local business relations by sector

Sector	Relations			
	Good	Reasonable	None	Bad
Employment & training	2	2	3	0
Advertising & design	0	6	5	0
Plant hire	7	3	0	1
Garages	10	2	0	0
Totals	19	13	8	1

2 non-responses.

The industrial divide in services is clear from Table 8. The sector contrasts are highly significant at 0.00536. Garages and plant hire companies are firmly sited in the local economy. Virtually all garages have good local relations. In Simmel's terms they are enmeshed within a web of 'supra-individually constrained' and therefore reliable relationships. The quantitative evidence closely underpins garage owners' own descriptions of the way they operate (above).

Not a single advertising or design agency described their local business links as good. If this observation is linked to designers' descriptions of their industry (above), then there is the strong suspicion that in Simmel's terms, these businesses are characterised by 'dyadic', non-regulated, and therefore unstable relationships. Moreover, when asked to describe business relations as 'formal' or 'friendly' 16 garages and plant hire firms answered 'friendly', but only four design and employment agencies thought of relations as 'friendly'.

PERSONALITY DIFFERENCES BY SECTOR?

An industrial divide between individualists and collectivists?
Is the way a business is conducted a reflection of its owner's personality, or rather, of

its sector? By posing this issue it is possible to develop a measure of the strength of the industrial divide in services. The three-section questionnaire contained one section on attitudes; and eight of the 39 items in this section of the questionnaire were aimed at eliciting personality traits. These attempted to distinguish 'individualists' from 'collectivists'. (Researchers into personality invariably use a far greater number of items — at least 20. This part of our research should therefore be regarded as highly provisional.) The items used were:

'I go out of my way to meet new people.'
'I would prefer to spend more time doing business at home.'
'If I had a choice I would rather spend a day on a deserted beach than a popular beach.'
'I like to go to social functions a lot.'
'There should be more emphasis on participation in team sports at school.'
'I like to read a lot for leisure.'
'Before making a decision, I am often sick with worry.'
'In a group, I tend not to take the lead in conversation.'

Answers to these questions might indicate the underlying personal predispositions of small business owners. Would the 'individualists' turn up in the sectors dominated by Type A (competitive) companies, and the 'collectivists' among the Type B (collaborative) companies? If the industrial divide is weak, then an individual could presumably conduct his or her affairs in a way that reflected their individual personality, that is, in a way that was suited to them. Alternatively, if the industrial divide is strong, then individuals would either have to temper their ways in order to fit the ruling industrial idiom, (or else leave for an industry to which they were more personally suited). Individualists might eschew what might seem to them as the stultifying suprapersonal constraints and communal duties of the garage and plant hire trades, preferring the intense, but transitory, dyadic relationships more characteristic of advertising and design or employment and training agencies. The collectivist might move in the other direction, choosing the dependable continuities of larger networks.

A plausible case could therefore be made for expecting to find few 'shy, private, or wary and anxious' personalities among garage owners, and few 'genial, trusting and outward looking' personalities among designers.

On balance, our provisional evidence does not support this view. It has already been shown that advertising and design, and employment and training agencies represent individuals locked in competition with each other and that collectivist behaviour is largely the domain of garages and plant hire. Yet the answers given to seven out of the eight personality items showed no significant differences. Those indicating individualist traits were fairly randomly distributed across both sides of the divide. Similarly, collectivist traits turned up as often among advertising and design, and employment and training agencies as they did among garages and plant hire firms. Only one personality trait seemed to show any kind of fit with industrial divisions: 'I like to go to social functions a lot.' Those who agreed tended to be from the plant hire and garage, Type B, industries. (The significance was rather low at 0.08702).

In other words, it appears from the data we have looked at so far, that the sector imposes a form of behaviour on the individual and that individuals do not choose their trade, nor the way they do business according to any prior personality traits they may have. Further research would be needed to test this fully. In so far as we have been able to measure it, the business is not a reflection of the owner.

There is an outline case for concluding that the industrial divide appears to be a strong determinant, constraining individuals to act in particular ways, whether it suits their personality or not. There is also a suggestion from the random personality distributions, that the experience of working in a Type A or Type B sector may have no effect on the 'underlying' personality. As far as we can tell from the data we have looked at so far, there are hardly any meaningful or significant differences between underlying personalities on one side of the divide compared with the other.

If the reader refers again to the advertisers' and designers' quotes s/he may detect a trace of regret among some designers, that the industry is so individualised. Might it be that this represents some tension for those individuals who are 'collectivists'?

Attitudes to technology on each side of the divide

There is much stronger evidence from our research, that specific attitudes towards technology do determine the destinies which individuals follow. Twenty-nine items in the attitudes section covered technology. The most sector-sensitive attitude was 'I like to pull apart and put back together gadgets' (significance = 0.00079). Three other attitudes came close to showing a significant distinction between sectors: 'New inventions will always be found to counteract the harmful effects of new technology' (significance = 0.05096); 'I often buy new equipment to stay ahead' (significance = 0.062350); and 'I try to read about new technology in my trade journals' (significance = 0.08957). A further factor suggested a distinction across the divide: 'I have contacts who I can turn to for advice on new technology' (significance = 0.09107). In each case garages and plant hire firms show up strongly.

In terms of the kind of persons who are found one side and the other of the divide, a highly significant difference is shown up when the personality trait 'I like ... social functions' is taken together with the attitudes to technology given above. Table 9 summarises this.

Table 9: ANOVA test of personality and attitude differences across the divide

Employment & training agencies	15.56
Advertising & design	16.83
Plant hire	19
Garages	21.17

Significance = 0.004; Fisher = 31.

This shows a highly significant separation between on the one hand, employment and training agencies, and advertising and design agencies, and on the other, plant hire and garages. The latter group are very definitely 'technophiles who like to party'!

TOWARDS A SYNTHESIS?

The value of a theory or model lies partly in its ability to simplify the world to the point at which the world becomes intelligible, from which point onwards, some generalisations can be made.

In this sense Simmel has worked well. There is a close fit with the co-operation/betrayal dynamic in plant hire noted earlier. The 'reputable operators group' are constrained to behave well towards each other. In contrast the 'lone cowboy owner-drivers' engage in a series of highly unstable one-off (dyadic) relationships at various building sites.

The reason why a 'rip-off' is more likely in dyadic business relationships than in triadic ones has been formally modelled and explained. We hypothesise that the collective pressure to behave well in larger groups makes the Type B idiom a comparatively more stable form of business relationship – just as multiplex rural communitarian systems impose customary stabilising standards and duties on farmers. We think that we have also explained why dyad relationships deliver and demand the most intense commitment, and that this leads to a mistrust of the one towards the other, in terms of the commitment which they can realistically expect.

The sure benefits which garages get from their large, homogeneous networks are to be compared with the potentially more dramatic gains and losses which dyadic relationships might deliver to heterogeneous user–supplier or asset exchanging partners.

Of course the world is never wholly as described by a model. Some features have to be left out. To describe the world completely would mean generating a model that was as complex as the world it was supposed to describe. And this would defeat the whole object of attaining a degree of intelligibility. We have to strike a balance somewhere between the complete representation of the domain we are looking at (as far as we can tell), and an over-simplified version of what is happening in it. Further, we have to make some evaluation of the relative 'research power' of theories which may not necessarily be in direct competition with each other.

In this paper, we have introduced other theories and levels of explanation which, while very different to Simmel, may have something to add. But they can only be admitted on the basis of their research power. In the synthesis, Simmel comes top. Other frameworks allowed for are 'effects at the level of technology'; 'the life and death of the local economy'; 'urban–rural differences' and 'psychology and personal disposition'. Of these, 'technology' is still an under-developed theme and 'urbanism–ruralism' a complete failure.

For the reasons just explained, models should not be made too complicated. Orthodox innovation models are certainly ruled out of any synthesis, because they do not seem to explain much of what we have seen. They are variously, wrong, weak, or irrelevant and have failed to earn a place. In particular we have also ruled out 'competitive-behaviour' and 'monopolistic-behaviour' economic models. The facts do not fit them.

SUBSTANTIVE CONCLUSIONS

1. The first crucial point is that the industrial divide in services can largely be explained in terms of the general laws which govern different kinds of relationship. The difficulties faced by advertising and design firms and by employment and training agencies, are the difficulties faced within any dyadic relationship. Apply Simmel to them:

> Because [dyads depend] on only two participants, the withdrawal of one would destroy the whole: A dyad depends on each of its two elements alone – in its death though not in its life: for its life it needs both, but for its death, only one. Hence the dyad does not attain the superpersonal life which, in all other groups creates among its members a sense of constraint.
>
> (Coser 1971, pp. 184–185)

But we also pointed out that despite the designers' specific repudiation of communitarian values, despite their strong sense of independence, they nevertheless depend on particular services from various suppliers. Simmel's argument was that in such dyads:

> The dependence of the whole on each partner is obvious; in all other groups duties and responsibilities can be delegated, but not in the dyad, where each participant is immediately and directly responsible for any collective action ...
>   The dyad relies on immediate reciprocity, but the triad can impose its will upon one member through the formation of a coalition between the two others ...
>
> (Coser 1971, ibid)

In these circumstances it is probably not surprising that designers remain wary of others; equally unsurprising, that garage owners are able to enjoy 'friendly' relations, safe in the knowledge that their business 'friends' are communally bound to behave well. Little wonder that in comparison with garages, designers are plagued by instabilities essential to the dyad, which, to recall Simmel 'for its life it needs both, but for its death, only one'.

Add in the specific, concrete, market organisation of a sector to the general features of all social relationships, and the industrial divide in services emerges as a major barrier, constraining the behaviour of those who fall either side of it, forcing them on the one side to play within either the Type A, competitive game rules, or on the other side to play the Type B, co-operative game rules.

2. Secondly, in terms of the debate between the 'new industrial districts' thesis and, the 'death of the local economy', we are agnostic. The recommendation is that the protagonists look carefully for inter- and intra-sector contrasts, before settling for one argument or the other. Clearly garages and plant hire firms are definitely in the local economy, and inhabit very real 'industrial districts'; most are Type Bs. However, advertising and design, and employment and training agencies have weak, or non-existent local or national links; most are Type As.

One or two exceptional Type Bs have been found in employment, and one or two exceptional Type As among garages and plant hire companies. These exceptions are theoretically useful because they are clearly operating under specifically heterodox conditions to the majority in their sector. They are exceptions which prove that the rules apply to the rest. There is some simplicity in the chaos (all Type Bs are in an industrial district, regardless of sector; all Type As have similar problems, regardless of sector), but great care is needed when entering this debate.

3. Finally we have found little evidence that personal predispositions have much effect on the way people do business; but there is rather stronger evidence that specific attitudes towards technology do determine the destinies which individuals follow.

NOTES

1. This is not a closely referenced paper, however a selection of sources drawn on during earlier work is included in the references.
2. 'Knock-ups' are preliminary design outlines.
3. A second Type B Employment Agency appeared in our pilot sample. The company specialised in training black workers, and like company (e) described above, had a large public sector presence. Although they had few direct competitors to talk to, the charismatic owner of the business had very strong and active links with a number of regional and national business organisations, and among black communities.

REFERENCES AND FURTHER USEFUL SOURCES

Abernathy W.J. (1982) Competitive Decline in US innovation: the Management Factor, Research Management, Vol. 25, No. 5, pp. 34–41.

Acs Z. and Audretsch D. (1990) Innovation and Small Firms, MIT Press, Cambridge.

Amin A. and Roberts K. (1990) The Re-emergence of Regional Economies?, Environment and Planning D, Vol. 8.

Aoki A. (1984) The Co-operative Game Theory of the Firm, Clarendon Press, Oxford.

Arensberg C.M. and Kimball S.T. (1968) Family and Community in Ireland, Harvard University Press, Boston.

Auerbach P. (1989) Vertical Integration, Planning and the Market, APEX Economic Discussion Papers, No. 2, Kingston Polytechnic, Kingston upon Thames.

Ball M. et al (1989) The Transformation of Britain: Contemporary Social and Economic Change, Fontana Books, London.

Barnekov T. and Rich D. (1989) Privatism and the Limits of Local Economic Policy, Urban Affairs Quarterly, Vol. 25 December, pp. 212–238.

Barras R. (1986) Towards a Theory of Innovation in Services, Research Policy, Vol. 15, No. 4, pp. 161–173.

Barras R. (1990) Interactive innovation in financial and business services: the vanguard of the service revolution, Research Policy, Vol. 19, No. 5, pp. 215–237.

Bessant J. (1982) Influential factors in manufacturing innovation, Research Policy, Vol. 11, No. 2.

Blackburn R., Curran J. and Jarvis R. (1990) Small firms and local networks: some theoretical and conceptual explorations, paper presented to 13th Small Firms Policy and Research Conference, Harrogate, November.

Boddy D. and Buchanan D. (1983) Organizations in the Computer Age, Gower, Aldershot.

Brody H. (1974) Inishkillane, Penguin, Harmondsworth.

Brown L. (1981) Innovation Diffusion: A New Perspective, Methuen, London.

Burns T. and Stalker G. (1961) The Management of Innovation, Tavistock, London.

Campagni R. (1990) Local milieu, uncertainty and innovation networks: towards a new dynamic theory of economic space, paper presented to Seminar on Network Innovators, University of Quebec, Montreal.

Carlisle J. and Parker R. (1989) Beyond Negotiation, John Wiley, Chichester.

Carter C. and Williams B. (1957) Industry and Technical Progress, OUP, Oxford.

Casson M. (1991) The Economics of Business Culture, Game Theory, Transaction Costs and Economic Performance, Clarendon, Oxford.

Castells M. (1977) Towards a Political Urban Sociology, in Captive Cities, ed. Harloe, M., Wiley, London.

Castells M. (1978) City Class and Power, Basingstoke, London.

Cattell R. (1978) The Scientific Use of Factor Analysis in Life and Behavioural Sciences, Plenum Press, New York.

CEST (1991) The Management of Technological Collaboration, Centre for Exploitation of Science and Technology, Manchester.

Child J. and Loveridge R. (1990) Information Technology in European Services, Basil Blackwell, Oxford.

Clark P. and Staunton N. (1989) Innovation in Technology and Organization, Routledge, London.

Clarke S. (1988) Overaccumulation, class struggle and the regulation approach, Capital And Class, Vol. 36, pp. 59−92.

Collier D. (1983) The service sector revolution: the automation of services, Long Range Planning, Vol. 16, No. 6, pp. 10−20.

Cooke P. (1988) Flexible Integration, Scope Economies and strategic Alliances, Environment and Planning D, Vol. 6, No. 3.

Coser L. (1971) Masters of Sociological Thought, Harcourt Brace Jovanovich, New York.

Curran J. (1986) Bolton Fifteen Years On: A Review of Small Business Research in Britain 1971−1986, Small Business Research Unit, London.

Curran J. and Burrows R. (1988) Enterprise Britain: A National Profile of Small Business Owners and the Self-employed, Small Business Research Trust, London.

Curran J. and Burrows R. (1989) Shifting the Focus: Problems and approaches to studying the small enterprise in the services sector, Paper presented at 12th National Small Firms Policy and Research Conference, Barbican.

Curran J., Blackburn R. and Woods A. (1991) Profiles of the Small Enterprise in the Service Sector, ESRC Centre for Research on Small Service Enterprises, Kingston Business School, Kingston upon Thames.

Daniel W. (1987) Workplace Industrial Relations and Technical Change, Frances Pinter, London.

Dickson K., Lawton Smith H., Smith S. and Woods A. (1990) Sizing up your partner: expectations and realities in inter-firm collaboration, paper presented at 13th Small Firms' Policy and Research Conference, Harrogate, November.

Dickson K., Lawton Smith H. and Smith S. (1990) The small firm perspective on inter-firm collaboration for innovation, in The Co-operation Phenomenon: Prospects for Small Firms and the Small Economies, ed. O'Doherty D., Graham and Trottman, Dublin.

Dickson K., Lawton Smith H. and Smith S. (1989) Inter-firm collaboration and innovation: strategic alliances or reluctant partnerships?, in Frontiers of Management: Research and Practice, ed. Mansfield R., Routledge, London.

Dickson K., Lawton Smith H. and Smith S. (1991) Bridge over troubled waters: problems and opportunities in inter-firm research collaboration, Technology Analysis and Strategic Management, Vol. 3, No. 2.

Eysenck H. and Eysenck S. (1969) Personality Structure and Measurement, Routledge & Keegan Paul, London.

Fleck J. (1984) The Adoption of Robots in Industry, Physics in Technology, Vol. 15, No. 1.

Flynn R. (1981) The Local State and Capital: Some Aspects of Incorporation in Strategic Planning, paper presented to BSA/PSA Political Sociology Conference, Sheffield, January.

Freeman C. (1982) The Economics of Industrial Innovation, 2nd Ed. Frances Pinter, London.

Gershuny J. (1979) The informal economy: Its role in the division of labour, Futures, February.

Gershuny J. and Miles I. (1983) The New Service Economy, Frances Pinter, London.

Gildner G. (1988) The Revitalisation of Everything: the Law of the Microcosm, Harvard Business Review, March–April, pp. 49–61.

Graham N. (1989) 1977–1987: A Decade of Service, Employment Gazette, Vol. 97, No. 1.

Griliches Z. (1958) Hybrid corn: an exploration of the economics of technological change, Econometrica, Vol. 25, pp. 501–522.

Hakansson H. (Ed) (1987) Industrial Technological Development: A Network Approach, Croom Helm, London.

Harvey D. (1973) Social Justice and the City, Edward Arnold, London.

Hayek F.A. (1960) The Constitution of Liberty, Routledge & Keegan Paul, London.

von Hippel E. (1976) The dominant role of users in the scientific instrument innovation process, Research Policy, Vol. 5, No, 3.

von Hippel E. (1987) Cooperation between rivals: informal know-how trading, Research Policy, Vol. 16, No. 4, pp. 291–302.

von Hippel E. (1988) The Sources of Innovation, OUP, Oxford.

Jones C. and Novak T. (1980) The State and Social Policy, in Capitalism, State Formation and Marxist Theory, ed. Corrigan P., Quartet Books, London.

Jewkes J. et al (1958) The Sources of Invention, Macmillan, London.

Kamien M. and Schwartz N. (1982) Market Structure and Innovation, Cambridge University Press, Cambridge.

Kelly P. and Kranzberg M. (Eds) (1978) Technological Innovation: A Critical Review of Current Knowledge, San Francisco Press.

Klein B. (1977) Dynamic Economics, Harvard University Press, Cambridge.

Kuznet S. (1953) Economic Change, Norton, New York.

Langrish J. et al (1972) Wealth From Knowledge, Macmillan, London.

Lash S. and Urry J. (1987) The End of Organised Capitalism, Polity Press, Cambridge.

LBS Small Business Bibliography (1988) London Business School.

Mansfield E. (1968) Industrial Research and Technological Innovation, Norton, New York.

Marshall N. (1990) The dynamics of producer services, in Spatial Context of Technological Development, eds Cappelin R. and Nijkamp P., Avebury Press, Aldershot.

Marquand J. (1983) The changes to distribution of service employment, in The Urban and Regional Transformation of Britain, ed Goddard J. and Champion A., Methuen, London.

Massey D., Quintas P. and Wield D. (1991) High-tech. fantasies: science parks, in Society, Science and Space, Routledge, London (forthcoming).

Mcloughlin I. and Clark J. (1988) Technological Change at Work, Open University Press, Milton Keynes.

Mole V. and Elliott D. (1987) Enterprising Innovation; An Alternative Approach, Frances Pinter, London.

Morgan K. and Sayer A. (1988) Microcircuits of Capital, Polity Press, Oxford.

Nelson R. and Winter S. (1977) In search of a useful theory of innovation, Research Policy, Vol. 6, No. 1.

Northcott J. (1982) Microelectronics in Industry: What's Happening in Britain, Policy Studies Institute, London.

Oakey R. (1984) High Technology Small Firms: Regional Development in Britain and the United States, Frances Pinter, London.

O'Connor J. (1973) The Fiscal Crisis of the State, St Martin's Press, New York.

OECD (1981) The Measurement of Scientific and Technical Activities, Frascatti Manual 1980, Organisation for Economic Co-operation and Development.

Offe C. (1973) The Abolition of Market Control and the Problems of Legitimacy, Kapitalistate I, III.

Offe C. (1974) Structural Problems of the Capitalist State in German Political Studies ed von Beyme, Vol. 1 Sage, Beverley Hills.

Offe C. (1985) Disorganised Capitalism, Polity Press, Cambridge.

Offe C. and Ronge V. (1975) Theses on the theory of the State, New German Critique, Vol. 6, pp. 137–147.

Olleros F-J. and Macdonald R. (1988) Strategic alliances: managing complementarity to capitalise on emerging technologies, Technovation, Vol. 7, pp. 155–176.

Pavitt K. (1984) Sectoral Patterns of Technical Change; Towards a taxonomy and a theory,

Research Policy, Vol. 13, No. 4.

Pahl R. (1984) Divisions of Labour, Basil Blackwell, Oxford.

Pickvance C. (Ed) (1976) Urban Sociology, Critical Essays, Methuen, London.

Piore M. and Sabel C. (1986) The Second Industrial Divide: Possibilities for Prosperity, Basic Books, New York.

Poulantzas N. (1976) The Capitalist State, a Reply to Milliband and Laclau, New Left Review, Vol. 95, pp. 63−83.

Preston J. (1977) Industrial Medway; an Historical Survey, Published by Private Subscription, Rochester.

Quinn J. (1988) Technology in services: past myths and future challenges, Technological Forecasting and Social Change, Vol. 34, No. 4, pp. 327−350.

Rainnie A. (1991) Flexibility and Small Firms: Prospects for the 1990s, Hatfield Business School Working Paper.

Robinson T. (1990) Partners in delivering the goods; the changing relationship between large companies and their small suppliers, 3i's, London, Mimeo.

Rogers E. (1983) Diffusion of Innovations, Free Press, New York, 3rd edn.

Rosenberg N. (1977) Perspectives on Technology, Cambridge University Press, Cambridge.

Rothwell R. and Zegveld W. (1982) Small and Medium Sized Manufacturing Firms: Their Role and Problems in Innovation, Frances Pinter, London.

Sabel C. (1990) Skills without a place: the reorganisation of the corporation and the experience of work, Paper presented to Annual Conference of the British Sociological Association, University of Surrey, Guildford, April.

Sayer A. (1989) Postfordism in question, The International Journal of Urban and Regional Research, Vol. 1, No. 3.

Schumpeter J. (1942) Capitalism, Socialism and Democracy, Harper & Row, New York.

Scott M. (1989) Management and Industrial Relations in Small Firms, Research Paper No. 70, Department of Employment.

Shaw R. (1986) Research into the consumer adoption of new service technologies: a critical review, Prometheus, Vol. 4, No. 1, pp. 5−67.

Sharp M. and Holmes P. (1989) Strategies for New Technology; Case Studies from Britain and France, Philip Allan, Hemel Hempstead.

Simmel, G. *see* Wolf, K.

Smith S., Dickson K. and Lawton Smith H. (1990) How Was It For Them? High Technology Research Collaboration and the Constraints of Disorganised Capitalism, Paper presented to the Annual Conference of the British Sociological Association, University of Surrey, Guildford, April.

Smith S. (1985) A Political Economy of Urbanisation and State Structure: Urban and Industrial Change in Two Selected Areas, Doctoral Dissertation, University of Kent, Canterbury.

Smith S. (1990) Review of Robinson T. (1990) International Small Business Journal, Vol. 9, No. 1, pp. 93−101.

Smith S. and Wield D. (1988) Banking on the new technology: co-operation, competition and the clearers, in New Perspectives on the Financial System, ed. Harris L. Croom Helm, London.

Stoneman P. (1983) The Economic Analysis of Technological Change, OUP, Oxford.

Teece D. (1986) Profiting from technological innovation: implications for integration, collaboration, licensing and public policy, Research Policy, Vol. 15, No. 4.

Townroe P. (1986) Technological Change in the Service Sector: Urban and Regional Implications, in Technological Change, Employment and Spatial Dyamics, ed. Nijkamp P. Springer-Verlag, Berlin.

Trist E. et al (1963) Organisational Choice, Tavistock, London.

Utterback J. (1979) The dynamics of product and process innovation in industry, in Technological Innovation for a Dynamic Economy, eds. Hill C. and Utterback J. Pergamon, Oxford.

Utterback J. and Abernathy W. (1975) A dynamic model of process and product innovation, Omega Vol. 3. No. 6.

Williams B. et al (1986) Attitudes to New Technologies and Economic Growth, Technical Change Centre, London.

Wilkinson B. (1983) The Shopfloor Politics and New Technology, Heinnemann, London.

Wolf K. (Ed. & trans.) (1950) Simmel G. Quantitative aspects of the group, in the Sociology of

Georg Simmel, Free Press, New York.

Wood P. (1990) The service sector, Geography, Vol. 75, No. 329, pp. 364–368.

Woods A. (1989) Technical Paper No 1, ESRC Centre for Research on Small Service Sector Enterprises, Kingston Business School, Kingston upon Thames.

Woodward J. (1965) Industrial Organisation: Theory and Practice, OUP, Oxford.

8.

Technical Entrepreneurs in the Service Sector:
The Growth of Small Technical Consultancies in the United Kingdom

Dylan Jones-Evans and David Kirby

INTRODUCTION

Traditional economic theory has emphasised the importance of scale economies in industrial organisation, and for some time the propensity has been for companies to organise themselves into large units. More recently, there has emerged a tendency for large firms to contract in size, and to externalise certain corporate activities (Howells & Green 1986). This may be due to recessionary forces reducing the demand for manufactured goods, resulting in rationalisation within larger organisations, with certain divisions peripheral to the core manufacturing operations being sold off. Alternatively, it has been suggested that the process of externalisation may be a consequence of growing demand and the generation of new activities (Perry 1990). However, most of the reasons put forward to explain this phenomenon, and the concomitant growth of the smaller firm, have been related to factors affecting the strategic orientation of the larger organisation. These include the decreasing importance of fixed costs over time (Kleijweg & Thurik 1991), the increased need for flexibility (Acs & Audretsch 1990, Brock and Evans 1989) and increasing specialisation (Perry 1990).

An additional factor may be the increasing influence of technology on corporate strategy. Technological progress is playing a dominant role in the stimulation of rapid industrial development (Gold 1987, Horwitch and Thietart 1987) but larger firms are finding access to certain technological avenues becoming increasingly more difficult. This is because of the growing diversity and complexity of modern technology and technological practices — Abetti (1991) has suggested that 90% of present technical knowledge has been generated during the past 55 years, and that technical knowledge will continue to increase exponentially, probably doubling every 30 years. As Gershuny (1987, p.111) states:

> as tasks become more specialised they require more expertise, and it is not always possible for even the largest of manufacturing concerns to support new specialities.

Such organisations have, therefore, no option but to look outside their internal resources for the appropriate expertise to keep pace with the rapid rates of technological evolution. This development is a natural consequence of the movement from a skill-intensive to a knowledge-intensive industry (Stonier 1983), consequently resulting in an increase in the information intensity of the manufacturing process (Green and Howells 1988).

An increasingly popular method for such organisations to gain access to this expertise is through strategic partnering. This is when two or more companies form a partnership where each company can provide the other with either capital, technology or other resources for a specific purpose (Feulner 1992). This can allow the accomplishment of mutually beneficial goals such as the funding of new research and development, acquisition of state-of-the-art technology, or penetration of new markets (Pelander and Hauser 1991, Gugler 1992). For many firms, entering into some sort of collaborative arrangement with other organisations has become a necessary step towards improving their competitive position. This is particularly true of research-intensive companies that frequently participate in such strategic alliances, especially in the area of pre-competitive research (Litvak 1990, Forrest and Martin 1992).

Thus strategic alliances are being used as a mechanism for increasing the speed at which new technology is developed, enabling many companies to extend their new ideas along the technological spectrum (Link 1990, Sprackland 1992). Several studies have been undertaken which examine such partnerships in a variety of industries, including the computer industry (Littler and Wilson 1992), the pharmaceutical industry (Cahill et al 1992), new materials (Hagedoorn and Schakenraad 1991), biotechnology (Fildes 1990), aerospace (Green et al 1991, Nordwall 1991), telecommunications (Hausmann 1991) and information technology (Hagedoorn and Schakenraad 1992). However, they have tended to concentrate on the co-operative partnerships between larger corporations. This is despite evidence that suggests that for manufacturing firms competing in technologically intensive industries, one option in sustaining efficient performance is the use of small independent consultants to raise the awareness of particular technologies, and assist in the implementation of certain technological systems (Eastwood 1989).

A source of such highly skilled services is naturally an environment where there is an abundant source of scientific and technological expertise. One such source is obviously academia, where individuals in science and engineering departments are often at the forefront of technology. Previous research has examined, in some detail, the technology transfer between academia and industry (Doutriaux and Peterman 1982, Samsom and Gurdon 1990). However, such research has tended to examine the transfer of technology in the form of products or processes, rather than as a specific technological expertise applied to a defined industrial problem. This is despite evidence of increased university—industry interaction with regard to consultation on research and development (Geisler et al 1991), with academics finding themselves in the role of consultant (Furnham & Pendleton 1991).

It has been suggested elsewhere that the function of technical consultancy may be carried out efficiently by technologically advanced small firms which possess the requisite skills and equipment (Bailly et al 1987, Dickson et al 1990). Various studies have indicated that the small-firm sector is providing an increasing number of technological innovations and contributing significantly to employment within high technology sectors (Robson and Townsend 1984, Rothwell 1985, 1986, Acs and Audretsch 1987, 1988). This has led to technologically innovative small firms finding increasing favour as vehicles for economic regeneration, especially in the manufacturing industry.

Various policy reasons have been put forward to explain why small companies involved in technologically innovative activities should be supported. They include:

1. many such small firms have been responsible for significant technological innovations and seem to have created unusually fertile climates for effective research and development (Cooper and Bruno 1977);
2. research and development (R&D) is carried out more efficiently in small technology-based companies (Cooper 1964);
3. the quality of jobs provided in new-technology-based firms is significantly better than those in traditional manufacturing industries (Monck et al 1988);
4. the new products introduced to the market by new firms or the new ventures of existing firms produce greater employment and more exports for the economy (Utterback et al 1982). Thus the formation of new companies can be seen as an indicator of the general economic and competitive health of manufacturing in a country, both in

terms of the actual employment they provide in aggregate, and the 'one-off' employment gain that can occur when small firms experience rapid growth (Oakey and
Rothwell 1986);

5. in ageing Western economies, such small companies are considered to be important
   as knowledge-intensive industries, aiding the transformation from a skill-based to a
   knowledge-based economy (Stonier 1983, Doutriaux and Simyar 1987);
6. during periods of technological change, large establishments and large companies
   cease to grow and expand, and SMEs, owing to their greater flexibility, are in a better
   position to face uncertainty (Maillat and Vasserot 1988);
7. innovative SMEs have above-average levels of employment growth, even in declining
   sectors (Meyer-Krahmer 1985).

Not surprisingly, there has been extensive research into the economic role of such
ventures in the United Kingdom (Rothwell and Zegveld 1983, Oakey 1984), but it has
concentrated on those entrepreneurs involved solely in product or process development
within their own companies. Whilst current research by Jones-Evans and Steward (1991)
has attempted to build on the contemporary knowledge available on such enterprises,
the research has revealed that the 'technological competence' of technical entrepreneurs —
the sufficiency of skill or qualification on which the small innovative enterprise is
based — may be used to provide technical services to other companies. In most cases,
the income from external consultancy is used to fund internal product development
within the small innovative firm, and may, in some cases, be preferable to other more
traditional sources of funding for such enterprises. This supports findings by Whitley
(1987) which have indicated that the problem-solving skills within these companies can
be used either to deal with clients' problems directly, as in the traditional mode of
professional work, or used to generate other outputs that are then sold to customers.

Therefore, despite indications that technical entrepreneurs may be providing service
sector consultancy, there has been comparatively little research in the UK that has
investigated this phenomenon, especially compared with research carried out in other
countries (Aje 1988, Hull and Slowinski 1990, Mouleart et al 1991). One exception is the
work by Howells (1987) on the growth of computer services in the UK, of which computer consultancy is a major sector. However, this study examined the industry as a
whole, and .did not investigate the specific role of consultancies.

SIGNIFICANCE OF THE RESEARCH

In the last decade, there has been a growing appreciation of entrepreneurs and the
important role that smaller companies play in the British economy, with the number of
small companies in the UK growing significantly. This growth has been accompanied
by an expansion in the range and diversity of technology during the same period,
with the resulting emergence of a relatively new type of business venture, namely the
technology-based small firm. Most of the research on this type of enterprise has examined
those companies involved in product or process development, rather than the transfer of
a particular technical expertise to other organisations. This is despite evidence demonstrating that:

1. those firms offering technical services to the community or undertaking R&D activities,
   have 'a very high marginal rate of productivity per employee, sales growing quickly
   with the number of persons involved' (Doutriaux 1987, p.286);
2. there is an increasing demand for new service industries from the manufacturing
   sector (Gershuny and Miles 1983, Wood 1991) consequent upon the needs to reduce
   costs and improve productivity to maintain competitiveness (Handy 1985);
3. the growth of small firms in professional business services stands out as the single
   most important component of the rapid growth of small service sector businesses in
   the 1980s (Keeble et al 1991).

4. many large companies have found that they can increase their efficiency, flexibility and innovativeness by relying more on small firms for certain materials and services. Likewise, many small firms are expanding their market opportunities and their access to capital by doing business with major companies (Henricks 1991, Gilbert 1991, McKee 1992).

Thus research examining this service niche will provide an insight into the processes involved in the development of this phenomenon, and contribute to the overall understanding of the processes of service sector growth as well as the relationship between small businesses and the large organisations which they serve, certainly in the United Kingdom. As Marshall (1988) has observed:

> In general, a limited view has been taken of the role of services in production. When combined with a failure to deal adequately with the internal and external difficulties in measuring transactions, this has severely limited the value of the work

> (p. 250)

TECHNICAL CONSULTANCIES

There is no recognised definition of a 'technical consultancy'. The Standard Industrial Classification (Central Statistics Office 1979) recognises three service activities in which technical consultancies could possibly be located, namely computer services (SIC 8394), professional and technical services not elsewhere specified (SIC 8370), and business services (SIC 8395). However, computer services also include data processing services, recruitment and training, and software development, whilst professional and technical services incorporate architects, chartered surveyors and consulting engineers. Business services account for mainly management consultants and market research organisations (Keeble et al 1989). Therefore, there is no activity heading specifically identifying technical consultancies, and consequently, official statistics cannot be analysed directly to chart the growth of this group.

Additionally, it has been suggested that technical consultants could exist in small technology-based manufacturing firms, and in research and development organisations (Jones-Evans and Steward 1991). An investigation of these two sectors where such companies are to be found could also examine the environment from which small technical consultancies are born. As Rajan (1987) has demonstrated, a significant proportion of the new self-employed consultants were previously engaged in the manufacturing sector in a specialist capacity.

This paper examines the four sectors in which technical consultancies are believed to thrive, namely high-technology manufacturing, computer services, professional/technical services, and R&D. To identify the high-technology manufacturing firms, the methodology devised by Butchart (1987) has been adopted — those SIC sectors with above-average R&D intensity, and above-average proportion of scientists, professional engineers and technicians in the workforce (see Table 1).

TECHNICAL CONSULTANCIES IN THE UK — A PRELIMINARY ANALYSIS OF FOUR SECTORS

To investigate the possible growth of small technical consultancies, data from the biennial Census of Employment has been utilised. This enables an examination of the overall employment change between the four sectors, in order to determine any shift from traditional manufacturing industry towards more service-oriented sectors.

More importantly, it permits an analysis of the number of data units and employees in employment, which will reveal any movement away from large-firm employment towards smaller specialist firms, as well as demonstrating the growth of new firms in the different sectors.

Table 1: High technology industries in the UK (by SIC industry description)

2514 Synthetic resins & plastic materials	3453 Active components & electronic sub-assemblies
2515 Synthetic rubber	3640 Aerospace equipment manufacturing & repairing
2570 Pharmaceutical products	3710 Measuring, checking & precision instruments & apparatus
3301 Office machinery	3720 Medical & surgical equipment & orthopaedic appliances
3302 Electronic data processing equipment	3732 Optical precision instruments
3420 Basic electrical equipment	3733 Photographic & cinematographic equipment
3441 Telegraph and telephone apparatus & equipment	7902 Telecommunications
3442 Electrical instruments & control systems	8370 Professional & technical services not elsewhere specified
3443 Radio & electronic capital goods	8394 Computer Services
3444 Components other than active components mainly for electronic equipment	9400 Research & Development

Adapted from Butchart (1987).

Italics – Industrial sectors classed as 'high technology manufacturing' sectors (for the purposes of this research, telecommunications is also included).

A data unit does not readily correspond to the commonly used terms 'firm', 'company', or 'business', as it includes units with employees which roughly correspond to workplaces. This is because of the way that the data is collected – through paypoints in the Inland Revenue's PAYE (Pay As You Earn) system, with each PAYE point asked to provide details of the number of employees in each worksite and its distinct industrial activity. In larger organisations, there could be more than one paypoint in the organisation, and this could affect the data. In smaller companies, it is expected that the data unit will be equivalent to the firm and include all the employees working there.

It must also be noted that with the gathering of data on the small data unit, the Census of Employment was conducted on a sample basis, from 1984 onwards. Although all units with 25 or more employees were polled, a sample of 1 in 5 was taken of those units with 24 employees or fewer, with the data obtained from this sample grossed up to give an estimate for total employment. However, the effect of sampling on the overall accuracy of the Census of Employment (1989) is very small. Therefore the figures are an estimate, albeit an accurate one, of the employment in the smaller data units.

TOTAL UK EMPLOYMENT

Analysis reveals that overall employment in the four sectors that would be expected to spawn technical consultancies has remained roughly constant in the period 1981–1989 (Table 2). However, the employment structure of the four sectors has changed dramatically. The greatest increase in terms of employment has been in 'professional services' – over 100,000 employees. Following the effects of the recession of the early 1980s on manufac-

Table 2: Change in employment in 'Technical Consultancy Sectors' 1981–1989

SECTOR	Sept 1981	Sept 1989	Change	% Change
HI-TECH MANUFACTURING	1,115,878	1,008,090	−107,788	−9.7
PROFESSIONAL SERVICES	168,814	273,928	105,114	62.3
COMPUTER SERVICES	54,783	137,743	82,960	151.4
RESEARCH & DEVELOPMENT	120,836	97,223	−23,603	−19.5
TOTAL	1,226,219	1,291,083	64,864	3.8

Source: Department of Employment.

turing industry within the UK, it is not surprising that the greatest fall in employment has been in those sectors classified as 'high technology manufacturing'.

The resulting increase in professional services can only be attributed partly to the decrease in employment in the manufacturing and R&D sectors. For example, in the manufacturing sector the externalisation of services began with the contracting out of mainly non-skill tasks in such services as catering, cleaning and security (Marshall 1988). Nevertheless, it is suggested here that a significant proportion of those employed in professional services was previously employed either in the R&D sector or the high-technology manufacturing sector.

With regard to the computing services sector, it is proposed that the growth in employment is due to the increasing range of applications of the information technology sector, ranging from computer-aided design and manufacture within the manufacturing industry, to computerised stock-taking within the service sector. There would seem to be two major reasons for the considerable percentage change in employment (+150%). First, many of the major computer services operators in the UK market have risen out of the in-house computing service departments within large multinational corporations. Howells (1987) shows that many of the key computer service and software operations in Europe have come from internal computer service departments through a sell-off or management buy-outs. Secondly, the number of graduates with information-technology and software-related degrees has been steadily increasing throughout the decade. This, coupled with the growing appreciation in the UK of entrepreneurship as a viable career option, has resulted in the establishment of numerous small computer based firms.

TECHNICAL CONSULTANCIES BY SIZE OF FIRM

As stated, the figures for data units employing fewer than 25 employees are based on a sample (1 in 5) of smaller units, and therefore provide only an estimate of the overall employment in those firms. Also, unlike the main Census of Employment, data unit size analysis is only available from the years 1987 and 1989, so an examination can be made only of growth in that particular period, rather than over a longer time (as in Table 2). Despite such constraints, these figures give an indication of the growth in employment in small companies in those sectors in which technical consultancies are located.

There has been an overall growth in both employment and the number of data units in the high-technology manufacturing sector. As Table 3 reveals, the larger 'company' still dominates the sector, accounting for 77% of the total employment (for those units with more than 100 employees, the average number of employees per unit in 1989 was 385). However, for those businesses employing fewer than five people, there has been a modest growth of nearly 20% in the number of data units and employees during

Table 3: Number of units and employees* by size of firm in high technology manufacturing firms, 1987–1989

	Size according to number of employees					
	1–4	5–24	25–49	50–99	Over 100	Total
1987						
Units	6 002	5 936	1 618	1 172	2 008	16 736
Employees	13 000	65 900	56 300	82 800	778 400	996 400
1989						
Units	7 092	6 264	1 702	1 193	2 024	18 275
Employees	15 200	70 000	59 700	82 800	779 400	1 007 100

Source: Department of Employment.

* Confidentiality rules regarding the Census of Employment dataset require all figures reproduced (relating directly to employment) to be rounded to the nearest 100. This does not apply to figures relating to number of units.

this period, with the average number of employees in 1989 for units with fewer than 100 employees being 14. This suggests that despite a growth in the number of small manufacturing firms, the larger unit still dominates this particular industrial sector where technical consultancies might be expected to grow.

This is also the case with those companies in the research and development sector (Table 4). Again, large companies account for nearly 80% of the total employment in the sector, with the average number of employees in the larger unit (>100 employees) being over 360. However, the number of employees in the sector has fallen by nearly 15 000 in the two years (a decrease of 13%) with the greatest reduction in the number of units being in the larger firm (>100 employees). Despite this declining trend, the number of very small businesses (one to four employees) in the sector (although still only accounting for 1.5% of the total employment in 1989) has grown considerably, with the number of businesses increasing by nearly 45% in two years. This suggests that research and development employees could be moving from larger organisations and establishing their own companies.

In contrast, both the computing services and the professional/technical services sectors are dominated by smaller companies. In 1989, data units employing fewer than 25 employees accounted for nearly half the employment in the professional/technical service industry (Table 5), whilst those companies with fewer than 100 employees accounted for 2/3 of the total employment in the computing services sector (Table 6).

All company size-bands in these two sectors have experienced growth in the period 1987−1989, with the number of large companies (>100 employees) enjoying an average growth of over 20%. However, the most dramatic growth in the computer services sector has been for the very small firms (those employing fewer than five employees). Between 1987 and 1989, the number of data units in this size-band has grown by nearly

Table 4: Number of units and employees* by size of firm: SIC 9400: research & development. 1987−1989

	Size according to number of employees					
	1−4	5−24	25−49	50−99	Over 100	Total
1987						
Units	478	491	155	112	230	1 466
Employees	1 100	5 700	5 300	8 000	91 100	111 100
1989						
Units	681	497	135	111	211	1 636
Employees	1 400	5 800	4 700	7 700	77 700	97 200

Source: Department of Employment.

* See Table 3.

Table 5: Number of units and employees* by size of firm: SIC 8370: professional/technical services, 1987−1989

	Size according to number of employees					
	1−4	5−24	25−49	50−99	Over 100	Total
1987						
Units	17 937	7 133	984	463	282	26 798
Employees	35 900	72 200	33 000	31 400	61 500	234 100
1989						
Units	23 451	8 589	1 163	477	331	34 010
Employees	43 900	85 700	39 800	32 800	71 700	274 000

Source: Department of Employment.

* See Table 3.

Table 6: Number of units and employees* by size of firm: SIC 8394: computer services

| | Size according to number of employees | | | | | |
	1−4	5−24	25−49	50−99	Over 100	Total
1987						
Units	8 727	2 233	458	253	158	11 830
Employees	14 600	24 400	15 800	17 900	35 900	108 400
1989						
Units	15 259	2 868	528	287	202	19 145
Employees	23 600	30 300	18 500	19 300	46 000	137 700

Source: Department of Employment.

* See Table 3.

75%, with the growth in the number of employees being almost equivalent to that employed by data units with more than 100 people. Despite the fact that large companies are offering excellent employment packages to new graduates and current employees alike, it would seem that a considerable number of computer specialists are choosing to set up their own firms.

CONCLUSION

The aim of the paper has been to examine the environment for the growth of technical consultancies. The examination of the four sectors where technical consultancies might be expected to be found − high technology manufacturing firms, computer services, professional technical services and R&D − has revealed that in the period 1981−1989, there was a considerable overall shift in employment in these four sectors towards technical services and computer services. Investigation of the growth by size of firm between 1987 and 1989 showed a significant increase in employment in small firms across all four sectors. More importantly, it revealed an increase in the overall numbers of very small firms, suggesting a high rate of new business formations. This may be due to externalisation by larger companies creating opportunities for employees to establish specialist organisations serving their former employers. Alternatively, it may result from the rapid advancement of technology, creating specialist niches in which small businesses can trade successfully.

Although this paper has not proved conclusively the growth of small technical consultancies, it suggests considerable growth in the number of small firms operating in high technology sectors where such consultants would be situated. In order to determine the precise nature of this phenomenon and the processes at work, further research is required. Accordingly, it is intended to undertake a programme of interviews with a sample of small technical consultancies drawn from the North East of England, focusing on the entrepreneurial teams involved in such ventures. The relationship of such companies with their major large firm clients will also be considered, through interviews with the executives of the larger partner. This will build on the previous knowledge of technical entrepreneurs by examining the phenomenon as a technical service rather than a technical producer, whilst enhancing the body of knowledge on the role of such professional service sector businesses, especially with regard to the strategic role of such individuals and organisations in large firm corporate policy. It will also provide information on the processes by which technical consultancies are formed, the mechanisms by which they grow and develop, and their relationship with larger firm clients, especially why large firms use consultants as opposed to developing expertise in-house. In so doing, the research will contribute to the body of understanding on one of the most significant growth sectors of the UK economy in recent years.

ACKNOWLEDGEMENTS

The authors would like to acknowledge the support of the Nuffield Foundation.

REFERENCES

Abetti P. (1991) The impact of technology on corporate strategy and organisation: illustrative cases and lessons, International Journal of Technology Management, Special Publication on the Role of Technology in Corporate Policy, pp. 40–58.

Acs Z.J. and Audretsch D.B. (1987) Innovation, market structure & firm size, Review of Economics and Statistics, Vol. 69, pp. 567–575.

Acs Z.J. and Audretsch D.B. (1988) Innovation and firm size in manufacturing, Technovation, Vol. 7, pp. 197–210.

Acs Z.J. and Audretsch D.B. (1990) Small firms in the 1990's, in Acs Z.J. and Audretsch D.B. (eds) The Economics of Small Firms: A European Challenge, Kingston upon Thames, Kluwer Academic.

Aje J.O. (1988) The process of hiring and firing a technical consultant, Engineering Management International, Vol. 5, No. 2, pp. 101–105.

Bailly A.S., Maillat D. and Coffey W.J. (1987) Service activities and regional development: some European examples, Environment and Planning A, Vol. 19, pp. 653–668.

Brock W.A. and Evans D.S. (1989) Small Business Economics, Small Business Economics, Vol. 1, pp. 7–20.

Butchart R.L. (1987) A new UK definition of the high technology industries, Economic Trends 400, February, pp. 82–88.

Central Statistics Office (1979) Standard Industrial Classification, HMSO, London.

Cahill S., Caligaris R. and Williams D. (1992) Have pharmaceutical companies missed the boat on biotechnology? Medical Marketing and Media, Vol. 27, No. 1, pp. 28–38.

Cooper A.C. (1964) R&D is more efficient in small firms, Harvard Business Review, Vol. 42, No. 3.

Cooper A.C. and Bruno A.V. (1977) Success among high technology firms, Business Horizons, Vol. 20, pp. 16–22.

Dickson K., Lawton Smith H. and Smith S. (1990) Research Collaboration in Industry, Frances Pinter, London.

Doutriaux J. and Peterman B.F. (1982) Technology Transfer and Academic Entrepreneurship, Proceedings of the 1982 Frontiers of Entrepreneurship Research Conference, Wellesley, MA, Babson College, pp. 430–448.

Doutriaux J. (1987) Growth pattern of academic entrepreneurial firms, Journal of Business Venturing, Vol. 2, pp. 285–287.

Doutriaux J. and Simyar F. (1987) Duration of comparative advantage accruing from start-up factors in high tech entrepreneurial firms, Proceedings of the 1987 Frontiers of Entrepreneurship Research Conference, Wellesley, MA, Babson College, pp. 436–451.

Durham K. (1989) Technology and Business Development, International Journal of Technology Management, Vol. 3, No. 6, pp. 657–665.

Eastwood R. (1989) Manufacturing industry, consultants and 1992, Industrial Management & Data Systems, No. 5, pp. 14–18.

Feulner E.J. (1992) Choosing the right friends, Chief Executive, Vol. 74, pp. 14–15.

Fildes R.A. (1990) Strategic challenges in commercialising biotechnology, California Management Review, Vol. 32, No. 3, pp. 63–72.

Flaig S.L. (1992) The Virtual Enterprise: Your new model for success, Electronic Business, Vol. 18, No. 6, pp. 153–155.

Forrest J.E. and Martin M.J.C. (1992) Strategic alliances between large and small research intensive organisations: experiences in the biotechnology industry, R&D Management, Vol. 22, No. 1, pp. 41–53.

Furnham A. and Pendleton D. (1991) The Academic Consultant, Journal of General Management, Vol. 17, No. 2, pp. 13–19.

Geisler E., Furino A. and Kiresuk T.J. (1991) Towards a conceptual model of co-operative research: patterns of development and success in university-industry alliances, IEEE Transactions on Engineering Management, Vol. 38, No. 2.

Gershuny J. (1987) The future of service employment, in The Emerging Service Economy, ed.

Giarini O., Oxford, Pergamon Press, pp. 105–126.

Gershuny J. and Miles I. (1983) The New Service Economy: The Transformation of Employment in Industrial Societies, Frances Pinter, London.

Gilbert N. (1991) Strategic alliances spur small business R&D, Financier, Vol. 15, No. 6, pp. 18–21.

Gold B. (1987) Technological innovation and economic performance, Omega, Vol. 15, No. 5, pp. 361–370.

Green A.E. and Howells J.R. (1988) Information services and spatial development in the UK economy, Tijdschrift voor economische en sociale geografie, Vol. 79, No. 4, pp. 266–278.

Green J.A.S., Brupbacher J. and Goldheim D. (1991) Strategic partnering aids technology transfer, Research Technology Management, Vol. 34, No. 4, pp. 26–31.

Gugler P. (1992) Building transnational alliances to create competitive advantage, Long Range Planning, Vol. 25, No. 1, pp. 90–99.

Handy C. (1985) The Future of Work: A Guide to a Changing Society, Basil Blackwell, Oxford.

Hagedoorn J. and Schakenraad J. (1991) Inter-firm partnerships for generic technologies – the case of new materials, Technovation, Vol. 11, No. 7, pp. 429–444.

Hagedoorn J. and Schakenraad J. (1992) Leading companies and networks of strategic alliances in information technologies, Research Policy, Vol. 21, No. 2, pp. 163–190.

Hausmann J.A. (1991) Joint ventures, strategic alliances and collaboration in telecommunications, Regulation, Vol. 14, No. 1, pp. 69–76.

Henricks M. (1991) The Power of Partnering, Small Business Reports, Vol. 16, No. 6, pp. 46–57.

Horwitch M. and Thietart R.A. (1987) The effect of business interdependencies on product R&D-intensive business performance, Management Science, Vol. 33, No. 2, pp. 178–197.

Howells J. (1987) Developments in the location, technology and industrial organisation of computer services: some trends and research issues, Regional Studies, Vol. 21, No. 6, pp. 493–503.

Howells J. and Green A.E. (1986) Location, technology and industrial organisation in UK services, Progress in Planning, Vol. 27, pp. 83–184.

Hull F. and Slowinski E. (1990) Partnering with technology entrepreneurs, Research Technology Management, Vol. 33, No. 6, pp. 16–20.

Jones-Evans D. and Steward F. (1991) How does previous experience contribute to entrepreneurial success – an examination of technical entrepreneurs as a case study, Proceedings of the ENDEC World Conference on Entrepreneurship and Innovative Change, Singapore, 3–5 July 1991, pp. 19–24.

Keeble D., Bryson J. and Wood P. (1991) Small firms, business services growth and regional development in the UK – some empirical findings, Regional Studies, Vol. 25, No. 5, pp. 439–457.

Kleijweg A. and Thurik R. (1991) Are there decreasing economies of scale over time in Dutch manufacturing?, Research Paper 9101, Research Institute for Small & Medium Sized Businesses in the Netherlands, Zootermeer.

Lawrence H. (1991) Marriages of Convenience, CFO: The Magazine for Senior Financial Executives, Vol. 7, No. 7, pp. 28–36.

Link A.N. (1990) Perspectives on co-operative research: Learning from US experiences, International Journal of Technology Management, Vol. 5, No. 6, pp. 731–738.

Littler D. and Wilson D. (1991) Strategic alliances in computerised business systems, Technovation, Vol. 11, No. 8, pp. 457–472.

Litvak I.A. (1990) Industry R&D Alliances – a key to competitive survival, Business Quarterly, Vol. 55, No. 1, pp. 61–64.

Maillat D. and Vasserot J-Y (1988) Economic and territorial conditions for indigenous revival in Europe's industrial regions, in High technology industry and innovative environments – the European Experience, eds Keeble D. & Aydalot P. London, Routledge, pp. 163–183.

Marshall J.N. (1988) Services and Uneven Development, Oxford University Press, Oxford.

McKee B. (1992) Ties that bind large and small, Nation's Business, Vol. 80, No. 2, pp. 24–26.

Meyer-Krahmer F. (1985) Innovation Studies and Regional Indigenous Behaviour, Regional Studies, Vol. 19, No. 6, pp. 523–34.

Monck C.S.P., Porter R.B., Quintas P., Storey D.J. with Wynarczyk P. (1988) Science Parks and the growth of high technology firms, Croom Helm, London.

Mouleart F., Chikhaoui Y. and Djellal F. (1991) Locational behaviour of French hi-tech consultancy firms, International Journal of Urban & Regional Research, Vol. 15, No. 1, pp. 5–24.

Nordwall B.D. (1991) Electronic Companies form Alliances to Counter Rising Costs, in Aviation Week & Space Technology, Vol. 134, No. 24, pp. 151—152.

Oakey R. (1984) High Technology Small Firms, Frances Pinter, London.

Oakey R.P. and Rothwell R. (1986) The contribution of high technology small firms to regional employment growth in Regional Industrial Change, eds Amin A. and Goddard J.B., London, Allen & Unwin, pp. 256—84.

Pelander E. and Hauser M. (1991) Joint ventures: Pulling the right pair from the pile, Corporate Cashflow, Vol. 12, No. 8, pp. 24—31.

Perry M. (1990) Business service specialisation and regional economic change, Regional Studies, Vol. 24, No. 3, pp. 195—209.

Rajan A. (1987) Services — the 2nd industrial revolution, Butterworth, London.

Robson M. and Townsend J. (1984) Trends and characteristics of significant innovations and their innovators in the UK since 1945, Science Policy Research Unit, University of Sussex, August, (mimeo).

Rothwell R. (1985) Innovation and the Smaller Firm, paper presented to the First International Technical Innovation and Entrepreneurship Symposium, Utah Innovation Foundation, Salt Lake City, September.

Rothwell R. (1986) The role of small firms in technological innovation, in The Survivial of the Small Firm Vol 2 — Employment, Growth, Technology and Politics, eds Curran J., Stanworth J. and Watkin D. Gower, Aldershot. pp. 114—139.

Rothwell R. and Zegveld W. (1983) Innovation and the Small to Medium Sized Firm, Frances Pinter, London.

Samsom K.J. and Gurdon M.A. (1990) Entrepreneurial scientists: organisational performance in scientist-started high technology firms, Proceedings of the 1990 Frontiers of Entrepreneurship Research Conference, Wellesley, MA, Babson College, pp. 437—451.

Sprackland T. (1992) Puttin' on the Ritz, Electronic Business, Vol. 18, No. 2, pp. 20—28.

Stigler G. (1951) The division of labour is limited by the extent of the market, Journal of Political Economy, Vol. 59, pp. 185—193.

Stonier (1983) The Wealth of Information: A Profile of the Post-Industrial Economy, Methuen, London.

Utterback J.M., Roberts E., Meyer M., Martin A. and Leonard-Barton D. (1982) Comparison of new technology based firm formation. Frontiers of Entrepreneurship Research, Babson College, pp. 519—528.

Whitley R. (1987) The Role of New Knowledge in Technical Skills and Practices, Manchester Business School Working Paper No. 144.

Wood P.A. (1991) Flexible accumulation and the rise of business services, Transactions of the Institute of British Geographers NS 16, pp. 160—172.

9.

STAGES OF GROWTH AND ENTREPRENEURIAL CAREER MOTIVATION

Colin Gray

INTRODUCTION

There are many economically and personally valid reasons why small-firm founders may not want their businesses to expand, but strong evidence indicates that the main reason is connected to the founders' attitudes towards growth and control. This, in turn, is linked to their main motivation for being in business on their own account which a wide variety of surveys and studies consistently identify as the desire to be independent, apparently a far stronger drive than financial motivation (Bolton Report, 1971; Stanworth and Curran, 1973; Department of Employment 1989; Small Business Research Trust (SBRT) 1990). However, it is also clear that 'independence' has quite different meanings for different types of new firm founders (Gray, 1990; 1991).

Apart from the frequently expressed desire 'to be my own boss', independence can range from a rather defensive 'leave me alone' to a more dynamic desire to 'create my own enterprise' or 'be responsible for my own decisions'. Not surprisingly, the more dynamic types of independence tend to become more evident as the size of firm increases. This will be partly due to the self-employed who want to be left alone or those who value their personal autonomy above the commercial imperatives or the social demands of operating a well-run business. These owners are likely actively to avoid employing others or becoming overly committed to clients or customers. On the other hand, owners with a more dynamic concept of independence are likely to seek actively to employ others so as to create supportive business environments for themselves. However, it is not wise to be too prescriptive in attributing causality to self-reported motives, especially if they are recorded at an early stage of a self-employed career.

According to classic motivation theory, many apparently growth-oriented owners will begin to slacken off as they near or attain their original targets (whether explicitly stated or implicitly 'felt'), even though their earlier rate of growth may have been rather swift. Others will seek satisfaction in other fields. It is for these reasons that the rate of growth of a small firm might be expected to decline over time (or as firms reach a certain size). Some economists feel that the rate of workforce growth will slow as efficiency improves with the owner/managers learning lessons from experience or delegating to various functional managers within the firm (Simon and Bonini 1958).

However, some successful owners will prefer to be in a position to sell their businesses, allowing themselves to enjoy the fruits of their earlier labours. By and large, they will be content for the firms they created to progress to higher stages of development under new management (this is common among restaurateurs and hoteliers). Other owners will modify or raise their expectations as a result of their successful organisation of other people and management of a business. Running a small business successfully can engender the desire to run a big business successfully. These owners are potential candidates for continued growth provided they gain their satisfaction from business success. If their main enjoyment lies in organising other people or starting new projects, they are likely to grow up to but not beyond the point the business demands more professional, as opposed to personal, management systems. Along with the legal and teaching professions, this is a fertile breeding ground for budding politicians of all shades and at all levels.

Even with capable and successful small firm managers, therefore the desire for independence can impede further growth if internal delegation or external equity investment are seen as a threat to personal control. The same attitudes can adversely affect plans to merge or sell all or part of the founder's enterprise. Consequently, the independence motive will influence at least four stages of entrepreneurial development from the initial decision to start a new business to the ultimate possibility of exchanging control of an incorporated company and selling out for an appropriate financial reward.

STAGES OF BUSINESS GROWTH

There are a number of stage models of business development which usually share certain features, especially those based on the product life cycle. In general, stage models share an underlying assumption that the ultimate goal of a growing small firm owner is to develop the business into a large, multi-functional corporation and that progression, if not inevitable, is usually linear. An early example is that of McGuire (1963) who developed a five-stage 'small business' development model based on Rostow's (now largely discredited) stage theories of economic development which outlined the progression as: (i) traditional small company, (ii) planning for growth, (iii) take-off from existing conditions, (iv) drive to professional management, and finally (v) mass production marked by a 'diffusion of objectives and an interest in the welfare of society'.

Without analysing this model in any detail, it is fairly evident that each stage is riddled with unsupported assumptions, starting with the idea that most small firms are incorporated, and that 'traditional' firms are likely candidates for planned, entrepreneurial growth, and ending with mass production and social welfare as desired small business targets. As this paper will seek to demonstrate, there is little support for these assumptions. Most small firms are services organised as sole-traders or partnerships with limited business growth objectives (which certainly do not include a social welfare role). The latest (1991) Labour Force Survey revealed not only that there had been a 4% decline in self-employment during 1991, but also that 70% of the 3,282,000 self-employed employed only themselves, and that only 1.5% had grown from sole-trader status to employing more than two other people over the year, in many cases family members rather than externally recruited employees (Campbell and Daly 1992). Stage (i) firms are, therefore, fairly rare and the take-off in stage (iii) even rarer with not much activity taking place in stage (ii). Furthermore, stages (ii) and (iv) — planning for growth and drive to professional management — represent the greatest, as yet unresolved, challenges to professional enterprise trainers and policy-makers.

The evident weakness of this type of stage model lies in its fundamental neo-classical economic assumptions which ignore the reality of small business management and the fact that only a tiny minority of small firms ever grow to a size where internal functional divisions and professional top management teams are in any way feasible. Even as a model for entrepreneurial development it appears to be too static and unreal. It is assumed that a management learning process occurs but, by and large, these models do not provide an explanation of why the firm was founded in the first place and what relation there is between the founding motivations and objectives and subsequent developments.

A well-known model, which attempts to link business objectives and organisational structures and styles to different stages of growth, has been developed by Neil Churchill and Virginia Lewis (1983). Stage (i) existence – directly managed personally by the owner, simple organic structure; (ii) survival – more complex structure with some delegated tasks, supervised by the owners; (iii) success – functional management has appeared and the owner is concerned about maintaining profitability but also concerned about whether future growth is a personal aim; (iv) take-off – having decided on growth the firm acquires a more divisional management structure (with or without the original owner); (v) resource maturity – internal systems and complexity reveals a firm that is concerned about obtaining maximum return on investments.

The Churchill and Lewis model is more flexible but essentially retains a big-business approach in that the strategies linked to each stage are those that imply the small firm owner intends to transform the business into a large corporation. As a model of how large firms might have developed from small origins it may work as a theoretical model but it seems to fly in the face of empirical evidence. This is not merely a matter of the small firm owner's personal motivation but also the fact that many modern large firms, with a few notable exceptions mainly in fashions and hi-tech, are planned and founded as reasonably sized operations from the start.

In fact, stage development models of growth are much more models of firm growth rather than models of individual entrepreneurial or even small firm manager development. Furthermore, they are usually under-developed theoretically. Whether stated explicitly or not, they are based on two dimensions – size of firm (usually defined in terms of workforce) and relative maturity (usually defined in terms of management structure complexity). The studies reported in this paper suggest that managers' attitudes towards growth could be a powerful intervening variable. This contrasts with most stage models which basically ignore the owner or manager as economic actors treating them instead as descriptive devices, almost as markers on a notional growth curve. The lack of relevance to smaller firms has also drawn criticism. Stanworth and Curran (1976) commented on the lack of rigour in stage models and suggested this was because they lacked 'empirical underpinning'. The samples upon which their generalisations are based are usually tiny, they often rely not on longitudinal data (which would seem to be essential) but on retrospective single point observations and they are insufficiently linked to other studies (such as thorough econometric studies of the type mentioned above).

A different approach more attuned to the reality of small firm decision-making, a 'crisis point' five-stage model, outlined a linear progression from a small young firm to a large mature firm in the form of a series of successive crises that have to be resolved before progress can be achieved (Greiner 1972) – crises of leadership, autonomy, control, red tape and so on. Greiner's model is ragged at the upper limits because the final stage(s) are left open-ended but it does provide a series of choice points and introduces the idea that growth or non-growth may be a matter involving the owner's volition. Sue Bates and Peter Wilson (1989) reported to the 12th National Small Business Policy and Research Conference another choice-point model. Their four-point model is much more directed at the earlier stages of small firm growth and is very owner-oriented. Point (i) awareness of the need for strategy – without conscious recognition of the need for an explicit strategy there will be little systematic, formal management development; (ii) willing to loosen control – growth will be more likely if the owner delegates other management functions; (iii) limits to owner's competencies – a management team is more likely to be developed if the owner recognises his or her own limits; (iv) role of external agents – an effective management team is unlikely to be constructed until the owner accepts that external intervention can be beneficial.

This provides a clue as to why so few firms pass beyond the 20–25 employee growth barrier. To employ even just one other human being (except perhaps another family member where the term 'employ' may be fairly loose) is quite a major step for many people which is one reason why less than 1/4 of self-employed have externally recruited employees. For those who do employ others, management can remain fairly informal –

often mainly an extension of the owner — up to about a half-dozen employees, but from about say five employees to around 20–25 there has to be a certain amount of sub-division of labour and the delegation of specific tasks to key employees or partners. Beyond this point it becomes organisationally and psychologically difficult to delegate tasks without also delegating some authority to make independent decisions. It is not too difficult to understand the transition to a more professional management stage, but the transition from self-employment to a microfirm of one to four employees and from there to a small business with say five to 25 employees, which has the resources and can meaningfully think in terms of transition to a medium-sized firm, is very under-researched. This paper examines some of these size effects in relation to personal motivation of owners and attitudes to growth, control and business with particular attention to recently founded surviving (say four to 10 years of trading) small business owners (with five to 25 employees).

Looking at the key decisions that many small firm owners have to face if they embark on a growth track suggests that a model based on five stages or decision-points — at any one of which the owner may refuse the next hurdle — is useful as a framework for discussing the growth potential and likely growth trajectories of certain small firms. The more useful aspects of earlier stage models can be captured under the following five categories:

1. startup (including attempting a management buy-out);
2. survival (exhibiting the decision and drive to continue in business);
3. take-off (whether or not to go beyond personal control);
4. professionalise (introduce a devolved organisational and management structure);
5. transformation (shift from being a small firm to a larger enterprise).

This paper examines how the small-firm owner's career motivation affects the transition from one stage to the next. The assumption is that the owner's business objectives and personal motivations will be significant factors determining whether small firms actually do manage to grow successfully through these five stages. However, it is recognised that most of the very smallest firms are essentially one-product operations and — in the absence of new product development — the fifth stage can usually be substituted eventually for decline or (where the owners manage to sell or merge) exit. Strong motivation on the part of the owner will obviously be linked to a successful passage from start-up to survival though the effects need not be a simple linear causal move from motivation to performance. It is highly unlikely that motivation and performance are independent variables because successful survival will positively affect most owner's future expectations and motivations. The focus of this paper is on the next two phases — transition from survival to take-off and then from take-off to a more delegated professional approach.

METHODOLOGY

The original data for this paper have been gathered through various quarterly postal surveys of small business owner-managers conducted by the Small Business Research Trust (SBRT). The SBRT surveys a sample composed of the memberships of Britain's larger small business representative organisations, chambers of commerce and trade, enterprise agencies and the SBRT's own database of 8,000+ small and medium-sized businesses, most with fewer than 50 employees. New start-ups are under-represented but firms with growth potential and experience are well represented which, for present purposes, is a strength.

The complex influence of the independence motive during the growth stage will be examined in relation to the 639 overlap of respondents from some 1,350 owner-manager respondents to the special question on career motivation and business objectives in a 1990 SBRT quarterly survey and some 1,700 owner-manager respondents to a special question on growth orientation in 1991. This allowed for personal motivation to be crossed against growth orientation plus the actual movement in sales turnover and employment to be monitored. Of the 452 growth-oriented and growth-averse respondents who completed both surveys, 307 also completed a follow-up survey examining personality and motivational, as well as personal background, variables. For the full overlap sample of 639 respondents, Table 1 reveals little difference between growth-oriented and growth-averse small-firm owners in relation to personal motivation.

The negligible difference on the key independence variable is not too surprising given the heterogeneity of the independence motive which is examined in more detail, together with other personal motivations, in the following sections. The implications of the earlier studies using the full sample were discussed in a paper presented to the 14th National Small Business Policy and Research Conference. To simplify analysis and concentrate on the key motivational issues of growth, this study is focused only on the 156 growth-oriented and 151 growth-averse respondents, and the various categories of the personal motivation and business objectives variables have been collapsed into: motivation (external pressures, financial motives, independence, other) and objectives (business targets such as growth in profits and sales, personal security goals, lifestyle, other). Apart from noting the almost even split between the two groups, it is interesting to note that the response rate from the growth-oriented respondents was slightly higher. Confining attention to the follow-up sample of 307 growth-oriented and growth-averse firms, the nucleus of two quite different approaches towards running a small business are apparent in Table 2.

Security objectives include 'protecting standard of living' and 'securing assets for the future', neither of which have a particularly adventurous ring to them (although this is not to say that entrepreneurs may not be motivated by such considerations) and it can be seen that business owners with these objectives are just as driven by financial motives as owners with more obvious economic objectives such as sales or profits

Table 1: Business owners' personal motivation and growth orientation

Motivation	Growth orientation (column percentages)			
	Growth oriented	Growth averse	Other	Total
No alternative	5	6	10	7
Family tradition	1	7	3	4
Independence	56	56	51	55
Security	9	7	6	7
Make money	22	17	22	20
Total (row%)	232 (36)	240 (38)	167 (26)	639 (100)

Table 2: Owners' business objectives by personal motivation

Motivation	Objectives				
	Business	Security	Lifestyle	Other	Total (%)
External	6	14	5	2	27 (9)
Financial	31	32	22	2	87 (28)
Independent	51	47	63	8	169 (55)
Other	3	3	16	1	23 (8)
Total (%)	91 (30)	96 (31)	106 (35)	13 (4)	306 (100)

Chi-square = 25.43; d.f. = 9; significance, $P < 0.0025$.

maximisation. Not surprisingly, owners with security business objectives are more likely than owners with more economic business objectives to have chosen their self-employed career because of family pressure or fear of unemployment. Although independence remains as the most important career motive for all groups, neither of these two groups are as strongly concerned about independence as people in business to support a lifestyle. Again, not surprisingly, far fewer 'lifestylers' (20%) admitted to financial motives compared with more economically minded owners (34%).

This highlights the importance of attitudes associated with a 'business culture' or 'being business minded' in determining the exact nature of growth or entrepreneurial motivation. The importance of these attitudes – which could very well clash with other cultural values subsumed under the 'lifestyle' heading – is more clearly outlined in Table 3 showing significant differences between the business objectives set by growth-oriented and growth-averse small business owners.

The impressive predominance of business/economic objectives among growth-oriented owners and their evident low standing among the growth-averse is significant at $P < 0.000$. Although industry differences ensured that there was no statistically significant connection between growth orientation and actual growth of workforce over the 18 months between surveys, the importance of business cultural values in influencing how independence may be defined by firms with growth potential is highlighted by Table 4 which outlines differences between owners who are business-centred and those who are more concerned about the non-business sides of their lives.

These differences were significant and suggest that those who prefer to define their interests and independence in business terms are more likely to want to pass through the various stages of entrepreneurial growth. These are likely to provide the bulk of small firm owners who transform into owners of larger-small (25–100 employees) and medium-sized (100–500 employees) firms where delegation, division of labour and formal systems become increasingly evident factors of survival and success. However, business centrality may not necessarily be such a significant factor in the early stages – particularly during start-up and during the transition from survival to the take-off 'springboard' – the transformation from microfirm to small business.

Table 3: Business objectives and growth orientation

Objectives	Growth orientation		
	Growth oriented	Growth averse	Total (%)
Business/economic	75	16	91 (30)
Security	39	57	96 (31)
Lifestyle	35	71	106 (35)
Other	7	6	13 (4)
Total (row%)	156 (51)	150 (49)	306 (100)

Table 4: Business objectives and centrality of business to the owner

Business centrality	Objectives				
	Business/economic	Security	Lifestyle	Other	Total (%)
Non-business	14	27	39	4	84 (28)
Business	77	66	65	9	217 (71)
Total	91 (30)	93 (31)	104 (35)	13 (4)	301 (100)

Chi-square = 14.29; d.f. = 6; significance, $P < 0.027$.

Factors associated with the transition from survival to the take-off and up to the professionalise stages are examined through analysing key responses from the 307 small-firm owners, equally split between growth-oriented and growth-averse on the two main variables — firm-size and maturity of firms according to number of years trading. Following the Labour Force Surveys in recognising the essential differences between self-employed sole traders, microfirms of one to four employees, the economic resilience of firms with around a half-dozen employees and the watershed two dozen employee mark, the size bands are: sole-trader, 1—2 employees, 3—4 employees, 5—9 employees, 10—14 employees, 15—24 employees and 25 or more employees. Table 5 which compares fulltime workforce sizes in early 1990, at the onset of the recession, and in mid-1991 gives a measure of the labour market shifts in the active small firm sector.

There have clearly been some movements between bands but the most interesting feature of Table 5 is that, despite the recession, the distributions have remained remarkably stable. Indeed, the 102 respondents who shed staff over the period were almost matched by the 92 who grew. It is of particular interest to note that the most turbulence occurs between the microfirm band of 3—4 employees and the next stage — the 5—9 employee small businesses, with significant growth from sole-trader start-ups to surviving microfirms and from small businesses into the 'springboard' small business band of 15—24 employees.

Whether these shifts are a function of motivation or time will be explored in the following sections. The maturity age bands have been influenced by VAT registration—deregistration analysis: young (1—3 years trading, which includes maximum vulnerability peak failure rates), 4—10 years where survival rates have stabilised, 11—20 years when firms are seen to be well established, 21—30 years which represents maturity and 31 years or more which should include most traditional and inter-generational firms. The independent variables which are the focus of attention include: personal motivation and attitudes towards independence, internal delegation, personal control and external equity finance (which should provide useful data on the likely influence of the independence motive on strategies for realising the value of the owner's enterprise).

RESULTS

In keeping with the dimensions that feature in the stage-models discussed above, progress is measured by size of workforce and, in the absence of detailed organisational and marketing data, maturity can be taken to be a function of age in years of trading. As Table 6 indicates there is a significant link between the age of the firm and its size.

With sole-traders accounting for 70% of the self-employed in Britain and microfirms with 1—5 employees accounting for another 21%, it is clear that the SBRT sample — with

Table 5: Shifts in fulltime workforce size 1990 to 1991

1990 FT employees	Fulltime workforce 1991 (employees)							
	Sole	1—2	3—4	5—9	10—14	15—24	25+	Total
Sole	26	10	4	0	0	0	0	40 (13)
1—2	12	33	7	2	0	0	0	54 (18)
3—4	2	10	39	8	1	0	0	60 (20)
5—9	0	5	9	45	5	1	0	65 (21)
10—14	0	0	1	6	13	7	1	28 (9)
15—24	0	0	0	2	7	13	2	24 (8)
25+	0	0	1	0	0	5	29	35 (11)
Total	40	58	61	63	26	26	32	306
(%)	(13)	(19)	(20)	(21)	(9)	(9)	(11)	(100)

Chi-square = 722.37; d.f. = 36; significance, $P < 0.0000$.

Table 6: Age of firm by size of firm (fulltime employees) in 1991

Size (FT employees)	Age of firm (years trading)					
	Startup 1–3	Survival 4–10	Established 11–20	Mature 21–30	Consolidate 31+	Total (%)
Sole trader	1	22	10	3	2	38 (13)
1–2	2	34	16	4	2	58 (19)
3–4	3	36	14	3	5	61 (20)
5–9	1	26	18	8	9	62 (21)
10–14	0	7	13	3	3	26 (9)
15–24	0	5	15	5	1	26 (9)
25+	0	2	12	7	11	32 (11)
Total (%)	7 (2)	132 (44)	98 (32)	33 (11)	33 (11)	303 (100)

Chi-square = 69.67, d.f. = 24, $P < 0.000$.

about 1/3 in these smaller bands — really is a sample of small-business owners. Furthermore, virtually all the sample has passed through the critical stage of start-up yet 3/4 of the sample have been trading through the height of the 'enterprise culture' years but are young enough to respond without becoming too mature as organisations. However, growth above the two-dozen employee barrier is clearly linked with age of firm and may be more due to the passage of time than any particularly proactive desire to grow. Also, more than half the sample (52%), especially those in the four to 10 year survival band, seem content to remain as microfirms or sole-traders.

This suggests that even in this sample of active small firm owners, the entrepreneurial drive to create a large enterprise was not a strong motivation for founding the firm. However, the desire for growth, even if not strong enough to promote development beyond the 25-employee barrier, does seem related to size. Table 7 compares the growth-oriented and growth-averse owners according to the size of their firms during the first survey in 1990, before the recession became widely acknowledged.

The size-effects in relation to attitudes to growth are clear and it is not surprising that these trends are statistically significant. The sole-traders and microfirms were clearly less concerned about growth and it can be seen that once again the reasonably established small businesses in the five to nine employee band are the most growth-oriented. Whether their stronger interest in business growth translates into a desire to take-off and pass through the 25-employee growth barrier and become professionally managed medium-sized firms is not so clear. Respondents were asked about their future career intentions and Table 8 shows that there are significant size-effects.

With the five to nine employee band accounting for roughly 1/4 of the respondents

Table 7: Growth orientation and size of firm in 1990

Size (FT employees)	Growth orientation		
	Growth oriented	Growth averse	Total (%)
Sole trader	9 (3)	31 (21)	40 (13)
1–2	18 (12)	36 (24)	54 (18)
3–4	27 (17)	33 (22)	60 (20)
5–9	37 (24)	28 (19)	65 (21)
10–14	21 (13)	7 (5)	28 (9)
15–24	19 (12)	5 (3)	24 (8)
25+	25 (16)	10 (7)	35 (11)
Total (%)	156 (100)	150 (100)	306 (100)

Chi-square = 41.44; d.f. = 6; significance, $P < 0.000$.

Table 8:　Future career intentions by size of firm (fulltime employees)

Size (FT employees)	Future career intentions					
	Other	Self-employed	Small firm director	Big firm director	Employee	Total (%)
Sole trader	4	31	4	0	1	40 (13)
1–2	5	40	9	1	3	58 (19)
3–4	9	33	17	0	2	61 (20)
5–9	12	27	21	2	1	63 (21)
10–14	4	11	9	2	0	26 (9)
15–24	1	8	15	0	2	26 (9)
25+	4	5	19	1	3	32 (11)
Total (%)	39 (13)	155 (51)	94 (31)	6 (2)	12 (4)	306 (100)

Chi-square = 63.91; d.f. = 24; significance, $P < 0.0000$.

who wish to become managers or directors of small and large firms, it appears there are some grounds for applying a stage-model approach at the early stages of growth. However, very few of even this active 1/3 of the sample have ambitions eventually to run a large firm. Except for three firms which grew over the 18-month period, the firms with more than 25 employees were already at that size. At the level of the larger and very small sizes, the stage model approach seems to break down.

It is immediately clear that the self-employed sole-traders are not very ambitious with only four (10% of all sole-traders) expressing a desire to become the directors or managers of a small business, thus confirming the pattern in Table 5 where most of the sole-traders had remained as sole-traders. This was not simply a question of opportunity because, as Table 6 demonstrates, all bar one had been in business for more than four years. A similar picture is recorded for the smallest microfirms with one to two employees. On balance, it seems these patterns of development are mainly a function of personal motivation rather than of experience linked with age as suggested by size-maturity (as opposed to decision point) stage models. Certainly, there is no statistically significant linkage between the number of years trading and the future career intentions nor between the age of respondents and workforce size. However, there is evidence that a personal life cycle effect may be operating on attitudes towards growth with the younger respondents tending to be more growth-oriented than the older respondents ($P < 0.000$). There is no statistically significant linkage between the age of respondents and the main objectives they select for their businesses but, as Table 9 shows, there is a link between the age of respondent and the personal motivations for being in business.

This strengthens the case for linking small business growth decisions to the personal life-cycles of the founders and managers rather than to more mechanistic models based on size. The independence motive dominates the more active and growth-oriented 35–44 year group but financial motivations are also important (though relatively less so than they are for the older not so growth-oriented respondents). The inherent conflict between the increasing organisational complexities related to size and the owner's personal motivations can be seen in Table 10 on the vital question concerning delegation.

The overall reluctance of small-firm owners to give up personal control inside their firms is clear (and even stronger if the likely socially desirable effects to report a more participative approach are taken into account). It is important to note, however, that this tendency to be directive in management style is more evident among owners who set 'lifestyle' as a business objective than it is amongst owners who set business/economic objectives or those who see their businesses as a form of security. Given the fact that growth implies an evolution to more devolved management, it is not surprising that growth-oriented owners are twice as likely to be delegative than growth-averse owners (although directive management styles dominate both groups). By contrast, a forced-

Table 9: Owners' personal motivations and age of respondents

Age (years)	Motivations				
	External	Financial	Independence	Other	Total (%)
25−34	0	8	9	2	19 (6)
35−44	3	27	49	2	81 (27)
45−54	11	20	56	5	93 (31)
55−64	6	26	45	9	86 (28)
65+	6	6	6	5	23 (8)
Total (%)	27 (9)	87 (29)	167 (55)	23 (8)	301 (100)

Chi-squared = 35.25; d.f. = 15; significance, $P < 0.002$.

Table 10: Business objectives by management style

Objectives	Management styles		
	Directive	Delegative	Total (%)
Business/economic	54	37	91 (30)
Security	63	30	93 (31)
Lifestyle	81	23	104 (35)
Other	9	3	12 (4)
Total (%)	207 (68)	93 (31)	300 (100)

Chi-square = 13.98; d.f. = 6; significance, $P < 0.03$.

choice question concerning control in relation to external forces − prefer personal control vs accept outside equity − which also addresses an important determinant of future growth, did not discriminate significantly between the growth-oriented and the growth-averse.

CONCLUSIONS

Although only a minority of firms actually grow and actual growth curves are not likely to be particularly smooth, the life-stage model provides a useful description of the process of growth and entrepreneurial development. It provides the (i) start-up and (ii) survival stages as convenient homes for the vast majority of the self-employed. It identifies where entrepreneurial firms fit on the curve, in relation to other businesses, and it clearly outlines the points at which more professional management structures need to be introduced as the business expands. Failure to introduce appropriate management systems is one major reason why expanding firms fail and fall off the curve.

Because severe doubts have been raised about whether many small firm owners actually want to develop their firms into larger businesses, however, it seems that workforce-size/maturity stage models may not be the most appropriate to describe small firm growth. It is clear that some small-firm owners are more business-minded and more steeped in a business culture than others. It is also clear that many growth-oriented firms are more business minded and that this more proactive approach to business is manifested in a greater awareness of the need to address the key issues of continued growth − the need to delegate and the need to seek external equity finance. Fortunately, some evidence has also been presented which suggests that survival and the uplift that comes from successfully running a business may itself help provide the impetus for some future growth.

This seems to be especially true of the microfirms with 3−4 employees and the smaller businesses with five to nine employees, but definitely not true of most sole-traders or even the very small microfirms. However, it also seems true that few of the more active small firms actually want to grow beyond a barrier, say at the 25 employee mark, where the nature of the firm and their own management tasks are transformed. The implication for public policy is that fewer resources should be spent on encouraging new start-ups but more on helping the self-employed and small microfirms employ and manage other people. At the other end of the scale, there may be a case to be made for facilitating the sale of successful small businesses — perhaps through regional business brokers — to professional teams and the re-investment of the successful ex-owners' capital and skills in boosting the growth prospects of strategically important microfirms. The success of any such scheme would, of course, depend on whether it matched the personal motivations of a sufficient number of successful small-business owners.

REFERENCES

Bates S. and Wilson P. (1989) Turning Points in Business Growth; Implementing Management Development in Small Business, Paper presented to the 12th National Small Firms Policy and Research Conference, London, November.

Bolton J. (1971) Small Firms — Report of the Committee of Inquiry on Small Firms, Cmnd 4811, HMSO, London.

Campbell M. and Daly M. (1992) Self-employment into the 1990s, Employment Gazette, June.

Churchill N. and Lewis V. (1983) The five stages of business growth, Harvard Business Review, May—June, pp. 30—50.

Department of Employment (1989) Small Firms in Britain, London.

Gray C. (1990) Business Independence — impediment or enhancement to growth in the 1990s?, Paper presented to the 13th National Small Firms Policy and Research Conference, Harrogate, November.

Gray C. (1991) Growth-orientation and the small firm, Paper presented to the 14th National Small Firms Policy and Research Conference, Blackpool, November.

Greiner L. (1972) Evolution and revolution as organizations grow, Harvard Business Review, July—August, p. 37.

McGuire J. (1963) Factors Affecting the Growth of Manufacturing Firms, Bureau of Business Research, University of Wisconsin, Seattle.

NatWest Quarterly Survey of Small Business in Britain (1990—1992) Volumes 6—8, Small Business Research Trust, London/Milton Keynes.

Simon H. and Bonini C. (1958) The size distribution of American firms, American Economic Review Vol. 48, September, pp. 607—617.

Stanworth J. and Curran J. (1973) Management Motivation in the Smaller Business, Gower, Aldershot.

Stanworth J. and Curran J. (1976) Growth and the small firms — an alternative view, Journal of Management Studies, Vol. 13, No. 2, May, pp. 95—110.

10.

'KEEPING IT IN THE FAMILY': Small Firms and Familial Culture

Monder Ram and Ruth Holliday

INTRODUCTION

The family enters the domain of work in a variety of ways. This paper discusses the actual significance of the family at the level of the workplace within the context of small firms, a setting which is suffused with the notion of the family in both actual and meta-phorical senses: not only do small firms often rely on family ties in, for example, recruit-ment (Maguire 1988); they are also frequently described by workers and managers as being 'like a family' (Rainnie 1989).

There have been a range of studies that have deployed metaphors and labels with familial connections. Newby (1977) for example, has used the term 'paternalism' to describe the nature of work relationships between farmers and farm workers. Scase and Goffee (1982) identified 'fraternalism' as the dominant mode of relations between owners and their skilled construction employees operating in particular product and labour market circumstances. Rainnie (1989) saw management's emphasis on the 'family' as a means of exerting discipline over workers in the small clothing and printing firms that he studied. However, despite the references to the family and familial terms, these studies have sought to present a picture of the general nature of social relations rather than an analysis of the impact of the family or specific 'family' culture on the shopfloor.

Within the ethnic business literature, there has been an even more pronounced as-sociation between the family and the firm, but a parallel neglect of the dynamics of the family at work. The family has often been seen as critical to the success of minority enterprise (Mars and Ward 1984, Ward 1987). This is particularly evident in accounts that derive from what Phizacklea (1984) has termed the 'sociology of ethnic relations school'. The approach accords primacy to ethnic solidarity and, in the case of Asians, would suggest that 'cultural' features like the ideology of self-help, the operation of fraternal networks and the importance of the family unit are integral to the development of minority enterprise.

Studies in the tradition of the sociology of ethnic relations school highlight the fact that migrants/immigrants are neither passive nor victims and can actively deploy their particular cultural resources to their advantage. However, they neglect the impact of racism which has been shown to be an equally if not more important factor in pushing ethnic minorities into self-employment and keeping them in peripheral market locations (Jones et al 1989). Furthermore, resource-based accounts in the tradition of Werbner (1984) obscure the fact that minority labour power is gendered (Phizacklea 1990). Anthias' (1983) study of Greek Cypriots' involvement in the rag trade sharply illustrates that the exploitation of minority women is crucial to the survival of such firms. The intensive use of female labour is underpinned by an ideology that emphasises family and community. In highlighting the plight of minority women in these situations, these studies provide a useful corrective to gender-blind accounts of ethnic business. Despite the pervasiveness of the 'family firm' label, labour power in this context is clearly gendered. But although such accounts help to highlight that the family is more a resource for men than women, they do not explore the concrete ways that the family operates on the shopfloor. The gendered nature of the family firm is exposed, but its impact on day-to-day relations at work is not.

This paper explores the impact of the family and of 'family' culture on concrete shopfloor processes. 'Family' members may be blood relatives or those enculturated into the family metaphor. Thus, small firm workers may not be related to other workers in, or owners of, the family firm but may nevertheless identify as 'one of the family'. The paper focuses on the ways in which the 'family' influences different processes in small firms, namely, management organisation and recruitment. Family culture is then discussed in more detail.

METHODOLOGY

The 6 companies used in this research were all small manufacturing firms. Those studied by Monder, companies A, B and C, were Asian-owned clothing firms, and Ruth's were an all-woman clothing manufacturer (Wellmaid), an engineering company supplying filtration equipment to the gas and oil industries (Techeng), and an electronics firm (Transformer Ltd).

We have very different backgrounds, both personally and academically. We have also been working on very different projects, centred respectively on employment relations and operations management. We have different ethnic backgrounds and different genders. We have also researched different kinds of firms. However, one thing that we do have in common is our methods, a mixture of direct and participant observation and interviews.

Access
Getting into small companies with a view to undertaking qualitative research over a long period is extremely difficult. Securing the consent of notoriously hard-pressed employers to enter the workplace and generally observe and participate in day-to-day shopfloor life over an extended period of time is an onerous undertaking. This may be why shopfloor studies focusing on internal processes are quite rare. In the case of minority businesses the problem is compounded since such firms tend to be concentrated in the recesses of the economy and because of racism within society.

However, neither of us experienced problems of this kind. Both of us used the 'opportunistic' approach advocated by other researchers (Bresnen 1988, Buchanan et al 1988, Crompton and Jones 1988) in which contacts, friends and relatives were used to the full. This also involved us being 'insiders' to varying degrees in order to make these contacts. Monder was an insider by virtue of his ethnicity and detailed knowledge of the clothing industry, as well as coming from a respected family in the local Asian community which has been immersed in the clothing sector for many years.

For Ruth, insider status was less tenable. Rather than familial contacts, access was secured through the playing of 'bargaining cards'. Bargaining cards can be skills/knowledge brought to the study setting — work experience, business school contacts and so on. As Gary Stockport found out, the organisations in his study were more interested in the researcher than the research, in terms of what they can get out of him (Stockport and Kakabadse 1992). Ruth's principal bargaining card was more straightforward: she was allowed access to study and interview in return for her labour. Thus, she had very few problems in this respect. Only one company flatly turned her down and another asked her to come back later as they were presently involved in a major crisis. The three other companies which she approached accepted immediately; in fact one company complained that she could not start earlier than she did.

The negotiation of access, however, is not a once-and-for-all agreement but a continuous process of winning people's trust. There was a range of considerations and issues in establishing trust in both studies. That said, our particular backgrounds and the terms upon which access was secured allowed us, in different ways, to get 'inside the culture' (Oakley 1981). Operating from such a position, the complex and negotiated nature of shopfloor processes was evident; and an integral part of such processes was clearly the family. It permeated many facets of shopfloor life; the following sections discuss its impact on management organization, recruitment and the pattern of control.

MANAGEMENT ORGANISATION

The family in management

The companies in Monder's research were all family-owned concerns with members of the family occupying the key management and supervisory positions within the firms. Typically, the company would be managed by the men in the family and the machinists would be supervised by the women in the family, who were often the spouses of the managers. In Ruth's research there was also evidence of substantial family involvement in the firms. For example, at Wellmaid the company was owned by three women, two of whom were sisters. Transformer Ltd was owned by a husband whose wife was also a director and company secretary of the firm. Techeng had been owned by a father who had passed the business on to his son.

The intensive use of familial labour within key positions in the firm has often been viewed as critical to the 'success' of Asian enterprise (Mars and Ward 1984, Ward 1987). Two basic reasons have usually been put forward to explain this. Firstly, family labour is cheap and relatives are prepared to work for long hours (Boissevain et al 1990). Secondly, family occupation of managerial roles is seen to ease the problem of managerial 'control'. In their study of minority clothing firms in London, Paris and New York, Morokvasic et al (1989) make the point that running a business with relatives and co-ethnics for partners resolves the problems of trust and delegation. These rationales were evident in the reasons given by employers for the prominence of the family in firms in the current studies. According to Sig, a partner in company B:

> The burden is shared — finance, trust, risk — it's all shared. I'm not the owner of the factory, but I worry if production is not coming out or if the accounts are not in order. If one of us has to go somewhere, then we know that there's someone left in the factory that we can trust. You can rely on family members to do the work, you can't really do that with ordinary workers.

Suneta, the wife of Gel, the de facto MD of company C, was placed in a position of responsibility because of familial ties. She was given the job of sample machinist because the company needed someone that they could 'trust' to tell them how difficult a particular garment was to assemble and what would be a fair rate for the job. Her views on the complexities of garments were integral to the calculation of the piece-rate. This was similarly the case at Wellmaid where Mary, a director and sister of one of the other directors, would sew sample garments and was then trusted to determine the piece-rate.

Familial labour — a constraint

The intensive use of familial labour was thus an important means of managing the enterprise in this context. Extensive familial involvement is depicted as a boon to management, primarily because it is cheap and supervision is made easier (Ward 1987). Viewed in this way, the 'rationality' of the use of family labour seems beyond contention. However, the use of the family in key positions can, in important respects, serve to constrain management.

Some of the brothers in company C were not competent to hold the positions that they occupied but they were retained regardless. This was the comment of the only non-brother in a management role:

> They're bosses but not all of them have the skill. Take Dev [a brother] for example. They spent £20,000 on a machine for him to run yet it's not making any money. They can't tell him to bugger off because he's a member of the family, but if it was me who was not pulling his weight, they'd soon tell me to piss off.

Similarly, at Wellmaid, the pattern cutter said of Mary, the sister of one of the directors and then a supervisor in the firm: 'Mary has got enough problems of her own, without sorting out anyone else's'. It was a running joke at the factory that Mary was incompetent, and this was worsened by Mary's stressed and nervous disposition. However, as a family member it would have been impossible for her to have been sacked despite the fact that she obviously couldn't cope. Eventually, Mary actually resigned and now works at the factory as a part-time machinist. The company had to wait for Mary to decide to leave, rather than dismissing her, which would probably have saved her a lot of worry.

The brother with overall responsibility in company C stated that one of the problems of having so many members of the family in the business is that they 'take too many liberties'. On one occasion, the youngest brother, who was regarded as something of a 'playboy', was actually sacked. He was soon reinstated however because the parents applied pressure on the brother in charge. Clearly, 'controlling' a family member was not a simple process.

Gender

The 'family' therefore was not the undiluted resource as which it is frequently presented; it could also constrain management in certain circumstances. Management organisation was further complicated by the role of gender, both in terms of the nature of women's jobs and in terms of the status attributed to them. Much of the management of the place of work was the responsibility of women members of the 'family'. Women's manage-ment of the internal processes of the firm, however, often meant balancing a chaotic production system and the conflicting pressures of the shopfloor and management, as well as shouldering the bulk of the responsibilities in the domestic sphere. Despite the rigours of these essentially managerial tasks, women were still supervisors rather than managers in these family firms.

In company A the wife of the proprietor and his two daughters-in-law were all involved in the running of the family business. For a number of years, the proprietor's wife virtually ran the family retail business (an offshoot of the manufacturing operation). Despite her central role in this enterprise, she was not paid a direct wage, instead being allocated a sum of pocket money by the proprietor. The daughters-in-law spent most of their time supervising a group of machinists. They were responsible for ensuring that everyone was supplied with work, looking after administrative matters and working as machinists themselves. In addition to these tasks, the daughters-in-law were expected to shoulder the domestic responsibilities of the household, which, given the fact it was a fairly large extended family, were considerable. The 'wages' that they received for performing this bewildering array of functions was whatever they earned on piece-rate as machinists. This was often negligible since most of their time was taken up on jobs other than sewing. It was expected that their husband or mother-in-law would provide them with an allowance for personal expenditure.

Despite the low level of direct wages, the three women (the proprietor's wife and the two daughters-in-law) played a crucial role in the day-to-day management of the firm's financial resources. For example, the takings of the various parts of the family business would be left with the proprietor's wife for safe keeping. Other than taking money out for household expenditures, she was not supposed to do anything with these funds. In reality, however, she played an active role in the management of these resources, switching funds around various parts of the family enterprise.

The daughters-in-law were responsible for negotiating, calculating and paying the wages of the machinists. They too would often be involved in the handling of the company's financial resources when it came to the payment of wages. They would bargain over the rate for the garment, responsibility for mistakes and the allocation of work. Yet, despite this immersion in the day-to-day financial matters of the business, they had little responsibility for the overall management of company resources.

Thus, family women are somewhat invisible in their roles as managers in small companies, but is this so for the families of women entrepreneurs? Watkins and Watkins (1986) argue that entrepreneurs are likely to be the progeny of entrepreneurial families, although this does not necessarily mean in continuation of the established family business. They add that the male entrepreneur is likely to have a traditional-style marriage with a wife who plays a subservient and supportive role, both in the home, by (single-handedly) bringing up a family, and working in the firm during the early stages of its existence. This usually involves doing the books for the company or undertaking secretarial, cleaning or packing work. Janet Finch's (1983) research adds the entertainment of business associates to the list of supporting duties. In contrast, female entrepreneurs are far more likely to be single. But, as Watkins and Watkins (1984, p. 224) discovered, even when the female entrepreneur was married:

> in those few cases where the husband was involved with the business it was usually in an ad hoc, peripheral, 'expert' role rather than a supportive, subservient one.

This pattern was apparent in one of Ruth's case studies where the wife of the owner-manager was also a director. However, Ruth only discovered this very late on in her fieldwork as this woman was never referred to in terms of her business role. When she questioned the owner of the company he explained that his wife was a 'sleeping partner', but that in fact she was more 'dormant than sleeping'. When questioned further he conceded that she was actually company secretary, and thus prepared the management accounts and so on. Furthermore, although she once had a permanent job within the company, she had given this up in order to secure another position elsewhere in order to fund the company through a particularly hard time. Thus she was responsible for 'facilitating' the survival of the business.

Jane Wheelock justifies the term familial economic unit by pointing out that many women facilitate the survival of their partners' businesses through their domestic labour, which is not explicitly financially rewarded (Wheelock 1991). Thus women play critical roles in the survival of family businesses, through both formal, but unacknowledged roles within the firm, and through their unpaid facilitating roles in the domestic sphere. They are very influential in a number of ways and yet because their roles are not usually formally recognised their input is frequently ignored by researchers of small businesses.

RECRUITMENT

Employers in both studies used the word-of-mouth method of recruitment. As is the case in most small firms, the grapevine was still the most effective system of recruitment. Generally, the process entailed the owners asking their workers to encourage friends and relatives to come to work for them. The whole process was very informal; application forms or formal interviews were rarely used. These particular channels of recruitment made it more likely that the workers recruited would be from the workers' familial and social milieux.

Such informality in recruitment through the use of family, community and workforce connections has often been viewed as a means of furthering management's control over the workforce, and that qualities such as 'reliability' and 'conformity' were guaranteed through family discipline and obligation (Dick and Morgan 1987). The utility to management of features like stability and discipline are beyond doubt and help to explain the continued prevalence of informal recruitment practices even in large organisations

(Collinson et al 1990, Maguire 1988). However, informality can have unintended consequences which may militate against the very advantages that informal recruitment is supposed to provide.

By allowing the workforce so much autonomy in attracting new workers, management in both the current studies were effectively ceding considerable discretion over eventual recruitment decisions. Many of the workers from the case study companies had been with the firms for a number of years. They had developed their own norms, understandings and patterns of working. Given the dynamics of the production system, which relied on the interdependence of workers for its effectiveness, it would have been extremely difficult for new recruits to survive for any length of time unless they fitted into existing configurations of social relations at work. For example, in company B in Monder's research, two workers who management recruited at particularly 'busy' times were effectively 'forced' out by the existing workforce. The recruits were undoubtedly competent, but one was a West Indian and the other was a Muslim whereas the existing workforce was predominantly Punjabi. In Ruth's study too the inability to fit into existing norms despite technical competence was also evident. For instance, Raj, owner of Transformer Ltd. said:

> I mean at one time we had a guy who was a first class able man, but he was a misfit because his attitude was all wrong: he didn't have any sense of humour, and he was a trouble-maker, so we had to part company.

To use Jenkins' (1986) point regarding 'suitability' and 'acceptability', it was evident that newcomers to the firms in both studies needed to be 'suitable' in the technical sense of being able to do the job, and 'acceptable' in terms of being able to 'fit in' — but 'acceptable' to a significant degree to workers as well as management.

The mutuality that such a recruitment process implies was evident in the current studies. In both cases there were instances where management felt an 'obligation' to employ family members despite there not being a pressing need for new workers in a strictly economic sense. At Techeng the accounts supervisor's daughter became pregnant by her boyfriend. He was unemployed, so the accounts supervisor went to the directors and asked them to find him a job. This they did and he was employed as a labourer and odd jobber. His tasks ranged from cleaning the factory, to gardening, to fetching snacks and making tea.

'FAMILY' CULTURE

The paper so far has predominantly discussed the ways in which family members are deployed in small businesses and their various work roles. Thus, we have shown that the impact of family at work is complex and cannot necessarily be seen as an uncomplicated resource for management. However, our research suggests that 'family' culture is not simply a product of employing family members and can be cultivated without a predominance of blood ties. Thus, even firms which employ no family members can still identify as a 'family firm'.

Analyses of small firms have frequently acknowledged the existence of a family culture. These appear to take two extreme views. First came the 'small is beautiful' hypothesis of employment relations (Ingham 1970) which described companies as being 'like happy families'. Indeed this philosophy appears to have been taken on board not only by academics but by small firms themselves. In response to this Rainnie (1989) stressed the disharmony of such companies portraying the image of the harsh, autocratic and patriarchal management. However, our studies have shown that the notion of 'family' culture is a more complex and negotiated phenomenon than these polarised views suggest. There are instances from our research which might serve to highlight this autocratic patriarchy of 'family firms'. At Techeng, for example, the finance director told of a new employee:

One man who came along and tried to start a union was fired because of that, because really they just create animosity. I think a trade union is a sign of bad management. If management is incapable of operating its personnel management without a union then you've got something wrong, seriously wrong. We've never had unions.

Therefore, taken purely from an owner's perspective, it might be expected that harsh management regimes exist which will not tolerate diversity or resistance. Perhaps the predominant theories of simple autocratic management in small firms have arisen through a tendency to interview only owners of companies or their nominees. However, managerial control in small companies, although in some ways made more autocratic or patriarchal through family involvement or the creation of a family culture, also acts to dilute managerial power.

There was much evidence in Ruth's research of key or core members of the firms, that is those that have been with the company for a long time or those who had family connections, who were identified very strongly with the 'family' culture. This identification, or position within the family milieux, entitled these employees to preferential treatment, as Chris at Techeng explained:

> Well you've got the old campaigners like Judy and Stan and Mike ... they're like a little family unit. All the other latecomers are ... well it's difficult to get in. The old campaigners, they're a law unto themselves, they come and go and all the newcomers are frightened to do anything wrong. I daren't ask for any time off to go to the dentist and they're rolling in late and going home early. It's one set of rules for one and another set for another.

Furthermore, this affiliation did not only entitle key members to privileges but also affected the way in which their relationships were conducted. For example, a key member might argue over some management decisions, or may even refuse to perform certain tasks which they found boring or unpleasant. Thus, family membership also entitled employees to negotiate their duties.

There is evidence, however, that the status of core women is still lower than that of core men. This also replicates gender roles within the family. In two of the companies there were 'key' women. At Techeng Judy had been with the company since she was sixteen and was certainly considered 'one of the family'. As one of the directors said:

> There isn't anyone in the organisation that I could delegate to except Judy, who's invariably the best at running the place. She could easily run the company I think. I would hate having to replace Judy because I view her as one of my vital supports in running the business, just the peace of mind that I have. I mean I've moved Judy around the company, she's been the buyer, Alan's secretary, she's been in charge of the accounts, she's now managing to whip Mike into shape in his quality management.

Judy had actually achieved the rather equivocal title of Document Control Manager. However, she was still paid less than all of the other (male) managers in the company. Although this was a very important job, it remained very much internal to the company, with no outside dealings. When this was put to the finance director, he replied: 'She's paid quite well, she's on £10,000 now and she's not qualified in any way. You find a girl at thirty with no qualifications in [this city] that's paid more.'

Thus, Judy is compared not to other managers within the company, some of whom were not qualified either, but rather with other 'girls' in other firms in the city. Furthermore, her title of manager has only been in place for one year, although she has been with the company for sixteen years.

A further aspect of gender in the workplace is the status attributed to women's jobs. Ruth was surprised when she undertook her fieldwork at Wellmaid that she was allocated the task of pattern cutting which is often regarded as being highly skilled and usually done by men. One thing which Ruth was not allowed to do was to sew as this was seen as too highly skilled. Thus, these tasks were attributed reverse status to the same tasks in Monder's case study firms where men always did the pattern cutting. This adds weight to Phizacklea's (1990) assertion that pattern cutting is viewed as skilled, simply because it is normally undertaken by men, and that conversely sewing is seen as semi-skilled as it is predominantly done by women. In the all-woman Wellmaid, such a gendered division of labour could not exist.

Our work lends support to our assertion that women in small firms are often attributed roles that simulate the gendered division of labour within the family. These roles are in turn rewarded accordingly, influenced by the male 'breadwinner' and female 'actual or potential wife and mother' ideology (Phizacklea 1990, p. 23). This in turn explains why these roles are valued and yet taken for granted and thus not rewarded fiscally or in terms of status within the company.

Thus, a family culture may be cultivated by owner-managers in order to promote trust and increase the degree of alignment between the goals of managers and employees. This can be seen as a rational policy on the part of managers. As a result those who join the company must fit into the family culture or leave. However, the maintenance of a family culture can be seen as irrational in that valuable resources are wasted. For example, in the perpetuation of the gendered division of labour, the talents and skills of women are wasted, both in terms of their being blocked from certain jobs and as they become demotivated through continuing low pay and status in relation to their male co-workers. However, it must be recognised that women and other workers are not purely passive in the face of autocratic management, and that key workers can hold power over management in certain situations. Thus, in family firms employing family members, and in those identified with a familial culture, power relationships are negotiated. The term 'negotiated paternalism', which Monder first used to describe the pattern of social relations in his study, would therefore appear to have wider currency as it was equally applicable to Ruth's cases.

CONCLUSION

The purpose of this paper has been to explore the significance of the family at work in the small firm setting. Small firms are saturated with the ideology of the family, but its actual impact at the level of the workplace is a question that has received little attention. We have argued that the family is of considerable importance to the organisation of the workplace, but not simply as a cover-up for managerial autocracy on the one hand, nor a signifier of harmony on the other. Rather, the 'family' contains complexities and contradictions which mean that its dynamics at work will be contingent and negotiated.

Picking up the degree of negotiation, the dynamics of the 'family' and the actual complexity of life on the shopfloor was attributable in large part to the methods used in researching the studies. This enabled the stereotypes and 'rationalities' of the workplace to be observed in action and located within their context. Our studies have thus linked the concepts of the family firm, the irrationality of management, and the low status of women; and identified the concept of 'negotiated paternalism' as a means of understanding the pattern of social relations in such settings.

REFERENCES

Anthias F. (1983) Sexual divisions and ethnic adaptation: the case of Greek−Cypriot women, in One Way Ticket, ed. Phizacklea A., Routledge and Kegan Paul, London.

Boissevain J. et al (1990) European trends in ethnic business, in Ethnic Entrepreneurs, eds. Waldinger R., Aldrich H., Ward R. and Associates, Sage, London.

Bresnen M. (1988) Insights on site: research into construction project organisations, in Doing Research in Organizations, ed. Bryman A., Routledge & Kegan Paul, London.

Buchanan D., Boddy D. and McCalman J. (1988) Getting in, getting on, getting out and getting back, in Doing Research in Organizations, ed. Bryman A., Routledge and Kegan Paul, London.

Collinson D., Knights D. and Collinson M. (1990) Managing to Discriminate, Routledge, London.

Crompton R. and Jones G. (1988) Researching white collar organisations: why sociologists should not stop at case studies, in Doing Research in Organizations, ed. Bryman A., Routledge and Kegan Paul, London.

Dick B. and Morgan G. (1987) Family networks and employment in textiles, Work, Employment and Society, Vol. 1, pp. 225–246.

Finch J. (1983) Married to the Job, Allen and Unwin, London.

Ingham G. (1970) Size of Industrial Organisation and Work Behaviour, Cambridge University Press, Cambridge.

Jenkins R. (1986) Racism and Recruitment, Cambridge University Press, Cambridge.

Jones T. et al (1989) Ethnic Communities and Business Needs, Commission for Racial Equality, London.

Maguire M. (1988) Work, Locality and Social Control, Work, Employment and Society, Vol. 2. pp. 71–87.

Mars G. and Ward R. (1984) Ethnic business development in Britain, in Ethnic Communities in Business, eds. Ward R. and Jenkins R., Cambridge University Press, London.

Morokvasic M. et al (1989) Business on the ragged edge, in Ethnic Entrepreneurs, eds. Waldinger R. Aldrich H. Ward R. and Associates, Sage, London.

Newby H. (1977) Paternalism and capitalism, in Industrial Society: Class Cleavage and Control, ed. Scase R. Allen and Unwin, London.

Oakley A. (1981) Interviewing women: a contradiction in terms, in Doing Feminist Research, ed. Roberts H., Routledge and Kegan Paul, London.

Phizacklea A. (1984) A sociology of migration or 'race relations'? A view from Britain, Current Sociology, Vol. 32 pp. 206–218.

Phizacklea A. (1990) Unpacking the Fashion Industry: Gender, Racism and Class in Production, Routledge, London.

Rainnie A. (1989) Industrial Relations In Small Firms: Small Isn't Beautiful, Routledge, London.

Scase R. and Goffee R. (1982) 'Fraternalism' and 'Paternalism' as employer strategies in small firms, in Diversity and Decomposition in the Labour Market, eds. Day G., Caldwell L., Jones K., Robbins D. and Rose H. Gower, Aldershot.

Stockport G. and Kakabadse A. (1992) Using ethnography in small firms research, in Small Enterprise Development; Policy and Practice in Action, eds. Caley K., Chell E., Chittenden F. and Mason C. Paul Chapman, London.

Ward R. (1987) Resistance, accommodation and advantage: strategic development in ethnic business, in The Manufacture of Disadvantage, eds. Lee G. and Loveridge R. Open University Press, Milton Keynes.

Watkins J. and Watkins D. (1984) The female entrepreneur: her background and determinants of business choice – some British data, in The Survival of the Small Firm, (Vol One: The Economics of Survival and Entrepreneurship), eds. Curran J., Stanworth J. and Watkins D. Gower, Aldershot.

Werbner P. (1984) Business on trust, in Ethnic Communities in Business, eds. Ward R. and Jenkins R. Cambridge University Press, London.

Wheelock J. (1992) The flexibility of small business family work strategies, in Small Enterprise Development; Policy and Practice in Action, eds. Caley K., Chell E., Chittenden F. and Mason C. Paul Chapman, London.

11.

GAMBLING ON ENTREPRENEURSHIP

Martin R. Binks and Philip A. Vale

INTRODUCTION

This paper focuses on the specific, supply-side issue of finance. The relevance of the supply of finance is readily apparent following the bullish behaviour of financiers and clearing banks in the buoyant 1980s, leading to embarrassed and bearish positions in the early 1990s. A policy initiative is proposed that if successful would:

- close debt and equity gaps;
- be less dependent on the state of the economic cycle;
- go some way to matching the nature and character of the source of finance with the particular type of investment;
- engender more appropriate financial structures amongst investee businesses.

Facets of the proposed financing initiative have not been thoroughly resolved: further discussions and deliberations may also reveal unanticipated difficulties. The principal contribution of this paper however, is to underline the inappropriateness of current financial processes and provision.

This paper acknowledges that entrepreneurship plays a significant role within an economy. According to the economic theory of entrepreneurship accepted here, entrepreneurship is an activity that can lead economic growth. It is also accepted that the viability of new ventures is dictated by the state of resource markets which themselves reflect the state of the economy. In short, there is a recursive system whereby the economy determines the quantity and characteristics of entrepreneurship that is viable and where the quantity and characteristics of entrepreneurship influence the economy (Figure 1).

Policies designed to facilitate entrepreneurship should accommodate this dynamic and recursive system (Binks and Vale 1990a, b). It can be argued that policy to date in the UK, is at best suited to a static economic context (Binks and Vale 1991).

The dynamic nature of the UK economy is epitomised by periods of recession, depression, recovery and boom and by real trends in the value of the Gross Domestic Product. One outcome of the 'static' approach to policy is that viable entrepreneurship may be lost during particular phases of the economic cycle while entrepreneurship may be least facilitated when it is most needed and vice versa. More significantly, entrepreneurship with negative ramifications can be engendered during periods of recession and depression.

POLICY — A GENERAL OBSERVATION

Official commitment to many policies waxes and wanes according to the state of the

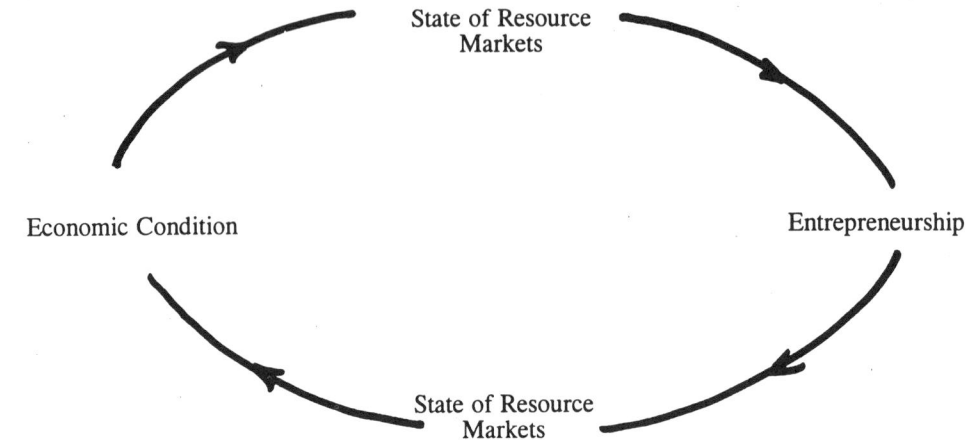

Figure 1: Interaction of entrepreneurship and the state of the economy.

economy. In particular, periods of recession or depression may see policies marginalised to satisfy Exchequer expedients. Welfare payments are known to rise when an economy is depressed: at the same time tax revenues decline. The inevitable pressure on the Public Sector Borrowing Requirement provides the stimulus for cost-saving measures. This response, perhaps in part justified, tends to be more a political one than an economic one. The arguments for counter-cyclical, fiscal budgeting are involved and not fully agreed upon. Nevertheless, failure to accommodate the impact of recession on entrepreneurship offers the prospect of curtailing business development and foregoing the tax revenues that would otherwise be available. In the extreme case, short-term policies to accommodate recession can exacerbate the unwanted condition.

It is irrational to starve the entrepreneurial motor of economic development at the time when the motor is needed most.

This basic observation is particularly pertinent in the case of the supply of finance for entrepreneurship. The UK Government is not a direct provider of significant funds for entrepreneurship but it does purport to instigate relevant initiatives and it does underwrite the Loan Guarantee Scheme. If the mechanism through which finance is available to new ventures is influenced by general economic conditions, then measures are required to ameliorate any negative implications.

It has been argued elsewhere that the economic significance of entrepreneurship does not reside exclusively with new businesses or with individual entrepreneurs (Binks and Vale 1990a). It is also accepted that entrepreneurship is a generic term that embraces activities with very different economic implications. Not all entrepreneurship is good for economic development although economic development will not occur without entrepreneurship.

For policy to be most effective and accommodate the dynamic aspect of the economy it is helpful to appreciate the different categories of entrepreneurship; the different ways in which they are affected by and impact on the economic cycle and the different funding characteristics implied. Without these distinctions being made, policy cannot be tailored appropriately.

CATEGORIES OF ENTREPRENEURSHIP

The origins and derivations of the categories of entrepreneurship described below are detailed elsewhere (Binks and Vale, 1990a).

It is significant to note from Figure 2 that it is only catalytic activity that introduces

ENTREPRENEURIAL ACTIVITY

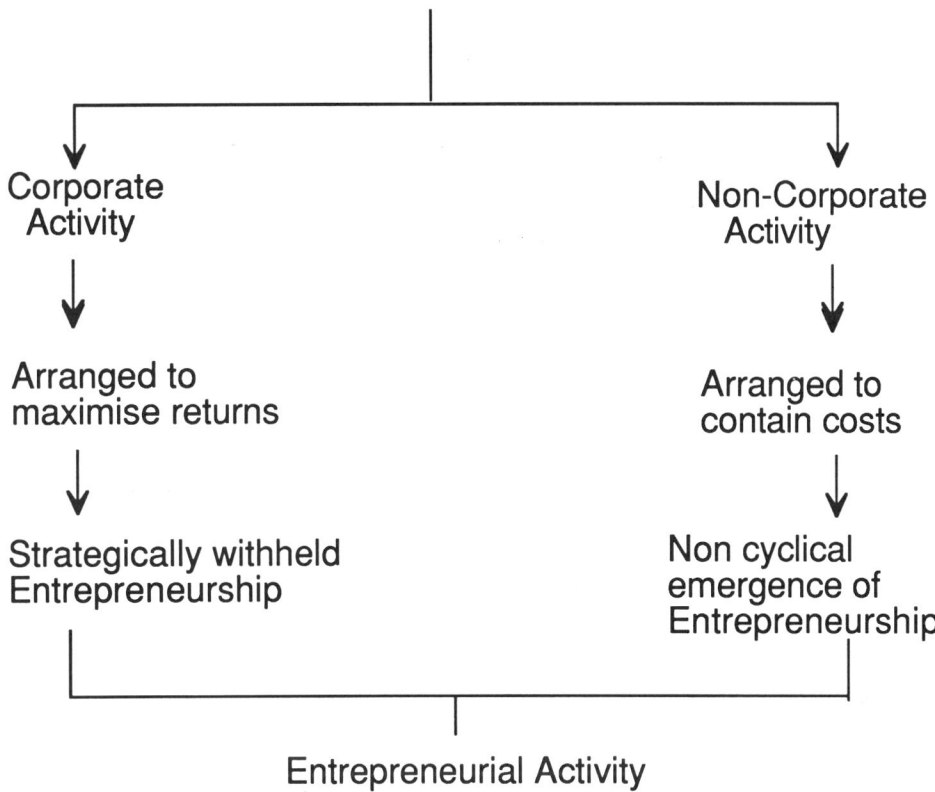

Figure 2: Entrepreneurial activity.

the potential for growth and that it is allocating activity that capitalises on that potential. In recessionary and depressed economic conditions these types of entrepreneurship are particularly crucial. It is also the case that catalytic activity will carry the highest degree of risk as there is no precedent or data on which to calculate risk. Allocating activity will carry substantial but less risk and refining activity is the least 'risky' variant of entrepreneurship.

In short, the economic requirement for entrepreneurship in recession is more precisely for those activities that carry the higher levels of risk, precisely when factor markets are most risk averse and conservative. In particular, the finance market will be most resistant to catalytic and allocating investment when the economic requirement for funding is most urgent.

To date these considerations have not been acknowledged by policy makers.

FINANCING ENTREPRENEURSHIP DESPITE THE FINANCE GAPS

It is well recognised that finance gaps act as a constraint on small businesses and entrepreneurship (Binks et al 1988, Edwards 1987, Wilson 1979). For catalytic and allocating events, the impact of these gaps can be particularly severe. In periods of economic recession and depression, supply-side considerations exacerbate the difficulties. Furthermore, corporate players strategically withhold events and place a heavier burden on

non-corporate catalytic and allocating events to aid recovery. The likelihood of entrepreneurship facilitating economic growth is reduced to a minimum at the time it is
required most.

The equity gap

The equity gap has long been recognised as one product of asymmetrical information
and uncertainty (Binks et al 1992). Provisions introduced on the basis of observations
made as long ago as 1931 by the Macmillan Committee have not closed the equity gap.
Despite the operations of what was the Industrial and Commercial Finance Corporation
(ICFC) and initiatives such as the Business Start-up Scheme (BSS) and the Business
Expansion Scheme (BES) the gap still exists for explicable reasons (Binks and Vale,
1990b).

The debt gap

A debt gap also arises as a result of information asymmetries in that the providers
of debt, primarily the banks, require collateral to ameliorate risk in the absence of a
highly informed relationship between the two parties. In the absence of a close banking
relationship and stable economic conditions, firms will find that they are unable to raise
loan finance without providing legally acceptable security.

   These finance gaps will not be closed in the short run because the changes involved
are medium to long term in their character while the high costs of effective relationship
banking dictate a minimum viable package of debt in the absence of security.

   In recognition of the difficulty some firms can have providing collateral, Government
introduced a Loan Guarantee Scheme as long ago as 1981. Despite the availability of this
initiative it has not fulfilled its potential. The perogative to offer the scheme lies with
the private institutions, mainly the clearing banks, that administer the funds. To date
there has been a reluctance to issue debt underwritten by Government guarantees.
Measures introduced in the Spring 1993 budget allow for a greater aggregate value
of guaranteed lending. It remains to be seen whether the banks respond to moral suasion.
Even if the banks respond positively, Figure 2 illustrates that debt is largely inappropriate
for the categories of entrepreneurship most likely to provide economic development.

The impact of recovery

In the event of an upturn in economic activity it can be argued that the failure rate of
businesses will accelerate rather than diminish; this expectation was first published
by Schumpeter in 1934. The main reasoning behind this view revolves around the
relationship between working capital requirements and the severely weakened balance
sheets of businesses that have been making trading losses, destocked and experienced
the devaluation of fixed assets – particularly property. In the absence of a strong financial
structure, over-trading is a very probable outcome.

   The extent to which the banks are able to accommodate further the liquidity requirements of small firms in particular may be insufficient to avoid lost growth and further
business closures. Many of the banks have suffered severe problems with bad debts as a
result of lending decisions made in the mid to late 1980s. They are concerned, therefore,
to ensure that high risk lending does not feature significantly in their portfolios. It is
unrealistic to expect the major clearing banks to allow many businesses to become
highly geared in the 1990s.

   In short, we can observe two quite distinct categories of entrepreneurship which may
be constrained by finance gaps in a recession and subsequent recovery. The first is non-
corporate entrepreneurial activities which engender catalytic or allocative change. The
second refers to the refinancing needs of surviving firms engaged in refining activity.

THE REQUIRED CHARACTERISTICS OF A NEW POLICY

Taken together the points raised imply a need for a new approach to funding policy. Familiar questions related to the characteristics or qualities of such a policy are raised. Outlined below are some of the more pertinent considerations.

- The first requirement of a new initiative should be that it is effective in the short run, as well as in the medium and longer term. By short run we refer to a period of up to two years.
- The policy should be able to accommodate the problems of evaluation due to asymmetrical information. This does not necessarily imply that the initiative would enable a more accurate calculation of risk. It should be accepted that the entrepreneurial risk is extremely difficult to quantify. But the funds could still be forthcoming with a sufficiently broad portfolio.
- The new structure should provide risk finance without creating the potential for abuse which was identified in the BSS and subsequently the BES.
- The source of funds provided must not be viewed as a 'provider of last resort'.
- The policy should be able to accommodate cycles in economic activity.
- The policy should be cheap to administer and simple in design.
- The policy should be developmental in its impact on existing institutions. Just as the LGS was designed in part to persuade banks to take a more income-geared or prospects-based approach to lending, so this policy should have a similar effect.
- The policy should be introduced on a permanent basis rather than an experimental one. The early designs of the loan guarantee scheme suffered from their experimental nature. It was unrealistic to expect banks to invest heavily in the training of personnel in order to apply such a scheme efficiently when its future was always in doubt.
- Finally, the policy should aim to be self-financing in the medium- to long-term. By this we do not mean to suggest that the design should be similar to the early versions of the loan guarantee scheme. The self-funding aspect should not be created by imposing a higher cost for funds on those who receive finance.

THE BASIC STRUCTURE OF THE POLICY

Users of the fund
Firms with entrepreneurial opportunities would be referred to the Entrepreneurship Fund by any relevant party such as banks, enterprise agencies, trusts, TECs, etc.

On referral to the scheme, projects would be subject to a comprehensive screening process. This would be based upon a knowledge-based system which would collect all the requisite information from the proposer/applicant as to the nature of the project envisaged. Having passed the initial screening process, proposers of projects would be interviewed by a panel of appropriate 'scrutineers' to examine the proposal in more detail, verify the realism of the assumptions made and to design appropriate funding packages.

As a result of this process, successful applications would be made an offer by the fund, specifying the amount of finance involved, the terms of its provision, monitoring and information requirement, the anticipated returns and their time profile.

FINANCE FOR THE ENTREPRENEURSHIP FUND

The proposed fund would have the twin purposes of financing high risk entrepreneurial developments and refinancing entrepreneurship in viable but financially weak businesses. The characteristic of the former investments would be uncertainty, or incalculable levels of risk, while the characteristics of the latter would be limited or unorthodox collateral.

To accommodate the fundamental differences between these two categories of investment there would most appropriately be two distinct sources of initial capital.

National enterprise lottery

National lotteries have proven to be a successful method for raising funds. The first source of finance for the entrepreneurship fund would arise as a result of the introduction of a national enterprise lottery. The underlying rationale for this approach is based upon the assumption that categories of entrepreneurship are most appropriately seen as a gamble. If it is not possible to assess or quantify the nature of that gamble or uncertainty by studying the projects concerned, then it is necessary to generate the supply of funds irrespective of the uncertainties of their allocation. The provisions of such a lottery would fulfil this objective. In effect, those participating in the lottery would be providing funds for entrepreneurship by pursuing the potential for very high returns which have a very low probability of occurring. Aside from the proven attraction of lotteries in general, the participants would have the additional motive of providing finance for entrepreneurial activity with the resultant economic benefits which this implies. Funds generated from the lottery would be used to finance entrepreneurship. Any future returns would revert to the lottery section of the Entrepreneurship Fund for re-investment.

Proposals which the screening procedures identified as refinancing or refining activity would be referred to a second section of the Entrepreneurship Fund.

Investor tax relief

Refinancing and funding refining types of entrepreneurial activity have more in common with the traditional notion of corporate investment. There are still levels of business risk however, and inadequate levels of collateral for conventional debt finance.

The second main source of finance for the entrepreneurship fund would attempt to attract investors by appealing to their desire for potentially higher returns in the medium and long term whilst also offering tax advantages. Investments in the fund would be fully tax deductible. Dividends received from the funds would also be tax deductible. These dividends would represent the total return from the portfolio of investments undertaken by this part of the fund. Such returns may be moderately low in the short run but could lead to very large returns in the medium to longer term.

A question still remains as to how effective such a policy could be in meeting the characteristics and quality objectives described above.

POLICY EFFECTIVENESS

The Entrepreneurship Fund could be established and effective in the short run by operating through existing financial institutions after negotiations to attract their selective or general co-operation.

Problems created by asymmetrical information could be reduced significantly through such a policy. In the case of new ventures funded through the lottery, the use of knowledge-based systems for both evaluation and monitoring would minimise information cost whilst countering abuse. Given the genuine uncertainty associated with entrepreneurial ventures where, by definition, no reliable data are applicable, the problem is not just one of differing information sets, but also that of an information vacuum. The likelihood of adverse selection could not be calculated, even if both principals' and agents' information sets overlapped exactly.

For re-financing proposals the same points apply as those above with respect to information costs. The levels of information available would be much greater due to previous trading information. The fund could provide equity finance without accepting any liability for future losses, thus limiting the impact of moral hazard.

Due to the simplicity and clarity of the scheme there would be less risk of the abuse of the tax relief. Much of the abuse which was avoided by the Business Start-up Scheme through overly rigorous qualifying criteria and which is attributable to the Business Expansion Scheme, arose due to the ability of individuals and fund managers to tie their investments to specific projects. Since the financial return from the proposed initiative refers to the total portfolio of investments made, this kind of project abuse could be avoided.

The screening processes which would be used in the implementation of such a scheme would mean that marginal cases would be rejected. The scheme would not be operated as a supplier of last resort although it would naturally attract many commercially unviable projects. The scheme would address the problem of finance gaps constraining viable projects; unviable projects would be rejected via the screening procedures.

The scheme will resolve some of the supply-side anomalies introduced by periods of general economic boom and bust. During periods of recession, the opportunity cost of investing in the fund will be lower, the alternatives available will tend to be depressed by existing market conditions. At the same time, refinancing requests will tend to be higher as companies become more prepared to sell equity in order to raise finance directly and so increase their ability to attract debt. There may, however, be fewer new ventures, and a lower demand for funds from the lottery. In periods of recovery and boom, the fund would attract more new ventures due to more buoyant economic conditions. Lottery funding would also be expected to rise. It is difficult to predict, reliably, the extent to which the demand for and supply of funds would be equated in practice but that can not be taken to mitigate the urgent requirement for an entirely new source and process of providing funds to entrepreneurial activity.

The Entrepreneurship Fund, once established, would be cheap to administer. By the appropriate use of knowledge-based systems the main cost of information collection and analysis would be low for the initial filtering system. The application of an appropriate panel of scrutineers meeting to interview applicants from their region would also be relatively efficient in the allocation of time in overcoming information asymmetries.

The scheme would be developmental in its impact on other institutions: there would be a demonstration affect. If the scheme were to be successful, existing institutional providers would attempt to prevent the loss of such potential. External equity providers such as venture capital and development capital institutions would attempt to reduce the costs of information collection. Banks would also be encouraged to adopt more efficient information systems. They would also be encouraged to provide financial products that involved an equity as well as a debt component so that they themselves could benefit from the upside gain of high-risk investment supported by low-cost information.

The proposed scheme would be very 'uncluttered' in design, simple in operation and permanent in its implementation, and it would become self-financing through returns on previous investments.

CONCLUSION

The arguments and recommendations outlined above focus upon the need for a new approach to policy with respect to the financing of entrepreneurship. We have outlined one possible scheme as an example of some of the qualities which we believe should be present in such an initiative.

In essence the scheme which is proposed would partly accommodate the economic cycle; it would recognise the innate gamble of some types of entrepreneurship; it would provide a medium or conduit through which the impact of finance gaps could be addressed.

The main strengths of the scheme arise from its simplicity. Catalytic and allocating events would be funded through a lottery. This is appropriate since the investment of funds in such ventures will always involve a gamble due to the levels of associated uncertainty. For those concerned with the refining and refinancing side of the scheme, the risk of investing in the scheme is spread across all accepted investments. The tax relief made available through the scheme provides an incentive to invest. The low cost of filtering provided by judicious applications of knowledge-based systems aids the reduction of information costs. The scheme will tend to encourage existing institutions to keep for themselves, more of the potential gains which could result from successful investments, by changing their own operating criteria.

REFERENCES

Binks M.R. and Vale P.A. (1990a) Entrepreneurship and Economic Change, McGraw Hill, London.

Binks M.R. and Vale P.A. (1990b) The Role of Entrepreneurship in Economic Change, Paper presented to the 13th Small Firms Policy and Research Conference, Harrogate, November.

Binks M.R. and Vale P.A. (1991) Entrepreneurship in Recession, Durham University Business School Occasional Paper No. 91101.

Binks M.R., Ennew C.T. and Reed G.V. (1992) Information Asymmetries and the Provision of Finance to Small Firms, International Small Business Journal.

Binks M.R., Ennew C.T. and Reed G.V. (1988) The Survey by the Forum of Private Business on Banks and Small Firms, in G. Bannock and E. Victor Morgan (eds), Small Businesses and Banks: A Two Nation Perspective, Forum of Private Business. Knutsford.

Edwards G.T. (1987) The Role of Banks in Economic Development, Macmillan, London.

Schumpeter J. (1934) The Theory of Economic Development, Harvard University Press, Cambridge, Mass.

Wilson H. (1979) The Financing of Small Firms: Report of the Committee to Review the Functioning of Financial Institutions, Cmnd 7503. HMSO, London.

12

Overcoming the Adverse Selection Problem:
Evidence and Policy Implications from a Study of Bank Managers on the Importance of Different Criteria Used in Making a Lending Decision

David Deakins and Guhlum Hussain

INTRODUCTION

Bank assessments of small-firm applications for loan finance are examples of decision-making under uncertainty incorporating asymmetric information for the provider and the client. The foundations of analysis of possible mismatches between supply and demand which can occur under these conditions have been laid down by Akerlof (1970). Writers have developed the significance of these conditions for finance theory using a principal-agent framework (Mirrlees 1974, 1975, Jensen and Meckling 1976, Holstrom 1979, Shavell 1979). However, the relevance of these insights is limited when considering the finance of small firms who have restricted access to financial markets. Concepts of moral hazard and adverse selection, however, are still important and have been further refined by later writers (Harris and Townsend 1981, Hellwig 1987, Magill and Shafer 1991).

Banks face moral hazard (monitoring problem) and adverse selection (risk-assessment problem) when dealing with small firm financial propositions (Stiglitz and Weiss 1981). It is possible to argue that these problems can lead to a credit glut (de Meza and Webb 1987), but there has been some work in the UK that has revealed the expected mismatches between providers (the commercial banks) and clients suggested by the theoretical papers (Binks et al 1988). Banks will find it difficult to overcome moral hazard because (for relatively small amounts of finance) it is not economic to devote resources to closely monitor ventures. However, we might expect banks to provide resources to overcome the adverse selection problem, for example, in staff development and training.

It is this adverse selection problem with which we are concerned. We argue that it arises either because the information set provided by the entrepreneur is incomplete or the bank manager chooses to use selective subsets of information that are inappropriate for risk assessment. It is also useful, in this context, to distinguish between start-up propositions and applications for additional finance from existing businesses. It is possible to hypothesise that bank managers will place more emphasis on the managerial and enterprise skills of the potential entrepreneurs for a start-up proposition since there is no financial track record. Our evidence is partly concerned with a start-up proposition but we do have some findings on the importance of different criteria on existing businesses.

It has been recognised that small-firm entrepreneurs will face liquidity constraints and rely heavily on bank credit (Evans and Jovanovic 1989, Walker 1989). Small-firm finance gaps which might result from liquidity problems and selection problems have been well documented (HM Government, 1931, 1971, 1979). However, these studies have concentrated on equity gaps and although these have narrowed (Bannock 1991), it is recognised that there is still a need to improve the provision of finance to reduce debt and equity gaps (Mason et al 1991).

The role of collateral is significant in bank assessments of small-firm propositions. In theory, given asymmetric information, it can be argued that collateral signals commitment from the entrepreneur. It can also be argued that it helps the bank manager with the moral hazard problem. In the literature on asymmetric information considerable attention has been given to the importance of signalling. Following Spence (1974), a number of writers have developed theoretical implications of the importance of signalling (Crawford and Sobel 1982, Quinzii and Rochet 1985, Cho and Kreps 1987). The importance of signalling commitment has also been recognised (Milgrom and Roberts 1982). In risk assessment of small firm propositions, collateral has a role in signalling commitment (Chan and Kanatas 1985). Collateral can also determine the level and maturity of debt in the small firm (Constand et al 1991).

This paper concentrates on whether bank officers are making the right decisions when assessing propositions from entrepreneurs. Whether they are depends, partly, on the quality of risk assessment and the importance of relevant criteria used. We believe that this is an area that has received little attention in the literature. Some previous research has been carried out on the importance of accounting ratios (Berry et al 1991) and on the relationship between the bank officer and the entrepreneur (Vyakarnam and Jacobs 1991), but little has been done on the significance and importance of criteria that are used by bank officers to make risk assessments. An interesting Swedish study has identified the importance of qualitative factors and bank officers' intuition in risk assessment (Green 1991). A NEDO study of bank lending decisions raised the importance of managerial training within banks (Doran and Hoyle 1986), but we believe that there are a number of fundamental policy issues that arise from our research which still need to be addressed by financial institutions and the Government.

RESEARCH METHODOLOGY

The problem faced by researchers in analysing the process of risk assessment of small-firm propositions by bank officers, is to observe, as near as possible, the actual conditions and process of decision-making. The limited research on bank lending decisions has not progressed beyond limited simulations of hypothetical situations (Berry et al 1991). This can be contrasted with research into decision-making by investment analysts, where methods have progressed from postal questionnaires (Lee and Tweedie 1981, Arnold and Mozier 1984) to participant observation and protocol analysis (Day 1986) and a case study (Gniewosz 1990). An opportunity arose to use a real business plan for a start-up venture. This provided the basis for an analysis of the importance of different criteria used by bank officers. To achieve this we took on the role of entrepreneurs seeking a funding decision. We were able to secure co-operation from a number of commercial banks which allowed us to record the opinions of 30 bank officers. We included some general questions on criteria that might be used by officers to assess both start-up and existing businesses. We give a brief account of the main findings before concentrating on the policy implications.

FINDINGS

The presentation of the main findings is organised around three sections. Firstly, we present a selection of the important criteria that were used to assess our start-up proposition. Secondly, we recorded bank managers' opinions of important criteria which may be used in general for any proposition, whether for start-up, or for additional funds. Thirdly, we include our observations on the role of collateral because we believe that this has implications for policy. The reader should note that we concentrate on the findings that have policy implications. A full discussion of the importance of all criteria that were used in risk assessment is given in our research report (Deakins and Hussain 1991).

Decisions on the proposition and criteria used

We found a remarkably even split between those managers that were prepared to fund the proposition and those that were not. Fifty per cent were prepared to help. We allocated the bank managers' decisions to an arbitrary scale with greater than 5 indicating a positive desire to go ahead with the proposition. Less than 5 indicates that the manager was not prepared to help. Table 1 shows the distribution of the decisions. All the bank managers required collateral to fund the proposition which accounts for the highest score of 8.

We might hypothesise that there may be some divergence of opinion especially for a start-up proposition. However, Table 1 shows a wide range of scores indicating a remarkable divergence of opinion about our venture. There was, also, considerable variation in the approach of managers. The reasoning behind decisions was variable. For example, reasons for rejection included; under-capitalisation, too speculative, insufficient information and the unfavourable economic climate.

Table 2 gives a selection of criteria that were used in descending order of importance. This table shows that important managerial and strategic information was only used by a small minority of officers. It also shows that certain subsets of information were given a disproportionate importance. For example, 66% of managers required a forecasted balance sheet and profit and loss account, even though, for our proposition, this would have yielded little additional information not provided by the cash-flow forecast. Information on the personal and managerial characteristics of the entrepreneurs was given a low weighting. This bias in approach meant that information concerning management skills, abilities and business training was discounted. For example, only 10% of officers were concerned about the transferability of managerial skills from a large to a small enterprise. This contrasts with evidence provided by ACOST who found 'managers recruited from large companies did not operate effectively in the small firm context' (ACOST 1990, p. 16).

Managers took a short-term view. Despite the proposition providing cash flow forecasts for four years, the major concerns were with the first 12 months and with the relatively high gearing. Bank managers sought, generally, to ease the equity problem through a reliance on personal collateral of the proprietors.

Importance of criteria for all propositions

Table 3 reveals the rank order of criteria as assessed by the bank managers. These

Table 1: Bank officers' decisions

Score out of 10	Number of Officers
0	1
1	4
2	4
3	3
4	3
5	1
6	3
7	10
8	1
9	0
10	0
Total	30

Note: see text for explanation of scale.

Table 2: Criteria used or sought on the start-up proposition

Information	Percentage of managers
Gearing	83
Entrepreneurs' personal financial position	73
Forecasted balance sheet and P&L Acc	66
Entrepreneurs' contacts in industry	60
Entrepreneurs' drawings	63
Timing of income payments	60
Contingency plans	57
Entrepreneurs' personal collateral	50
Market research	50
Entrepreneurs' qualifications/careers	43
Cash flow assumptions	40
Entrepreneurs' starting separately	37
Role of IT consultant	33
IT development costs	27
Business/managerial strategy	13
Enterprise and small business experience	10

Note: these are selective criteria. The full range of bank managers' questions is analysed and discussed in our research report (Deakins and Hussain, 1991).

Table 3: Importance of criteria used to assess lending propositions

Criteria	Rank order	Mean score	Standard deviation
Trading experience	1	4.43	0.5
Projected income	2	4.37	0.85
Existing profitability	3	4.3	0.6
Equity stake	4	4.18	0.69
Repayment of previous loans	5	4.12	0.76
Gearing	6	3.82	0.95
Client an existing customer	7	3.78	0.76
Net profit to sales	8	3.75	0.89
Previous loans	=9	3.73	0.69
Personal guarantees	=9	3.73	0.69
CVs of clients	11	3.7	0.76
Trade debtors	12	3.65	0.71
Liquidity ratios	=13	3.62	0.85
Gross profit to sales	=13	3.62	0.85
Trade creditors	15	3.57	0.85
Charge on personal assets	16	3.55	0.65
Fixed charge on business assets	17	3.52	0.91
Floating charge	18	3.00	1.07

Note: 6 point scale used from 0 to 5.

criteria are those that would apply to all propositions; both start-up and existing concerns. There are a number of observations on this table:

1. There is little correlation between the importance of the criteria in Table 3 and the criteria that were important in the analysis of our start-up venture. For example in Table 3 trading experience and projected income are ranked highly. It might be expected that these would be more highly rated with our proposition. This may be because these criteria would have a different order of ranking for a purely start-up venture and our high gearing was sufficient to cause that to be the major concern. However, given that the strength of our proposition was the experience and qualifi-cations of the entrepreneurs, we might expect more managers to treat it favourably.

2. The variances in ranking (as indicated by the standard deviations) are high, indicating a large variance between individual managers on the ranking of the importance of different criteria. Thus the rank order given in Table 3 cannot be construed as representative of any particular bank or bank manager.
3. We did not find any significant association between the ranking of criteria by the managers and the decision on the proposition.
4. Managers discussed other factors and several stressed that it is obviously the 'mix' of criteria that will be important when assessing a proposition.
5. Managers also rated as important the character and personality of the client and the entrepreneur's ability to 'sell' the proposition to the manager.
6. Mnemonic guides (such as CAMPARI and PARSER) were mentioned but not generally used and were seen primarily as an aid for inexperienced managers.

With some managers (not the full sample due to time constraints) we discussed the major factors that might cause rejection of a proposition. The most important reasons are shown in Table 4. This table shows that the amount of equity and gearing probably plays a more significant role than that indicated by Table 3, particularly as a discriminating factor between those propositions that are accepted and those that are rejected.

We did include some additional questions about the importance of different criteria for new entrepreneurs and here too, experience of product or service provided rated very highly. It seemed to be a virtual precursor for a successful new venture for most of the officers. Thus a client's previous experience or trading record had a dominant pre-eminence in criteria which are used in risk assessment of lending propositions for both existing and new small business ventures.

The role of collateral

The potential of the role of collateral for signalling commitment on the part of the entrepreneur has been mentioned in the introduction. It might appear from Table 3 that this potential has been over-rated, yet none of the bank officers were willing to proceed with our application for funding without commitment to pledge substantial personal collateral. It can also be argued that the pledging of such collateral on the part of the entrepreneur reduces the moral hazard problem for the bank associated with subsequent monitoring. We suspect that collateral plays a more important role than that indicated by Table 3, particularly as a discriminating factor for decisions on new ventures.

Table 2 shows that the highest score in favour of the proposition was 8; this was accounted for by none of the officers being willing to proceed without taking a charge on personal property of the proprietors. Thus, without collateral, our proposition would have been unsuccessful in obtaining finance. The reasons for this requirement on the part of commercial banks are understandable, it reduces their exposure on propositions that can be perceived as high risk (and introduces additional incentives on entrepreneurs). However, there is also a danger that the requirement can reduce the sophistication of

Table 4: Reasons for rejection of propositions

Criteria	Percentage of managers
Under-capitalisation/gearing	57%
Lack of experience/track record	38%
Poorly prepared business plan	33%
Management ability	29%
Serviceability	21%
Lack of security	24%

Note: sample n = 21.

risk analysis and also contribute to the liquidity constraints that are faced by small firms and new entrepreneurs as mentioned in the introduction. Rather perversely, requiring collateral can contribute to the adverse selection problem, since it can be used as a surrogate for more important information concerning the risk of a proposition for decision-making of bank officers.

There are also strategic implications for an economy if potentially viable propositions are not receiving funding because the entrepreneurs concerned lack personal assets that can be used as collateral. Attempts in the UK to reduce such entry barriers for new and existing small firm ventures, by introducing government schemes (for example, the Small Firms' Loan Guarantee Scheme (SFLGS) and Business Expansion Scheme (BES)), have generally had a low take-up and have met with, at best, limited success (Harrison and Mason 1989). The implications are that there are still small-firm finance gaps; but more importantly, inappropriate decisions may be made in risk assessment.

THE ADVERSE SELECTION PROBLEM

The adverse selection problem is well known, and the NEDO report identified a number of possible reasons why this problem occurs (Doran and Hoyle 1986), including: rejection of a satisfactory business plan, acceptance of an unsatisfactory business plan, judgement of character at fault, inappropriate financial structure and the potential lack of security. Our finding, though, is that there are large variances in approach between bank officers in the weighting given to different characteristics of a proposition and a disproportionate emphasis on selective financial criteria.

The result of these approaches, in the UK, is that bank officers are overly concerned about making Type II errors, that is, taking on propositions from entrepreneurs that turn out to be business failures. This means that they will also be making Type I errors: turning away entrepreneurs who will be business successes and profitable for the bank. Our conclusion is that the sophistication of risk analysis, by bank officers in the UK, is inadequate to prevent adverse selection occurring. We are not surprised at the large-scale provision for bad debts that the UK banks have had to make, at the present time, following lending decisions that were made during the mid-1980s when the UK economy was a lot stronger. Inadequate breadth and importance of different criteria have been, at least partly, responsible.

We believe that there are measures that the banks can take that will reduce the occurrence of adverse selection. Obviously, it can never be eliminated since it is a well-defined problem in conditions of uncertainty with asymmetric information. Rather than present conclusions we discuss policy implications of our findings that include our main conclusions and recommendations.

POLICY IMPLICATIONS

The measures that the banks can take concern their training and staff development and their organisation. In addition we believe that there is a role for state schemes such as the Small Firms' Loan Guarantee Scheme, but in a rather modified form. The emphasis on collateral also has strategic implications.

Bank training and staff development

The emphasis on financial management leads to a non-specialist approach to risk assessment. In the UK, bank officers are generalists rather than specialists. Banks treat the small business sector as homogeneous which contrasts with evidence that the sector is heterogeneous (Curran and Burrows 1988, Curran et al 1991).

The relative discounting of the importance of managerial subsets of information, reported above, was reflected in a non-specialist approach and policy to decision-making by the officers. Officers preferred to rely on information that could be interpreted generally across different types of industry, for example, balance sheet ratios and forecasted income. For our proposition only 7% of the officers could have been considered to have a working knowledge of the industry. Only one officer questioned the role of an IT consultant proposed by our proposition, yet this role was important to the success and growth strategy of the venture. Lack of knowledge of particular industry sectors and IT applications can only contribute to the problem of asymmetric information and inability to adequately assess risk for small-business propositions.

The traditional role of a bank manager as a non-specialist can be understood when banks will want staff to deal with general customers and the local branch to deal with the account, yet it also contributes to the problems of both adverse selection and moral hazard, since officers will not have specialised industrial sector knowledge to make good decisions, nor will they be able to adequately interpret subsequent business performance.

There are some examples of the banks recognising the importance of specialisation. For example, the National Westminster Bank employs some 50 plus 'Technology Managers', who specialise in assessing high-tech applications. If a new technology entrepreneur approaches the bank for a funding decision, the technology manager will make an initial assessment and then, if he/she wishes to progress with the application, outside consultants are used to make the risk assessments. The entrepreneur has to agree to pay the consultancy fee with no guarantee of eventually receiving funding. Follow-up discussions with the Bank revealed that training is limited. Each technology manager receives only 2−3 days specific training. Also the referral system is not ideal since there is no specific requirement for any individual manager to refer a high-tech client to a technology manager.

That one bank has attempted some specialisation means that it must foresee some potential benefits, both in attracting new business and reducing adverse selection. Yet, to get the full benefit of specialisation banks must take on board the implications for networking of branches and pooling of staff skills and expertise. Greater specialisation carries with it obligations for individual branches to network effectively and pool the skills of different managers within a region. In follow-up discussions with representatives of the banks we have discussed the possibility of banks drawing on outside specialists to aid decision-making in risk assessment. A greater willingness on the part of banks to employ outside consultants could bring benefits in some cases.

Banks also need to address training issues of their staff in risk assessment. We believe that our findings concerning the focus of managers on certain financial information reflects their training. If this is the case, then training needs to be more balanced, to improve the importance and assessment of managerial skills. The interpretation of financial accounting information has its place and has the advantage of relative objectivity, but more emphasis needs to be placed on the interpretation of management information. Our experience is, that in some cases, this information is ignored and does not enter the risk assessment equation.

In addition, there is a lack of consistency. Attitudes and approaches to different sets of information varied considerably between managers. Whether our proposition was acceptable or not, depended on which manager was approached. The message for entrepreneurs was obvious, it can pay to approach a number of different banks and managers. Yet this must be a cause for concern for the banks. Attempts to control inconsistency through, for example, mnemonic guides or a reporting system to higher officers appeared not to work. We suggest that more effective control measures could be achieved through detailed guidelines for bank officers concerned with small business risk assessment.

Bank officers probably do not see risk assessment of small businesses as a career in itself, although we welcome attempts at some specialisation through creation of 'Small Business Manager' (or equivalent) posts. These posts are often held for a rather limited period and this relatively quick turnover of staff can create problems in the SME community. There is evidence in research that we are undertaking that this lack of continuity can lead to some loss of business for the banks. The lack of continuity that arises in the treatment of small business applications is again a problem of consistency that can be tackled both through the training of staff and in general through an appropriate strategy for human resource management.

The combination of the non-specialist approach and the reliance on a narrow range of information on which to base their assessment meant that officers relied on their experience when making lending decisions. Although banks try to control this rule of thumb decision-making by having their own guidelines for officers and requiring them to report decisions to superiors, officers will use their own intuition based on their previous experience. Where a decision has been successful in the past, it is likely to be repeated, yet the sophistication of risk analysis behind this decision may be weak.

Branch networking and organisation

We asked managers whether they attempted to hold a portfolio of advances. This was generally interpreted to mean maintaining a portfolio of industrial sector lending. Individual branches did not hold a sector portfolio, but were aware of head office portfolio management. However, officers did admit to being required to monitor their portfolio of debts and they were restrained in their decision-making by the need to meet targets set by head office for bad debts and for 'hard-core' lending.

Thus, we found the potential of portfolio management underdeveloped. Banks could allow a network of branches to carry a portfolio of loans that allows for more flexibility in the treatment of risk. We are not asking banks to increase risk, rather to consider the concept of a balanced portfolio of risk. Traditionally banks have to achieve a high success rate due to relatively low margins, hence their concern with the need to control for Type II errors. This contrasts with the approach of venture capitalists who might look for very high returns from relatively few successes. There is some scope for more flexibility in the approach of the banks to risk assessment. Propositions that are perceived as relatively high risk do not have to be automatically turned away (assuming that they have growth potential). The use of a portfolio approach in a network of branches would offer more flexibility than an individual branch considering a perceived high risk application.

The present portfolio approach of banks also leads to some anomalies. The monitoring of industrial sectors, for example, means that applications from a specific industrial sector will always have a perceived level of risk associated with that sector. Propositions can be favourably/unfavourably treated according to characteristics associated with their industrial sector rather than the specific features of the individual proposition.

The reliance on personal collateral

The ability of the entrepreneur to provide personal collateral is given a disproportionate importance in risk assessment. Considerable collateral is required if gearing is higher than the banks' preferred ratio of 1:1. This requirement obviously reduces exposure and risk for the bank but contributes to the financial constraints that entrepreneurs face, as mentioned in the Introduction. If a potential entrepreneur, seeking to launch a new venture, does not have considerable personal property, he/she will find it very difficult if not impossible to raise finance and fall into the finance gaps that have been mentioned before.

The consequences of this reliance on personal collateral are only too apparent at the present time. Although it now seems that the small firms sector has been responsible for the creation of the majority of jobs in the 1980s (Daly et al 1991), the small firms sector is also characterised by a great deal of volatility (Robson and Gallagher 1992). Recent figures showing record bankruptcies are testimony to this. There are a number of problems that result from the requirement for personal collateral:

1. Banks are first in the queue of secured creditors in bankruptcy. When a business is in difficulties there may be a tendency to 'pull the plug' without adequate assessment of the firm's long term prospects.
2. Other small firms will often be unsecured creditors. By contrast they are last in the queue in bankruptcy and can often get into difficulties if a large debtor has gone into bankruptcy. This can produce a domino effect, further deepening the effect of the recession.
3. The value of personal collateral depends on property values. These were inflated in the boom years of the mid-1980s. Coupled with Government encouragement to enter business and promotion of the enterprise culture, soaring property values must have encouraged people to enter business who were perhaps ill-equipped to deal with recessionary times. However, their ability to provide security will have persuaded the bank to lend money. The collapse of property values has meant that business owners who have since gone into liquidation, have been left with very little wealth, and in some cases, destitute. The social cost of this 'volatility of small firms' is too often ignored.
4. Potentially viable businesses that do not contain collateral are ignored. This problem has not been solved by schemes of last resort lending such as the SFLGS. Attitudes of the managers that we interviewed to the SFLGS varied considerably, but in all cases the Scheme was rarely used. This confirms other evidence that take-up rates on this scheme and others is relatively low (Harrison and Mason 1989). The BES, designed to attract more equity investors has now been withdrawn.

That banks should rely on the provision of collateral is only to be expected. We cannot solve these problems by expecting the banks to give loans that are not backed in some way by collateral. We can hope that the banks will improve their risk assessment by a more balanced approach and through better training of their staff. However, they will still require collateral in many cases. Positive measures that can be taken include the following:

1. Raising the profile of the SFLGS. Applications for funding should be referred by an independent body rather than by the banks.
2. A replacement scheme for BES needs to be introduced that will encourage equity investment in small manufacturing firms (not property firms).
3. We found evidence of some close liaison between the banks and Enterprise Agencies. There is considerable scope for more co-operation between the banks and the support agencies. An initiative involving the Midland Bank and Enterprise Agencies has recently been launched and is to be welcomed. Government encouragement and possible funding for such schemes should be provided.

REFERENCES

ACOST (1990) The enterprise challenge: overcoming barriers to growth in small firms, HMSO, London.

Akerlof G. (1970) The market for lemons: qualitative uncertainty and the market mechanism, Quarterly Journal of Economics, Vol. 89, pp. 488−500.

Arnold J. and Mozier P. (1984) A survey of the methods used by UK investment analysts to appraise investments in ordinary shares, Accounting and Business Research, Vol. 14, No. 55, pp. 195−207.

Bannock G. (1991) Venture Capital and The Equity Gap, National Westminster Bank, London.

Berry A., Faulkner S., Hughes M. and Jarvis R. (1991) Financial Information, The Banker and The Small Business, Occasional paper No. 14, Brighton University Business School (mimeo).

Binks M., Ennew C. and Reed G. (1988) The Survey by the Forum of Private Business on Banks and Small Firms, in: Banks and Small Businesses: A Two Nation Perspective, eds Bannock G. and Morgan V. Forum of Private Business, Knutsford.

Chan Y. and Kanatas G. (1985) Asymmetric Valuations and the Role of Collateral in Loan Agreements, Journal of Money Credit and Banking, Vol. 17, No. 1, pp. 84–95.

Cho I-K. and Kreps D. (1987) Signalling games and stable equilibria, Quarterly Journal of Economics, Vol. 102, pp. 179–221.

Constand R., Osteryoung J. and Nast D. (1991) Asset-Based Financing and the Determinants of Capital Structure in the Small Firm, in Advances in Small Business Finance, ed Yazdipore, R., Kluwer, Kingston upon Thames.

Crawford V. and Sobel J. (1982) Strategic information transmission, Econometrica, Vol. 50, pp. 1431–1451.

Curran J. and Burrows R. (1988) Enterprise in Britain: a national profile of small business owners and the self-employed, Small Business Research Trust, Cambridge.

Curran J., Blackburn R.A. and Woods A. (1991) Profiles of the small enterprise in the service sector, Paper presented to the 14th National Small Firms' Policy and Research Conference, Blackpool.

Daly M., Campbell M., Robson G. and Gallagher C. (1991) Job creation 1987–89: the contributions of small and large firms, Employment Gazette, November, pp. 589–594.

Day J. (1986) The use of annual reports by UK Investment Analysts, Accounting and Business Research, Vol. 16, No. 64, pp. 295–307.

Deakins D. and Hussain G. (1991) Risk Assessment By Bank Managers, Birmingham Polytechnic Business School (mimeo).

de Meza D. and Webb D. (1987) Too much investment: a problem of asymmetric information, Quarterly Journal of Economics, Vol. 102, pp. 281–292.

Doran A. and Hoyle M. (1986) Lending to Small Firms: a Study of Appraisal and Monitoring Methods, NEDO, London.

Evans D. and Jovanovic B. (1989) An estimated model of entrepreneurial choice under liquidity constraints, Journal of Political Economy, Vol. 97, No. 4, pp. 808–827.

Gniewosz G. (1990) The share investment decision process and information use: an explanatory case study, Accounting and Business Research, Vol. 20, No. 79, pp. 223–230.

Green E. (1991) Entrepreneurs, their future business concept and credit rating: an intuitive understanding of a total situation, Entrepreneurship and Regional Development, Vol. 3, No. 3, pp. 281–304.

HM Government (1931) Report of The Committee on Finance and Industry (Macmillan Report), Cmnd 3897, HMSO, London.

HM Government (1971) Report of The Committee of Inquiry on Small Firms (Bolton Report), Cmnd 4811, HMSO, London.

HM Government (1979) Interim Report on The Financing of Small Firms (Wilson Report), Cmnd 7503, HMSO, London.

Harris M. and Townsend R.M. (1981) Resource allocation under asymmetric information, Econometrica, Vol. 49, pp. 33–64.

Harrison R.T. and Mason C.M. (1989) The role of the Business Expansion Scheme in the UK, Omega, Vol. 17, pp. 147–157.

Hellwig M. (1987) Some recent developments in the theory of competition in markets with adverse selection, European Economic Review, Vol. 31, pp. 319–325.

Holstrom B. (1979) Moral hazard and observability, Bell Journal of Economics, Vol. 10, pp. 74–91.

Jensen M. and Meckling W. (1976) Theory of the firm: managerial behaviour, agency costs and ownership structure, Journal of Financial Economics, Vol. 3, pp. 305–360.

Lee T.A. and Tweedie D.P. (1981) The institutional investor and financial information, Institute of Chartered Accountants in England and Wales, London.

Magill M. and Shafer W. (1991) Incomplete markets, in The Handbook of Mathematical Economics, eds Hildenbrand W. and Sonneschein H., Vol. IV, Elsevier North Holland, Amsterdam.

Mason C., Harrison R. and Chaloner J. (1991) Informal Risk Capital in the UK, Venture Finance Research Project, Working Paper No. 2, University of Southampton.

Milgrom P. and Roberts J. (1982) Limit pricing and entry under incomplete information: an equilibrium analysis, Econometrica, Vol. 50, pp. 443–459.

Mirrlees J.A. (1974) Notes on welfare economics, information and uncertainty, in Essays in Economic Behaviour Under Uncertainty, eds Balch M., McFadden D. and Wu S., Elsevier North Holland, Amsterdam.

Mirrlees J.A. (1975) The theory of moral hazard and unobservable behaviour-Part 1, Nuffield College, Oxford (mimeo).

Quinzii M. and Rochet J.C. (1985) Multidimensional signalling, Journal of Mathematical Economics, Vol. 14, pp. 261−284.

Robson G. and Gallagher C. (1992) The interaction between small and large firms in UK job creating, 22nd ESBS Conference, Amsterdam.

Shavell S. (1979) Risk sharing and incentives in the principal-agent relationship, Bell Journal of Economics, Vol. 10, pp. 55−73.

Spence A.M. (1974) Market Signalling, Harvard University Press.

Stiglitz J. and Weiss A. (1981) Credit rationing in markets with imperfect information, American Economic Review, Vol. 71, pp. 393−410.

Vyakarnam S. and Jacobs R. (1991) How Bank Managers Construe High Technology Entrepreneurs, Paper presented to 14th National Small Firms Policy and Research Conference, Blackpool,

Walker D. (1989) Financing the Small Firm, Small Business Economics, Vol. 1, pp. 285−296.

13.

OVERDRAFT LENDING AND BUSINESS STARTS:
An Empirical Investigation on UK Data

Robert Cressy

INTRODUCTION

An overdraft is a UK lending facility (US equivalent: 'line of credit') which provides the option of borrowing by a person or business up to a maximum amount (the overdraft limit) over a fixed period (usually less than one year) at a fixed margin over base agreed at the outset. An up-front arrangement fee is usually paid to set up the facility (the Loan Commitment Fee in US terminology). Interest paid on drawn-down funds is calculated on a daily basis at the Base rate plus the agreed margin as long as the borrower remains within the agreed limit.[1] If the borrower exceeds the overdraft limit at any point during the term of the overdraft another rate of interest may, at the discretion of the bank manager, apply to the 'unauthorised' portion of borrowing for the period during which the limit is exceeded. This penal rate is a flat rate (i.e. is independent of base rate) and is usually much higher than would be paid on authorised borrowing and is identical across borrowers.[2]

Overdraft borrowing is the most common form of institutional finance used by the small business.[3] Several reasons have been advanced to explain this fact. Firstly, an overdraft provides flexibility by allowing the borrower in the light of subsequent product market conditions and interest rates to decide whether to borrow and if so at what level. Secondly, through the fixed margin overdrafts also allow the borrower some insurance against subsequent deterioration in his credit rating. Finally, overdraft facilities, in combination with up-front fees can help overcome the moral hazard problem implicit in lending under asymmetric information.[4]

Despite a now large theoretical literature on lending under asymmetric information[5] the empirical inter-relationships between overdraft lending, interest rates, security levels, equity participation, background characteristics, and subsequent business success have never been systematically explored. The small amount of empirical work done on loan commitments (Ham and Melnik 1987, Melnik and Plaut 1986, Avery and Berger 1991) has laboured under huge informational lacunae. None of the published studies have been able to allow for the potentially complex web of interdependencies existing between the various commitment contract terms and other endogenous variables or to control for a sufficiently wide range of exogenous variables.[6] Currently published results must therefore be considered at best preliminary.

The present paper examines the empirical characteristics of overdraft contracts using a new firm-bank database from a nationwide random sample of UK business starts. The use of start-up data has the advantage of highlighting the methods banks use to overcome the problems of lending under asymmetric information; the businesses have little or no track record.

Interdependencies between initial overdraft contract terms, entrepreneur equity inputs and subsequent survival chances are explored. These contract and para-contract variables are related to some important background characteristics of the businesses representing human capital and collateralisable assets.

METHODOLOGY AND DATA

To avoid sample selection bias it is necessary to establish whether the sample of borrowing businesses to be studied is randomly selected from the full sample of businesses. The probability of both requesting and using an overdraft bank facility was therefore estimated on the full sample (borrowers and non-borrowers). Ordinary least squares was then used to estimate bivariate relationships between contract terms (overdraft limits, interest margins, collateral requirements and owner equity involvement) and to relate these variables to important exogenous variables representing human capital, and collateral availability.

The data
The data used is based on a questionnaire put to a nationwide random sample of some 2000 start-ups opening business accounts for the first time at the National Westminster Bank of Great Britain in 1988.[7] Replies to some 35 questions were recorded. These questions included information on the backgrounds of the businesses and their proprietors, sources of finance used to start the business, current banking requirements and the status of the bank official conducting the interview. In addition, quarterly bank accounts data on the business is available recording initial and subsequent borrowing conditions (levels, interest rates, collateral required etc.) of the businesses. Finally information on account cessations including bankruptcies of the businesses up to eight quarters later is available.

The remainder of the paper is organised as follows. Section 3 defines the variables of the system. Section 4 provides the empirical estimates and Section 5 interprets and evaluates the findings. A final section overviews the results.

EMPIRICAL ANALYSIS

An overdraft contract consists of values assigned to the following variables and which legally bind the bank and business in their subsequent relationship: overdraft limit, interest margin, security level, duration of the facility and arrangement fee for the facility. In the start-up tracking exercise (STE) dataset arrangement fees are a direct function of the limit; hence they have no statistical role in the estimation.[8] Currently no data is available on duration of overdrafts and this feature of the contract has therefore been ignored.

Two additional 'endogenous' variables are modelled, personal equity inputs of the entrepreneur and the survival probability of the business account. These are of relevance to the overdraft contract because both affect survival chances of the business and therefore both parties' returns to the contract, although they generally have no legal status in the terms of the contract.

Each variable used in the analysis is measured at the business account opening stage. This is also the date of start-up for some 80% of the businesses considered.[9]

Endogenous variables
PERFIN = 1 if the business used 'personal money or savings' to start up and is 0 elsewhere.
ODLIM = the overdraft limit (£) set for the business.
ODLIM2 = (ODLIM)**2.
MARG1 = the margin over base (%) set for borrowing on overdraft.

SEC = 1 if the overdraft is secured and 0 elsewhere.
PRES921 = 1 if the business account ceased in the period 1988q1−1992q1 and 0 elsewhere.

Exogenous variables
AVAGE = arithmetic mean age of the proprietors at start-up.
AVAGE2 = (AVAGE)**2.
AVHEQ = arithmetic mean house equity of the proprietors at start-up stage.
AVQUAL = average academic qualifications of the proprietors (see Appendix for details).

PROBABILITY OF USING AN OVERDRAFT FACILITY

Estimation took the form of a profit equation estimated on the complete set of background characteristics available in the STE database using the full sample (borrowers and non-borrowers). This provides a sample selection equation for the system.[10] The hypothesis that the probability of using an overdraft is constant across observations could not be rejected. Thus we conclude that the subsample of overdraft borrowers is randomly selected from the sample of start-ups. Estimates of overdraft contract parameters on the subsample of borrowers (see below) will therefore be free from selection bias.[11]

UNIVARIATE DISTRIBUTIONS

Tables 1−5 provide the univariate distributions of owner equity participation rates, overdraft limits, overdraft margins, overdraft security and business survival rates. These are discussed in turn.

Owner equity participation rates
From Table 1 some 43% of overdraft users used personal savings/money of the proprietors (PERFIN) at start-up.[12] These financial inputs are used both singly and in combination with other sources of finance.[13] Personal equity inputs are thus an important source of initial capital and are used by almost half of the business start-ups that approached the bank for overdraft finance.[14]

Table 1: Distribution of start-up owner equity inputs (PERFIN), 1988

PERFIN	Frequency	Percentage frequency
0	289	57.1
1	217	42.9

Table 2: Distribution of start-up overdraft limits (ODLIM), 1988

ODLIM(£)	Frequency	Percent
100	18	3.8
250	9	1.9
500	58	12.1
1000	87	18.2
2500	134	28.0
5000	60	12.6
10 000	61	12.8
25 000	37	7.7
50 000	6	1.3
100 000	7	1.5
>100 000	1	0.2

Overdraft limits

Table 2 shows the distribution of overdraft limits (ODLIM) set at the account opening stage for the subsample of start-ups that took overdraft facilities. Since the scale is approximately geometric the distribution is skewed to the right. The minimum limit is £50 and the maximum £100 000 with an average (median) overdraft limit of some £1750. The amounts used are surprisingly small until one realises that some 88% of the businesses are sole traders or partnerships with one or two employees.

Overdraft margins

Table 3 presents margins (MARG1) over base rate (BRATE) set at start-up.[15] The distribution is roughly symmetrical, possibly bimodal, with a minimum of 2.5% above base and a maximum of 9% above base. The average (median and mode) margin is about 5%, though there is apparently another mode at 7%. This implies an average margin about 2% higher than reported for small firms in general.[16] The spread of rates around the mean is also larger than commonly reported for small businesses. Both these results may however arise because the figures represent margins set rather than paid.[17]

Overdraft collateral requirements

Overdraft limits may be either manager-secured, manager-unsecured, head office limit or under report.[18] An overdraft limit is said to be secured if the bank can call upon tangible assets to recoup drawn down funds in the event of default. An example is a second mortgage on the business owner's house.[19]

For the present analysis we define a security variable SEC taking the value 1 if either manager or head office secured limit has been imposed and 0 elsewhere. Table 4 shows the distribution of SEC. It is clear that the vast majority (some 80%) of start-up overdraft borrowing is unsecured. This is almost certainly because the limits are too small for security to be worth 'perfecting', i.e. for its value to be assessed by the bank.[20] Fees for

Table 3: Distribution of start-up overdraft margins (MARG1), 1988

MARG1(%)	Frequency	Percentage frequency
2.5	12	2.5
3	27	5.6
3.5	13	2.7
4	46	9.6
4.5	14	2.9
5	134	28.0
5.5	85	17.8
6	19	4.0
6.5	1	0.2
7	125	26.2
7.5	0	0.0
8	0	0.0
8.5	0	0.0
9	1	0.2

Table 4: Distribution of start-up overdraft security rates (SEC), 1988

SEC	Frequency	Percentage frequency
0	365	78.8
1	98	21.2

the latter passed on to the business would make the cost of an initial loan prohibitive and discourage potentially profitable customers.

Survival rates of accounts

Table 5 shows the survival rates of accounts in the period 1988q1–1989q4. An account is said to survive to a particular quarter if it is still open at the originating branch at the end of that quarter. Non-survival of accounts may take the form of non-trading, discontinuation of the business without bankruptcy, bankruptcy/insolvency, and to a much lesser extent takeover and account transfers.[21]

Note that only some 43% of borrowers starting up in 1988 survive until 1992q1. In other words 2/3 of the 1988 start-ups had ceased within approximately three-and-a-half years of their inception.[22]

BIVARIATE RELATIONSHIPS

Bivariate statistics show how the various endogenous variables relate to overdraft limits, security and age of proprietors respectively. These relationships are also modelled in a set of quadratic regressions to enable significance tests to be performed and to gauge the potential importance of individual explanatory variables. A number of facts emerge.

Survival and age of proprietors

Survival (mean PRES921) has an initially strong positive association with age of the proprietors (AVAGE): 'older is more beautiful'. Thus a three-and-a-half year survival rate of 30% at age 20 years rises to 70% at age 50 years (Table 6). However the statistics also show that survival rates tail off after about the age of 50. By the age of 65 they have fallen to approximately their level at age 20 (33%). This implies an inverted U-shaped relationship between survival and age and this relationship is confirmed in the OLS regression of Table 7. Proprietor age explains some 50% of the variance of survival rates.

Table 5: Distribution of start-up three-and-a-half year survival rates (PRES921)

PRES921	Frequency	Percentage frequency
0	236	49.4
1	242	50.6

Table 6: Mean three-and-a-half year survival rates (PRES921) by age of proprietors, 1988

AVAGE	Frequency	PRES921 (mean)
15	0	0.000000
20	37	0.297297
25	89	0.438202
30	82	0.500000
35	95	0.473684
40	94	0.489362
45	40	0.575000
50	33	0.696970
55	15	0.666667
60	7	0.571429
65	3	0.333333
70	0	0.000000

Table 7: OLS estimates of survival (PRES921) against proprietor age (AVAGE)

Variable	Parameter estimate	PR > |T|
AVAGE	0.021322	0.0001
AVAGE2	−0.000186	0.0024

Goodness-of-fit statistics		
R-squared	*R*bar-squared	Prob>*F*
0.5099	0.5078	0.0001

The positive side of the relationship of survival to age arises because maturity brings wage and business experience (general 'human capital') enhancing business skills and thereby survival chances. Age also brings responsibilities[23] which provide a moral and economic push to business continuation and reduces transfer earnings into wage employment, locking the mature proprietor into his or her business.[24] Finally mature proprietors are more likely to invest personal equity in the business and to place security for loans (see below). Finally there is evidence of a trade-off between security and equity inputs in the eyes of the bank: both serve (to different degrees) as 'hostages to fortune' (see below for more detail).

The negative side of the relationship between survival and age partly reflects the eventual dominance of human physical decline over growing business experience: whilst the young have much energy and little experience, the old have much experience but less energy. However the negative side of the relationship also reflects the fact that some proportion of self-employment in the retirement age group is part-time work and a decline in business conditions will not be so readily met by the extra hours that might be forthcoming in younger proprietors.[25]

Survival and borrowing levels

Survival rates (estimated by PRES921) seem to be higher for larger borrowers (measured by ODLIM), being approximately twice as high for overdrafts of £25K than overdrafts of £50 (Table 8). This result is of interest but, as we shall see, may simply reflect the fact that larger borrowers are older, have more assets and can borrow more. Survival may thus be influenced not by initial borrowing but by age of proprietors.[26] Furthermore a quadratic regression of survival on overdraft limit (Table 9) is not statistically significant. Thus we are forced to conclude that big borrowers are not 'beautiful' in the survival sense of the term.

Table 8: Mean business survival rates (PRES921) by overdraft limit (ODLIM), 1988

ODLIM(£)	Frequency	PRES921 (mean)
50	15	0.333333
100	3	0.333333
250	18	0.555556
500	53	0.358491
1000	111	0.459459
2500	106	0.575472
5000	66	0.530303
10 000	69	0.536232
25 000	23	0.652174
50 000	7	0.571429
100 000	7	0.571429

Table 9: OLS estimates of survival (PRES921) against overdraft limit (ODLIM)

Variable	Parameter estimate	PR > |T|
Intercept	0.472218	0.0001
ODLIM	0.000005587	0.1439
ODLIM2	−4.03085E-11	0.2792

Goodness-of-fit statistics		
R-squared	Rbar-squared	Prob>F
0.0051	0.0009	0.2986

Survival and security posted

A regression of survival rate on security (Table 10) indicates that higher security does increase survival chances as predicted by the theory of moral hazard. Thus proprietors with security for loans are more committed to their business and have the will to make it succeed. They have more to lose than borrowers with similar loans but no security posted with the bank (e.g. younger borrowers).

Margins and overdraft limits

A clear negative relation between average margin (mean MARG1) and overdraft limit (ODLIM) emerges (Table 11), implying that bigger overdrafts get smaller margins above base. This may reflect (i) fixed costs (mainly legal fees and manager time) of setting up an overdraft spread over a larger (potential) lending amount; (ii) a lower probability of

Table 10: OLS estimates of survival (PRES921) against security (SEC)

Variable	Parameter estimate	PR > |T|
Intercept	0.468254	0.0001
SEC	0.156746	0.0060

Goodness-of-fit statistics for PERFIN equation		
R-squared	Rbar-squared	Prob>F
0.0159	0.0138	0.0060

Table 11: Mean start-up overdraft margins (MARG1) by overdraft limit (ODLIM)

ODLIM(£)	Frequency	MARG1 (mean)
50	15	6.100000
100	3	5.500000
250	18	6.638889
500	53	6.122642
1000	111	5.644144
2500	106	5.402123
5000	66	5.219697
10 000	69	4.623188
25 000	23	3.673913
50 000	7	3.714286
100 000	7	3.000000

failure associated with larger businesses, i.e. borrowers.[27] We shall see later that the first explanation is the more plausible of the two. The relationship between margins and limits is a U-shaped one (see OLS regression in Table 12).

Security and overdraft limits

Larger overdrafts (ODLIM) are more likely to be required to post security (SEC) (see Table 13). The rate of securitisation rises from 0.0% below £500 to above 95% for limits over £25 000. Once more regression analysis confirms the relationship to be statistically highly significant. The effect of overdraft limit on security is also quantitatively important, explaining some 34% of the variation in security rates across businesses (OLS regression in Table 14).

Table 12: OLS estimates of margin (MARG1) against overdraft limit (ODLIM)

Variable	Parameter estimate	PR > |T|
Intercept	7.654800	0.0001
ODLIM	−0.000196	0.0001
ODLIM2	1.3498695E-9	0.0001

Goodness-of-fit statistics for PERFIN equation		
R-squared	*R*bar-squared	Prob>*F*
0.0818	0.0779	0.0001

Table 13: Mean start-up overdraft security rates (SEC) by overdraft limit (ODLIM), 1988

ODLIM(£)	Frequency	SEC (mean)
50	14	0.000000
100	3	0.000000
250	18	0.000000
500	52	0.019231
1000	110	0.054545
2500	106	0.141509
5000	62	0.225806
10 000	63	0.444444
25 000	21	0.952381
50 000	7	1.000000
100 000	7	1.000000

Table 14: OLS estimates of security (SEC) against overdraft limit (ODLIM)

Variable	Parameter estimate	PR > |T|
Intercept	0.043580	0.0166
ODLIM	0.000034017	0.0001
ODLIM2	−2.15205E-10	0.0001

Goodness-of-fit statistics		
R-squared	*R*bar-squared	Prob>*F*
0.3432	0.3404	0.0001

Security and margins

The previous two results suggest that security (SEC) and margins (MARG1) may be negatively correlated. Table 15 suggests there is in fact a strong negative relation between margins and security levels amongst start-up borrowers. An OLS regression (Table 16) also confirms this to be statistically significant. This result may reflect bank managers' own remarks that they are willing to lend larger amounts of money without security provided the margin is raised to reflect the extra risk/exposure to the bank.

Personal equity involvement and overdraft limit

Personal equity involvement (PERFIN) has a weak U-shaped relationship with the Limit (ODLIM) (see Table 17). Smaller borrowers reduce equity involvement as the limit rises but after a limit of £500 is reached equity becomes a steeply increasing function of the overdraft limit. This may be accounted for by the theory of control-aversion (Cressy, 1992c). Smaller borrowers prefer to substitute own for borrowed funds as wealth increases thereby reducing perceived bank control over their affairs. These businesses probably do not grow significantly. Larger borrowers however find that the utility of extra profits outweighs the extra control associated with borrowing. They are the growers and borrow more to fund growth as owner wealth increases.

An alternative explanation is that the bank sees security and entrepreneurial equity inputs as (imperfect) substitutes: if it cannot (for cost reasons) impose security on small overdrafts then to ensure 'commitment' on the behalf of the entrepreneur the bank may require more personal equity to be invested.

Table 15:   Mean start-up overdraft security rates (SEC) by overdraft margin (MARG1)

MARG1	Frequency	SEC (mean)
2	1	0.000000
2.5	10	0.700000
3.0	27	0.740741
3.5	12	0.333333
4	44	0.613636
4.5	14	0 500000
5	130	0.169231
5.5	80	0.025000
6	16	0.000000
6.5	1	0.000000
7	107	0.065421
7.5	0	0.000000
8	0	0.000000
8.5	0	0.000000
9	56	0.071429

Table 16:   OLS estimates of margin (MARG1) against security (SEC)

Variable	Parameter estimate	$PR > |T|$
Intercept	7.311371	0.0001
SEC	−2.674079	0.0001

Goodness-of-fit statistics for PERFIN equation		
R-squared	Rbar-squared	Prob$>F$
0.0570	0.0550	0.0001

Table 17: Mean start-up personal equity participation (PERFIN) by overdraft limit (ODLIM), 1988

ODLIM(£)	Frequency	PRES921 (mean)
50	10	0.500000
100	7	0.571429
250	20	0.400000
500	67	0.298507
1000	116	0.405172
2500	112	0.482143
5000	69	0.492754
10000	70	0.385714
25000	22	0.590909
50000	7	0.142857
100000	6	0.666667

House equity and age of proprietors

House equity (AVHEQ), a proxy for available security, is an inverse U-shaped function of owner age (AVAGE), first increasing steeply until about age 45 and then declining until retirement.[28] The regression analysis of house equity on age (Table 19) indicates a strong relationship between the two:[29] older proprietors have been in the housing market for longer than their younger colleagues, thus incurring the benefit of rising house prices for longer. The oldest proprietors entering as part-timers from retirement may have less 'human capital' and be less likely to own a house, or one with a high

Table 18: Mean start-up house equity (AVHEQ) by age of proprietors, 1988

AVAGE	Frequency	AVHEQ (mean)
20	25	7010.0
24	64	26941.4
28	81	51085.5
32	65	58076.4
36	72	71872.7
40	80	84723.7
44	40	107437.5
48	27	91134.6
52	18	71763.9
56	13	79053.8
60	4	137500.0
64	6	22000.0

Table 19: OLS estimates of average house equity (AVHEQ) against proprietor age (AVAGE)

Variable	Parameter estimate	PR > |T|
Intercept	−177008	0.0001
AVAGE	11557	0.0001
AVAGE2	−124.329947	0.0001

Goodness-of-fit statistics		
R-squared	Rbar-squared	Prob>F
0.0908	0.0869	0.0001

equity value. Once more the relationship is inverse-U indicating that there is an 'optimal' age as far as owner house equity of borrowers is concerned.

Security and age of proprietors

Regressing security against proprietor age (Table 21) we find the relationship roughly parallels that for the house equity regression: older proprietors are more likely to place security for loans up to a certain age and after that the probability declines. However this may well reflect both 'supply' and 'demand' factors: whilst the bank (for a given loan size) is perhaps as likely to ask for collateral of young and old borrowers, a younger or middle-aged borrower is more likely to be prepared to place it than one facing retirement in a relatively short period.

SUMMARY AND CONCLUSIONS

This paper has identified the empirical characteristics of overdraft lending to UK start-ups. The picture that emerges is this.

The bank wishes to lend to proprietors that are committed to their business and wish it to succeed. Maturity (middle age) of proprietors was shown to be the key to this process. Mature proprietors have more assets to invest via accumulated savings and more security available via house equity than younger or older proprietors ('tailenders'). Thus they can be lent more than the 'tailenders' without incurring much, if any, extra risk. They are thus offered more money and lower interest rates. Mature proprietors also have less outside alternatives than younger colleagues to switch to if the going gets

Table 20: Mean start-up collateral posted (SEC) by age of proprietors (AVAGE)

AVAGE	Frequency	SEC (mean)
20	25	0.000000
24	63	0.079365
28	81	0.209877
32	61	0.262295
36	67	0.208955
40	76	0.250000
44	40	0.200000
48	25	0.320000
52	18	0.388889
56	13	0.153846
60	4	0.000000
64	6	0.000000

Table 21: OLS estimates of security (SEC) against proprietor age (AVAGE)

Variable	Parameter estimate	$PR > |T|$
Intercept	−0.677870	0.0015
AVAGE	0.045680	0.0001
AVAGE2	−0.000546	0.0004

Goodness-of-fit statistics		
R-squared	Rbar-squared	Prob>F
0.0382	0.0341	0.0001

rough. The bank in turn has good reason to require security from these proprietors due to the incentive effects it provides. Slightly surprising is the finding that survival chances of the business are not influenced by initial borrowing and margins charged. This result is however robust and survival may well turn out to be influenced by subsequent borrowing parameters as yet undetermined.

NOTES

1. Two qualifications need to be added here. Firstly, there is sometimes a split level of the overdraft. Below the split, a lower margin is charged; above it a higher margin. Secondly, banks often operate minimum rates which set lower bounds to the interest rate charged and are fixed at the outset.
2. Since the advent of unauthorised borrowing is normally accompanied by a letter of admonition from the bank manager at the client's cost, the effective rate of interest on marginal unauthorised borrowing is understated by the method of margin calculation used below.
3. For example, in the case of startups, overdrafts constitute about 60% of lending (Cressy 1992a).
4. See for example, Boot, et al (1987), Berger, et al (1992), Melnik and Plaut (1986).
5. See Thakor (1989) for an excellent survey.
6. Recent contributions to the empirical literature include: Ham and Melnik (1985) who use microdata to examine the demand for loan commitments in a sample of large American firms. The dependent variable was desired borrowing, and this was regressed against sales, interest cost, borrowed reserves, and collateral dummy. Melnik and Plaut (1986) use a sample of 92 American loan commitments to regress commitment size against risk premium, commitment duration, commitment fee, current ratio, collateral and firm size dummy. Avery and Berger(1991) use aggregate bank-level data to examine the determinants of the ratio of non-performing loans to total loans, the ratio of charge-off loans to total loans and the ratio of net income to total assets. These performance measures are to be explained by a set of loan commitment variables (ratio of used loans against commitments; ratio of unused commitments to total loans) and a set of control variables (e.g. ratio of loan types likely to be used for commitments; ratio of agricultural to total loans; ratio of demand deposits to total assets). Keasey and Watson (1992) examine UK small business lending behaviour on a UK database that combines business accounts and bank account data. They regress interest margins against measures of firm size and loan size (etc.). Their work is of considerable interest in attempting to relate background information of the businesses to borrowing characteristics. However they do not deal explicitly with overdraft contracts, the subject of the present paper, and their analysis is confined to limited companies.
7. These questions relate to the nature of the business, the backgrounds and qualifications of the proprietors, the sources of finance used to start up and the initial banking requirements of the owners. A full analysis of the database is found in Cressy (1992a).
8. They may play a role via the 'true' cost of funds since the latter will include all payments associated with the loan, not simply interest. See below.
9. Other types of start-up defined in the STE database are purchase of an existing business and upgrading of a business from part- to full-time or from Personal to Business account.
10. The estimated results are available from the Author.
11. In common language, any empirical statement about *actual* borrowers has been shown to be equally applicable to *potential* borrowers.
12. The total number of borrowing firms differs across tables due to missing values for some variables.
13. Most businesses used only one or two sources of finance to start up. The most

common combination used was personal and bank finance. No business used more than four sources. See Cressy (1992b) for details.

14. The data presented here are of course binary. However, the quantitative importance of personal finance is confirmed by a later sample in the same database.

15. Strictly these are the first margins over base since the overdraft may have a split level above which a different interest margin applies. The percentage of ODLIMs with a split however is very small at the startup stage and so the distinction has been ignored.

16. See e.g. Keasey and Watson (1992) who report a margin of around 3% above base.

17. The margin is paid only if the overdraft is actually drawn down. Some businesses hit by large margins may decide ex post not to use their facility. A future paper will explore this issue.

18. A manager-unsecured limit is one without security of any form. Small overdraft limits (e.g. up to £5K in 1988, the majority of this sample as can be seen from Table 1 above) would be of this kind.

    Head office secured limits are imposed when the manager cannot lend up to the amount proposed without higher authority. These limit types constitute only a few percent of the start-up sample.

    Under Report means that the account has given cause for concern and is currently being investigated usually at regional office level. Thus the decision has been removed from the branch manager's control. Security review is part of that process.

19. Note that a personal guarantee by the owner is not in general considered security for an overdraft.

20. See Stanworth and Gray (1991), p.65.

21. Details of the breakdown of cessations are available in a forthcoming paper.

22. This compares with UK VAT statistics presented in Ganguly (1985), Table 27, showing approximately the same percentage of VAT new registrations deregistering within two years. The period of analysis for the VAT data is 1974–1982.

23. E.g. a family to support, a house mortgage to pay.

24. Some 20% of account cessations are in the form of business discontinuances rather than bankruptcies or insolvencies.

25. A regression of the number of full-time employees against age of proprietors indicates a strong inverse U-shaped relationship between the two.

26. Insofar as borrowing is correlated with project size a correlation of survival and borrowing may simply reflect the fact that larger businesses are more diversified and hence less bankruptcy prone (Prais, 1973).

27. If margins reflect bankruptcy risk then higher risk to the bank may be compensated for by higher margins. In theory of course the charging of higher margins may itself increase the chances of failure. See below however for further discussion.

28. The figure of £137500 at age 60 is associated with a sample size of only 4.

29. An interesting confirmation of the importance of house equity in early business growth can be found in Black De Meza and Jeffries (1992).

REFERENCES

Avery R.B. and Berger A.N. (1991) Loan commitments and bank risk exposure, Journal of Banking and Finance, pp. 173–192.

Bates T. (1990) Entrepreneur human capital inputs and small business longevity, Review of Economics and Statistics, Vol. 72, No. 4.

Berger A.N. and Udell G.F. (1990) Collateral, loan quality and bank risk, Journal of Monetary Economics, Vol. 25, pp. 21–42.

Berger A.N., Udell G.F. and Wolken J.D. (1992) Spot Versus Forward Contracting in Small Business Working Capital Financing, Federal Reserve, April.

Black J., de Meza D. and Jeffreys D. (1992) House Prices, The Supply of Collateral and the Enterprise Economy, Working Paper under ESRC funded project 'The Functioning of Capital Markets under Uncertainty'.

Boot A., Thakor A.V. and Udell G.F. (1987) Competition, risk neutrality and loan commitments,

Journal of Banking & Finance, Vol. 11, pp. 449–471.

Buck A.J., Friedman J. and Dunkelberg W.C. (1991) Risk and return in small business lending: the case of commercial banks, in: Advances in Small Business Finance, ed. Yazdipour R., Kluwer, Netherlands.

Cressy R.C. (1992a) Characteristics of Business Proprietors and their Startups, SME Centre Working Paper, Warwick Business School.

Cressy R.C. (1992b) Business and Proprietor Characteristics, Complementary Finance Sources and Bank Lending: The Case of UK Business Starts, SME Centre Working Paper No. 8, Warwick Business School, July.

Cressy R.C. (1992c) Borrowing and Control: A Theory of Business Types, SME Centre Working Paper No. 11, Warwick Business School, November.

Evans D. and Jovanovic B. (1989) An estimated model of entrepreneurial choice under liquidity constraints, Journal of Political Economy, Vol. 97, No. 4, pp. 808–827.

Evans D. and Leighton L. (1989) Some empirical aspects of entrepreneurship, American Economic Review, Vol. 79, No. 3, June, pp. 519–535.

Ganguly P. (1985) UK Small Business Statistics and International Comparisons (ed. G. Bannock) Paul Chapman Publishing, London.

Ham J.C. and Melnik A. (1987) Loan demand: an empirical analysis using micro data, Review of Economics and Statistics, pp. 704–709.

Hutchinson P. and Ray G. (1986) Surviving the financial stress of small enterprise growth, in: The Survival of the Small Firm, eds Stanworth J. and Watkins D., Gower, Aldershot.

Jovanovic B. (1982) Selection and the evolution of industry, Econometrica, Vol. 50, No. 3, May.

Keasey K. and Watson R. (1992) Investment and Financing Decisions and the Performance of Small Firms, Study Commissioned by National Westminster Bank.

Leeth J.D. and Scott J.A. (1989) The incidence of secured debt: evidence from the small business community, Journal of Financial and Quantitative Analysis, Vol. 24 (September), pp. 379–393.

Maddala G.S. (1983) Limited Dependent and Qualitative Variables in Econometrics, Cambridge University Press.

Melnik A. and Plaut S. (1986) Loan commitment contracts, terms of lending and credit allocation, Journal of Finance, Vol. 61, No. 2, June.

Prais S.J. (1973) The Evolution of Giant Firms in Britain, Cambridge University Press, Cambridge.

Reid G.C. (1991) Staying in business, International Journal of Industrial Organisation, Vol. 9, pp. 545–56.

Stanworth J. and Gray C.(eds) (1991) Bolton 20 Years On, Paul Chapman, London.

Stiglitz J.E. and Weiss A. (1981) Credit rationing in markets with imperfect information, American Economic Review, Vol. 71, No. 3, pp. 393–410.

Thakor A.V. (1989) Strategic issues in financial contracting: an overview, Managerial Finance, Summer, pp. 39–58.

14.

Payment Periods and Cash Flow in the UK, Germany and France

Francis Chittenden, Anthony Kennon and Suneil Mahindru

INTRODUCTION

> The credit given by suppliers is a useful source of finance for all firms and should be used to the limit, that is, the point where the supplier threatens to stop deliveries, or the rate of discounts not obtained becomes higher than the interest paid on other available sources of finance, or than the rate of profit earned on assets.

This statement (Westwick, 1987) is a succinct expression of a business culture which places immediate financial advantage above contractual obligations. It has become commonplace in the UK, as well as other countries. As a result, there is concern from those who are disadvantaged by late payment, including many small businesses, that existing remedies are ineffective.

This report looks at the reasons for granting commercial credit, the importance of payment practices and the impact which late payment has on suppliers and the overall economy. It provides an economic analysis to determine the likely effects of prompter payment in the UK and elsewhere.

This examination is conducted from the viewpoint that current business culture ranks financial advantage above contractual obligations. Although late payment is in many ways an issue of business ethics, the best way to reduce its incidence would be to reduce its financial advantage. The quotation above encapsulates the motivation behind most late payments, and also identifies the most compelling motivations for paying. Since suppliers withholding delivery damage themselves as well as their customers, financial inducements to prompt payment are more likely to be effective. The economy as a whole will be shown to benefit from prompt payment.

THE IMPORTANCE OF PAYMENT PRACTICES

The value of a company can be calculated as the net present value of its future cash flows, discounted for risk (Modigliani and Miller, 1958). It is generally accepted that, all things being equal, the longer a debt is outstanding beyond its due date, the greater the likelihood of eventual non-payment. Therefore late payment reduces the value of companies, both by delaying the cash flows and by increasing the risk of non-payment, and therefore the risk inherent in the firm.

There are many ways to calculate the return which a company generates on the assets it employs (Holmes and Sugden 1990), e.g. return on total assets, return on net assets, return on fixed assets. Particularly relevant to the performance of a company needing additional working capital is return on financeable assets, because this measures the ability to cover the cost of such finance.

RETURN ON FINANCEABLE ASSETS

Return on financeable assets (ROFA) is calculated as follows:

ROFA = Net profit/(fixed assets + stocks + WIP + debtors − creditors).

This is a particularly strong measure of performance as it provides a link between profits and cash flow, both of which are important for continuing success. This link can be demonstrated by examining the similarity between the calculation of ROFA and the internal cash flow stream generated (from operations) by firms.

Cash flow = Net profit + depreciation ± fixed assets ± stocks and WIP ± debtors ± creditors

ROFA (and cash flow) can be increased by increasing net profit or creditors, or by decreasing fixed assets, stocks and work in progress, or debtors.

Figure 1 shows the way in which net profit and the constituents of net working assets build towards overall ROFA, expressing all figures as a percentage of total assets. Fixed assets have been omitted for the sake of clarity, but their relative importance is shown in Table 1.

It can be seen that profit is often relatively small in comparison to debtors and creditors (for small non-manufacturers profit was non-existent), and the presumption must be that many companies can achieve bigger improvements to ROFA by managing cash flows than by improving profit margins. Peter F. Drucker (1977) has written:

Working on the productivity of capital is the easiest and usually the quickest way to improve the profitability of a business, and the one with the greatest impact.

The importance of cash flow management is, in any case, widely recognised both for large, quoted companies and small firms, but for different reasons. For large companies it is known that stock market valuations are dependent on the cash-flow stream generated; whilst for small firms cash-flow management is critical because such businesses have fewer equity resources and limited access to external finance.

PRICE AND PAYMENT TERMS

To improve ROFA, a firm can negotiate better prices, which will improve net profit. Alternatively, negotiating on payment terms, can produce a more significant increase in

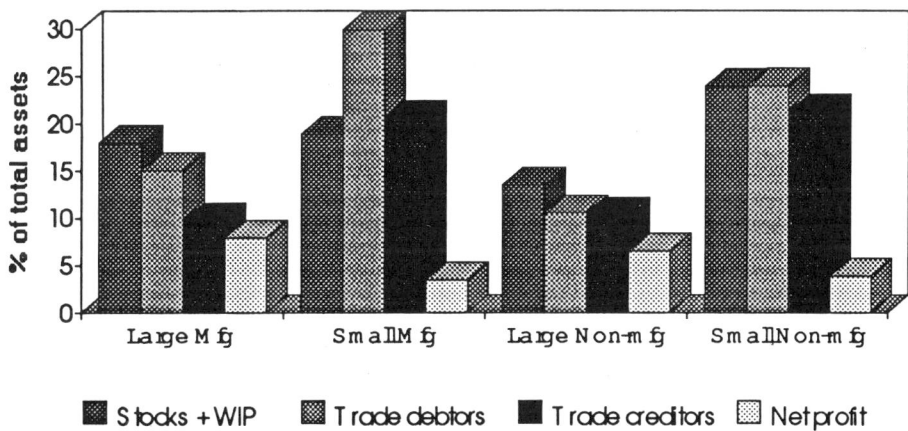

Figure 1: Contribution of net profit and net working assets to overall ROFA (average of 1987–1990 figures). Source: Business Monitor MA3.

Table 1: Balance sheet structure 1990

	Large mfg %	Large non-mfg %	Small mfg %	Small non-mfg %
Fixed assets				
Net tangible assets	34.6	55.4	33.1	24.9
Intangible assets	5.9	4.2	0.3	0.5
Investments	10.8	3.6	1.1	6.4
Total net fixed assets	51.3	63.3	34.5	31.8
Current assets				
Stocks and WIP	15.8	12.5	16.7	21.2
Trade debtors	13.4	9.6	29.0	24.5
Other debtors due <1yr	6.5	6.1	7.9	14.7
Debtors due after >1yr	1.5	1.2	0.1	0.3
Investments	2.6	2.3	0.5	1.0
Cash at bank & in hand	8.8	5.0	11.4	6.5
Total current assets	48.7	36.7	65.5	68.2
Total fixed & current assets	100.0	100.0	100.0	100.0

	Large mfg %	Large non-mfg %	Small mfg %	Small non-mfg %
Capital & long term liabilities				
Shareholders' interests	37.8	46.3	36.8	25.2
Minorities & provisions	12.1	4.0	2.1	0.5
Loans	12.4	17.6	4.6	10.1
Other creditors & accruals	4.0	2.5	2.4	3.3
Total capital & long term liabilities	66.3	70.5	45.9	39.2
Current liabilities				
Bank loans & overdraft	6.9	5.1	11.2	11.8
Directors' short-term loans	0.0	0.0	0.6	2.7
Other short-term loans	1.2	2.0	0.7	1.3
Trade creditors	8.8	9.0	22.0	21.5
Other creditors & accruals	11.8	8.8	13.8	18.8
Dividends & interest due	1.6	1.5	0.1	1.1
Current taxation	3.4	3.2	5.7	3.7
Total current liabilities	33.7	29.5	54.1	60.8
Total capital & liabilities	100.0	100.0	100.0	100.0

Source: *Business Monitor* MA3 23rd issue, Tables 8 & 9, excluding oil.

ROFA. Since a less sophisticated business is likely to understand clearly the impact of price on profits, but not necessarily to know how payment terms will affect ROFA, it is probable that payment terms are easier to alter by negotiation, when price has become immovable.

It is also likely that any payment which is made later than the agreed terms will not be (generally) perceived as significantly damaging to the supplier, whereas a change in price of a few percent would immediately be seen as impacting profit. Economic rationality suggests that since price and payment terms are two aspects of the same reward to a supplier, any alteration in one will lead to a compensating adjustment of the other. Whilst there is little doubt that this trade-off is made in the medium term, either through management decision, or the gradual liquidation of businesses failing to adapt to the new contractual arrangements, there appears to be a period of adjustment from which slow-paying customers benefit in the short term. This is an area worthy of further research.

Late payment has therefore become commonplace because it is not seen as a breach of contract terms in the same way as an equivalent change in price. Late payment is 'normal', perhaps because the culture of this country has changed — it has become customary to pay credit cards on the latest day permissible, not to pay the telephone bill before the red reminder, and so on. In these consumer instances, payment is not made until the sanction (application of interest charges, disconnection) is about to be applied. In commercial contracts, where sanctions are known to be cumbersome and expensive to apply, many, if not most, companies have discovered that late payment can be practised, apparently without penalty.

REASONS FOR COMMERCIAL CREDIT

Commercial credit has two basic functions, economic and administrative, which are mutually beneficial to customer and supplier. However, commercial credit may also be an expression of customer dominance, which benefits only the customer.

Economic

As goods are sold and re-sold down the supply chain from primary producer to retailer, each link in the chain holds stocks, and thus incurs a working capital requirement. This has to be financed, and it has been common practice for centuries that suppliers do so where it is in their interest. In order to maximise sales, the supplier provides credit to the customer, covering the anticipated time between delivery and resale. The economic benefits to both parties, i.e the minimised costs of stock-holding for the customer, and broader distribution for the supplier, occur due to shifting the working capital requirement from customer to supplier.

Business Monitor MA3 shows that large firms comprise a greater proportion of manufacturing than non-manufacturing enterprises, and that large firms have more fixed assets than small firms. This provision of commercial credit down the supply chain may be linked to the fact that large manufacturing firms will normally be in a better position, with greater fixed assets, to borrow from the banks than small, wholesale or retail firms. The UK banking system, certain specialist components excluded, tends to manage the risk of extending credit to small firms by lending against assets (Binks 1991). Of these assets, stocks are generally one of the least valuable elements of security, due to the difficulty and expense of continued monitoring by a lender.

As a result of the relative unattractiveness of stocks as a basis for raising external finance, commercial credit has been important to economic growth in the past. Today's commercial world, with minimum stock levels, more frequent distribution (often daily or even twice-daily), just-in-time manufacturing, etc., has reduced the amount of working capital required to finance stocks, and increased the speed of stock-turn. An extreme example of this can be found in supermarket retailing, where the largest chains have a negative working capital requirement because goods are sold for cash within hours or a very few days of delivery, and payment terms are rarely below 30 days. Such payment terms are a reflection of the strong commercial position enjoyed by UK supermarkets, which account for a significant percentage of the total distribution channels for most foods.

Administrative

The administrative reasons for offering commercial credit are aimed at minimising costs, and include security (think of the difficulties in arranging collection of cash on delivery for all sales!), reduced paperwork (one invoice/statement per month), and assurance of quality (by allowing time for goods inward testing/checking).

Administrative reasons for credit remain valid, and some organisations are reputed to have difficulty in paying within a short period, so complex have their procedures become. Increasing usage of electronic document interchange (EDI) and more responsive computer systems should reduce the minimum elapsed time required between invoicing and payment. It can be argued that any company with systems able to control frequent deliveries has no reason for failing to pay invoices quickly.

DOMINANT CUSTOMERS

Since the mutually beneficial economic and administrative justifications for commercial credit indicate that credit requirements should, if anything, be diminishing, the explanation for retaining or increasing commercial credit levels must lie with the strength of the negotiating position of certain customers.

If a product is in short supply, the supplier may be commercially dominant. If there are many alternative sources of supply, the customer is dominant and will be able to control negotiations. Because of the importance of cash flow this dominance will probably find expression in credit terms as well as price.

Therefore the original (economically beneficial) reasons for commercial credit have become less important, and in the short term apparent customer dominance (economically detrimental) may become more significant. Without this factor, more frequent deliveries and more sophisticated computer systems should, all things being equal, have reduced the requirement for commercial credit.

The amount and terms of commercial credit granted to a firm's customers determine the level of trade debtors in the balance sheet. The amount granted can be assumed to be dependent on sales, so that the payment terms agreed (assuming prompt payment) will be the effective determinant of a company's trade debtors. Various sources (including EC DG XXIII (1992), Intrum Justitia (1990) and the Forum of Private Business (1987)) show that the terms normally offered by UK suppliers are 30 days, which might be expected to be sufficient to accommodate the economically beneficial reasons for commercial credit.

Dominant customers, who impose longer payment terms than economically or administratively justifiable, therefore weaken the balance sheets of their suppliers. This is detrimental to the national economy, as well as to the suppliers. In some instances, companies have failed because of the default of one major customer. The conclusion which must be reached is that many are constrained in their commercial decisions (investment, expansion, employment, etc.) by unjustifiably long payment terms.

RELATIONSHIP BETWEEN STOCKS, DEBTORS AND CREDITORS

If the economic reasons for trade credit are the most important, it would be expected that a direct correlation would exist between changes in stocks and work in progress, and changes in trade creditors. If, on the other hand, other reasons are driving the amount of trade credit, then a weaker correlation could be anticipated between changes in stocks and trade creditors, coupled with a stronger correlation between changes in trade debtors and trade creditors.

In order to test this hypothesis, correlation analysis was conducted on seven years data (1984—1990) drawn from Dun & Bradstreet *Key Business Ratios*. The results are shown in Table 2.

This table shows that during this period, for all sectors except services, a stronger relationship exists between debtors and creditors (max or min — see below for calculation) than for stocks and creditors. For all sectors except services the relationship between debtors and creditors is significant at the 99% level. A similar relationship between stocks and creditors is apparent only in the retail sector. Thus it appears that the main driver for trade credit has become the level of debtors, in place of stocks.

IMPACT OF LATE PAYMENT

Late payment requires an increase in working capital for the creditor company, which may be obtained from one of four sources:

1. increased debt, resulting in reduced profits and reduced borrowing capability;
2. increased equity, which devalues existing investors' stakes if returns are unchanged;
3. reduced investment in the future, constraining the company's long-term performance;
4. or an increase in days credit taken from suppliers, which 'exports' the problem.

It should be noted that in the case of increasing equity, a further injection of capital by the owners is likely to be the only source available to most SMEs in the current economic climate.

If a firm elects, or through financial stringency is forced, to keep its working capital constant, then any late payment by debtors must be balanced by late payment to creditors. Unless the firm sells for cash, e.g. retailing, trade debtors will represent the vast majority of a company's incoming cashflows, and must be used to pay regular commitments such as rent, interest on borrowings, and payroll, in addition to trade creditors. The only one of these items which can easily be delayed (think of the consequences of paying wages late) is trade creditors, and to the extent that trade creditors are less than trade debtors, the resulting outgoing delay must be greater than the incoming delay. Thus if working capital is kept constant, late payment multiplies — not only in money, but also to a greater extent in time.

If trade debtors exceed trade creditors, then keeping working capital constant in the face of late receipt of payment is only possible to a limited extent. Due to the multiplier

Table 2: Relationship between stocks, debtors and creditors

		Debtors	Stocks
GB Ltd	Creditors Min	0.9175 $P=0.002$	0.7209 $P=0.034$
	Creditors Max	0.1851 $P=0.367$	−0.3536 $P=0.218$
Agriculture	Creditors Min	0.6086 $P=0.046$	−0.2092 $P=0.326$
	Creditors Max	0.8746 $P=0.005$	0.5755 $P=0.088$
Manufacturing	Creditors Min	0.9707 $P=0.000$	0.6983 $P=0.040$
	Creditors Max	0.2676 $P=0.281$	−0.5730 $P=0.107$
Wholesalers	Creditors Min	0.9255 $P=0.001$	0.5544 $P=0.098$
	Creditors Max	0.5432 $P=0.104$	−0.0559 $P=0.453$
Retailers	Creditors Min	0.9836 $P=0.001$	0.8157 $P=0.013$
	Creditors Max	0.8302 $P=0.010$	0.7205 $P=0.034$
Services	Creditors Min	0.7038 $P=0.039$	0.8657 $P=0.006$
	Creditors Max	−0.3229 $P=0.240$	0.2135 $P=0.323$

Source: *Key Business Ratios* 1984—1990.
P = Single tailed probability.

effect just described, the point at which creditors apply sanctions will be reached sooner than the point at which sanctions are applied to debtors, assuming that such application of sanctions is related primarily to the time element.

PAYMENT PRACTICE AND ECONOMIC CONDITIONS

Dun & Bradstreet *Key Business Ratios* (see Table 3) shows that there has been a reduction in both collection period (debtor days) and creditors to sales between 1988 and 1990. This is not necessarily the same as improved payment practice. The reduction in collection period may be a reflection of shorter credit periods granted, or a reduction in the proportion of sales to which credit terms apply. Creditors to sales would also improve if profit margins increased. However, the major reason for this reduction in debtor days and creditors to sales is probably stricter credit management.

Economic rationality suggests, and several sources have confirmed, that when the risk of non-payment increases, as in times of recession, professional credit managers chase harder and earlier for payment, thereby trading administrative expense for certainty of payment. Evidence from Lombard NatWest Factors (Table 4) shows that their average collection period shortened from 23 to 19 days between 1990q4 and 1992q3. Overdue accounts therefore decreased from 49.1% to 39% of total debts outstanding. This underlines the importance of professional credit management.

Dun & Bradstreet *Key Business Ratios* also shows that the gap between trade debtors and trade creditors widened in 1990. This means that, despite aggregate reduced debtor days, late payment is a problem of increasing severity, because of the difficulty of passing delays on to creditors. At the same time, *Business Monitor* MA3 shows that short-term bank lending and overdrafts have not risen significantly between 1989 and 1990, so the increased working capital requirement has not been funded by borrowing.

It is not unreasonable to imagine that, if large and professionally managed companies are placing increased emphasis on credit control, the effect is to encourage customers to prioritise payment of invoices from these companies. To the extent that this is the case, companies who do not, or are unable to, apply equally increased pressure for prompt payment will be disadvantaged. The overall figures, therefore, are likely to conceal instances of increasing debtor days amongst the commercially weaker enterprises.

These factors may well explain why the issue of late payment has become so prominent in the last two years – although it appears to be diminishing in volume, its effects are hitting much harder. Reduced trading profits are causing tighter cash flows; with banks reluctant to increase lending and enterprises wishing to reduce uncertainty, the result for many companies is being caught in a squeeze between their suppliers and customers.

DIFFERENTIAL EFFECTS ON SMEs

Small firms tend to be more highly geared than large firms, as shown by Bolton (1971) and several studies since (see Table 1), primarily because they have less equity in the balance sheet. It is also widely accepted that small firms have greater difficulty raising money. Due to higher gearing and lower fixed assets, SMEs are a less attractive lending

Table 3: Trends in payment periods 1984–1990

Great Britain	1984	1985	1986	1987	1988	1989	1990
Trade debtors (days)	32.2	31.2	30.2	30.8	31.6	30.9	30.3
Trade creditors (days)	25.1	19.4	16.7	16.4	14.7	13.9	12
Collection period (days)	58	56.1	56	56.9	58	56.9	53.3
Creditors to sales (days)	40.5	37.4	36.1	36.6	36.7	35.7	32.8

Source: Dun & Bradstreet *Key Business Ratios*.

Table 4: Trends in collection practices

	1990q4	1991q1	1991q2	1991q3	1991q4	1992q1	1992q2	1992q3
Debt turn	66	66	64	63	65	62	62	62
Collection period (beyond due date)	23	21	20	19	18	16	16	15
Average credit extended	43	45	44	44	47	46	46	47
Overdues as % of total debt	49.1	40.1	39.8	39.0	38.0	36.1	34.3	32.4

Source: Lombard NatWest Factors Limited.

proposition; restricted access to the financial markets and an aversion to external equity participation make share capital more difficult to raise.

For an SME, the balance sheet structure is different from that of large firms:

1. Fixed assets are lower, and debtors are higher;
2. Shareholders' interests and long-term loans are lower;
3. Bank overdrafts, short-term loans and creditors are higher.

Because shareholders' interests and long-term loans are a smaller percentage of the SME's liabilities, it appears that there is less scope for accommodating late payment by increasing equity or long term debt. It has often been argued that many, if not most, SMEs in the UK are undercapitalised.

Therefore the two main avenues open to an SME suffering from late payment are to increase short-term bank borrowing, or delay payments to creditors. It has been shown that delaying payments to creditors cannot be taken beyond a certain point. Bank borrowing is easier to arrange in times of economic growth than recession, and it may be that late payment has become a more important issue over the last few years, precisely because bank borrowing for increased working capital has become more difficult.

A further consideration in the cycle of late payment is to consider the different motivations of large businesses and SMEs. It has been demonstrated (Prais, 1976) that increasing concentration of industrial ownership in the UK has not increased plant size, so that the merger logic of economies of scale does not apply to production. It does apply, though, to finance. A large company enjoys considerable financial economies of scale over an SME. Typically, it can borrow at a rate which is two or three percentage points lower, and its bank is less likely to demand collateral security. Therefore the cost to an SME of late payment is higher, and so is the benefit of being, in turn, a late payer.

LATE PAYMENT AND SIZE OF COMPANY

It has already been shown above that small companies have greater trade creditors than large companies, relative to both stocks and total assets. They also have greater costs of, and lesser access to, bank borrowing. As a result, it would not be expected that small companies could, on average, pay their suppliers more promptly than large companies.

This conclusion is supported by the results of the Slow Payers Survey conducted by the Forum of Private Business (1989). Despite the popular contention that late payment is practised by large companies against small firms, this survey of small enterprises found that more respondents stated that they were owed most by small rather than large businesses.

The conclusion which must be drawn is that large companies may well be late payers, but SMEs are at least as bad and probably worse. In particular, SMEs have a greater incentive to pay late, and suffer greater pressures on their finances when payment to them is late.

ECONOMIC ANALYSIS

Having examined the reason that late payment of commercial credit is a serious problem in the UK economy, especially for small firms, the likely impact of any modifications in payment practices can be examined. Changes in payment practices, be they voluntary or statutory, will affect firms in different ways. The precise impact will depend on a variety of factors including the size of the company and the characteristics of the sector they are involved in. This section aims to evaluate the implications of reforms in payment practices, and determine which types of firms will benefit.

Data sources

The two main sources of data used for this analysis were Dun & Bradstreet *Key Business*

Ratios and the BDC database. *Key Business Ratios* provides financial data for a number of sectors in the UK economy based upon the published accounts of some 200,000 companies of all sizes. The BDC database contains the accounts of approximately 1,200 small companies in the UK, from 40 industry sectors. This data was grouped into four main industrial sectors, and values were calculated for the characteristics of an average firm in each sector. To complement the UK study, data on two major European countries was also used. The data comprised the accounts of a sample of French and German companies from DIANE and DAFNE respectively. These are databases containing publicly available accounts of commercial enterprises in the two countries, and in each case about 250 records were randomly chosen subject to sufficient information being available (i.e. incomplete records were rejected).

Table 5 shows the results from the BDC database together with the corresponding figures from *Key Business Ratios*. A characteristic of small-firm data is the wide ranging values, which often have the effect of distorting average figures. To avoid this problem the simple arithmetic mean was replaced by the median and an adjusted mean (calculated by omitting the top and bottom 5% of values). The results for individual sectors are broadly similar. This suggests that the BDC sample of small companies is a representative one, with characteristics similar to the whole industry. However, it is still important to remember that these aggregate figures disguise the wide diversity of results among small firms.

Sector implications

Key Business Ratios provides calculations of collection period (debtor days) and creditors to sales. Creditors to sales is not an accurate reflection of payment practices, being based on selling price rather than purchase cost. For meaningful analysis, the actual length of time taken to pay creditors must be calculated, and in order to do this, an approximation of the value of bought-in items must be made.

One simple approximation is to use the cost of goods sold, rather than sales. The resulting ratio, creditors to cost of goods sold, is termed 'minimum creditor days' for this analysis. Although it is a more realistic measure of the length of credit taken than the creditors to sales ratio, it is still likely to underestimate the true payment period. This is because cost of goods sold comprises two main elements: raw materials and direct labour costs. To the degree that cost of goods sold includes any labour costs, this ratio will be misleading.

Another estimate of raw material costs (including bought-in services) is achieved by subtracting total employee remuneration from the cost of goods sold. Because remuneration is likely to contain non-direct labour costs, the outcome will now exaggerate the true payment period. This measure is called 'maximum creditor days'.

Although it is not possible to pinpoint actual payment periods in this way, these two ratios provide the bounds between which the true figure must lie. Results of these calculations, performed on data from *Key Business Ratios*, are presented in Table 6.

Taking, for example, a statutory maximum credit period of 30 days, it can be estimated, at the aggregate level, the extent to which firms in a sector might be expected to benefit or suffer from compliance with this policy. Benefits will occur when the increase in funds caused by lower trade debtors exceeds the reduction in funds caused by a lower figure for trade creditors. The outcome of this change would be a reduction in the net working assets financed by the business.

In the *Key Business Ratios* sectors examined, only agriculture and retail businesses would suffer from the need to finance an increased net working assets requirement. Retailing is likely to suffer from any reduction in payment terms simply because debtor days are already below the 30 day limit. Companies in all other sectors would in aggregate enjoy improved cash flow as a result of paying suppliers in 30 days and collecting payment from customers in the same time period (see Table 7).

Table 5: BDC and KBR ratios

		Gross profit to sales	Net profit to sales	Stocks to sales	Trade debtors to sales	Trade creditors to sales	Net working assets to sales	Calc net working assets to sales	Fixed assets to sales	ROFA
Manufacturing	Median	30.8	3.2	7.5	16.6	9.1	14.0	15.0	12.0	11.8
	Adj Mean	29.8	1.3	10.0	16.0	10.9	15.7	15.1	20.8	3.5
	KBR 1990	34.3	1.1	10.3	17.9	10.2	18.0	18.0	19.4	2.9
Wholesale	Median	23.3	1.4	8.3	12.0	7.1	15.4	13.2	5.6	7.2
	Adj Mean	24.2	0.5	12.5	12.9	9.1	16.4	16.3	13.3	1.7
	KBR 1990	27.0	(0.1)	10.2	15.5	10.2	15.5	15.5	9.4	(0.4)
Retail	Median	24.6	2.2	9.5	5.3	6.8	10.5	8.0	8.9	13.0
	Adj Mean	23.5	2.3	12.3	6.5	7.2	12.4	11.6	14.4	8.7
	KBR 1990	28.6	0.3	11.4	3.3	6.4	7.9	8.3	13.5	1.4
Business services	Median	49.3	5.7	0.8	15.4	5.2	11.2	11.0	13.1	23.7
	Adj Mean	47.2	7.4	7.4	17.5	13.5	13.2	11.4	52.5	11.6
	KBR 1990	48.6	(1.1)	3.4	14.7	7.3	10.8	10.8	19.5	(3.6)

Table 6: Payment periods by sector

1990	Great Britain	Agriculture	Manufacturing	Wholesale	Retail	Services
Collection period	53.3	31.9	65.5	56.8	11.9	53.6
Creditors to sales	32.8	26.9	37.4	37.1	23.3	26.7
Min creditor days	50.2	41.6	56.9	50.8	32.6	51.9
Max creditor days	80.4	67.8	100.8	63.2	41.8	160.8

Source: derived from *Key Business Ratios*.

Table 7: Impact of reducing credit periods

1990	Great Britain	Agriculture	Manufacturing	Wholesale	Retail	Services
Net benefit-min cr days	10.1	−5.6	17.8	11.6	−1.9	12.3
Net benefit-max cr days	2.7	−13.1	9.2	7.3	−6.6	1.9

Results are expressed in terms of days sales. Source: derived from *Key Business Ratios*.

Small firm implications

Having examined the effect on the major sectors of the economy, the BDC database was used to evaluate the differential effect on small firms in each sector. The results confirm the *Key Business Ratios* analysis and show that the only sector which does not benefit on average is retail — there are no agricultural firms in the BDC database. The impact on business service companies is approximately neutral and the remaining two sectors, manufacturing and wholesale, are net beneficiaries of the reduction in credit periods.

Due to the diversity of small firms, comprehensive analysis requires scrutiny of the effects on individual firms within each sector. Table 8 outlines the results for several sub-sectors within the four industrial sectors. It may be seen that average results conceal a wide range of impacts which will be felt by firms in each sector. Sectors which benefit from a reduction in credit periods may contain several firms which actually suffer, and vice versa. However, on aggregate, businesses will enjoy the advantages of improved cash flow.

EUROPEAN COMPARISON

A similar study of payment practices and the impact of any reforms was conducted for France and Germany, to determine whether the impact of late payment is similar in other European countries. The results in Table 9 suggest that the UK is not alone in this respect.

As far as Germany is concerned, a limit to the length of credit would have a beneficial effect on companies' cash flows. Over a four year period, from 1988 to 1991, the average firm would benefit by the equivalent of approximately 28 days worth of sales (22 after

Table 8: Sectoral impact of 30 day credit period

Sector	Average net benefit (min creditor days)	Winners	Losers	Neutral	Sample total
Computer services	12.04	12	8	1	21
Household goods retail	(14.55)	1	18	11	30
Food wholesale	1.16	12	6	7	25
Clothing & footwear wholesale	4.04	11	10	3	24
Clothing & footwear manufacture	47.70	10	6	7	23
Chemical manufacture	(4.82)	9	13	3	25

Source: derived from BDC database.

Table 9: Impact of reducing credit periods to 30 days in France and Germany

		1991	1990
France	Net benefit	7.1	10.3
	VAT adjusted	3.7	5.8
Germany	Net benefit	28.1	29.6
	VAT adjusted	22.1	23.3

Results are expressed in terms of days sales. Source: Derived from DIANE and DAFNE.

adjusting for VAT). This value has remained remarkably constant, and the number of firms benefiting has outweighed those suffering by between 3:1 and 4:1.

French figures also suggest a similar situation, but not to the same extent. The benefit to cash flows has gradually fallen from approximately 25 days of sales in 1988 to under 10 days (4 days after adjusting for TVA) in 1991. Also the ratio of winners to losers is between 2:1 and 1:1. These results are not totally as expected since late payment in France is considered to be at least as bad as the situation in the UK. One possible explanation is that the accuracy of the French results may be suspect because of the wide variations observed in the French data. Nonetheless French companies would benefit from reduction to 30 days credit extended and received.

CONCLUSIONS

By adjusting creditors' days so that they are stated in terms of inputs, the likely consequences of any changes in payment practices may be estimated. If the maximum credit period in the UK was 30 days, agriculture and retailing would suffer an increase in the level of net working assets which required financing, whilst all other sectors in the study would benefit and in certain cases (e.g. manufacturing) the liquidity position of businesses would improve and the level of finance required to expand when the economy moves out of recession would be substantially reduced. However these aggregate figures disguise the fact that there will be a range of outcomes in any one sector, as demonstrated with the BDC small company data. The European data also shows that shorter payment periods would be of overall benefit to businesses in Germany and France.

There is one constraint to this analysis, the arbitrary choice of the 30 day limit. The economic justification for extending trade credit rests upon the twin premises of administrative efficiency and the provision of financial support for stock holding, thus easing

Table 10: Stock holding periods

Sector	Stock turnover (median) ×	Gross profit %	Adjusted stock turnover ×	Stock turn days
Great Britain	11.4	34.6	7.45	49
Construction	15.6	28.7	11.12	33
Agriculture	5.3	35.3	3.43	106
Mining	19.4	32.4	13.11	28
Manufacturing	9.7	34.3	6.37	57
Transport & communications	81.0	34.4	53.14	7
Wholesale	9.8	27.0	7.15	51
Retail	8.8	28.6	6.28	58
Real estate & investments	1.7	50.8	(1.70)	215
Services	29.8	48.6	15.30	24

Source: derived from Dun & Bradstreet _Key Business Ratios._

the movement of goods down the supply chain. Table 10 shows the length of stock-holding periods based upon the cost of goods sold and balance sheet stock figures supplied by *Key Business Ratios*.

This data shows that for the economy as a whole, average stock days in 1990 stood at 49, with a spread from 24 days in services to 106 days for agriculture. It has already been seen that these figures have been gradually declining, and this trend should be encouraged to continue until the optimum level is reached.

In addition the need for administrative efficiency, particularly amongst SMEs who generally have less sophisticated administrative resources, is of great importance. To propose a statutory payment period of 30 days would place an additional burden on many businesses as payments would require to be prepared on a number of occasions during any monthly accounting cycle.

It is, therefore, worth considering the introduction of a longer period of time, such as 45 days, which would both equate more closely with the average period of stock holding and provide greater administrative flexibility. If the requirement was that accounts should be settled by the end of the month following that in which delivery took place this would provide the option for businesses to trade on monthly terms, thus minimising the administrative burden, at the same time as providing an average payment period of 45 days which would be very close to the average length of time for which stocks are held in the economy.

ACKNOWLEDGEMENTS

The research on which this paper is based was funded by National Westminster Bank PLC, whose support is gratefully acknowledged. The views expressed do not necessarily reflect those of the sponsoring organisation.

REFERENCES

Binks M. (1991) Bolton 20 Years On, Chapter 4, Eds Stanworth J. and Gray C., Paul Chapman, London.

Bolton J. (1971) Committee of Enquiry on Small Firms, Cmnd 4811, HMSO, London.

DG XXIII (1992) On the Problem of the Time Taken to Make Payment in Commercial Transactions, Commission of the European Communities, Staff Working Paper, SEC (92) 2214, Brussels.

Drucker P.F. (1977) People and Performance, Pan Books, London.

Forum of Private Business (1987) Slow Payers Report, Knutsford.

Holmes G. and Sugden A. (1990) Interpreting Company Reports and Accounts, 4th Edn, Woodhead Faulkner, Cambridge.

Intrum Justitia (1990) Getting Paid, Intrum Justitia, London.

Modigliani F. and Miller M.H. (1958) The Cost of Capital, Corporation Finance and the Theory of Investment, American Economic Review, Vol. 48, pp. 261−297.

Prais S.J. (1976) The Evolution of Giant Firms in Britain, Cambridge University Press, Cambridge.

Westwick C.A. (1987) How to Use Management Ratios, 2nd edn, Gower, Aldershot.

15.

SUPPORT FOR MATURE SMEs:
Developing a Policy Agenda

David Smallbone, David North and Roger Leigh

INTRODUCTION

This paper is concerned with policy support for mature SMEs and in particular with the use of external assistance as a means of extending the resource base of the firm. Limited management resources is one of the disadvantages of small size and thus from time to time, SMEs might be expected to turn to individuals and/or organisations outside the firm for assistance. Owners and managers of SMEs cannot be expected to be equally proficient in all aspects of management. Effective use of outside agencies may be able to help the firm to deal with specific problems and/or to contribute to the overall strategic development of the company. Outside help may be provided by public or semi-public agencies or by private sector organisations as a result of a normal market transaction. A third possibility is that the assistance is delivered by a private sector organisation but is partly funded by the state (as in the case of subsidised consultancy).

The empirical evidence cited in this paper is based upon some of the findings of a project which is part of the ESRC's Small Business Research Initiative. Although the main aim of the project has been to examine how firms in the study have developed over time adapting to changing circumstances, we also investigated the extent to which firms used external advisors and consultants during the study period. The firms were drawn from 8 manufacturing sectors and their mature nature is reflected in the fact that to be included, a firm had to be in existence in 1979 and was therefore at least 10 years old at the time of the interviews in 1990/1. The other definitional criteria were that in the base year (1979) the firm had to be independently owned and employing less than 100 employees. A total of 306 firms were interviewed drawn from 3 types of location: 126 from Greater London, 100 from outer metropolitan locations (in Hertfordshire and Essex), and 80 from remote rural areas (mainly in northern England). Two particular characteristics of the data base should be emphasised: first that by including firms drawn from 3 different support environments we have a broad base of support experience on which to draw, and secondly that the random selection of firms within the sectors means that we have firms with varying degrees of growth orientation, a variety of performance characteristics and different experience with external agencies.

'External assistance' was defined in the survey as 'help relating to either specific business problems or the development of the business which was received from individuals or organisations outside the firm'. These could include both formal and informal contacts and our aim was to include the full range of elements in the 'business support system' in order to avoid overemphasising the importance of any particular type of agency or organisation. However, in an attempt to focus on those contacts which have some importance to the firm, we only include in this paper those responses where managers were able to point to specific examples of assistance received during the period 1979–90. Help which took the form of only information provision or signposting was therefore not included.

The rest of the paper is divided into two main sections. We first present a summary of the nature and extent of the external assistance used by firms over the decade. This is followed by a discussion of some of the policy issues raised by the survey with the aim of contributing to the development of a policy agenda for improving the external support offered to this type of firm.

FIRMS' USE OF EXTERNAL ASSISTANCE: SOME SURVEY EVIDENCE

Fifty-five percent of all firms were able to identify some form of external assistance which had been received (see Table 1). This means that nearly half the firms were virtually self sufficient over a 10 year period, relying solely on their internal management resources to guide the business. Remote rural firms showed the highest propensity to use outside support (66%) and firms in London[1] the lowest (44%); a variation which is explained mainly by the stronger presence of public sector support organisations in the remote rural areas, and the Rural Development Commission[2] (RDC) in particular. In fact outside of the remote rural areas, external support for established SMEs is almost entirely delivered by private sector sources.

PRIVATE SECTOR SOURCES

The use of paid consultants

Paid consultants were the most commonly used single source of 'assistance': as Table 1 shows, 75 firms (25%) used consultants on a total of 101 different occasions. Although in the majority of cases, the purchase of consultancy was a market transaction with the firm bearing the full cost of the consultant's fee, in a third of them firms received a subsidy under the DTI's Enterprise Initiative (EI). The most common types of consultancy used by firms were in business planning and design/product development (see Table 2). The use of design and product development consultancies was mainly by London-

Table 1: Firms using external assistance from different sources during the 1980s

Sources of assistance	London		OMA		Rural		All firms	
	No.	%	No.	%	No.	%	No.	%
Public & semi-public agencies*	7	6%	14	14%	44	55%	65	21%
Paid consultants	28	22%	34	34%	13	16%	75	25%
Banks & accountants	20	16%	17	17%	14	18%	51	17%
Informal sources†	6	5%	13	13%	8	10%	27	9%
Trade associations & Chambers of Commerce	8	6%	13	13%	4	4%	25	8%
Other sources	9	7%	6	6%	3	4%	18	6%
Firms using external assistance‡	58	46%	57	57%	53	66%	168	55%
Number of firms in panel	126	100%	100	100%	80	100%	306	100%

* Public and semi-public agencies include enterprise agencies, local authorities, the Small Firms Service and the RDC.
† Informal sources include friends, business associates and members of the family other than those who are directly involved in the business.
‡ This is the total number of different firms using external assistance. Since some firms used more than one source, the figure is less than the total for the column.

Table 2: Types of paid consultancy

Type of consultancy	London panel	OMA panel	Rural panel	All firms
Business planning	6	12	4	22
Marketing	2	7	1	10
Design/product development	15	5	1	21
Manufacturing systems	3	3	2	8
Financial information systems	3	1	1	5
Quality managememt	3	5	6	14
Other	8	9	4	21
Total number of consultancies	40	42	19	101
Number of firms using consultants	28	34	13	75

based electronics and instruments firms which needed to maintain a programme of product development in order to remain competitive but were too small to invest heavily in R&D in-house.

A key issue is the extent to which outside assistance is actually implemented by the firm and has some positive impact on the business. In view of the fact that some payment by the firm was involved, it is not surprising that in the majority of cases managers had attempted to at least 'partially' implement consultants' recommendations. In 2/3 of cases managers said they were either 'satisfied' or 'extremely satisfied' with the consultancy and in 52% of cases, managers judged that the consultancy had made a positive impact on their business, such as by 'increasing sales' (17 firms) and 'cost savings' (10 firms). However, both the level of implementation and the reported satisfaction with the consultancy received did tend to vary with the type of consultancy. In particular it was the business-planning consultancies which appeared to be the most difficult to deliver effectively: for example 45% of business-planning consultancies were not implemented at all compared with only 15% of the other types of consultancy. The problems with this type of consultancy appear to be a combination of its more challenging 'root and branch' nature, the 'in and out' method of delivery and the circumstances in which firms turn to consultants for help of this sort. In contrast, the most effective uses of consultancy tended to be those cases where the consultant was employed to address a specific issue or problem where a tangible objective could be identified (such as the design, product development or quality management consultancies).

Whilst the overall level of satisfaction with and implementation of consultancy was generally high, the causes of dissatisfaction given by a minority and the problems of implementation do help us to understand how the effectiveness of the use of consultants by small firms can be increased. One of the most common complaints made by managers was that the consultants' expertise was either inadequate or that the consultant simply did not understand the business. Other reasons given for partial implementation were that the consultants' recommendations were judged too expensive to introduce completely, or were impractical in some way.

In terms of small-firms' policy, the subsidised consultancy under the Enterprise Initiative reflects a shift away from support for business start-ups towards assisting more established firms (Stanworth and Gray 1991). In view of the fact that the 34 subsidised consultancies (received under the EI) compares with only four firms which had made use of either the Loan Guarantee Scheme or the Business Expansion Scheme, it would certainly appear that the EI has extended the scope and the take-up of government policy for established SMEs such as these. One aim of the EI is to 'pump-prime' the market for consultancy by encouraging firms which have not used consultants previously to employ consultants for the first time. Our evidence suggests that there is an additionality effect since in 70% of cases of subsidised consultancy, managers stated that they would not have used consultants for the particular project in the absence of a subsidy.

However, an important finding is that the level of implementation of subsidised consultancies was below that of the non-subsidised variety. It also appeared that the overall level of satisfaction with and success of the subsidised consultancies was below that of the non-subsidised type. Whilst this may be partly explained by the higher proportion of subsidised consultancies which involved firms using consultants for the first time, as well as by the higher proportion of the more challenging 'business planning' type, the fact remains that in a third of cases managers were clearly dissatisfied with what they had received. When the reasons for their dissatisfaction are examined it is clear that the quality control over the delivery of the subsidised consultancy has still to be improved. Too often the consultants appeared to the clients to lack the necessary detailed knowledge of the conditions in their sector, or the constraints on their type of business that hindered implementation.

Finally, some knowledge of the propensity of different types of SME to use paid consultants may help to inform policy makers interested in targeting small-business support policies more effectively. In general it was the larger firms which showed the highest propensity to use consultants and the smallest firms the lowest (see Table 3). The reasons are partly to do with the cost of paying consultants but are also affected by the characteristics of the type of consultancy offered which very small firms often find difficult to make effective use of.

It also appeared that the use of paid consultants was more common in the better performing firms which supports the finding that fast-growth firms are more likely to have a wider range of external contacts than firms with lower levels of performance (Storey et al 1989). We classified firms into one of five performance groups based mainly on their real turnover growth between 1979 and 1990.[3] Whereas a third of the high growth firms had used paid consultants, only a fifth of firms in each of the other performance groups had done so. It is not clear though if better performing firms are simply more 'open' to advice and thus more likely to use external sources to extend their internal resource base, or if consultants make a sufficient impact on the firm to materially affect growth.

There was also some sectoral variation: in the more science- and technology-based sectors (i.e. instruments, electronics and pharmaceuticals) approximately half the firms had used consultants over the period but in the more craft-based printing, clothing and industrial plant sectors, only one in seven firms had done so. The existence of trained managers in a company was another factor which appeared to increase the likelihood of the firm using both paid consultants and public or semi-public agencies, suggesting that increasing the extent of management training in SMEs and their use of external support are mutually supportive policy objectives.

Table 3: The use of external assistance and firm size

1990 Employment	All sources	Public semi-public	Paid consult	No external assist	All firms No.	%
1–9	52%	(32%)	(10%)	48%	102	100%
10–19	61%	(18%)	(31%)	39%	67	100%
20–49	54%	(16%)	(29%)	46%	90	100%
50+	60%	(14%)	(43%)	40%	42	100%
Total	56%	(22%)	(25%)	44%	301	100%

The figures shown in brackets for assistance received from public and semi-public agencies and consultants are included in the total shown in the 'All sources' column.

Banks and accountants

Seventeen per cent of firms had received assistance from banks or accountants over the decade. This figure excludes routine contacts with banks to discuss loans, or with accountants to discuss annual accounts, unless these contacts led to advice being offered which went beyond the initial purpose of the meeting.

Not surprisingly, in most cases assistance received from banks tended to be stimulated by a financial issue or problem of some sort. In some cases this was associated with an expansion of the business perhaps initiated by an approach to the bank for finance for an investment such as the purchase of a new machine. In others it was the result of a financial crisis which in some instances was sufficiently serious to threaten the survival of the company. Whatever the initial stimulus, the type of assistance received from the bank typically involved either financial analysis or business planning. In some cases, more specialised assistance was received from banks such as help with costing, help in planning market research from the bank's small business advisory service or help with export documentation from a bank's international department.

As in the case of the banks, the role of accountants was normally focused initially on some aspect of finance which typically had wider implications for the development of the business. These include cases where an accountant had helped to assemble a financial package to fund an acquisition or relocation and also cases where an accountant's advice was central to the survival, recovery or re-orientation of the business. In other instances, more routine tax advice or recommendations for improvements in accounting procedures had resulted in the manager being able to identify some tangible benefit for the business.

In view of the centrality of financial questions to the growth and survival of small firms, bank managers and accountants are potentially an important point of entry into a support system for SMEs. Unfortunately the publicity given to the role of the banks in contributing to the failure of small firms in the current recession makes it difficult for this potential to be developed in the short term, since small business managers tend to see the bank in an adversarial rather than a supportive role. This would seem to be doubly unfortunate since our evidence suggests that when firms do look to banks (or accountants) for more than routine assistance they are usually satisfied with the outcome. For such firms the role of the bank was more than just a source of finance although this may have been the reason for the initial approach. Of course there were some firms where managers were very critical of the banks, accusing them (together with the Government) of having encouraged a 'credit flood' by lending indiscriminately and then squeezing credit as interest rates rose. Some managers also accused the banks of being too distant from their customers and not interested in small companies as businesses, only as risks. Thus whilst the banks are a potentially important element in the external support system for small firms, they clearly still have some way to go to tune themselves more finely to the needs of small manufacturing businesses.

Other non-public sector sources

Surprisingly perhaps, only 8% of firms had received external assistance from either a trade association or Chamber of Commerce over the period, indicating that in the UK these organisations are viewed by managers as fairly weak and a limited source of support for SMEs. This compares with the help available to firms in some other European countries such as Germany (Bennett and Krebs 1991) or parts of Italy where sector-based support organisations have been established with participation from both regional and local government and from producer associations (Brusco and Righi 1989).

Whilst only 9% of managers were able to point to examples of external assistance having been received from either friends, business associates or members of the family (other than those who were directly involved in the business), where such sources had been used it was common for managers to be able to point to tangible benefits for the business. These cases included the use of someone in whom the owner or manager had both trust and confidence as either a mentor or a confidant in the making of key decisions, or as a source of specialist 'professional' advice (at either low cost or no cost to the firm). The nature of these contacts meant they were likely to be ongoing, providing help and support with implementation as well as with diagnosis and recommendations for action. This meant there was a greater likelihood of the assistance making both a short-term impact on the business as well as contributing to the learning experience of the manager. There is an important lesson here for improving the effectiveness of the use of consultants and external advice in small firms in general, in that the continuity of contact and the confidence that comes from it, are important factors in successful delivery of external aid.

PUBLIC AND SEMI-PUBLIC AGENCIES

Twenty-one per cent of all firms received some form of external assistance from one or more of the public or semi-public support organisations (i.e. an enterprise agency (EA), the Small Firms Service (SFS), a local authority or the RDC) at some time during the 10 year period (see Table 4). However, a firm's propensity to use, and its assessment of, this type of support organisation varied considerably between the three types of location. Whereas 55% of remote rural firms had received some form of assistance from a public or semi-public agency and the reported level of satisfaction and impact was generally high, in the urban areas (where the majority of small firms are located) the level of contact was much lower. Only 6% of firms in Greater London had used such an organisation, and most of those which had could not identify any positive impact or benefit for their business. It must be a matter of some concern that public sector agencies have failed to establish a more active presence and involvement with the majority of established small firms in the urban and metropolitan areas. The main explanation for the contrast lies in the difference in the type of agencies which predominated in the different areas together with associated differences in delivery methods (see Table 4).

The Rural Development Commission

The most commonly used public sector agency was the Rural Development Commission (RDC) whose role in small business support is particularly focused on the remote rural areas (see Table 4). Whilst the types of assistance offered by the Commission have varied in detail through time and also between the Rural Development Areas[4] (RDA) and the non-designated rural areas, it currently includes: premises provision; advice (both general business counselling and the provision of specialist advisory services);

Table 4: Firms receiving external assistance from public and semi-public agencies

Sources of assistance	London	OMA	Rural	All firms
Enterprise agencies	0	3	3	6
Small Firms Service	2	8	0	10
Local authorities	5	1	7	13
Rural Development Commission	–	4	38	42
Number of different firms*	7 (6%)	14 (14%)	44 (55%)	65 (21%)
Number of firms in panel	126 (100%)	100 (100%)	80 (100%)	306 (100%)

* Since some firms used more than one source, the figures in this row may be less than the totals for the columns.

loans (for buildings and capital equipment); grants (e.g. for exhibition participation and marketing consultancy); and training.

In view of the level of use reported by managers, some of the distinctive features of the approach used by the RDC are highlighted below:

1. Many of the firms which had used the RDC had developed a relationship with the agency over a period of time: for example 43% of firms which had used the RDC were able to point to more than one type of assistance being received.
2. The RDC is also more proactive (at least in the RDAs) than the other public and semi-public agencies covered in the study. If support agencies are to be successful in identifying the needs of mature SMEs and to stand any chance of persuading busy managers of the potential advantages of external assistance, they need to operate proactively: to get to know their potential clients and to 'sell' their services to sometimes sceptical business owners and managers.
3. Assistance received from the RDC frequently included some form of financial benefit for companies, or at least the prospect of it: 45% of firms which used the RDC actually received some form of direct financial assistance and if those making unsuccessful applications are included, the proportion rises to 60%. The 'carrot' effect of a tangible benefit such as finance is a distinct benefit in gaining entry to firms, and one that can be used by the agency to encourage firms to take up other aspects of external support designed to improve the competitiveness of the business.

The advantage of having an established agency offering a variety of types of external assistance was reflected in the fact that in the majority of firms which used the RDC, managers were positive about the assistance received, and judged it had made some tangible impact on their business. In 71% of cases, managers said they were 'satisfied' with the assistance received and in 59% of cases managers judged that RDC assistance had made a tangible impact on the performance of the firm. This contrasts markedly with the Small Firms Service for example, where managers reported satisfaction in only 29% of cases and a tangible impact in just one case.

Enterprise agencies, the Small Firms Service and local authorities

Only 2% of firms had received assistance (other than signposting) from an enterprise agency (EA) over the period, despite the fact that national coverage is claimed for these agencies (Business in the Community, 1988). Whilst EAs may be aiming to diversify their activities away from a focus on assisting new business start-ups, there is no evidence from this survey that managers of established SMEs see these agencies as relevant to their needs. Other studies have also referred to the low level of use of EAs by the small business population as a whole (Macmillan et al 1990, Curran et al 1991). Only 3% of firms had used the Small Firms Service (SFS) and with one exception the contribution of the assistance received to the development of these firms was very limited, and generally below that of the other sources of external assistance reported in the study. The main problems tended to be associated either with aspects of delivery (such as the delay between the initial contact with the SFS and the submission of its report) or with the characteristics of the advisers (such as a lack of an understanding of the resource constraints operating on the managers of SMEs). Consultancy (whether free or paid for) which is ineffectively delivered can cause more harm than good, since it can confirm the prejudices which some small business managers have against looking for outside help and can result in a negative demonstration effect. The SFS was particularly poor in this respect, on this evidence.

A further 4% of firms had some kind of assistance from their local authority over the period which in most cases was related either to premises and/or involved some form of grant or loan. However the extent to which local authorities set out to provide support for established SMEs varies considerably between areas, often reflecting area designation which offers the local authority some potential for attracting additional central Government resources (e.g. urban programme authorities in London).

As with private sector support, firms making use of public sector agencies h&
distinct features. In fact, small firms were more likely to have used a public
public agency than the larger firms (see Table 3). Since it was the smallest firm
showed the lowest propensity to use paid consultants, it might appear that 'no
'low cost' support from public sector sources is compensating for a deficiency in the
consultancy market. Closer examination however, shows that firms' use of public and
semi-public agencies is very much concentrated on the use of the RDC (which accounted
for 59% of the total number of uses of public and semi-public agencies). In terms of
performance characteristics, it was the 'strong growth' (Group 2) firms which showed
the highest propensity to have used public or semi-public sources of assistance although
once again this is almost entirely attributable to the activities of the RDC in the remote
rural areas. The majority of firms in this performance group were relatively young firms
which had grown rapidly over the decade and whilst it is encouraging to find that the
RDC is supporting these small growing businesses, similar firms of this type outside the
remote rural areas appear to be much less adequately catered for by the public sector
and yet seem unwilling to use the private sector.

There was also evidence that the use of public and semi-public agencies tended to
be highest in the sectors where the use of paid consultants was generally low (i.e. in
the craft-based furniture, clothing and industrial plant sectors). It appeared that these
agencies seemed generally more user-friendly to managers with a craft background than
did 'professional' consultants, and perhaps public sector agency staff are also more
comfortable with these craft-based businesses. In sum, public sector agencies appear
to have focused on those types of firm which show a lower propensity to use paid consultants particularly the smaller firms in the craft-based sectors. Nevertheless it is only
in the remote rural areas that the public sector is providing an alternative to paid consultancy for any type of firm. If the activities of the RDC are excluded, then the role of
the public sector in delivering support to established SMEs appears very marginal
indeed in the UK in the 1980s.

DEVELOPING A POLICY AGENDA

In this final section of the paper, we attempt to contribute to the development of a
policy agenda for improving support for mature SMEs by considering a number of
policy issues arising from the survey evidence.

The case for strengthening support networks for mature SMEs

On the basis of our survey evidence, 45% of established SMEs had not used external
assistance at all over a 10 year period, and of the 55% that did, very few regularly used
assistance from any source. Whilst the reported frequency of such contacts may vary
with the precise definition of 'contact' used, these results confirm the picture which
emerges from other recent studies which show 'little extensive participation in networks
of any kind' (Curran et al 1991, Curran & Blackburn 1992).

This raises the question of whether or not a 'support gap' exists. When we asked
managers if there had been problems over the decade where external assistance could
have been useful but was not available, the fact that 25% were able to point to particular
problems demonstrates that some latent demand exists for a strengthening of support
networks although not an overwhelming one. However, a more convincing argument
for strengthening support for firms of this type can be based on the need to mobilise
more of the growth potential of the sector.

Such a rationale can be developed using evidence drawn from the study as a whole
which suggests that mature manufacturing firms have both an underlying resilience in
coping with external environmental change and a potential for growth which makes
them an appropriate focus for policy. In London for example (where the longitudinal
nature of our data base enabled survival rates to be accurately calculated over the 10
year period), 58% of firms which were in existence in 1979 survived until 1990 (North et

al 1991). Of the 306 firms in the panel as a whole, 54% showed real turnover growth over the decade and 37% more than doubled it. This is important from a policy perspective, since employment generation was closely related to output growth, being particularly concentrated in those firms which more than doubled their real turnover growth between 1979 and 1990. In fact 83% of the additional jobs created in the panel as a whole were created in firms which more than doubled their real turnover over 10 years (North et al 1992).

Target groups for external support

If mature SMEs such as these are to achieve their potential, it will be necessary to make some attempt to widen the scope of what small business owners and managers see as being within their reach. In many ways this is the most challenging aspect since in so many small firms, managers set themselves modest goals for the evolution of the business based on survival and satisfaction rather than growth. Our previous analysis has demonstrated the high risks associated with conservative survival strategies (although in some sectors growth can itself be a high risk strategy) (North et al 1991). Whilst it is true that the independence of small business owners means there is often resistance to external advice, there is at the same time a significant number of managers who are willing to listen to proposals which may be of benefit to them. Indeed it was not uncommon for firms to report that the in-depth interview they gave us had some thera-peutic value, by forcing them to analyse the development of the firm in a way which made them realise more of the underlying strengths and weaknesses of the business. The role of the external agency here is to encourage more small business owners to raise their aspirations for the development of their businesses. This will involve raising confidence levels and helping managers to identify the threats and opportunities facing their businesses.

At the same time there are particular types of mature SME which would seem to justify priority support. One target group would seem to be those firms that are trying to grow but failing to achieve it (27% of firms in this study were aiming for growth but failed to achieve it over a 10 year period). Better marketing of support services to make it clear that agencies are not just interested in 'start-ups' or 'firms in crisis' would help. Ambitious entrepreneurs often have an image of themselves as self-sufficient and com-petent that makes it difficult for them to seek assistance from agencies which they do not associate with business success or with business values (e.g. local authorities, SFS, DTI). This is an important aspect for the Training and Enterprise Councils (TECs) to address in the way in which they set out to market their services.

A second target group are those firms which are growing strongly but which have weaknesses or problems which may threaten the long term development of the company. These are the 'strong growth' firms in our performance classification (Group 2) which include firms which have either yet to achieve the minimum size necessary to give them the resilience to resist external shocks, and/or those in which high turnover growth has been at the expense of consistent profitability. The growth performance of this group of firms over 10 years indicates their potential but their size and other characteristics suggest that they may need help if their development over a long period of time is to be secured. Our Group 2 category contains some interesting cases which illustrate the point made by other writers that many fast growth firms need supporting (Storey and Johnson, 1987).

For example, whilst only 21% of firms in the study as a whole reported that a shortage of development finance had acted as a major constraint on the development of the business during the late 1980s, the figure rose to 37% in the 'strong growth' category (Group 2); 49% of this group stated that finance had held back the firm to some extent (compared to 33% of all firms). The growth performance over 10 years of this group of firms is an indication of their dynamism and development potential, but assistance may be required if this potential is to be realised.

The distinctive support needs of mature SMEs

Successful targeting of assistance for established SMEs needs to recognise the more specialised requirements of this group in comparison with new or very young businesses. This is one reason why local enterprise agencies have been relatively unsuccessful in reaching this type of firm. Assistance with marketing plans or manpower planning for a firm which has already been trading for at least 10 years places considerably greater demands on the specialist expertise of an agency than is placed by the typical start-up business. Unfortunately, as other studies have found, networking between support agencies such as EAs is generally poorly developed (Deakin 1991). The new 'one-stop shops' (to be piloted with DTI support from April 1993) are a response to the problem of over-proliferation of small business support agencies and services, although it remains to be seen whether they will be able to successfully deliver the type of specialist support which is required by established SMEs such as these.

One aspect of this need for specialist support which was reported by a number of owners and managers we interviewed is the need for specialist sectoral expertise, particularly in cases where the assistance is in the field of marketing or business policy. This is important not least because the outside agency must be capable of talking on 'equal terms' with the prospective client to gain credibility, which is also recognised in another recent study of support systems (Carswell 1990). In addition, as we have argued elsewhere, the sector defines factor and technology choices and also influences the opportunities for growth and the type of growth strategy likely to be successful (Leigh et al 1991). Sector-based support and advice has not merely a higher chance of being acceptable to clients, thus encouraging take-up, but also of making more of a real impact on the business. However, external advice and consultancy for established SMEs needs to be more than just informed by sectoral conditions. Ideally, it should be delivered by sector experts and marketed to firms as part of a sectoral initiative.

The role for the public sector

As we have shown, only 1/5 of firms had received external assistance from a public or semi-public sector agency over the decade and these were heavily concentrated in the rural areas. Of course, since 1988 the focus of the Government's support for this type of firm has been the subsidised consultancy offered through the DTI's Enterprise Initiative. In view of the criticisms of the SFS made by managers, the apparent failure of enterprise agencies to successfully reach these established firms and the fact that paid consultancy is the most commonly reported single source of external assistance, such a strategy would seem to be an appropriate one.

At the same time there does appear to be a 'gap' in the support offered since the smallest firms made little use of consultants.

For firms which are under-represented in the consultancy market, the public sector agencies can play an important role and in the RDAs in particular, the RDC appears to be successfully reaching a cross-section of established SMEs of different types. Outside of the remote rural areas there needs to be a more concerted attempt to provide support for such firms, arguably by using the more intensive delivery methods characterised by the RDC. It is doubtful if individual TECs have either the resources or the expertise to offer the kind of support needed by firms of this type. There has to be co-ordinated provision and it has to involve specialist advisers and consultants working intensively with relatively small panels of firms which they come to know on a continuing basis.

The role for banks and accountants

From the evidence presented here, banks have an important potential role to play as a point of entry for firms into the support system leading either to delivering further business support themselves, or to referring clients to alternative sources of advice. Many significant aspects of business development require both finance and an element of financial planning, and banks and accountants have an additional advantage in that they do tend to have on-going relationships with firms. Routine contacts can lead to more extensive assistance particularly when triggered by a critical event which may have important financial implications for the firm.

If banks are to be effective as a point of entry however, there needs to be both an efficient referral system and a lead organisation within a local economy capable of co-ordinating it (Segal, et al 1988). An active Chamber of Commerce might conceivably play this role, although there is no evidence from this study that these organisations were fulfilling this role on any scale during the 1980s. The creation of the TECs is too recent to have been a factor in the period covered by this study although this function is one they may be able to perform in the future.

Improving the delivery of consultancy

There is a clear need to improve the effectiveness of the delivery of consultancy in general and of subsidised consultancy in particular. The limitations of mainstream consultancy of the 'in and out' variety are particularly exposed where the problem being addressed involves business planning and/or marketing since this can often point to the need for a fundamental review of the business. To be successful, this type of consultancy clearly requires managers to be able to successfully implement consultants' recommendations. In the smallest firms in particular, consultancy needs to be seen as a process, since sustained contact is potentially more valuable than consultancy of the 'one-off' variety. This is because a major part of the benefit from consultancy must come from the development of knowledge in the managers themselves and thus be part of his/her learning experience.

Increasing the effective use of consultancy in SMEs is partly dependent on raising the level of management skills of owners and managers themselves. Unless managers have the skills to be able to understand and implement consultants' recommendations, the impact of the consultancy on the performance of the business is likely to be marginal. Two-thirds of firms in this study had no trained managers and only 23% of firms had managers who had participated in more than the occasional training seminar. We have already demonstrated that firms with trained managers are more likely to look outside the firm for help when they face problems which they cannot adequately deal with from their own resources. Thus our evidence suggests that raising the level of management training would help to increase the effectiveness of the use of consultants in SMEs.

There appears to be particular problems with the delivery of subsidised consultancy. Improving quality control in the delivery of subsidised consultancy is important if a negative demonstration effect is to be avoided (Segal et al 1991). There are still too many reports of consultants who do not have either sufficient knowledge of the particular sector and/or sufficient awareness of the constraints which operate on small-business managers. The higher level of reported dissatisfaction with, and the lower impact of, the subsidised consultancies must be a cause for concern despite any additionality benefits the EI may have had in persuading a wider group of firms to use consultants than have previously done so. Thus for consultants to be effectively employed in SMEs, the minimum conditions required are for competent consultants who have experience of the particular requirements and constraints affecting small firms, and also that the owners and managers of the firms themselves have the skills to be able to understand and implement consultants' recommendations. Unless these conditions are also addressed there is little point in simply increasing the number of firms which use consultants since there may be negative demonstration effects.

Finally, the above implications for policy highlight a number of other key issues. On the one hand, in the absence of an effective system of Chambers of Commerce or trade associations in the UK on the continental model, the development of a comprehensive and integrated network of business support services must be a priority. At what geographical scale such networks are best defined and operated in order to avoid problems of duplication and overlap and to balance economies of scale in delivery against a local knowledge and client access is an important but difficult issue.

On the other hand, we must also continue to strive to encourage more small business owners and managers to think of the longer term development of their businesses. The effective use of external assistance and consultancy is associated with a desire on the part of the owner to manage the assets of the company rather than simply running a production unit which requires him/her creating more time to manage. It is also necessary to break down the perception of self-sufficiency and the suspicion of outsiders which is common in many small firms. All these aspects need to be addressed if small firms are to benefit from external economies of scale in the area of management skills and resources.

NOTES

1. A more detailed examination of the use of external assistance by London firms together with an analysis of the effects of other types of government policy is available in Smallbone, Leigh & North (1991).
2. The Rural Development Commission (RDC) was formed in 1988 as a result of a merger between the Council for Small Industries in Rural Areas (COSIRA) and the Development Commission. COSIRA was established in 1968 in order to increase the advice and financial help available for small businesses in rural areas. RDC is used in this paper to refer to either COSIRA (pre 1988) or the RDC in the post 1988 period.
3. Each firm was assigned to one of 5 performance groups based mainly on the change that occurred in real turnover between 1979–90; additional criteria were used to identify the 'high growth' and 'strong growth' firms however and the performance groups were defined as follows:

    'High growth' (Group 1): firms which more than doubled their turnover in real terms over the decade, that reached a size by 1990 likely to ensure continuing viability (£0.5 m turnover) and that were consistently profitable in the latter part of the decade.
    'Strong growth' (Group 2): firms that at least doubled their turnover in real terms over the decade but failed to either reach a large enough size and/or to maintain the consistent profitability needed to be in Group 1. Their 'success' was arguably less secure than that of the high growth firms in that they remained small and lacked consistent profitability. Nevertheless on the criterion of sales growth they were clearly successful.
    'Moderate growth' (Group 3): firms which increased turnover in real terms by a factor of between 1.5 and 2 over the decade.
    'Stable firms' (Group 4): firms that stayed at about the same size in terms of the real value of their output having increased their turnover by a factor of between 1.0 and 1.5. These are survivors rather than growers.
    'Declining firms' (Group 5): firms which actually declined in terms of their real turnover over the 1979–90 period. These were the weakest of the surviving firms in the panel.

    Note that the adjustments made by firms with different levels of performance over the decade are analysed in Smallbone, Leigh & North 1992; and Smallbone, North & Leigh, 1992.
4. Rural Development Areas (RDAs) are designated areas which have serious economic and social problems. The main criteria used for designation are: unemployment rates above the national average, an inadequate range of available employment opportunities, declining population, net outmigration of young people, age structure biased towards the elderly, poor access to services and facilities. The approach used by the RDC in RDAs aims at integrated development with an emphasis on social as well as economic initiatives.

ACKNOWLEDGEMENTS

The Economic and Social Research Council's Small Business Research Initiative includes financial contributions from Barclays Bank, Commission of the European Communities

(DG XXIII), Department of Employment, and the Rural Development Commission. The views expresssed in this paper do not necessarily reflect those of the sponsoring organisations.

REFERENCES

Bennett R.J. and Krebs G. (1991) Local Economic Development: Public Private Partnerships Initiatives in Britain and Germany, Belhaven Press, London.

Brusco S. and Righi (1989) Local government, industrial policy and social consensus: the case of Modena, Italy, Economy and Society Vol 18, No 4, pp 405–424.

Business in the Community (1988) The Future for Enterprise Agencies, BITC, London.

Carswell M. (1990) Small firm networking and business performance, Paper presented to the 13th UK Small Firms Policy and Research Conference, Harrogate, November.

Curran J., Jarvis R., Blackburn R. and Black S. (1991) Small Firms and Networks: Constructs, Methodological Strategies and Preliminary Findings, ESRC Small Business Research Initiative Working Paper, Small Business Research Centre, Kingston Polytechnic, Kingston Upon Thames.

Curran J. and Blackburn R. (1992) Small Firms and Local Economic Networks: Relations between Small Firms and Large Firms in Two Localities, Kingston University Business Paper Series, Kingston University, Kingston Upon Thames, May.

Deakin D. (1991) Effective Networks of Agency Support for Small Businesses, Paper presented to the 14th National Small Firms Policy and Research Conference, Blackpool, November.

Leigh R., North D. and Smallbone D. (1991) Adjustment Processes in High Growth Small and Medium Size Enterprises: a Study of Mature Manufacturing Firms in London during the 1980s, Working Paper No 2, ESRC Small Business Research Initiative, Middlesex Polytechnic Project.

Macmillan K., Curran J. and Downing S. (1990) Government consultations with small business owners: empirically evaluating communications strategies, International Small Business Journal, Vol. 8, No. 4, pp 14–32.

North D., Leigh R. and Smallbone D. (1991) A Comparison of Surviving and Non-Surviving Small and Medium Sized Manufacturing Firms in London during the 1980s, Working Paper No 1, ESRC Small Business Research Initiative, Middlesex Polytechnic Project.

North D., Smallbone D. and Leigh R. (1992) Employment and Labour Process Changes in Manufacturing SMEs during the 1980s, Paper presented at the ESRC Small Business Research Initiative Seminar, University of Warwick, September.

Segal, Quince and Wicksteed (1988) Encouraging Small Business Start-Up and Growth, HMSO, London.

Segal, Quince and Wicksteed (1991) Evaluation of the Consultancy Initiatives: Second Stage, HMSO, London.

Smallbone D., Leigh R. and North D. (1991) The External Assistance and Policy Support Experience of Mature Manufacturing Firms in London during the 1980s, Working Paper No 4, ESRC Small Business Research Initiative, Middlesex Polytechnic Project.

Smallbone D., Leigh R. and North D. (1992) Managing Change for Growth and Survival: a Study of Mature Manufacturing Firms in London during the 1980s, Working Paper No. 3, ESRC Small Business Research Initiative, Middlesex Polytechnic Project.

Stanworth J. and Gray C. (1991) Bolton 20 Years On: The Small Firm in the 1990s, Paul Chapman Publishing, London.

Storey D. and Johnson S. (1987) Job Generation and Labour Market Change, Macmillan, Basingstoke.

Storey D., Watson R. and Wynarczyk P. (1989) Fast Growth Small Businesses: Case Studies of 40 Small Firms in North East England, Research Paper No 67, Department of Employment.

16.

Issues in Supporting Enterprise and Training in Asian SMEs:
A Case Study from the Inner City

Monder Ram and John Sparrow

INTRODUCTION

The launch of the Training and Enterprise Councils (TECs) in 1990 focused attention on the provision of support for enterprise and the supporting infrastructure for new and developing businesses. The need for a co-ordinated development of a strategy of enterprise support has been well documented (Segal, et al 1988; Moran 1989). TECs have clearly stated the need for an effective strategy of enterprise training and support for new and developing businesses (Training Agency 1990). They have an opportunity to develop and implement such a strategy.

The present network of support, despite some advances in regional co-operation, remains based upon individual agency provision of blanket support. This has led to criticisms of duplication of provision and the lack of a strategic focus (Segal, et al 1988). The potential entrepreneur and small business owner is faced with a bewildering range of agencies that have a reactive policy of support provision. Commentators have called for a more proactive role for support providers (Oakey, et al 1991). It has been demonstrated that the relatively low profile of support provision means that existing and potential entrepreneurs have low levels of awareness of the existing support provision (Carswell 1990).

The central issue concerns the ways in which existing resources of support agencies can be utilised to provide an effective system within which each agency has a clearly defined role. At issue here therefore are firstly, the establishment of potential bases for structuring post start-up support, and secondly, the establishment of mechanisms for reaching clients in terms of the chosen aspects of support in the framework.

Enterprise Agencies for example can provide services ranging from basic business counselling to major business support with purpose-built premises. Additional small business support is provided by the Small Firms Service, local authorities, regional agencies such as the Welsh and Scottish Development Agencies, and through various programmes organised by TECs. There are training and development programmes and counselling provided by colleges, firms, Chambers of Commerce and the Rural Development Commission. It is not surprising that this system of support has been described as a diverse and often confusing range of alternatives (Moran 1989).

POTENTIAL BASES FOR TARGETING SUPPORT

Smallbone (1990) argued that resources might be used more effectively if support was used more selectively. There are a number of criteria which have been suggested as bases for the selective targeting of support. Suggested groups have included developing businesses (Storey, 1987), high technology firms (Moore 1989), and female entrepreneurs (Hartshorn and McClure 1990). In addition there are ground-swell suggestions that support should be targeted at winners. And anyway, isn't support being targeted by the TECs offering particular products or initiatives? Is there a complete set of bases upon which support might be structured rather than particular or topical good ideas? Sparrow and Deakins (1990) conducted a study of developing small businesses to identify the factors which seemed to be associated with differences in their growth paths. The groups of businesses listed in Table 1 were found to face distinct issues.

Blanket and reactive support to any and all businesses does not seem to be an optimal strategy. But upon what basis might one choose between structuring support on these various alternative bases? Which would be a better basis? The targeting of support to address particular management skills (such as people management or marketing) and incidentally the general basis used implicitly by TEC programmes? Or ethnic groupings of business owners? Or industrial classification of the business? etc. Deakins and Sparrow (1991) investigated this issue with 150 Enterprise Agencies. They found that support was being targeted in terms of some bases more than others (see Table 1). But why these bases? The study found evidence that the priorities were very largely beliefs and did not even bear any relationship to the stated abilities of the Enterprise Agencies. What about value added? Can this be used as a basis to prioritise support? What about political acceptability? Is there a mathematical solution which can account for the most variation in business development? These are some of the questions which must now be addressed.

MECHANISMS FOR REACHING TARGETED CLIENTS

It has been noted how the array of services available to SMEs is potentially bewildering. It has also been noted how most support agencies manage their activities on a reactive basis, i.e. responding to specific requests from SMEs. If support is to be targeted, what implications follow for the way services are promoted? How can the specific needs of selected client groups be identified? It seems likely that the uniform approach to product marketing implicit in TEC initiatives will not be optimal for each client sub-group. If a mechanism is developed, could/should it provide a focus for other potential services

Table 1: Bases upon which enterprise support can be targeted

Client groups*	Percentage of agencies currently targeting†
Different age groups	26
Different genders	13
Marital status	0
Ex-employed vs unemployed	11
Trading status	1
Use of unwaged help	0
Different industrial sectors	1
Employers vs non-employers	1
Turnover groupings	1
Receiving Government support	0
Finance source categories	2
Resource constraints	0
In/not in sheltered premises	0
IT absorption	1
Particular management skills	4
Ethnic grouping	9

* Sparrow and Deakins (1990).

† Deakins and Sparrow (1991).

(including other non-targeted initiatives) in a one-stop fashion? The present study addresses these issues by examining the support needs of Asian SMEs and the current approach to providing support by the local TEC and Chamber of Commerce.

THE STUDY

A detailed description of the rationale and methodology of the study is given elsewhere (Ram and Sparrow 1992; Ram 1992). Despite the prominence of ethnic minority firms in the local economies of regions across the country, there has been relatively little research on the concrete needs of Asian enterprise. Marlow (1992) has attributed this to the difficulties of gaining access into firms located in the 'peripheral' sections of the economy and the persistence of racism in wider society. The little that has been done tends to be based upon 'shallow' postal questionnaire assessments of specific issues. The study examined the approaches of 50 Asian SMEs towards enterprise and training develop-ment and their views upon current support provision. The study was more than a statistical exercise. It was intended to give a genuine 'feel' for the way in which Asian employers operated. Hence the way in which the research was conducted was far from simple; it was not a linear or one-way process where participants responded to an aloof interviewer. The research approach required a certain amount of flexibility. For example employers often asked about the availability of grants, general business issues and were curious about the first author's family and personal background. It was important to respond openly to such questions; not to have done so would have militated against establishing rapport and trust.

'Getting in' was not simply a question of looking up employers in the appropriate directories and pleading for interviews. Such directories did not exist and given the type of issues under scrutiny, any cold-calling type of approach was unlikely to meet with success. Furthermore, allied to the generic research access issues of getting the 'right' respondents with time and opportunity to talk are the additional considerations of ethnicity and cultural diversity. For instance, one employer told the first author, 'I'm only talking to you because I know your family. If you were white I wouldn't talk to you.' The utilisation of such an informal and intuitive approach made it easier to negotiate the cultural context of the field. Employers were generally quite willing to talk at length about the development of their businesses, management and relationships with external bodies. We also elicited the views of officers of the local TEC and Chamber of Commerce towards the issue of targeting support.

PROVIDER VIEWS UPON TARGETING SUPPORT FOR ASIAN SMEs

The specification of an enterprise system targeted for Asian SMEs would need to address two broad sets of factors. These are the broad infrastructure and objectives of support (i.e. providers' conceptions of their practical and political environment) and the needs of Asian businesses. It seemed that there were several strongly-held conceptions within the TEC and Chamber which were implicit in the current approach to enterprise and training development. These conceptions included:

- the notion that there are national programmes of value to businesses in general;
- the notion that local information and support services which have evolved for businesses have developed most of the basic services and approaches to delivery which are necessary for businesses;
- the importance of integration and control in service provision. A general reluctance to see many autonomous units developing from the core;
- that the size of a section manager's job is preferably defined to fit a standard profile of existing management status positions, salaries and reporting frameworks;
- that a radical proposal to depart from all of the above preferences (as a client-led

(rather than programme-led) autonomous unit might be) might raise so many additional concerns as to thwart development of any kind. For example the whole strategic issue of identifying a complete set of bases for segmenting service provision (e.g. high-tech firms, women at work, etc.) might be raised.

An Asian Business Unit (ABU) had been established in the area in 1991 and had grown out of a recognition that Asian businesses were playing an important role in the local economy but that their needs, aspirations and problems were not fully understood or catered for by existing support agencies. As one TEC officer commented, the setting up of the ABU was regarded as a 'good thing'. The precise role of the ABU, its position *vis-à-vis* TEC and its particular relevance to the Asian business community were not clearly established. The fact that there was commitment to some form of delivery mechanism in the area may distinguish the area from others. It is not believed however that this limits the relevance of the arguments and findings for other localities.

An examination of the ABU's initial aims and objectives strongly indicated that its principal function was to promote TEC and, to a lesser extent, Chamber services within minority firms. Although there were other aims relating to the development of management skills, raising awareness of legislation and meeting Asian business needs, the objectives were to be measured primarily in terms of Asian employers' involvement on existing initiatives. For example, there were targets for NVQs, business planning kits and youth and adult training placements; interest had to be generated in a sales mission to Europe; and a certain number of business guidance interviews had to be held.

Important though these services and corresponding targets are, the degree to which they resonated with the concerns of Asian businesses in the locality could be doubted. Precise targets were set, but the basis upon which they had been devised and their relevance to the Asian business community was questionable. The aims and objectives seemed to reinforce the image of the ABU's manager as a 'TEC salesman' rather than the conduit through which the needs of Asian businesses are expressed and addressed. In addition to the general lack of appropriateness in the initial aims, they constituted a bazaar of objectives which were so disparate that there was no synergy between them. Action upon any one was at the potential expense of any other.

ASIAN BUSINESS CHARACTERISTICS WHICH CHALLENGE THE EFFICACY OF UNIFORM REACTIVE SUPPORT

The study identified many features of Asian businesses which challenge the appropriateness of standard provision of general programmes. These are summarised under the headings: Market characteristics; Approaches to recruitment and management development; Desired role for support agencies; Attitudes towards outside support; Awareness and use of support agency services; Perceptions of understanding by support agencies.

Taken together these findings cast severe doubt upon the efficacy of a blanket approach towards enterprise and training initiatives by support agencies.

Market characteristics
Two major findings were made here. These were:
1. the pervasiveness of institutionalised racism.

> As an Asian broker, I've suffered. To be competitive, we need as many agencies as we can [agencies are secured from major insurance companies; this enables a broker to offer a wider range of policies and keener prices]. But there are certain insurance companies who won't deal with Asians. I think there's prejudice; they know most of my clients are Asian so they won't deal with us.

2. the competitive and in many cases closed market location of Asian firms.

> Employers using intermediaries were often producing goods of high quality that

were being sold in reputable chain stores. Yet many still found it necessary to utilise agents, and it was clear that being Asian was a major reason for this.

> You could feel that they [chain store buyers] didn't want to buy off you because of the colour of your skin.

> As soon as they see us Asians, they think we're in the cheap end of the market. I've approached them; they've given me appointments, but I'm usually out of the store in 10 minutes. Yet, our quality is far superior to theirs but we still can't get in.

Figure 1 reveals the proportion of firms (70%) operating in ways other than directly to the open market.

There was a widely expressed need for assistance in the areas of marketing and market intelligence in order to overcome some of these unique barriers.

Approaches to recruitment and management development
The study also identified clear ethnicity in recruitment and management with implications for training/development support. Although many firms were 'successful', most managers claimed that they would not recruit at management level. Ninety-six per cent of employers were only interested in recruiting at the operative level. Yet many of the employers who would not recruit managerial staff were experiencing problems in managing credit control, design, production and quality-related issues. Figure 2 shows the general approaches to training amongst the Asian businesses. There is a high emphasis upon development within their own resources and community.

Desired role for support agencies
The owners were invited to consider what role they would like to see support agencies (like the Chamber and TEC) actually play. 50% of employers claimed that they wanted such organisations to provide advice, expertise and assistance in the areas of marketing and market intelligence. For example, a manufacturer of jeans asserted that:

> Marketing and sales should be the role of external bodies. The Chamber should be making introductions and interface more with the chain stores and customers.

Another clothing manufacturer made the point that the Chamber should 'Keep in touch and offer assistance on export and market trends'.

A property developer stated that outside bodies like the Chamber should be: 'much more active in promoting business'.

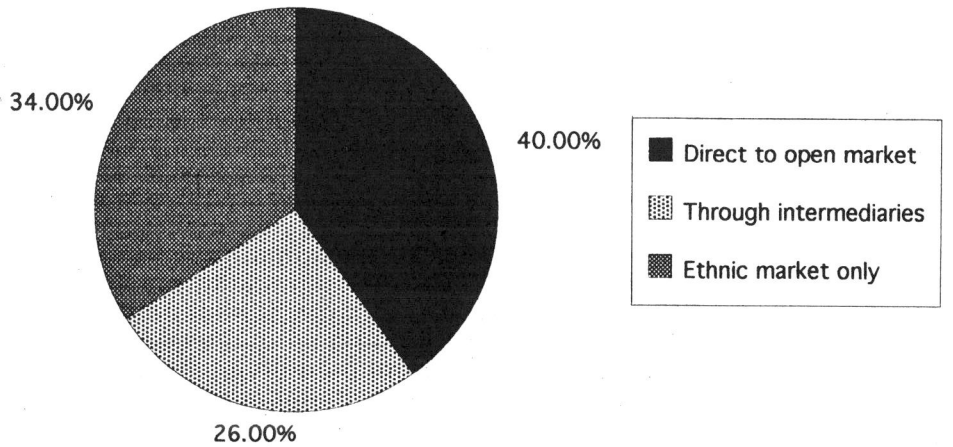

Figure 1:   The positioning of Asian firms in operations with the open market.

Figure 2: General use of training approaches by Asian businesses.

The other roles included being much more proactive in tackling skill shortages and some clothing employers argued for more direct action in tackling the limited availability of skilled sewing machinists. Engineering employers claimed that there should be more relevant short courses on offer. Some firms wanted courses designed specifically to meet their needs.

Attitudes towards outside support

Three quarters of employers had neither used consultants nor engaged in any form of externally linked management training. Figure 3 shows the findings for use of trainers and consultants. Only 6% had taken any initiative in the form of externally supported management training, and this was usually in the form of an occasional short course. Primary criticisms of external training were lack of relevance and expense. Twenty-two per cent of firms had made use of consultants in the past. In most of these cases, they were used to tackle problems in production, although two employers had taken advantage of the BGT Option 3 programme and a further two owners were using consultants to initiate the process of implementing BS 5750. The reasons offered for not using consultants were similar – lack of relevance, lack of need, expense and confidentiality. Although some employers acknowledged that consultants and trainers had something to offer, the burden of these constraints far outweighed any perceived value they could bring to the owners' businesses.

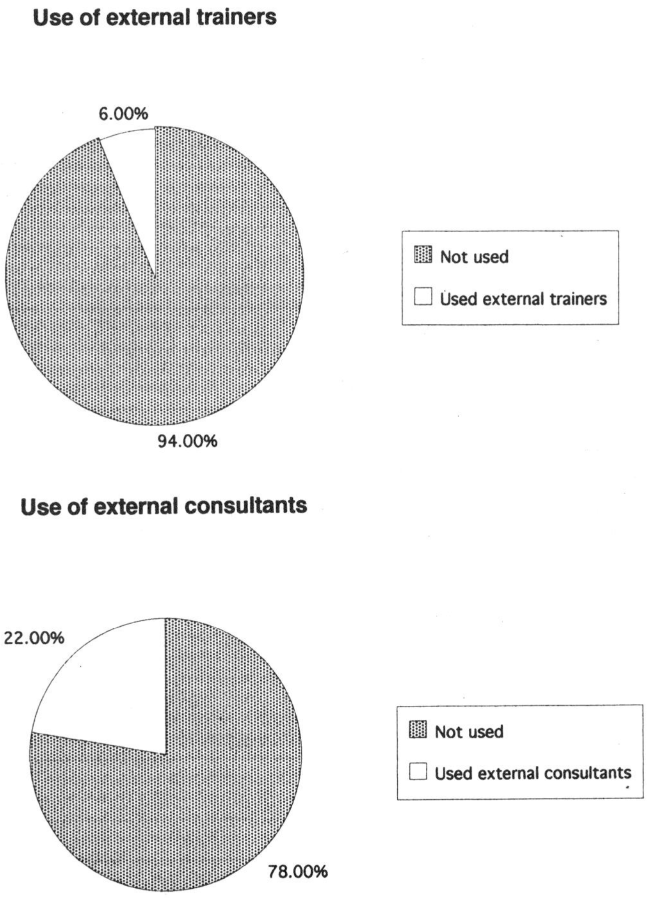

Use of external trainers

6.00%

- Not used
- Used external trainers

94.00%

Use of external consultants

22.00%

- Not used
- Used external consultants

78.00%

Figure 3: Use of trainers and consultants.

Awareness and use of support agency services

The owners were also asked about the range of enterprise and training initiatives currently on offer, and about the TEC and Chamber as providers generally. Figure 4 shows that there was a lack of awareness of support agencies; an unfavourable impression of such agencies.

Employers were asked to recall any initiatives or policies by TEC and the Chamber that they may have come across. With regard to TEC, only four owners could recollect any initiative. One employer had taken on a youth trainee, another had actually been on the TEC board, while the remaining two had been approached by consultants.

In relation to the Chamber, only one could remember any initiative. He had noted some reference to business development seminars in the local press. Hence, 49 employers could not recall any Chamber initiative designed to help their business.

Employers were asked to relate their personal experiences of TEC and the Chamber, i.e. direct contact. Only three (6%) employers had any direct experience of TEC. Most employers did not know that TEC existed, and those that did were not aware of TEC's function.

Fifty-six per cent of employers had had direct contact with the Chamber of Commerce. Of these 21% felt that the Chamber had been useful and helpful, especially in the provision of translation services and export documentation. However, 79% of employers that had had contact expressed negative views. Many from this group complained of the lack of Chamber attention to their problems. Others claimed that the Chamber tended to be emphasising their social role to the detriment of assistance with real business problems.

In terms of correspondence from the support agencies, 92% of employers could not recall receiving any correspondence from TEC. Four per cent had read the TEC material. The remaining 4% had discarded the material. Forty-eight per cent of employers could not recall receiving any correspondence from the Chamber. Twenty per cent had read it and 32% had thrown it away.

Perceptions of understanding by support agencies

Employers were asked the extent to which they believe that the TEC and Chamber understood the problems of an Asian small business like theirs. Results are summarised in Figure 5.·

Ninety-two per cent of employers had not had any contact with TEC, so could not comment. Four per cent found TEC quite helpful while the remaining 4% did not think that TEC was relevant to them.

Experiences with Chamber of Commerce

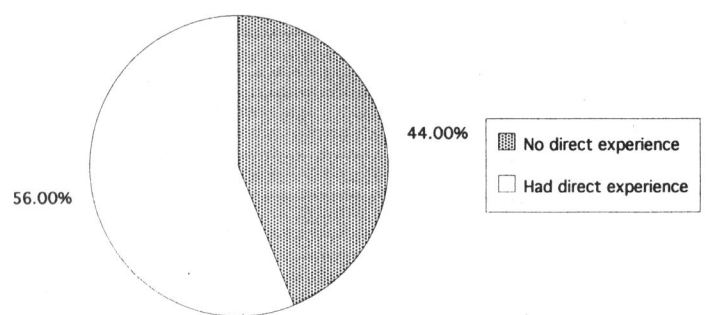

Figure 4: Knowledge and experience of TEC and Chamber and reaction to correspondence.

Experiences with TEC

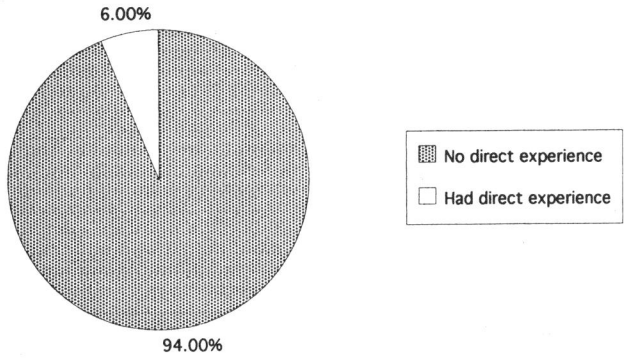

Response to Chamber of Commerce correspondence

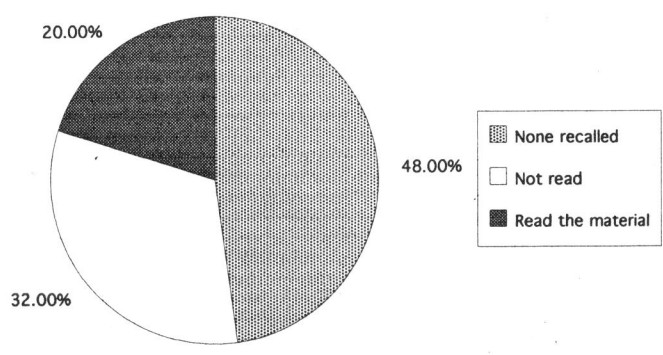

Response to TEC correspondence

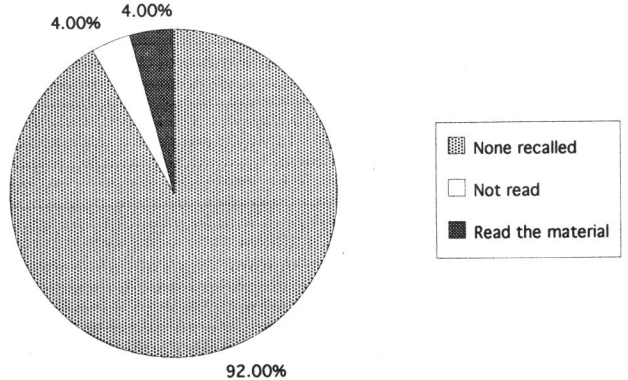

Figure 4: Cont'd

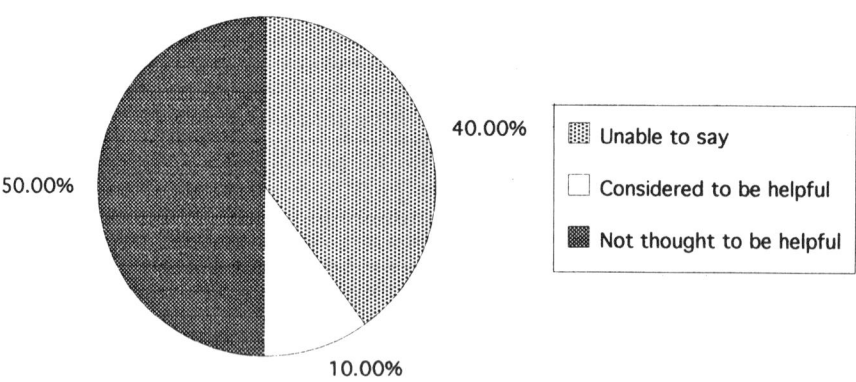

Chamber of Commerce's understanding of Asian Businesses

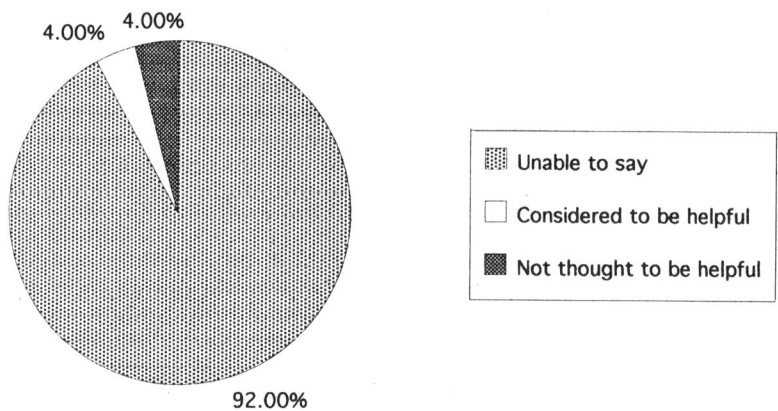

TEC's understanding of Asian Businesses

Figure 5: Perceptions of understanding of support agencies.

Forty per cent of employers had not had any contact with the Chamber. Ten per cent felt that the Chamber were helpful, in things such as keeping them informed on business issues. Fifty per cent of employers were highly critical of the Chamber's understanding of their business.

Many employers were of the opinion that the assistance provided by the Chamber was too generalised to be of use to them: 'They are a list broker'; 'They were not relevant to us'.

Taken together we feel that the findings of the study provide sufficient information to warrant the avocation of a targeted approach towards enterprise and training support.

A MECHANISM FOR TARGETED SUPPORT FOR ASIAN SMEs

The concerns expressed by the respondents in this study patently indicate a mismatch between the needs of many Asian firms and a standard product-oriented approach by support agencies. An approach is advocated which we feel applies in the locality we examined, but will also be applicable to other areas with large Asian business communities. We suggest the following five roles for a targeted approach:

A higher profile focal point

The results starkly illustrate many Asian employers' lack of awareness of the role, function and (in a significant number of cases) the identity of external agencies. The channels of communication used by TECs and Chambers may fail to alert many Asian firms to their services. There are at least two forms of response to these shortcomings:

1. The production of documentation in different languages;
2. a specific local unit (e.g. Asian Business Unit) becoming much more active in promoting itself within the local Asian business community.

It seems clear from the study that the preference for an interpersonal approach rather than a formal approach within Asian businesses would cast doubt on the utility of investment in separate document production.

In relation to the second alternative, there is no substitute for establishing personal contact with employers. It is likely that this increase in profile will have a general awareness raising effect which will increase involvement with enterprise and training development.

A focused support agency offering integrated services

An Asian Business Unit (ABU) should be an agency constituted on the basis of a target group of clients. It could interface with parent bodies in the terms upon which they are structured. This structure is likely to reflect the prevailing budget heads (through major programmes). An ABU could present the uniform and integrated face to the Asian business community which conveys the benefits of support through endemic networks. Services which may currently appear fragmented to clients can be presented in a more integrated manner.

As such an ABU could provide monitoring of the local Asian business community. It should establish a much needed database profile of the Asian businesses in the community. Interviews with TEC officers in the study revealed there was very little information on minority firms in the area. Base-line data on the numbers of minority businesses, their background, structures, turnover, profitability, growth and potential employment is a prerequisite for effective support to minority firms.

Additionally, an ABU should ascertain the needs of local Asian businesses; not simply on a one-off (programme-led) basis, but through an ongoing process of integrated business counselling. In this way, it will be possible to get a more accurate picture of the real concerns of the employers and to respond accordingly.

An agency configured to maximise value for money in Asian enterprise development

An ABU should begin the process of segmenting the Asian business community. Asian firms, like small firms *per se*, are not a homogeneous grouping with uniform requirements. They will be in different sectors and at different stages of development. The unit should be sufficiently close to the firms to initiate this process of differentiating firms according to relevant criteria. By assuming such a position, the unit can play an informed and important role in channelling relevant support to firms who could most effectively utilise it. This proactive strategy should help to ensure that the most appropriate firms, in terms of growth for example, would receive particular forms of targeted support. Value for money in training and enterprise support needs to be highlighted. The monitoring of effectiveness of support within different segments of the Asian business community is a prerequisite. The overall study (Ram and Sparrow, 1992) identified many bases upon which Asian firms could in themselves be segmented. The viability of addressing particular initiatives to these groupings needs to be evaluated.

Providing marketing support for businesses

At present, the demand for formal packages of training and education is minimal. The general process of awareness raising may however prove useful in this regard. However, one area in which an ABU could have a more direct impact is marketing support. Many employers stated that they would welcome assistance in the area of marketing and market intelligence. The unit through its links would be in a good position to offer such assistance. This form of enterprise support rests upon the true localness and integration in the community of support services. It requires a real information system concerning businesses and their products and services. Credibility is however all important. It is not sufficient merely to provide advice on presentation and packaging. A concerted effort needs to be made to establish relevant data bases of potential customers, and assistance needs to be given in making contact with buyers. This is a difficult undertaking, and it undoubtedly has implications in terms of resources. Success in these terms will be the indicator that Asian businesses will use to assess the unit however. This service would provide the opportunity for establishing credibility with local firms. Once that has been achieved, then initiatives in other areas, like management training, can be pursued more effectively. Trying to lead with programmes is not considered to be a viable strategy.

Combating discrimination

In tackling the problem of finding new markets, the issue of racism in its various guises will have to be addressed. This is a difficult, if not intractable, problem. But clearly, an ABU, being in such close proximity to the victims, is ideally placed to highlight unfair discrimination when it occurs and campaign to eradicate it. In the context of the clothing industry, a start could be made by examining the role of agents more closely. To be credible in pursuit of this policy, an ABU and parent bodies must also look inwards and ensure that their own practices are in order. Good equal opportunity policy is exemplified by its total integration in all areas of an organisation's work. An analysis of the ethnic mix of TEC workforces might reveal a relatively low number of black employees and their concentration at the lower levels of the organisation. If one examines particular areas of TECs with responsibility for interfacing with employers, the position may be even worse.

CONCLUSION

This paper has presented arguments for the targeting of support for SMEs. It has discussed a variety of alternative bases for structuring support and summarised current practice in the UK. A study has been reviewed which shows the need for targeting in Asian business support and the ways in which such targeting can be addressed by local support providers. It is hoped that the arguments will be extended to other potential bases for targeting and to other localities.

REFERENCES

Carswell M. (1990) Small firm networking and business performance, Paper presented to 13th National Small Firms Policy and Research Conference, Harrogate, November.

Deakins D. and Sparrow J. (1991) Developing quality support for new and developing businesses, in Small Businesses and Small Business Development: A Practical Approach, R. Welford ed, European Research Press, Bradford.

Hartshorn C. and McClure R. (1990) Latent enthusiasm in women's business creation, Paper presented to 13th National Small Firms Policy and Research Conference, Harrogate, November.

Marlow S. (1992) The take-up of business growth training schemes in Britain, International Small Business Journal. Vol. 7, No. 1.

Moran P. (1989) Development of small business support services in the 1990's, Paper presented to 12th National Small Firms Policy and Research Conference, London, November.

Moore I. (1989) Government technology policy and innovation in small high-technology firms: evidence from biotechnology and scientific instruments, Paper presented to 12th National Small Firms Policy and Research Conference, London, November.

Oakey R.P., Cooper S.Y. and Biggar J. (1991) Improving product marketing in high technology small firms, Heriot Watt University Business School.

Ram M. (1992) Minority enterprise: continuing constraints, restricted choices, Paper presented to 15th National Small Firms Policy and Research Conference, Southampton, November.

Ram M. and Sparrow J. (1992) Research on the needs of the Asian Business Community in Wolverhampton, Report to TEC and Chamber, May.

Segal, Quince and Wicksteed (1988) Encouraging small business start-up and growth: creating a supportive local environment, HMSO, London.

Smallbone D. (1990) Success and failure in small business start-ups, International Small Business Journal, Vol. 8, No. 2.

Sparrow J. and Deakins D. (1990) The delivery of small business support: An analysis of areas for strategic intervention by business support services, British Academy of Management, Small Firms Policy Workshop, Manchester, April.

Storey D.J. (1987) The Performance of Small Firms, Croom Helm, London.

Training Agency (1990) Training in Britain: a study of funding activities and attitudes, HMSO, London.